New Deal Thought

THE AMERICAN HERITAGE SERIES

THE AMERICAN HERITAGE SERIES

New Deal Thought

Edited by

Howard Zinn

Boston University

Hackett Publishing Company, Inc.
Indianapolis/Cambridge

This book was originally published as a volume in the American Heritage Series under the general editorship of Leonard W. Levy and Alfred Young.

Printed in the United States of America

09 08 07 06 05 04 03 1 2 3 4 5 6 7

For further information, please address:

Hackett Publishing Company, Inc.
P.O. Box 44937
Indianapolis, IN 46244-0937

www.hackettpublishing.com

Cover design by Rick Todhunter and Abigail Coyle
Printed at Sheridan Books, Inc.

Library of Congress Cataloging-in-Publication Data

New Deal thought / edited by Howard Zinn.

p. cm.

Originally published: Indianapolis: Bobbs-Merrill, c1966

(The American heritage series).

Includes bibliographical references and index.

ISBN 0-87220-686-6 (alk. paper)—ISBN 0-87220-685-8 (pbk.: alk. paper)

1. United States—History—1933–1945—Sources. 2. New deal—

1933–1939—Sources. 3. United States—Social policy—Sources.

I. Zinn, Howard, 1922–

II. American heritage series (New York, N.Y.)

E806.N425 2003

320.973—dc22

2003056164

The paper used in this publication meets the minimum requirements of American National Standard for InformationSciences—Permanence of Paper for Printed Library Materials, ANSI Z39.48-1984

∞

To my mother and father

FOREWORD

This anthology assembles the contemporary writings not only of the New Dealers—the men who devised and executed the programs of the government in the era of Franklin D. Roosevelt—but also of the "social critics" who "gathered in various stances and at various distances around the Roosevelt fire." Here is a sampling of the famous movers and shakers of the 1930's: Thurman Arnold, Henry Wallace, Rexford Tugwell, David Lilienthal, Harry Hopkins, Harold Ickes, Frances Perkins, John Maynard Keynes, and of course Roosevelt himself. Here too are the voices of those who thought the New Dealers were going "too far" such as Walter Lippmann and Raymond Moley, and of those who thought they were not going "far enough"; like John Dewey, W.E.B. DuBois, Norman Thomas, Lewis Mumford, and Carey McWilliams.

A book about the 1930's, drawn from material of the era, it is also a book for our own time, assembled by an editor who believes that the past should "speak wisely to our present needs." To a remarkable extent the writings take up the unfulfilled programs of the New Deal which are still "on the agenda" of contemporary society or deserve to be on it: national economic planning, giantism in business, public support for the arts, Negro rights, security for the one third of a nation Roosevelt saw as "ill nourished, ill clad, ill housed." In his introduction Professor Zinn defines the boundaries of the New Deal's experimentalism and tries to explain why it sputtered out. The result is a book that captures the spirit of the New Deal—hopeful, pragmatic, humane—yet remains hardheaded about its accomplishments and failures.

This book is one of a series aiming to provide the essential primary sources of the American experience, especially of American thought. The series when completed will constitute a documentary library of American history, filling a need long felt among scholars, students, libraries and general readers for authoritative collections of original materials. Some volumes will illuminate the thought of significant individuals, such as James Madison or Louis Brandeis; some will deal with movements, such as the Antifederalists or the Populists; others will be organized around special themes, such as Puritan political thought, or American Catholic thought on social questions. Many volumes will take up the large number of subjects traditionally studied in American history for which surprisingly there are no documentary anthologies; others will pioneer in introducing new subjects of increasing importance to scholars and to the contemporary world. The series aspires to maintain the high standards demanded of contemporary editing, providing authentic texts intelligently and unobtrusively edited. It will also have the distinction of presenting pieces of substantial length which give the full character and flavor of the original. The series will be the most comprehensive and authoritative of its kind.

Alfred Young
Leonard W. Levy

CONTENTS

PART THREE • NATIONAL ECONOMIC PLANNING

PART FOUR • GIANTISM IN BUSINESS

PART FIVE • PUBLIC ENTERPRISE

PART SIX • ORGANIZING LABOR

PART SEVEN • THE FARMER

PART EIGHT • MINIMUM SECURITY

PART NINE • THE NEGRO

PART TEN • THE CONSTITUTION AND SOCIAL PROGRESS

INTRODUCTION

When we compel the past to speak, we want neither the gibberish of total recall nor the nostalgia of fond memories; we would like the past to speak wisely to our present needs. And so we have a good reason for trying to recapture some of the lost dialogue of the New Deal years—that which was carried on, with varying degrees of tension, inside and outside the Roosevelt circle.

The New Dealers themselves were articulate, humane, and on occasion profound. Among them were the "brains trust"* (Adolf A. Berle, Raymond Moley, Rexford Guy Tugwell), the cabinet members (Henry Wallace, Frances Perkins, Harold Ickes, and others), the administrators of the alphabetic agencies (Harry Hopkins, David Lilienthal, and others), the Congressional spokesmen (Robert F. Wagner, Hugo Black, and others). And above them all was Franklin D. Roosevelt himself. They had no clearly defined set of goals, beyond that of extricating the nation from the depression of 1929-1932. In the course of easing the crisis, however, they found themselves—pushed partly by the cries of alarm on all sides, partly by inner humanitarian impulses—creating new laws and institutions like the Tennessee Valley Authority, the social security system, farm subsidies, minimum wage standards, the National Labor Relations Board, and public housing.

These accomplishments were considerable enough to give many Americans the feeling they were going through a revolution, while they successfully evaded any one of a number of totalitarian abysses into which they might have fallen. So it is not surprising that the New Deal left a glow of enthusiasm, even adoration, in the nation at large.

*Moley and Tugwell both insist that the proper name is "brains trust," as originally used by James Kieran, a *New York Times* reporter, although the term became popular as "brain trust."

Yet, when it was over, the fundamental problem remained—and still remains—unsolved: how to bring the blessings of immense natural wealth and staggering productive potential to every person in the land. Also unsolved was the political corollary of that problem; how to organize ordinary people to convey to national leadership something more subtle than the wail of crisis (which speaks for itself); how to communicate the day-to-day pains felt, between emergencies, in garbage-strewn slums, crowded schools, grimy bus stations, inadequate hospital wards, Negro ghettos, and rural shacks—the environment of millions of Americans clawing for subsistence in the richest country in the world.

When the reform energies of the New Deal began to wane around 1939 and the depression was over, the nation was back to its normal state: a permanent army of unemployed; twenty or thirty million poverty-ridden people effectively blocked from public view by a huge, prosperous, and fervently consuming middle class; a tremendously efficient yet wasteful productive apparatus that was efficient because it could produce limitless supplies of what it decided to produce, and wasteful because what it decided to produce was not based on what was most needed by society but on what was most profitable to business.[1]

What the New Deal did was to refurbish middle-class America, which had taken a dizzying fall in the depression, to restore jobs to half the jobless, and to give just enough to the lowest classes (a layer of public housing, a minimum of social security) to create an aura of good will. Through it all, the New Dealers moved in an atmosphere thick with suggestions, but they accepted only enough of these to get the traditional

[1] In *The Affluent Society* (Boston: Houghton Mifflin Company, 1958), John Kenneth Galbraith has pointed eloquently to the American economy's emphasis on private rather than public needs. Michael Harrington's *The Other America* (New York: The Macmillan Company, 1963), and Leon Keyserling's *Poverty and Deprivation in the United States* (Washington, D.C.: Conference on Economic Progress, 1962) testify to continuing large blocs of poverty thirty years after the New Deal.

social mechanism moving again, plus just enough more to give a taste of what a truly far-reaching reconstruction might be.

This harsh estimate of New Deal achievements derives from the belief that the historian discussing the past is always commenting—whether he realizes it or not—on the present; and that because he is part of a morally responsible public, his commentary should consider present needs at the expense, if necessary, of old attachments. It is fruitless today to debate "interpretations" of the New Deal. We can no longer vote for or against Roosevelt. We can only affect the world around us. And although this is the 1960's, not the 1930's, some among us live very high, and some live very low, and a chronic malaise of lost opportunities and wasted wealth pervades the economic air.[2]

It is for today, then, that we turn to the thinking of the New Deal period. Although the New Deal gave us only fragments of solutions, it did leave us—perhaps because those were desperate years, and desperation stimulates innovation—with a public discussion more intense and more sweeping than any we have had before or since. People outside the New Deal entourage, invited or not, joined that discussion and extended the boundaries of political and economic imagination beyond those of the New Dealers—sometimes to the left, sometimes to the right, sometimes in directions hard to plot.

Among these were philosophers, writers, critics, lawyers, poets, college professors, journalists, dissident politicians, or commentators without special portfolio. Their names are still known today: John Dewey, Charles Beard, Reinhold Niebuhr, Paul Douglas, Stuart Chase, John Maynard Keynes, Norman Thomas, Oswald Garrison Villard, Heywood Broun, Max Lerner, Morris Cohen, Walter White, Edmund Wilson, Felix Frankfurter, John Steinbeck, John L. Lewis, Upton Sinclair.

[2] David Bazelon, in *The Paper Economy* (New York: Random House, Inc., 1963), and Robert Theobald, in *Free Men and Free Markets* (New York: C. N. Potter, 1963), give trenchant critiques of the American economy in the 1960's.

Their thinking does not give us facile solutions, but if history has uses beyond that of reminiscence, one of them is to nourish lean ideological times with the nectars of other years. And although the present shape of the world was hardly discernible in 1939, certain crucial social issues persist in both eras. Somehow, in the interaction between the ideas of the New Dealers themselves and those of social critics who gathered in various stances and at various distances around the Roosevelt fire, we may find suggestions or approaches that are relevant today.

I

The word "pragmatic" has been used, more often perhaps than any other, to describe the thinking of the New Dealers.[3] It refers to the experimental method of the Roosevelt administration, the improvisation from one step to the next, the lack of system or long-range program or theoretical commitment. Richard Hofstadter, in fact, says that the only important contribution to political theory to come out of the Roosevelt administration was made by Thurman Arnold, particularly in his two books, *The Symbols of Government* and *The Folklore of Capitalism.* Hofstadter describes Arnold's writing as "the theoretical equivalent of FDR's opportunistic virtuosity in practical politics—a theory that attacks theories."[4] As the chief expression of Roosevelt's "ideology," Arnold's work deserves some attention.

All through both his books, in a style of cool irony, Arnold cuts away at "preconceived faiths," "preconceived principles," "theories and symbols of government," "high-sounding prejudices," "traditional ideals," "moral ideals," "permanent cures."

[3] A representative statement is Arthur M. Schlesinger, Jr.'s, in *The Politics of Upheaval* (Boston: Houghton Mifflin Company, 1960), p. 649. "For Roosevelt, the technique of liberal government was pragmatic. . . . Nothing attracted Roosevelt less than rigid intellectual systems."

[4] Richard Hofstadter, *The Age of Reform* (New York: Alfred A. Knopf, Inc., 1955), p. 317.

In the last paragraphs of *The Symbols of Government,* he writes:

> So long as the public hold preconceived faiths about the fundamental principles of government, they will persecute and denounce new ideas in that science, and orators will prevail over technicians. So long as preconceived principles are considered more important than practical results, the practical alleviation of human distress and the distribution of available comforts will be paralyzed. . . . The writer has faith that a new public attitude toward the ideals of law and economics is slowly appearing to create an atmosphere where the fanatical alignments between opposing political principles may disappear and a competent, practical, opportunistic governing class may rise to power. . . .[5]

Because the Roosevelt administration did, in fact, experiment and improvise without a total plan, FDR's "pragmatism" has come, for many, to be the most important statement about the thinking of the New Dealers. This emphasis on the method rather than on the substance of that thinking tends to obscure what may be its greatest significance.[6]

Most statesmen experiment: Tsar Nicholas instituted a Duma, Lenin encouraged private enterprise for several years, Bismarck sponsored social welfare measures, Mao Tse-tung introduced back-yard steel furnaces, and George Washington supported a national bank. These examples show that experimentation can be linked to a variety of social ideals. Some statesmen engage in more experiments than others, and in a time of crisis one who is willing to undertake a vast number of them deserves commendation, as Roosevelt does. The truly important question that can be asked about the thinking of any government is: in what direction, and how far, is it willing to

[5] Thurman Arnold, *The Symbols of Government* (New Haven: Yale University Press, 1935), pp. 270-271.

[6] A notable exception is William E. Leuchtenburg, *Franklin D. Roosevelt and the New Deal* (New York: Harper & Row, 1963), pp. 344-346.

experiment? What goals, what ideals, what expectations direct that experimentation?

Thurman Arnold himself contributed to this misplaced emphasis on method rather than substance. He was so anxious to demolish old myths that stood in the way of the welfare measures of the New Deal that mythology itself became his chief concern. He was so intent on sweeping away old debris, that he became obsessed, ironically, with a folklore of his own, in which the idea of debris-clearing crowded out the concept of what he wanted to plant in the cleared area.

Examining Arnold's *The Symbols of Government,* one sees that what started him on a crusade against myths was that he sought to expose the symbolism that stood in the way of bringing cheap electric power to people and of instituting relief, public works, social security.[7] His strongest expression on social justice was his statement that: "Those who rule our great industrial feudalism still believe inalterably the old axioms that man works efficiently only for personal profit; that humanitarian ideals are unworkable as the principal aim of government or business organization; that control of national resources, elimination of waste, and a planned distribution of goods would destroy both freedom and efficiency."[8]

As was true of his associate, Thurman Arnold, FDR's experimentalism and iconoclasm were not devoid of standards and ideals. They had a certain direction, which was toward gov-

[7] *The Symbols of Government,* pp. 16, 110-111, 120. Hofstadter, in *The Age of Reform,* p. 318, analyzes the words that recur frequently in Arnold's books to show his movement away from the Progressivist moralism. Yet even to make this point he finds he must include the word "humanitarian" because it appears so frequently.

[8] *The Symbols of Government,* pp. 259-260. Arnold was so reluctant to admit he possessed a set of values that Sidney Hook, reviewing *The Folklore of Capitalism,* took him at his word (or rather at his emphasized words), and described him as one who believed "all standards and ideals are nonsense." *University of Chicago Law Review,* V (April 1938), 341-357.

ernmental intervention in the economy to prevent depression, to help the poor, and to curb ruthless practices in big business. Roosevelt's speeches had the flavor of a moral crusade. Accepting the nomination at the Democratic Convention of 1932, he said that "the Federal Government has always had and still has a continuing responsibility for the broader public welfare," and pledged "a new deal for the American people." In a campaign speech that year at the Commonwealth Club in San Francisco, he said: "Our government . . . owes to every one an avenue to possess himself of a portion of that plenty sufficient for his needs, through his own work." In his 1936 speech accepting the nomination, he spoke of the power of the "economic royalists" and said: "Our allegiance to American institutions requires the overthrow of this kind of power."

But FDR's ideas did not have enough clarity to avoid stumbling from one approach to another: from constant promises to balance the budget, to large-scale spending in emergencies; from an attempt to reconcile big business interests and labor interests (as in the National Recovery Act), to belated support for a pro-labor National Labor Relations Act; from special concern for the tenant farmer (in the Resettlement Administration), to a stress on generous price supports for the large commercial farmer (in the Agricultural Adjustment Act of 1938).

His ideas on political leadership showed the same indecision, the same constriction of boundaries, as did his ideas about economic reform. Roosevelt was cautious about supporting the kind of candidates in 1934 (Socialist Upton Sinclair in California, Progressive Gifford Pinchot in Pennsylvania) who represented bold approaches to economic and social change; and when he did decide to take vigorous action against conservative Congressional candidates in 1938, he did so too late and too timorously. He often attempted to lead Congress in a forceful way to support his economic program; yet his leadership was confined to working with the existing Congressional leadership, including many Southern conservatives who ruled important committees. Roosevelt's political daring did not extend to building new political forces among the poor, the unemployed, the tenant farmers, and other disadvantaged groups, with whose support he might have given the country a bolder economic program.

The circle of men around Roosevelt, the cabinet members and administrators, was an odd mixture of liberals and conservatives who often worked at cross-purposes. Rexford Guy Tugwell, a bold advocate of national planning to help the lower-income groups, was close to Roosevelt for several years; but so was Raymond Moley, who believed in a kind of planning more beneficial to business interests. Even the liberal New Dealers, with rare exceptions, hesitated to carry their general concern for the underprivileged too far. Frances Perkins, the Secretary of Labor, had the humanitarian instincts of a first-rate social worker, but she seemed often to be trailing behind the labor movement, rather than helping to give it direction. (The most advanced piece of New Deal labor legislation was the Wagner Act, but Secretary Perkins wrote later: "I myself, had very little sympathy with the bill.") Progressive Secretary of the Interior Harold Ickes was offset by conservative Secretary of Commerce Daniel Roper. And although Roper was succeeded in 1939 by Harry Hopkins, there remained in the cabinet a powerful force for fiscal conservatism and budget-balancing—Secretary of the Treasury Henry Morgenthau.

The experimentalism of the New Deal, in short, had its limits: up to these limits, Roosevelt's social concern was genuinely warm, his political courage huge, his humanitarian spirit unfailing; beyond them, his driving force weakened. Thus, by 1938, with the nation out of the worst of the depression, with a skeletal structure of social reform in the statute books, and with that year's Congressional elections showing a sudden waning of political approbation, the Roosevelt program began to bog down. As it slid to its close, it left behind a mountain of accomplishment, and ahead, mountains still unclimbed. Many millions—businessmen, professionals, unionized workingmen, commercial farmers—had been given substantial help. Many millions more—sharecroppers, slum-dwellers, Negroes of North and South, the unemployed—still awaited a genuine "new deal."

II

Why did the New Deal sputter out around 1938-1939? One important factor seems to be that the urgency of 1933-1935 was gone. By 1939, although there were still nine million unemployed, the sense of panic was over. After all, unemployment was normal in America. Harry Hopkins had said in 1937 that even in prosperity it was "reasonable to expect a probable minimum of 4,000,000 to 5,000,000 unemployed."[9] The American nation had developed over the years a set of expectations as to what constituted "normal" times; and by 1938 it was approaching these.

Hopkins' statement and the administration's inaction indicate that the ideals of the New Dealers did not extend very far beyond the traditional structure of the American economy. They had wanted to get out of the terrible economic despair of 1932 and 1933 and to establish certain moderate reforms. These aims had been accomplished. True, some of the New Dealers, including FDR himself, did speak of what still remained to be done. But once the nation was restored to close to the old balance—even if income was still distributed with gross inequality, even if rural and urban slums crisscrossed the land, even if most workingmen were still unorganized and underpaid, and a third of the nation still, in FDR's words, "ill-nourished, ill-clad, ill-housed"—the driving force of the New Deal was gone.

Why were the expectations and ideals of the New Deal (its folklore, its symbols, according to Thurman Arnold) so

[9] Harry Hopkins, "The Future of Relief," *The New Republic*, XC (1937), 8.

limited? Why did the New Dealers not declare that the government would continue spending, experimenting, and expanding governmental enterprises—until no one was unemployed, and all slums were gone from the cities, until no family received below-subsistence incomes and adequate medical care was available to everyone, until anyone who wanted a college education could get one? True, there were political obstacles to realizing such objectives, but to state them as *goals* would itself have constituted the first step toward overcoming those obstacles. For this might have enabled FDR to do what political scientist James MacGregor Burns asserts was not done: to build "a solid, organized mass base" among labor and other underprivileged groups.[10]

Humanitarianism pure and simple can go only so far, and self-interest must carry it further. Beyond the solicitude felt by the New Dealers for the distressed, beyond the occasionally bold rhetoric, there was not enough motive power to create a radically new economic equilibrium; this would have to be supplied by the groups concerned themselves; by the tenant farmers, the aged, the unemployed, the lowest-paid workers in the economy. Those who *did* organize—the larger farm operators, the several million industrial workers who joined the CIO—improved their position significantly. But as Paul Douglas, then an economics professor at the University of Chicago and now a United States Senator, wrote in 1933:

> Along with the Rooseveltian program must go . . . the organization of those who are at present weak and who need to acquire that which the world respects, namely, power. . . . Unless these things are done, we are likely to find the permanent benefits of Rooseveltian liberalism to be as illusory as were those of the Wilsonian era.[11]

[10] James MacGregor Burns, *Roosevelt: The Lion and the Fox* (New York: Harcourt, Brace & World, 1956), p. 376.

[11] "Rooseveltian Liberalism," *The Nation*, CXXXVI (June 21, 1933), 702-703.

Many organized movements sprang up in the 1930's, spurred by need and encouraged by the new atmosphere of innovation. The Townsend Movement sought $200 a month pensions for the aged. Father Charles Coughlin's panacea of "Social Justice" was heard by millions of radio listeners. Huey Long, the Louisiana Senator, excited many others with his "Share the Wealth" plan. The National Negro Congress, the Farmers Union, and the American Youth Congress all represented special needs and all hurled their energies into the boiling political pot in Washington.

But there was no political program around which these disparate groups could effectively unite. And many of them began to lose their thrust when their demands were partially met. Even the Congress of Industrial Organizations, the largest and most successful of those mass movements born in the depression and stimulated by New Deal legislation, came eventually to represent a special interest of its own.

The Madisonian argument that political stability would be assured in a federal republic of many states, because an uprising in one would die for lack of support, applied also in the economic sphere, where no single economic interest, fierce as it might be in its own domain, ever developed a concern wide enough to embrace society at large. Perhaps one reason is that in the United States every little rebellion, every crisis, has been met with enough concessions to keep general resentment below the combustible level, while isolated aggrieved groups fought their way up to the point of complacency.[12]

But if—as Paul Douglas forecasts—the underprivileged are the only ones who can supply the driving force for a sharp

[12] Gabriel Kolko, in *The Triumph of Conservatism* (New York: Free Press, 1963), pp. 302-304, advances his theory of "political capitalism," and distinguishes between "the rhetoric of reform" and its "structural results," and argues that what we call "reform" is really the use by capitalists of "a centralized state power to meet problems they could not solve themselves."

change in their condition, then it is probably the intellectuals of society who will furnish the theories, state the ideals, define the expectations. And so it is from those thinkers who clustered, half-friendly, half-reproachful, around the New Deal, their ideological reach less restrained, perhaps, by the holding of power, that our generation may find suggestions.

III

Almost immediately, with John Dewey, we are brought face to face with the proof that it is not the fact of experimentalism, but the definition of its boundaries, that is of supreme significance. He was one of the fathers of American pragmatism, the theoretician par excellence of the experimental method. In an article of 1918, he expressed the view of pragmatic experimentation that he held to the end of his life in 1952.

> The question is whether society . . . will learn to utilize the intelligence, the insight and foresight which are available, in order to take hold of the problem and to go at it, step by step, on the basis of an intelligent program—a program which is not too rigid, which is not a program in the sense of having every item definitely scheduled in advance, but which represents an outlook on the future of the things which most immediately require doing, trusting to the experience which is got in doing them to reveal the next things needed and the next steps to be taken.[13]

Roosevelt and Dewey were both experimentalists and they both operated within a range of ideals; but that range, for John Dewey, involved goals that went well beyond Roosevelt's farthest bounds. Roosevelt wrote to newspaper publisher Roy Howard on September 2, 1935, that his legislation was "remedial," described the New Deal program as involving "modifications in the conditions and rules of economic enterprise" and

[13] The article is quoted in Document 61.

said that: "This basic program, however, has now reached substantial completion." Undoubtedly he was bending over backward to satisfy an anxious and influential citizen. And his program did go on to embrace a minimum wage law, public housing, and other measures. But that was largely because of the momentum already created for reform and because of pressures among the public. The Roosevelt vision had been stretched almost to its limits.

In Dewey's 1935 lectures at the University of Virginia, he said:

> The only form of enduring social organization that is now possible is one in which the new forces of productivity are cooperatively controlled and used in the interest of the effective liberty and the cultural development of the individuals that constitute society. Such a social order cannot be established by an unplanned and external convergence of the actions of separate individuals, each of whom is bent on personal private advantage. . . . Organized social planning, put into effect for the creation of an order in which industry and finance are socially directed . . . is now the sole method of social action by which liberalism can realize its professed aims.[14]

Both Roosevelt and Dewey believed in moving step by step. But FDR wanted to preserve the profit system; Dewey was willing to reshape it drastically. Because Dewey's aim was larger, his steps were longer ones, taken two or three at a time, and were less haphazard. "In short," he said, "liberalism must now become radical. . . . For the gulf between what the actual situation makes possible and the actual state itself is so great that it cannot be bridged by piecemeal policies undertaken *ad hoc*."[15] Dewey was very conscious of the dangers of totalitarianism, but he believed that the spirit of free expression

[14] Reprinted in *Liberalism and Social Action* (New York: Capricorn Books, 1963), p. 54.

[15] *Ibid.*, p. 62.

could remain alive, even while liberalism went on to "socialize the forces of production."[16] Among pragmatists, apparently, crucial distinctions exist.

Part of Roosevelt's "pragmatism" was his rejection of doctrinaire ideas of the left.[17] Marxism was in the air all around him. Many intellectuals were enthusiastic about the Five Year Plans of Soviet Russia. British Marxists were influential: Harold J. Laski lectured and wrote extensively in the United States; John Strachey popularized the concepts of socialism in *The Nature of Capitalist Crisis* (1935) and other works. Some in depression-ridden America were attracted to Marxism's claims that society could be analyzed "scientifically": that economic crisis was inevitable where production was complex and gigantic, yet unplanned; that exploitation of working people was built into a system where private profit was the chief motive; that the state was not neutral but an instrument of those who held economic power; that only the working class could be depended on to take over society and move it towards a classless, strifeless commonwealth. A true pragmatist might at least have explored some of the suggestions of Marxist thought. Roosevelt's thinking, however, remained in a kind of airtight chamber that allowed him to regulate what currents he would permit inside—and Marxism was not one of them.

Nevertheless, to steer clear of the theories of the Marxists, as of the Hooverian folklore of "free enterprise," "thrift," and "laissez-faire," left a vast middle ground of which Roosevelt explored only one sector. Edmund Wilson, for instance, a social critic and essayist, also rejected Marxian dialectics; yet he tried to extract from it some truths. He wrote with apparent warmth of the idea that (as he put it, in an imaginary restatement of a more acceptable Marxism): ". . . if society is to survive at all,

[16] *Ibid.*, p. 88.

[17] Schlesinger, *The Politics of Upheaval*, pp. 176, 647.

it must be reorganized on new principles of equality."[18] Others, not Marxists, but more demanding in their notion of reform than was the New Deal, reconnoitered beyond its ideological fences.

Reinhold Niebuhr, a theologian and social philosopher who carried the Social Gospel to new borders in the 1930's, urged that "private ownership of the productive processes" be abandoned,[19] yet he hoped that through an alliance among farmers, industrial workers, and the lower income classes, the transition to a new order could be accomplished without violence. Stuart Chase, an economist who wrote a series of widely selling books in the 1930's, suggested that old alternatives had been swept aside by the onrush of technology, that the choice was no longer between capitalism and socialism; there was a need, he said, for some uncategorizable collectivist society whose "general objective will be the distribution of the surplus, rather than a wrangling over the ownership of a productive plant which has lost its scarcity position."[20]

William Ernest Hocking, a Harvard philosopher, asked for "collectivism of a sort," but neither the collectivism of a "headless Liberalism" or of a "heady" Communism or Fascism. He wrote: "What the State has to do with production is to drive into economic practice the truth that there is little or no capital whose use is not 'affected by a public interest.'" Hocking said: "Economic processes constitute a single and healthy organism only when the totality of persons in a community who have a right to consume *determine what is produced*. . . ."[21] Hocking was setting goals quite beyond the Rooseveltian ones.

[18] "The Myth of the Marxian Dialectic," *Partisan Review*, VI (1939), 66-81.

[19] *Reflections on the End on an Era*, quoted in Schlesinger, p. 158.

[20] "The Age of Distribution," *The Nation*, CXXXIX (July 25, 1934), 93-96.

[21] "The Future of Liberalism," *The Journal of Philosophy*, XXII, No. 9 (1935), 230-247.

Upton Sinclair, a muckraker since the early part of the century, preached a non-Marxist, home-grown socialism that attracted enough adherents to bring him very close to winning the gubernatorial election in California in 1934.[22] Sinclair prophesied that "in a cooperative society every man, woman, and child would have the equivalent of $5000 a year income from labor of the able-bodied young men for three or four hours per day."[23] This prophesy was certainly utopian in 1933, but such vision, even if it were going to be bent and modified in practice, might carry a program of social reform much further —and perhaps win more powerful blocs of electoral support— than did the more moderate goals of the New Deal.

A program may be pragmatic in its willingness to explore various means, yet be certain of its goals; it may be limited in how far it is willing to go, and yet be clear about the direction of its thrust. There is a difference between experimentation and vacillation. Robert MacIver, a distinguished social scientist, was impressed in 1934 by the variety of new institutions created under Roosevelt, but wondered if they meant "the inauguration of a period of social and cultural reformation." He asked: "The new institutions are here, but the essential point is—Who shall control them?"[24] There was uncertainty about the New Deal, particularly in its first two years, when the National Recovery Act set out to create large planning organizations for industry in which big business seemed to be making the important decisions. It led some liberals and radicals to see in it possible Fascist aims,[25] led some important business-

[22] He won easily in the primary over liberal George Creel, but then, lacking FDR's support, lost to an anti-New Dealer.

[23] Upton Sinclair, *The Way Out* (New York: Farrar & Rinehart, 1933), p. 57.

[24] Robert MacIver, "Social Philosophy," in *Social Change and the New Deal,* ed. William F. Ogburn (Chicago: The University of Chicago Press, 1934), pp. 107-113.

[25] For example, William Z. Foster, for the Communists; Norman Thomas, for the Socialists; and I. F. Stone, as an independent radical.

men to support it,[26] and kept political loyalties crisscrossed in a happy chaos.

After 1935 (although ambiguity remained in specific areas like trust-busting), the over-all direction of the New Deal became clear: it was sympathetic to the underprivileged, and to organized labor, and it was pervaded by a general spirit of liberal, humanitarian reform. But also the scope of the New Deal became clear. This limitation is shown in a number of issues that the New Deal faced, or sometimes tried to avoid facing, between 1933 and 1939: the problem of planning; the question of how to deal with monopolistic business; the controversy over deficit financing and the extension of public enterprise; the creation of an adequate system of social security.

IV

When Roosevelt told students at Oglethorpe University during his 1932 campaign that he was in favor of "a larger measure of social planning," it was not clear how large this measure was. Was he willing to go as far as his own advisor, Columbia professor Rexford Guy Tugwell? Tugwell attacked the profit motive, said that "planning for production means planning for consumption too," declared that "profits must be limited and their uses controlled," and said he meant by planning "something not unlike an integrated group of enterprises run for its consumers rather than for its owners." The statement, he said, that "business will logically be required to disappear" is "literally meant" because: "Planning implies guidance of capital uses. . . . Planning also implies adjustment of production to consumption; and there is no way of accomplishing this except through a control of prices and of profit margins." To limit

26 Russell Leffingwell, of J. P. Morgan and Company; Edward Filene, of the Boston mercantile family; Richard Whitney, president of the New York Stock Exchange; and many others.

business in all these ways, he said, meant in effect "to destroy it as business and to make of it something else."[27]

Raymond Moley, who played a direct role in shaping Roosevelt's early legislation, also deplored the lack of planning in the New Deal. But Moley was interested in planning for quite different groups. Tugwell was concerned with the lower classes' lack of purchasing power. Moley, although he too was moved by a measure of genuine concern for deprived people, was most worried about "the narrow margin of profit" and "business confidence."[28] In the end, Roosevelt rejected both ideas. Whatever planning he would do would try to help the lower classes, for example, the Tennessee Valley Authority. On the other hand, the planning would not be national; nor would it interfere with the fundamental character of the American economy, based as it was on corporate profit; nor would it attempt any fundamental redistribution of wealth in the nation. And the TVA embodied these too because it represented *piecemeal* planning.

David Lilienthal's defense of this method, in his book on the TVA, comes closest to the New Deal approach. "We move step by step—from where we are," wrote Lilienthal.[29] Not only was any notion of national economic planning never seriously considered, but after the TVA, the moving "step by step" did not carry very far. Housing developments and several planned communities were inspiring, but came nowhere near matching the enormity of the national need.

Ambiguity persisted longest in the policy towards monopoly and oligopoly. The NRA was a frank recognition of the usefulness—or at least, the inevitability—of large enterprise, when

[27] Rexford Guy Tugwell, "The Principle of Planning and the Institution of Laissez-Faire," *American Economic Review,* XXII, Supplement (March 1932), 75-92.

[28] Raymond Moley, *After Seven Years* (New York: Harper & Brothers, 1939), pp. 370-371.

[29] David Lilienthal, *T.V.A.: Democracy on the March* (New York: Pocket Books, 1944), Chapter 18, "Planning and Planners," pp. 206-213.

ordered by codes. The Securities Exchange Commission and the Public Utilities Holding Company Act moved back (but weakly, as William O. Douglas recognized at the time)[30] to the Brandeis idea of trying to curb the size and strength of large enterprises. Roosevelt's basic policy towards giantism in business, although he vigorously attacked "economic royalists" in 1936, remained undetermined until 1938, when he asked Congress for a sweeping investigation of monopoly. And although he was clearly returning to the idea of restraining the power of big business, one sentence in his message to Congress reveals his continuing uncertainty: "The power of the few to manage the economic life of the Nation must be diffused among the many or be transferred to the public and its democratically responsible government."

The first alternative was an obviously romantic notion; the second was really much farther than either Congress or FDR was prepared to go. Hence, the Temporary National Economic Committee, after hearing enough testimony to fill thirty-one volumes and forty-three monographs, was unwilling, as William Leuchtenburg writes, "to tackle the more difficult problems or to make recommendations which might disturb vested interests."[31] Roosevelt had come close to expressing, but he still did not possess, nor did he communicate to the nation, a clear, resolute goal of transferring giant and irresponsible economic power "to the public and its democratically responsible government." The restraints on the New Dealers' thinking is shown best perhaps by Adolf A. Berle, who said that prosperity depended on either a gigantic expansion of private activity or nationalization of key industries. Yet, knowing private industry was not going to fill the need, he did not advocate nationalization—nor did any other New Dealer.

Roosevelt was experimental, shifting, and opportunistic in his espousal of public enterprise and the spending that had to

[30] William O. Douglas, "Protecting the Investor," *The Yale Review*, XXIII (Spring 1934), 521-533.

[31] Leuchtenberg, *Franklin D. Roosevelt and the New Deal*, p. 259.

accompany such governmental activity. As James MacGregor Burns says: "Roosevelt had tried rigid economy, then heavy spending, then restriction of spending again. He had shifted back and forth from spending on direct relief to spending on public works."[32] The significant measure, however, was not the swings of the pendulum, but the width of the arcs. When FDR went all-out for spending, it was still only a fraction of what the British economist John Maynard Keynes was urging as a way of bringing recovery. An American Keynesian, Professor Alvin Hansen, was arguing that the economy was "mature" and therefore required much more continuous and powerful injections of governmental spending than was being given.[33]

Roosevelt himself had introduced into public discussion the idea of a "yardstick," which the Tennessee Valley Authority represented—a public enterprise that would, by competing with private producers, force them to bend more towards the needs of the consumer. (Later FDR tried, unsuccessfully, to get Congress to introduce "seven little TVA's" in other river valleys.) But the vast implications of the concept were left unexplored. When political scientist Max Lerner called for government-owned radio stations and government-subsidized newspapers to break into the growing monopolization of public opinion by giant chains, there was no response.[34] TVA, a brief golden period of federal theater, a thin spread of public housing, and a public works program called into play only at times of desperation, represented the New Deal's ideological and emotional limits in the creation of public enterprise.

It is one thing to experiment to discover the best means of achieving a certain objective; it is quite another thing to fail

[32] Burns, *Roosevelt: The Lion and the Fox,* p. 322.

[33] In late 1937, Secretary of the Treasury Henry Morgenthau, Jr., speaking to the American Academy of Political Science, said the 1933 emergency was over; now the budget could be balanced. He suggested cuts in public works, unemployment relief, and farm benefits.

[34] Max Lerner, "Propaganda's Golden Age," *The Nation,* CXLIX (November 11, 1939), 523-524.

to recognize that objective. The Social Security System, as set up, was not an experiment to find the best type of system. Roosevelt knew from the beginning that it was not the most effective way to handle the problems of poverty for the aged, the unemployed, and the helpless. Behind the basic political problem of getting the bill passed lay fundamental narrowness of vision. Social security expert Abraham Epstein pointed this out at the time,[35] and it was noted on the floor of Congress.[36] Henry E. Sigerist, a physician and student of welfare medicine in other countries, wrote patiently and clearly about the need for socialized medicine, answered the arguments against it, and explained how it might operate.[37]

Thus, if the concept of New Deal thought is widened to include a large circle of thinkers—some close to the administration itself, others at varying distances from it—we get not panaceas or infallible schemes but larger commitments, bolder goals, and greater expectations of what "equality" and "justice" and "security" meant.

V

For our view of the New Deal as a particularly energetic gyroscopic motion putting the traditional structure aright again, we have what the natural scientists might call a set of "controls"—a way of checking up on the hypothesis—one in the area of race relations, another in the experience of war.

In the field of racial equality, where there was no crisis as in economics, where the gyroscope did not confront a sharply titled mechanism, there was no "new deal." The special encumbrances of the depression were lifted for Negroes as for

[35] Abraham Epstein, " 'Social Security' Under the New Deal," *The Nation,* CXLI (September 4, 1935), 261-263.

[36] Congressman Henry Ellenbogen, of Pennsylvania, *Congressional Record,* August 19, 1935, pp. 13675-13677.

[37] Henry E. Sigerist, "Socialized Medicine," *The Yale Review,* XXVII (Spring 1938), 463-481.

many other Americans, but the *permanent* caste structure remained unaltered by the kind of innovations that at least threatened the traditional edifice in economics. The white South was left, as it had been since the Compromise of 1877, to deal with Negroes as it chose—by murder, by beatings, by ruthless exclusion from political and economic life; the Fourteenth Amendment waited as fruitlessly for executive enforcement as it had in all earlier administrations since Grant. Washington, D.C., itself remained a tightly segregated city. And the Harlems of the North continued as great symbols of national failure.

The warm belief in equal rights held by Eleanor Roosevelt, as well as by FDR himself, the appointments of Mary McLeod Bethune, Robert Weaver, and others to important secondary posts in the government, even the wide distribution of relief and WPA jobs, were not enough to alter the fundamental injustice attached to being a Negro in the United States. The disposition of the New Deal to experiment could have led to important accomplishments, but the clear goal of ending segregation, as with comparable objectives in economics, was never established.

With the coming of World War II, economic and social experimentation blossomed under Roosevelt's leadership and involved a good measure of national planning, jobs for everyone, and a vast system of postwar educational benefits to eighteen million veterans. There was little inhibition; new, radically different national goals were not required for the traditional objective of winning at war. With such an aim, policy could be fearless and far-reaching.

Some coming generation perhaps, while paying proper respects to the spirit of the New Deal, may find, as William James put it, "the moral equivalent of war"—in new social goals, new expectations, with imaginative, undoctrinaire experimentation to attain them. If, in such an adventure, the thought of the past can help, it should be put to work.

ACKNOWLEDGMENTS

My first thanks to Leonard Levy, for enlisting me in this project, and to Alfred Young, who gave immeasurable help every step of the way as a tireless and keen-minded editor-critic. I am grateful to Carl Degler and William Leuchtenburg for good advice at an early stage of the work. August Meier made some valuable suggestions in the field of Negro thought. My wife Roslyn Zinn, as always, was chief consultant.

CHRONOLOGY
1929-1939

October 1929: Wall Street stock market crash.

June 1932: Franklin D. Roosevelt, governor of New York, nominated for President by the Democratic Party Convention; he flies to Chicago to make an acceptance speech, promising "a new deal for the American people."

November 1932: Roosevelt defeats incumbent Herbert Hoover, with 27 million votes against Hoover's 15 million votes, carrying 42 states.

March 1933: Industrial production down to all-time low index of 56 (using 100 as "normal"). Unemployment at an all-time high, with close to 25 per cent of the labor force jobless. More than 5,000 banks closed down.

Roosevelt inaugurated as President.

Special session of Congress called by FDR, stays in session from March 9 to June 16, later to be known as the "Hundred Days."

Emergency Banking Relief Act gives President broad powers over banks and banking transactions.

Economy Act reduces salaries of government workers and veterans' pensions.

Civilian Conservation Corps established by Congress to provide work in reforestation and other outdoor jobs for 250,000 unemployed young people between the ages of eighteen and twenty-five.

April 1933: The United States goes off the gold standard to raise prices on American stock exchanges and commodity exchanges.

May 1933: Federal Emergency Relief Administration set up by Congress, with $500 million in grants to states and localities for relief. Harry Hopkins appointed Federal Relief Administrator.

Agricultural Adjustment Act provides for payment to farmers for reducing acreage on certain commodities.

Tennessee Valley Authority set up as independent public corporation to build dams and power plants to develop the Tennessee Valley area, providing cheap electric power and fertilizer.

June 1933: United States Employment Service set up to cooperate with state employment services in helping the unemployed get jobs.

Home Owners Loan Corporation set up to refinance mortgages and lend money to home owners.

Glass-Steagall Act creates the Federal Bank Deposit Insurance Corporation to guarantee individual bank deposits of less than $5,000.

National Industrial Recovery Act establishes the National Recovery Administration, under which industries would agree to fair competition codes, including (in section 7A) the right of collective bargaining for labor unions. Under the same act, the Public Works Administration was set up, under Secretary of the Interior Harold Ickes, with more than $3 billion to construct roads, buildings, and other projects.

October 1933: The Commodity Credit Corporation is set up to loan money to farmers on their crops.

November 1933: The Civil Works Administration is set up under the direction of Harry Hopkins to put 4 million jobless persons to work on various projects.

June 1934: The Securities and Exchange Commission established to license stock exchanges and regulate trading in securities.

Federal Communications Commission established to regulate interstate and foreign communications by telegraph, cable, and radio.

National Housing Act establishes Federal Housing Administration to insure bank loans for home building and repair.

January 1935: Roosevelt's annual message to Congress outlines program of public works, social security, and housing.

April 1935: Works Progress Administration set up under Harry Hopkins to create useful jobs, employs more than 3 million persons during the following year. Includes Federal Theater Project, Federal Writers' Project, and Federal Arts Project.

May 1935: Resettlement Administration set up by executive order, with Undersecretary of Agriculture Rexford G. Tugwell as administrator, to help the lowest strata of farm families through loans and the establishment of new communities.

Rural Electrification Administration set up by executive order to lend money for the construction of power lines in isolated rural areas.

Supreme Court declares the NIRA unconstitutional in the *Schechter Case.*

June 1935: National Resources Committee set up by executive order to collect data and make plans for the development of national resources.

National Youth Administration set up by executive order, as a part of WPA, under Aubrey Williams, to provide jobs for young people between the ages of sixteen and twenty-five and part-time jobs for needy students.

July 1935: National Labor Relations Act passed, setting up National Labor Relations Board to supervise elections in which workers would choose unions to represent them in collective bargaining.

August 1935: Social Security Act passed, providing for federal-state system of unemployment compensation, and federal system of old-age and survivors' insurance for old-age pensions.

Public Utility Holding Company Act passed to restrict the operations of holding companies in the field of public utilities.

Revenue Act of 1935 raised taxes on corporate profits and high individual incomes.

November 1935: Committee for Industrial Organization set up in AFL.

January 1936: Supreme Court declares Agricultural Adjustment Act unconstitutional in case of *U.S.* v. *Butler.*

February 1936: Soil Conservation and Domestic Allotment Act passed to replace the invalidated AAA, gives payments to farmers who practice soil conservation.

November 1936: Roosevelt re-elected over Republican candidate Alfred M. Landon, with 27 million votes to Landon's 16 million votes. New Democratic majority is 77-19 in the Senate, and 328-107 in the House.

December 1936: Sit-down strike for 44 days at General Motors plant, Flint, Michigan, organized by CIO.

January 1937: Roosevelt inaugurated for second term.

February 1937: Roosevelt submits to Congress plan for "court-packing," permitting an increase in the number of Justices on the Supreme Court.

March 1937: West Coast Hotel Co. v. *Parrish* upholds a Washington minimum-wage law, thus overturning precedent which voided such laws as a violation of due-process clause.

May 1937: Memorial Day Massacre, in which union demonstrators at Republic Steel plant in Chicago were fired on by police, resulting in 4 killed, 84 injured.

July 1937: Bankhead-Jones Farm Tenant Act establishes the Farm Security Administration, providing low-interest loans for tenant farmers, sharecroppers, farm laborers.

September 1937: Wagner-Steagall Act establishes U.S. Housing

Authority to give loans to local public agencies setting up housing projects, and subsidies to permit low rents.

February 1938: Agricultural Adjustment Act of 1938 provides loans to farmers for storing surplus crops.

April 1938: With business recession underway, Roosevelt asks Congress for expansion of WPA and other measures.

June 1938: Joint Congressional resolution, responding to FDR's request, sets up Temporary National Economic Committee under Senator Joseph C. O'Mahoney to investigate the concentration of economic power.

Fair Labor Standards Act passed, establishing minimum wages and maximum hours, and barring child labor, in interstate commerce.

January 1939: Roosevelt's annual message to Congress proposes no new domestic reforms, stresses international danger.

SELECTED BIBLIOGRAPHY

Original Sources

The most important single repository for material on the New Deal is the Franklin D. Roosevelt Library at Hyde Park, New York, which contains the papers of FDR himself, of other people connected with him, and various manuscripts and printed materials on the New Deal. Roosevelt's public statements have been published in a thirteen-volume series edited by Samuel Rosenman, *The Public Papers and Addresses of Franklin D. Roosevelt* (New York: Random House, 1938-50). Many of his personal letters have been reprinted in four volumes edited by his son, Elliott Roosevelt, *F.D.R.: His Personal Letters, 1928-1945* (New York: Duell, Sloan and Pearce, 1947-50).

Collateral Reading

There are various valuable memoirs written by people close to Roosevelt: Eleanor Roosevelt, *This I Remember* (New York: Harper & Brothers, 1949); Frances Perkins, *The Roosevelt I Knew* (New York: Viking Press, 1946); Rexford Tugwell, *The Democratic Roosevelt* (New York: Doubleday, 1957); Samuel Rosenman, *Working With Roosevelt* (New York: Harper & Brothers, 1952); Raymond Moley, *After Seven Years* (New York: Harper & Brothers, 1939); Harold Ickes, *The Secret Diary of Harold Ickes* (3 vols., New York: Simon and Schuster, 1953-54); John Morton Blum, *From the Morgenthau Diaries* (Boston: Houghton Mifflin, 1959); James A. Farley, *Behind the Ballots* (New York: Harcourt, Brace and Company, 1938).

There are two excellent one-volume studies that deal not only with the policies but with the thought of the New Deal:

William E. Leuchtenburg, *Franklin D. Roosevelt and the New Deal* (New York: Harper & Row, 1963); James MacGregor Burns, *Roosevelt: The Lion and the Fox* (New York: Harcourt, Brace & World, 1956). Arthur M. Schlesinger, Jr.'s two volumes, *The Coming of the New Deal* and *The Politics of Upheaval* (Boston: Houghton Mifflin, 1957-60) are rich with material on the thinking in and around the New Deal circle. Further volumes will carry the story beyond 1936. A multivolume biography of Franklin D. Roosevelt is being written by Frank Freidel, *Franklin D. Roosevelt* (Boston: Little, Brown and Company, 1952-56), of which three volumes thus far published carry FDR's life up to 1932. There are several provocative studies of the American past which devote some attention, and with keen perception, to the New Deal: Carl Degler, *Out of Our Past* (New York: Harper & Brothers, 1959); Richard Hofstadter, *The American Political Tradition* (New York: Alfred Knopf, 1948); Eric Goldman, *Rendezvous With Destiny* (New York: Alfred Knopf, 1952). A critical view of Roosevelt from the left is Mauritz A. Hallgren, *The Gay Reformer* (New York: Alfred Knopf, 1935). A critical view from the right is Edgar E. Robinson, *The Roosevelt Leadership, 1933-1945* (Philadelphia: Lippincott, 1955).

A picture of the nation during the depression years is provided by Irving Bernstein, *The Lean Years* (Boston: Houghton Mifflin, 1960), and Robert and Helen Lynd, *Middletown in Transition* (New York: Harcourt, Brace, 1937). An excellent account of economic conditions and economic policy during the New Deal years can be found in Broadus Mitchell, *Depression Decade* (New York: Rinehart & Company, 1947). A study of Roosevelt's early thinking on economic questions is Daniel Fusfeld, *The Economic Thought of Franklin D. Roosevelt and the Origins of the New Deal* (New York: Columbia University Press, 1956). An account and analysis of the economic collapse of 1929 is John Galbraith, *The Great Crash* (Boston: Houghton Mifflin, 1955).

The New Deal period is given some treatment in the perspective of the total development of American thought in Henry Steele Commager, *The American Mind* (New Haven: Yale University Press, 1950), and in Louis Hartz, *The Liberal Tradition in America* (New York: Harcourt, Brace, 1955). Some light is thrown on the thinking of the New Deal period in Leo Gurko, *The Angry Decade* (New York: Dodd, Mead & Co. 1947), in Alistair Cooke, *A Generation on Trial* (New York: Alfred Knopf, 1950), and in Max Lerner, *Ideas for the Ice Age* (New York: Viking Press, 1941).

Valuable discussions on the problem of government spending can be found in Seymour Harris (ed.), *The New Economics* (New York: Alfred Knopf, 1947) and in Alvin H. Hansen, *A Guide to Keynes* (New York: McGraw-Hill, 1953). The role of the Supreme Court in passing on legislation is analyzed in Robert K. Carr, *The Supreme Court and Judicial Review* (New York: Farrar & Rinehart, 1942). Useful background for understanding the Social Security bill can be found in Paul H. Douglas, *Social Security in the United States* (New York: Whittlesey House, 1936). A good collection of essays on labor in the Roosevelt period is Milton Derber and Edwin Young (eds.), *Labor and the New Deal* (Madison: University of Wisconsin Press, 1957). Background material for understanding the farm problem can be found in Murray Benedict, *Farm Policies of the United States 1790-1950* (New York: Twentieth Century Fund, 1953). Hallie Flanagan, *Arena* (New York: Duell, Sloan & Pearce, 1940) is a colorful study of the federal theater.

For further reading on specific subjects see the excellent bibliographies in the works of Burns, Leuchtenberg, and Schlesinger cited above.

Howard Zinn

Boston, Massachusetts
April 1966

PART ONE

PHILOSOPHIC SETTING

1 · Charles A. Beard: *The Myth of Rugged American Individualism*

Charles A. Beard (1874-1948) was one of the leading figures in American liberal scholarship in the first half of the twentieth century. An iconoclast historian with a broad interest in government and social philosophy, his books—*An Economic Interpretation of the Constitution* (1913), *The Rise of American Civilization* (1927), and many others—had a huge influence on students of his generation. The essay that follows was written at the height of the economic crisis following the 1929 stock market crash, while Herbert Hoover, a firm exponent of "rugged individualism" was still President. The Hoover doctrine was not simply a Republican dogma; many conservative Democrats held to it. For instance, in the same year in which Beard wrote this essay, banker Russell Leffingwell, a supporter of Franklin D. Roosevelt and the Democratic Party, wrote: "I think the cure for the depression is in hard work and thrift in our daily lives; in an effective demand on our governments, national, state and municipal, that they too stop squandering our money and reduce our taxes and public debts. . . ." All these ideas were part of the individualist creed. Beard's slashing critique in this essay is typical of both his style and his scorn of special privilege. Although

Beard later became an opponent of Roosevelt (mainly over foreign policy), this essay is close to the heart of New Deal thought. It reveals that even before FDR took office, the spirit of social concern that animated the New Deal was already part of the American intellectual heritage.

"The House of Bishops would be as much at sea in Minneapolis as at Atlantic City." This bit of delicious humor, all too rare in America's solemn assemblies, sparkled at a tense moment in the late conference of the Episcopalian magnates at Denver when the respective merits of the two cities as future meeting places were under debate. But the real cause of the caustic comment seems to have been a heated discussion, led by the Honorable George W. Wickersham, over a dangerous proposal to modify . . . the sacred creed of rugged American individualism. . . .

This is only one of many straws in the wind indicating a movement to exalt rugged individualism into a national taboo beyond the reach of inquiring minds. From day to day it becomes increasingly evident that some of our economic leaders (by no means all of them) are using the phrase as an excuse for avoiding responsibility, for laying the present depression on "government interference," and for seeking to escape from certain forms of taxation and regulation which they do not find to their interest. If a smoke screen big enough can be laid on the land, our commercial prestidigitators may work wonders—for themselves. . . .

Hence it is important to ask, calmly and without reference to election heats, just what all this means. In what way is the Government "in business" and how did it get there? Here we climb down out of the muggy atmosphere of controversy and face a few stubborn facts. They are entered in the indubitable records of the Government of the United States and are as evident as the hills to them that have eyes to see. Let us catalogue a few of them *seriatim* for the first time in the history of this adventure in logomachy.

1. Government Regulations of Railways, from 1887 to the last Act of Congress. How did the Government get into this business? The general cause was the conduct of railway corporations under the rule of rugged individualism—rebates, pools, stock watering, bankruptcy-juggling, all the traffic will bear, savage rate slashing, merciless competition, and the rest of it. If anyone wants to know the facts, let him read the history of railroading in the sixties, seventies, and early eighties, or, if time is limited, the charming illustrations presented in Charles Francis Adams' "A Chapter of Erie." And what was the immediate cause of the Government's intervention? The insistence of business men, that is, shippers, who were harassed and sometimes ruined by railway tactics, and of farmers, the most rugged of all the rugged individualists the broad land of America has produced. And the result? Let the gentle reader compare the disastrous railway bankruptcies that flowed from the panic of 1873, including bloodshed and arson, with the plight of railways now, bad as it is. Government regulation is not a utopian success, but it is doubtful whether any of our great business men would like to get the Government entirely out of this business and return to the magnificent anarchy of Jay Gould's age. President Hoover has not even suggested it.

2. Waterways. Since its foundation the Government has poured hundreds of millions into rivers, harbors, canals, and other internal improvements. It is still pouring in millions. Some of our best economists have denounced it as wasteful and have demonstrated that most of it does not pay in any sense of the word. But President Hoover, instead of leaving this work to private enterprise, insists on projecting and executing the most elaborate undertakings, in spite of the fact that some of them are unfair if not ruinous to railways. Who is back of all this? Business men and farmers who want lower freight

rates. There is not a chamber of commerce on any Buck Creek in America that will not cheer until tonsils are cracked any proposal to make the said creek navigable. Dredging companies want the good work to go on, and so do the concerns that make dredging machinery. Farmers are for it also and they are, as already said, the ruggedest of rugged individuals—so rugged in fact that the vigorous efforts of the Farm Board to instill co-operative reason into them have been almost as water on a duck's back.

3. The United States Barge Corporation. Who got the Government into the job of running barges on some of its improved waterways? Certainly not the socialists, but good Republicans and Democrats speaking for the gentlemen listed under 2 above.

4. The Shipping Business. The World War was the occasion, but not the cause of this departure. For more than half a century the politicians of America fought ship subsidies against business men engaged in the shipbuilding and allied industries. At last, under the cover of war necessities, the Government went into the shipping business, with cheers from business. Who is back of the huge expenditures for the merchant marine? Business men. Who supports huge subsidies under the guise of "lucrative mail contracts," making a deficit in postal finances to be used as proof that the Government cannot run any business? Business men clamor for three mail subsidies and receive them. Who put the Government into the business of providing cheap money for ship building? Business men did it. . . .

5. Aviation. The Government is "in" this business. It provides costly airway services free of charge and subsidizes air mail. Who is behind this form of Government enterprise? Gentlemen engaged in aviation and the manufacture of planes and dirigibles. Then the government helps by buying planes for national defense. Who is opposed to air mail subsidies? A few despised "politicians."

6. Canals. Who zealously supported the construction of the Panama Canal? Shippers on the Pacific Coast who did not like the railway rates. Also certain important shipping interests on both coasts—all controlled by business men. Who insisted that the Government should buy the Cape Cod Canal? The business men who put their money into the enterprise and found that it did not pay. Then they rejoiced to see the burden placed on the broad back of our dear Uncle Sam.

7. Highway Building. Who has supported Federal highway aid—the expenditures of hundreds of millions on roads involving the taxation of railways to pay for ruinous competition? Everybody apparently, but specifically business men engaged in the manufacture and sale of automobiles and trucks. Who proposes to cut off every cent of that outlay? Echoes do not answer.

8. The Department of Commerce, its magnificent mansion near the Treasury Department, and its army of hustlers scouting for business at the uttermost ends of the earth. Who is responsible for loading on the Government the job of big drummer at large for business? Why shouldn't these rugged individualists do their own drumming instead of asking the taxpayers to do it for them? Business men have been behind this enormous expansion, and Mr. Hoover, as Secretary of Commerce, outdid every predecessor in the range of his activities and the expenditure of public money. Who proposes to take the Government out of the business of hunting business for men who ought to know their own business?

9. The Big Pork Barrel—appropriations for public buildings, navy yards, and army posts. An interesting enterprise for the United States Chamber of Commerce would be to discover a single piece of pork in a hundred years that has not been approved by local business men as beneficiaries. When Ben Tillman shouted in the Senate that he intended to steal a hog every time a Yankee got a ham, he knew for whom the speaking was done.

10. The Bureau of Standards. Besides its general services, it renders valuable aid to business undertakings. Why shouldn't they do their own investigating at their own expense, instead of turning to the Government?

11. The Federal Trade Commission. Who runs there for rulings on "fair practices"? Weary consumers? Not often. Principally, business men who do not like to be outwitted or cheated by their competitors. If we are rugged individualists, why not let every individualist do as he pleases, without invoking government intervention at public expense?

12. The Anti-Trust Acts. Business men are complaining against these laws on the ground that they cannot do any large-scale planning without incurring the risk of prosecution. The contention is sound, but who put these laws on the books and on what theory were they based? They were the product of a clamor on the part of farmers and business men against the practices of great corporations. Farmers wanted lower prices. . . .

13. The Tariff. On this tender subject it is scarcely possible to speak soberly. It seems safe to say, however, that if all the business men who demand this kind of "interference"—with the right of capital to find its most lucrative course, industry and intelligence their natural reward, commodities their fair price, and idleness and folly their natural punishment—were to withdraw their support for protection, cease their insistence on it, then the politicians would probably reduce the levy or go over to free trade; with what effect on business no one can correctly predict. At all events there are thousands of business men who want to keep the Government in the business of protecting their business against foreign competition. If competition is good, why not stand up and take it?

14. The Federal Farm Board. This collectivist institution is the product of agrarian agitation, on the part of our most stalwart individualists, the free and independent farmers; but President Hoover sponsored it and signed the bill that created it. Now what is its avowed purpose as demonstrated by the language of the statute, the publications of the Farm Board,

and the activities carried out under its auspices? It is primarily and fundamentally intended to stabilize prices and production through co-operative methods. . . .

15. The Moratorium and Frozen Assets. The latest form of government interference with "the natural course" of economy is the suspension of payments due the United States from foreign powers on account of lawful debts and the proposal to give public support to "frozen assets." What was the source of inspiration here? American investment bankers having got themselves into a jam in their efforts to make easy money now demand government assistance. . . .

For forty years or more there has not been a President, Republican or Democrat, who has not talked against government interference and then supported measures adding more interference to the huge collection already accumulated. Take, for instance, President Wilson. He made his campaign in 1912 on the classical doctrine of individualism; he blew mighty blasts in the name of his new freedom against the control of the Government by corporate wealth and promised to separate business and government, thus setting little fellows free to make money out of little business. The heir of the Jeffersonian tradition, he decried paternalism of every kind. Yet look at the statutes enacted under his benign administration: the trainmen's law virtually fixing wages on interstate railways for certain classes of employees; the shipping board law; the farm loan act; federal aid for highway construction; the Alaskan railway; the federal reserve act; the water power act; and the rest of the bills passed during his regime. Only the Clayton anti-trust law can be called individualistic. No wonder Mr. E. L. Doheny exclaimed to Mr. C. W. Barron that President Wilson was a college professor gone Bolshevist! And why did Democrats who had been saying "the less government the better" operate on the theory that the more government the better? Simply because their mouths were worked by ancient memories and their actions were shaped by inexorable realities.

Then the Republicans came along in 1921 and informed the

country that they were going back to normalcy, were determined to take the Government out of business. Well, did they repeal a single one of the important measures enacted during the eight years of President Wilson's rule? It would be entertaining to see the sanhedrin of the United States Chamber of Commerce trying to make out a list of laws repealed in the name of normalcy and still more entertaining to watch that august body compiling a list of additional laws interfering with "the natural course of business" enacted since 1921. Heirs of the Hamiltonian tradition, the Republicans were not entitled to talk about separating the Government from business. Their great spiritual teacher, Daniel Webster, a pupil of Hamilton, had spoken truly when he said that one of the great reasons for framing the Constitution was the creation of a government that could regulate commerce. They came honestly by subsidies, bounties, internal improvements, tariffs, and other aids to business. What was the trouble with them in the age of normalcy? Nothing; they just wanted their kind of government intervention in the "natural course of industry." Evidently, then, there is some confusion on this subject of individualism, and it ought to be examined dispassionately in the light of its history with a view to discovering its significance and its limitatons; for there is moral danger in saying one thing and doing another—at all events too long. . . .

Closely examined, what is this creed of individualism? Macaulay defines it beautifully. . . . Let the Government maintain peace, defend property, reduce the cost of litigation, and observe economy in expenditure—that is all. Do American business men want peace all the time, in Nicaragua, for instance, when their undertakings are disturbed? Or in Haiti or Santo Domingo? Property must be defended, of course. But whose property? And what about the cost of litigation and economy in expenditures? If they would tell their hired men in law offices to cut the cost of law, something might happen. As for expenditures, do they really mean to abolish subsidies, bounties, and appropriations-in-aid from which they benefit? Speaking brutally, they do not. That is not the kind of economy in expenditures which they demand; they prefer to cut off a few dollars from the Children's Bureau. . . .

Do any stalwart individualists believe that simple creed now? Not in England, where Liberals, professing to carry on the Cobden-Bright tradition, vote doles for unemployed working people. Why not let idleness and folly get their natural punishment? Why not, indeed? There must be a reason. Either the individualists betray their own faith, or, as some wag has suggested, they are afraid that they might find themselves hanging to a lantern if they let the idle and the foolish starve, that is, reap the natural punishment prescribed by Macaulay. Nor do American individualists propose to let nature take her course in this country. There is no danger of revolution here; as Mr. Coolidge has said, "we have had our revolution"; yet business men agree with the politicians on feeding the hungry. It is true that they seem to be trying to obscure the issues and the facts by talking about the beneficence of private charity while getting most of the dole from public treasuries; but that is a detail. Although our rugged individualists advertise Macaulay's creed, their faith in it appears to be shaky or their courage is not equal to their hopes. Then why should they try to delude themselves and the public?

There is another side to this stalwart individualism that also deserves consideration. Great things have been done in its name, no doubt, and it will always have its place in any reasoned scheme of thinking. Individual initiative and energy are absolutely indispensable to the successful conduct of any enterprise, and there is ample ground for fearing the tyranny and ineptitude of governments. In the days of pioneering industry in England, in our pioneering days when forests were to be cut and mountain fastnesses explored, individualism was the great dynamic which drove enterprise forward. But on other pages of the doom book other entries must be made. In the minds of most people who shout for individualism vociferously, the creed, stripped of all flashy rhetoric, means getting money, simply that and nothing more. And to this creed may be laid most of the shame that has cursed our cities and most of the scandals that have smirched our Federal Government. . . .

The cold truth is that the individualist creed of everybody for himself and the devil take the hindmost is principally responsible for the distress in which Western civilization finds itself—with investment racketeering at one end and labor racketeering at the other. Whatever merits the creed may have had in days of primitive agriculture and industry, it is not applicable in an age of technology, science, and rationalized economy. Once useful, it has become a danger to society. . . .

2 · Upton Sinclair: *Production for Use*

Upton Sinclair (1878-), a novelist and long-time socialist, began his career as a "muckraker," in the era of Theodore Roosevelt. His most famous book, *The Jungle* (1906), brought the shocking conditions in the Chicago meatpacking industry to national attention. In a series of novels and works of nonfiction, he then attacked in turn the newspapers, the coal magnates, the oil industry, the prosecutors of Sacco and Vanzetti, and other targets of radical reform. In 1934, defying the regular conservative Democratic machine of California, Sinclair ran in the Democratic Primary for Governor of California. His imaginative and sweeping program was called EPIC—End Poverty in California. Sinclair occupied a place near the very left margin in the spectrum of New Deal thought. He hoped for Roosevelt's support in the 1934 election, but did not get it, and lost to the Republican candidate. The views expressed below, in the form of a letter to an imaginary friend, were circulated throughout California during the gubernatorial campaign. They may reveal why Franklin D. Roosevelt, a humanitarian but also a politician, did nothing to help Sinclair win.

My Dear Perry:

You understand by now my point of view, that the concentration of wealth in our society is an inescapable consequence of the system of private ownership and competition for profits. Like a diseased body, we are killed by the poisons of our own generating. The disease gets worse and worse every year, and the only remedy which will have permanent effect is to abolish private ownership of industry and production for profit, and substitute public ownership with production for use.

Here we have this enormous machine, the most perfect ever constructed in the history of our planet. Taking our own country, which is enough for us to deal with, we have natural resources without limit so far as concerns the immediate future. We have the skilled labor, we have the willingness to work, we have a government which preserves order and protects property—in short, we have everything necessary to a prosperous and happy communal life. Our problem is to take all this productive machinery and make it into one machine: to organize it and systematize its processes, making one process with one purpose, the production of all the necessities and comforts desired by our people, and the distribution of these upon a basis of justice and fair play.

Will you, Perry, say that you are unable to conceive of such a task? Will you say that the collective intelligence of our directing class would be unequal to it? As you know, we now have one great corporation which handles the whole telephone business of the United States. We have two corporations which handle our telegrams, and any one will admit that, but for the element of price competition, it would be more economical to have one telegraph company. We have many steel companies, but only one big one, and any steel man would admit that, but for the element of price competition, we could save a great deal of money by having one national steel trust.

We have one post office system and one express system. Why would it not be possible to have one banking system, one system for producing shoes, one system for distributing groceries to the people, one system for growing cotton and another for growing wheat? Does not your business mind immediately begin to grapple with the problem of forming such an organization in your own line? Does it not begin immediately to see all the wastes that could be cut out, the duplications of office buildings and clerical staffs, the wastes of competitive advertising, of competitive salesmen, of competitive shipping organizations? It doesn't make any difference whether you take two big concerns like Postal and Western Union, or whether you take two dairies or two laundries in a town, each with its rival delivery wagons in the same block, each with its competitive circulars littering our doorsteps and front lawns. . . .

You see what this means. If you take our whole system and eliminate the competitive elements and rationalize everything from top to bottom, as our production engineers understand how to do, we should with the same amount of labor have something more than three times the amount of wealth per capita; in other words, we should need to work less than one-third as many hours, which means that our working day would be two or three hours.

As a Socialist, I have been accustomed to tell my readers and audiences that in a coöperative society every man, woman, and child would have the equivalent of $5,000 a year income from the labor of the able-bodied young men for three or four hours per day. I was rarely believed, but I always said that I would take care of my health and live to see it. . . . The certain fact is that we have developed only a small part of our production powers, and are able to use only a small part of what we have developed: our steel plant working at twenty per cent capacity, our automobile plant thirty-two per cent, and so on. Let us make them all into public service institutions, and run them one hundred per cent, and then make all the improvements we can, and cut down our working hours and increase our income to whatever extent we find possible. That is a simple, common-sense proposition, and I am firm in my faith that our engineers will ultimately come to understand it, and that a considerable part of our business men will help the government in putting the job through.

There are two questions to be settled, or rather two groups of questions. First, how are we going to get the industries; and, second, how are we going to run them?

Before we can acquire the industries, it is necessary to have the will to acquire them. That is a matter of education; the job is being done for us by capitalism, which is squeezing the life out of our people, and eliminating more and more of them from industry, making it inevitable that sooner or later they will rebel.

For our leaders, the need is, in part, of understanding and, in part, of courage. Men brought up in a certain system inevitably try to continue in the old way. It means a sharp break with the past and a brand-new idea in the mind of a statesman like President Roosevelt. He has been trying to save business and restore it to its feet, and now he has to say: "I will wipe it out of existence and replace it with something better." The difference is fundamental, and there is no reconciling the two procedures.

For example, Roosevelt has just asked Congress to appoint a Tennessee Valley Authority to take over the Muscle Shoals plant and run it as a public service. Immediately there come before Congress the heads of all the private power plants in the South and point out that the result of this procedure will be to break the private power companies and render their stock worthless. This statement is absolutely true, and it applies to every step in the new path which the Government can take. If Roosevelt goes ahead planting forests, and if he makes economic use of these forests for the people, he will break the private lumber companies. If he takes over any bankrupt railroad and runs it in the public interest, he will wipe out all the competing railroads, and ultimately will have to take over the entire railroad system. If he permits postal savings banks to carry checking accounts, he will break the private banks. If instead of buying food and clothing for the unemployed, he puts them to work making their own food and clothing, he will find that all his efforts to raise prices of farm products will fail and he will have to socialize agriculture.

And so on into the tiniest cranny of the profit system. It is obvious why a statesman shrinks from embarking on this course, and it is also obvious why the masses, the bankrupt farmers and unemployed laborers and white-collar workers, should clamor for this same action. . . .

At the outset, the government should take only the principal industries, those which are essential to the social welfare, and especially those which have been holding up production. The President could obtain from Congress the right to take over all private industries which are unable to employ more than a certain percentage of their workers. The one essential is that everybody should be put to work, and that the goods should be produced which are necessary to the health and happiness of every person in the community. Provide work for all, and pay them adequate wages, and they will go to the stores and create a market for all products.

The great public service corporations present a special problem, for the reason that they have been accustomed to control our government, and own and run the political machines in most of our cities and states. They have not suffered so much from the depression, because they have a strangle hold upon the community; through their control of public commissions they have been able to keep up rates and protect themselves. The answer to them is found in the Muscle Shoals project. Once they realize that the government is determined to compete them out of business, their resistance will weaken.

Fundamentally, the problem is one of mass pressure. Let the people decide what they want, and they can get it, and nothing can stop them. We saw it happen in wartime, when the government declared a public emergency and took over the railroads and munitions plants. Now we have another kind of war, a war for the salvation of our people from starvation, and of our country from civil strife and revolution, and we have exactly the same need and the same right to act. . . .

3 · Reinhold Niebuhr: *After Capitalism—What?*

Reinhold Niebuhr (1892-), emerged in the 1930's as one of the nation's most powerful theological spokesmen for the "social gospel"—the idea that the church should be an active and radical opponent of those social institutions that bring poverty or injustice or war. As a pastor in Detroit, with many auto workers in his congregation, he had become conscious of the terrible personal consequences of economic depression. Both the depression in the United States and the rise of Hitler in Europe strengthened certain beliefs that he maintained throughout his writings: that there is a persistent element of evil in the nature of man; and that a socially conscious church must reckon with the fact of power in the world. Although he modified his views somewhat in the 1940's and 1950's, he con-

From Reinhold Niebuhr, "After Capitalism—What?" *The World Tomorrow,* XVI (March 1, 1933), 203-205. Reprinted with the permission of the author.

tinued to write books and essays—*The Irony of American History*, *Faith and History*, and others—that stressed political realism as an accompaniment to the vision of a just world. His essay below is a good illustration of the way in which the depression evoked in intellectuals the most radical components of their thinking. The work appeared just as Franklin D. Roosevelt was being sworn into office.

The following analysis of American social and political conditions is written on the assumption that capitalism is dying and with the conviction that it ought to die. It is dying because it is a contracting economy which is unable to support the necessities of an industrial system that requires mass production for its maintenance, and because it disturbs the relations of an international economic system with the anarchy of nationalistic politics. It ought to die because it is unable to make the wealth created by modern technology available to all who participate in the productive process on terms of justice. . . .

The most generally applicable judgment which can be made is that capitalism will not reform itself from within. There is nothing in history to support the thesis that a dominant class ever yields its position or privileges in society because its rule has been convicted of ineptness or injustices. Those who still regard this as possible are rationalists and moralists who have only a slight understanding of the stubborn inertia and blindness of collective egoism.

Politically this judgment implies that liberalism in politics is a spent force. In so far as liberalism is based upon confidence in the ability and willingness of rational and moral individuals to change the basis of society, it has suffered disillusion in every modern nation. As the social struggle becomes more sharply defined, the confused liberals drift reluctantly into the camp of reaction and the minority of clear-sighted intellectuals and idealists are forced either to espouse the cause of radicalism or to escape to the bleachers and become disinterested observers. The liberal middle ground has been almost completely wiped out in Germany. It is held today only by the Catholic party, a unique phenomenon in Western politics. In England only the free-trade liberals who managed to extricate themselves from the Tory embrace and the quite lonely and slightly pathetic Mr. Lloyd George stand in the liberal position. The English liberals who interpreted their position as a championship of the community of consumers against warring camps of producers have had to learn that the stakes which men have in the productive process outweigh their interests as consumers. Mr. Roosevelt's effort at, or pretension to, liberalizing the Democratic Party may be regarded as a belated American effort to do what Europe has proved to be impossible. Equally futile will be the efforts of liberals who stand to the left of Mr. Roosevelt and who hope to organize a party which will give the feverish American patient pills of diluted socialism coated with liberalism, in the hope that his aversion to bitter pills will thus be circumvented.

All this does not mean that intellectual and moral idealism are futile. They are needed to bring decency and fairness into any system of society; for no basic reorganization of society will ever guarantee the preservation of humaneness if good men do not preserve it. Furthermore, the intelligence of a dominant group will determine in what measure it will yield in time under pressure or to what degree it will defend its entrenched positions so uncompromisingly that an orderly retreat becomes impossible and a disorderly rout envelops the whole of society in chaos. That ought to be high enough stake for those of us to play for who are engaged in the task of education and moral suasion among the privileged. If such conclusions seems unduly cynical they will seem so only because the moral idealists of the past century, both religious and rational, have been unduly sentimental in their estimates of human nature. Perhaps it will be permitted the writer to add, by way of parenthesis, that he has been greatly instructed by the number of letters which have come to him in late months complaining that a religious radical ought not to give up his faith in human nature so completely lest he betray thereby his lack of faith in the divine. Classical religion has always spoken rather unequivocally of the depravity of human nature, a conclusion at which it arrived by looking at human nature from the perspective of the divine. It is one of the strange phenomena of our culture that an optimistic estimate of human nature has been made the basis of theistic theologies. . . .

The certainty that dominant social groups which now control society will not easily yield and that their rule is nevertheless doomed raises interesting problems of strategy for those who desire a new social order. In America these problems are complicated by the fact that there is no real proletarian class in this country. All but the most disinherited workers still belong to the middle class, and they will not be united in a strong political party of their own for some years to come. Distressing social experience will finally produce radical convictions among them, but experience without education and an adequate political philosophy will merely result in sporadic violence. We are literally in the midst of a disintegrating economic empire with no receiver in bankruptcy in sight to assume responsibility for the defunct institution. All this probably means that capitalism has many a decade to run in this country, particularly if it should find momentary relief from present difficulties through some inflationary movement. The sooner a strong political labor movement, expressing itself in socialist terms develops, the greater is the probability of achieving essential change without undue violence or social chaos.

One of the difficulties of the situation is that America may have to go through a period of purely parliamentary socialism even after Europe has proved that a socialism which makes a fetish of parliamentarism will not be able to press through to its goal. Though we will probably have to go through the experience of parliamentarism, we may be able to qualify our faith in it sufficiently to be pragmatic and experimental in the choice of our radical techniques. To disavow pure parliamentarism does not mean to espouse revolution. . . .

Prediction at long range may seem idle and useless. But it is important to recognize that neither the parliamentary nor the revolutionary course offers modern society an easy way to the mastery of a technological civilization. If this is the case, it becomes very important to develop such forms of resistance and mass coercion as will disturb the intricacies of an industrial civilization as little as possible, and as will preserve the temper of mutual respect within the area of social conflict. Political realists have become cynical about moral and religious idealism in politics chiefly because so frequently it is expressed in terms of confusion which hide the basic facts of the social struggle. Once the realities of this struggle are freely admitted, there is every possibility of introducing very important ethical elements into the struggle in the way, for instance, that Gandhi introduces them in India.

The inability of religious and intellectual idealists to gauge properly the course of historical events results from their constant over-estimate of idealistic and unselfish factors in political life. They think that an entire nation can be educated toward a new social ideal when all the testimony of history proves that new societies are born out of social struggle, in which the positions of the various social groups are determined by their economic interests.

Those who wish to participate in such a struggle creatively, to help history toward a goal of justice and to eliminate as much confusion, chaos and conflict in the attainment of the goal as possible, will accomplish this result only if they do not permit their own comparative emancipation from the determining and conditioning economic factors to obscure the fact that these factors are generally determining. No amount of education or religious idealism will ever persuade a social class to espouse a cause or seek a goal which is counter to its economic interest. Social intelligence can have a part in guiding social impulse only if it does not commit the error of assuming that intelligence has destroyed and sublimated impulse to such a degree that impulse is no longer potent. This is the real issue between liberalism and political realism. The liberal is an idealist who imagines that his particular type of education or his special kind of religious idealism will accomplish what history has never before revealed: the complete sublimation of the natural impulse of a social group.

Dominant groups will always have the impulse to hold on to their power as long as possible. In the interest of a progressive justice they must be dislodged, and this will be done least painfully and with least confusion if the social group which has the future in its hands becomes conscious of its destiny as soon as possible, is disciplined and self-confident in the knowledge of its destiny and gradually acquires all the heights of prestige and power in society which it is possible to acquire without a struggle. When the inevitable struggle comes (for all contests of power must finally issue in a crisis) there is always the possibility that the old will capitulate and the new assume social direction without internecine conflict. That is why an adequate political realism will ultimately make for more peace in society than a liberalism which does not read the facts of human nature and human history aright, and which is betrayed by these errors into erroneous historical calculations which prolong the death agonies of the old order and postpone the coming of the new.

It may be important to say in conclusion that educational and religious idealists shrink from the conclusions to which a realistic analysis of history forces the careful student, partly because they live in the false hope that the impulses of nature in man can be sublimated by mind and conscience to a larger degree than is actually possible, and partly because their own personal idealism shrinks from the "brutalities" of the social struggle which a realistic theory envisages. But this idealism is full of confusion. It does not recognize that everyone but the ascetic is a participant in the brutalities of the social struggle now. The only question of importance is on what side of the struggle they are. Think of all the kind souls who stand in horror of a social conflict who are at this moment benefiting from, and living comfortable lives at the expense of, a social system which condemns 13 million men to misery and semi-starvation. Failure to recognize this covert brutality of the social struggle is probably the greatest weakness of middle-class liberals, and it lends a note of hypocrisy and self-deception to every moral pretension which seeks to eliminate violence in the social struggle.

The relation of the sensitive conscience to the brutal realities of man's collective behavior will always create its own problem—a problem in the solution of which orthodox religion has frequently been more shrewd than liberalism because it did not over-estimate the virtue of human society, but rather recognized the "sinful" character of man's collective life. This problem has its own difficulties, and they ought not to be confused with the problem of achieving an adequate social and political strategy for the attainment of a just society or for the attainment of a higher approximation of justice than a decadent capitalism grants.

4 • Stuart Chase: *The Age of Distribution*

Stuart Chase (1888-   ), an economist and prolific writer, was one of the most influential popularizers of reform ideology in the

From Stuart Chase, "The Age of Distribution." *The Nation,* CXXXIX (July 25, 1934), 93-96. Reprinted with the permission of the publisher.

New Deal period. Early in his career he had helped investigate the meatpacking industry for the Federal Trade Commission; in the 1930's and 1940's he served as consultant for such New Deal agencies as the National Resources Committee and the TVA. Throughout his writings—*The Tragedy of Waste* (1925), *The Economy of Abundance* (1934), and many other widely selling books—he emphasized the idea that the American economy had reached a new stage in its development, which required a rational plan for the equitable distribution of the enormous amount of goods it was now possible to produce. The essay below summarizes his views on this point, and illustrates the extent to which many thinkers of the time, while avoiding the traditional doctrines of Marxist socialism, sought far-reaching changes in the capitalist system. (See Document 40.)

. . . The new physical conditions and facts are reasonably apparent and have repeatedly been called to our attention. There is no need to go into them at length here. They include: A compounding curve of invention; a vast per-capita increase in the consumption of inanimate energy; an industrial and agricultural plant far in excess of pecuniary market demand; a steady increase in output per man hour, resulting in a surplus of labor and technological unemployment; specialization of economic activity to the point where it now constitutes one interdependent network; population growing at a decrement; autarchy and the resulting decline of foreign trade.

With these facts firmly in mind, let us approach the concept "capitalism." What is it? I should define it as the private ownership of the means of production, and, by virtue of such ownership, a flow of free income in the form of profits, interest, rents, and royalties. After deducting living expenses, including certain outlays for conspicuous consumption, the pleasure and the duty of the capitalists has been to invest the balance in more means of production, the income from which, after deductions, is further reinvested, ad infinitum.

This stupendous rhythm of compounding indebtedness has not only been pleasurable to capitalists, but it has come to provide the balance wheel of the whole system. The prompt investment of the free income has provided wages and salaries for workers in durable-goods industries, with which income these workers have cleared the shelves of the consumers' goods produced in the same period. Equilibrium came to depend on compounding reinvestment in a compounding durable-goods sector, which distributed compounding purchasing power, with which a compounding volume of consumers' goods was cleared at a profit—which was once more reinvested. Accounting, insurance, actuarial, and banking practice are all predicated on this rhythm. Capitalism by its name connotes the investment and safe-guarding of capital, or the profitable accumulation of the means of production. It is a method harsh but pragmatic for building up a productive plant; for "developing" a given economic area. It belongs to an age where the problems of production are paramount.

But what of the time when the area should be at last "developed"; when the means of production should no longer be at a premium as a vehicle for profitable investment; when the exquisite mathematics of the compounding process should run clear off the map of physical realities? Capitalists have been too busy ever to answer these questions. Even today, with the compounding process seriously crippled, most capitalists prefer a mystic nostalgia for 1928 to any frank facing of their own formula.

Yet for all practical purposes, the problem of production is solved. The plant has lost its scarcity status, as witnessed by surpluses and excess capacity, a condition which was becoming ominous long before the depression. Further increases in the means of production are discouraged, owing to the poor prospects of realizable profits. Regard the sorry state of the durable-goods industries today, and the huge surplus of idle capital in the banks. But without an increase—duly compounded—in the means of production, durable-goods workers remain on the streets, their purchasing power all but gone. This so depresses the total volume of purchasing power that profits and free income are, for the system as a whole, inadequate to validate the values set on the present means of production. According to R. R. Doane, capital assets valued at $441,000,000,000 for the whole nation in 1929 dropped to $256,0000,000,000 in 1932. The decline of nearly two hundred billion registers an appalling shrinkage in the ability to validate.

With no sufficient means under the canons of "sound money" to extend markets and purchasing power, the system comes to a halt, the majestic rhythm stops. Presently it goes below the line into disintegration—as we have observed it for the past five years, both here and abroad. Capitalism cannot stand still without disaster. It must move forward to keep in equilibrium—like the Red Queen.

The simple conclusion seems to be that capitalism has fulfilled its function, the plant has been built to the limit of the sound-money framework, and the flow of free income is seriously jeopardized. Whether that body of enterprising individuals constituting the "control" (see Berle and Means) of this disintegrating system are also departing, is another question. Some, like Kreuger, Insull, Wiggin, and Mitchell, have gone; others may or may not follow. We shall return to them presently.

Consciously or unconsciously, economic thinking and economic action are now oriented towards distribution. The consumer is creeping to the center of the stage. Ways and means to furnish him with purchasing power form the outstanding problem of current statesmanship. Doles, subsidies, civil works, public works, controlled prices, pegged minimum wages are all aimed pragmatically, if without much theoretical blessing, at mass distribution, a distribution which bypasses the rigid formula of capitalism. The fact of the bypassing is amply evidenced by the piteous wails issuing from the sound-money camp.

Aids to distribution have taken two general forms—the artificial stimulation of purchasing power through government spending; the rationing of surplus products—like wheat, meat, potatoes—direct to the needy consumer. All Western nations are threatening their budget balances with one or the other of these devices. We use both in the United States, and the general opinion seems to be that we must use them far more freely. John Maynard Keynes recently advised the President that four hundred million, rather than the present one hundred million a month, was essential if the economic machine was to continue to operate.

These doles, driblets of relief, and feeble "make-work" projects can hardly be dignified with the title of "a distributive age." But they clearly mark the beginning of such an age, as Watt's wheezy old steam engine marked the beginning of the age of quantity production. If private business cannot distribute the surplus, the community must. The community is proceeding to do so, with comparatively little regard for budget balancing. Consumers must eat. There can be, I believe, no permanent retreat from this beginning. The tide of distribution must mount, at the cost of any and every "sound-money" barrier. . . .

I do not pretend in this brief exposition to enter the vast and vaulted grottoes of Marxian criticism. Marx was a great man. His economic vision was profound, perhaps to the point of foreseeing the collapse of capitalism at the hands of a surplus economy. His sociology was less profound, and his tactics, I believe, stand in need of extensive revision. The analysis of socialism in this article does not pretend to account for all that Marx did or did not say. It follows a simple pattern—the popular conception of socialism as evidenced by the linguistic behavior of most of its adherents.

Let us look more closely at the popular concept of "socialism." Its cardinal plank is also ownership—the social ownership of the means of production. It is thus a kind of anti-capitalism, developed in opposition to capitalism, in the age of scarcity when the problem of production was dominant. It proposed to wrench the monopoly of ownership in the scarce means of production away from private parties and vest it in the state. Most socialists appear to assume that the volume of goods is limited, and that the division should be more just. But under 1934 technological conditions, the potential volume of goods is all but unlimited.

What happens to anti-capitalism when capitalism degenerates; when a distributive economy undermines the strategic importance of the private ownership of the means of production? Socialism loses some of its own importance. . . .

The moral sanction of factory seizure was given by the doctrine that labor creates all wealth. This was roughly true in 1850. Today the mental labor of technicians harnesses inanimate energy to create far more wealth in total tonnage than is created by manual labor. The traditional toiler is passing from the productive picture at an alarming rate. Already in this country an adequate flow of physical goods could be produced by not more than one-fifth of the working population. Yet everybody must eat. A surplus economy is undermining rigid conceptions of the class struggle. The conflict is no longer primarily between producers and owners of the means of production; the ground has shifted to a point where mass consumption is sovereign to both, technologically as well as ethically. Class struggles we may have, but the lines must be reformed.

Socialism, narrowly interpreted, loses much of its drive and significance in a distributive age. In its broader aspects, namely distributive justice and community well being, it is of course greatly advanced, for mass distribution is a long step towards social justice. But the ancient strategies, the ancient objectives, the ancient hates, become less valid. This is depressing, if not infuriating, to those who have devoted their lives to capturing scarcity-age citadels. Capitalism has become a dear and necessary enemy. I call on any competent psychologist to check me on these observations. . . .

For a long time I have been searching for a social philosophy which would fit the modern facts. Thorstein Veblen started me on this quest. I have tried to hold to the facts no matter whose toes were stepped on. I have not been able to find any hope in an enlightened or reformed capitalism. This is not because all capitalists are low fellows, but because of the inflexibility of their compounding formula. A production system cannot fit a distribution age. I have been unable to find a realistic solution in the class-struggle tactics of socialism or communism, as popularly interpreted, because they too are production-age systems. . . .

This has thrown me back on the experimental method. Experimentation is a somewhat lonely business, lacking, as it does, the warm arms of faith and doctrine. Given the modern trend, however, what else can a fact follower do? There is no body of doctrine competent to deal with this trend. . . .

The formulation of a clean-cut philosophy and a social program for the age of distribution is coming. It will contain many elements broadly called socialistic. It may win the allegiance of many socialists, now vaguely disturbed with their own lack of progress. It will be strongly collectivist; it will nationalize certain key industries; it will work out a method of non-interest-bearing public credit, it will largely displace the profit motive—not for ethical reasons but to move the goods. A vast extension in the public-works sector appears to be inevitable. The general objective will be the distribution of the surplus, rather than a wrangling over the ownership of a productive plant which has lost its scarcity position. . . .

5 · John Dewey: *The Future of Liberalism*

John Dewey (1859-1952), one of the giants of American philosophy and for many years a professor at Columbia University, wrote extensively on philosophy, education, and social problems. In addition, he was an energetic battler for many of the liberal and radical causes of his day: for academic freedom, for political democracy, for a more equalitarian economy. The essay below was part of a symposium at a 1934 meeting of the American Philosophical Association, in which Dewey and the Harvard philosopher, William Ernest Hocking, exchanged their views on "The Future of Liberalism." Like Dewey, Hocking saw liberalism in crisis, needing a redefinition in a time of catastrophe, requiring a new discipline to achieve important social goals, while retaining the kernel of the liberal tradition—the spirit of free inquiry. Dewey's essay faithfully represents his lifelong commitment to experimentalism, to the conscious use of intelligence for the changing of society. In his stress on the compatibility of liberal thought and radical action, he reflected the growing impatience of reformers, in days of economic crisis, with gradualism in social change.

The emphasis of earlier liberalism upon individuality and liberty defines the focal points in discussion of the philosophy of liberalism to-day. This earlier liberalism was itself an outgrowth, in the late eighteenth and nineteenth centuries, of the earlier revolt against oligarchical government, one which came to its culmination in the "glorious revolution" of 1688. The latter was fundamentally a demand for freedom of the taxpayer from government arbitrary action in connection with a demand for confessional freedom in religion by the Protestant churches. In the later liberalism, expressly so called, the demand for

From John Dewey, "The Future of Liberalism," *The Journal of Philosophy,* XXII, No. 9 (1935), 225-230. Reprinted with the permission of the publisher.

liberty and individual freedom of action came primarily from the rising industrial and trading class and was directed against restrictions placed by government, in legislation, common law and judicial action, and other institutions having connection with the political state, upon freedom of economic enterprise. In both cases, governmental action and the desired freedom were placed in antithesis to each other. This way of conceiving liberty has persisted; it was strengthened in this country by the revolt of the colonies and by pioneer conditions.

Nineteenth-century philosophic liberalism added, more or less because of its dominant economic interest, the conception of natural laws to that of natural rights of the Whig movement. There are natural laws, it held, in social matters as well as in physical, and these natural laws are economic in character. Political laws, on the other hand, are man-made and in that sense artificial. Governmental intervention in industry and exchange was thus regarded as a violation not only of inherent individual liberty but also of natural laws—of which supply and demand is a sample. The proper sphere of governmental action was simply to prevent and to secure redress for infringement by one, in the exercise of his liberty, of like and equal liberty of action on the part of others.

Nevertheless, the demand for freedom in initiation and conduct of business enterprise did not exhaust the content of earlier liberalism. In the minds of its chief promulgators there was included an equally strenuous demand for the liberty of mind, freedom of thought and its expression in speech, writing, print, and assemblage. The earlier interest in confessional freedom was generalized, and thereby deepened as well as broadened. This demand was a product of the rational enlightenment of the eighteenth century and of the growing importance of science. The great tide of reaction that set in after the defeat of Napoleon, the demand for order and discipline, gave the agitation for freedom of thought and its expression plenty of cause and plenty of opportunity.

The earlier liberal philosophy rendered valiant service. It finally succeeded in sweeping away, especially in its home, Great Britain, an innumerable number of abuses and restrictions. The history of social reforms in the nineteenth century is almost one with the history of liberal social thought. It is not, then, from ingratitude that I shall emphasize its defects, for recognition of them is essential to an intelligent statement of the elements of liberal philosophy for the present and any nearby future. The fundamental defect was lack of perception of historic relativity. This lack is expressed in the conception of the individual as something given, complete in itself, and of liberty as a ready-made possession of the individual, only needing the removal of external restrictions in order to manifest itself. The individual of earlier liberalism was a Newtonian atom having only external time and space relations to other individuals, save that each social atom was equipped with inherent freedom. These ideas might not have been especially harmful if they had been merely a rallying cry for practical movements. But they formed part of a philosophy and of a philosophy in which these particular ideas of individuality and freedom were asserted to be absolute and eternal truths; good for all times and all places.

This absolutism, this ignoring and denial of temporal relativity, is one great reason why the earlier liberalism degenerated so easily into pseudo-liberalism. For the sake of saving time, I shall identify what I mean by this spurious liberalism, the kind of social ideas represented by the "Liberty League" and ex-President Hoover. I call it a pseudo-liberalism because it ossified and narrowed generous ideas and aspirations. Even when words remain the same, they mean something very different when they are uttered by a minority struggling against repressive measures and when expressed by a group that, having attained power, then uses ideas that were once weapons of emancipation as instruments for keeping the power and wealth it has obtained. Ideas that at one time are means of producing social change assume another guise when they are used as means of preventing further social change. This fact is itself an illustration of historic relativity, and an evidence of the evil that lay in the assertion by earlier liberalism of the immutable and eternal character of their ideas. Because of this latter fact, the *laissez-faire doctrine* was held by the degenerate school of liberals to express the very order of nature itself. The outcome was the degradation of the idea of individuality, until in the minds of many who are themselves struggling for a wider and fuller development of individuality, individualism has become a term of hissing and reproach, while many can see no remedy for the evils that have come from the use of socially unrestrained liberty in business enterprise, save change produced by violence. The historic tendency to conceive the whole question of liberty as a matter in which individual and government are opposed parties has borne bitter fruit. Born of despotic government, it has continued to influence thinking and action after government had become popular and *in theory* the servant of the people.

I pass now to what the social philosophy of liberalism becomes when its inheritance of absolutism is eliminated. In the first place such liberalism knows that an individual is nothing fixed, given ready-made. It is something achieved, and achieved not in isolation, but the aid and support of conditions, cultural and physical, including in "cultural" economic, legal, and political institutions as well as science and art. Liberalism knows that social conditions may restrict, distort, and almost prevent the development of individuality. It therefore takes an active interest in the working of social institutions that have a bearing, positive or negative, upon the growth of individuals who shall be rugged in fact and not merely in abstract theory. It is as much interested in the positive construction of favorable institutions, legal, political, and economic, as it is in the work of removing abuses and overt oppressions.

In the second place, liberalism is committed to the idea of

historic relativity. It knows that the content of the individual and freedom change with time; that this is as true of social change as it is of individual development from infancy to maturity. The positive counterpart of opposition to doctrinal absolutism is experimentalism. The connection between historic relativity and experimental method is intrinsic. Time signifies change. The significance of individuality with respect to social policies alters with change of the conditions in which individuals live. The earlier liberalism in being absolute was also unhistoric. Underlying it there was a philosophy of history which assumed that history, like time in the Newtonian scheme, means only modification of external relations; that it is quantitative, not equalitative and internal. The same thing is true of any theory that assumes, like the one usually attributed to Marx, that temporal changes in society are inevitable—that is to say, are governed by a law that is not itself historical. The fact is that the historicism and the evolutionism of nineteenth-century doctrine were only half-way doctrines. They assumed that historical and developmental processes were subject to some law or formula outside temporal processes.

The commitment of liberalism to experimental procedure carries with it the idea of continuous reconstruction of the ideas of individuality and of liberty in intimate connection with changes in social relations. It is enough to refer to the changes in productivity and distribution since the time when the earlier liberalism was formulated, and the effect of these transformations, due to science and technology, upon the terms on which men associate together. An experimental method is the recognition of this temporal change in ideas and policies so that the latter shall coördinate with the facts instead of being opposed to them. Any other view maintains a rigid conceptualism and implies that facts should conform to concepts that are framed independently of temporal or historical change.

The two things essential, then, to thorough-going social liberalism are, first, realistic study of existing conditions in their movement, and, secondly, leading ideas, in the form of policies for dealing with these conditions in the interest of development of increased individuality and liberty. The first requirement is so obviously implied that I shall not elaborate it. The second point needs some amplification. Experimental method is not just messing around nor doing a little of this and a little of that in the hope that things will improve. Just as in the physical sciences, it implies a coherent body of ideas, a theory, that gives direction to effort. What is implied, in contrast to every form of absolutism, is that the ideas and theory be taken as methods of action tested and continuously revised by the consequences they produce in actual social conditions. Since they are operational in nature, they modify conditions, while the first requirement, that of basing them upon realistic study of actual conditions, brings about their continuous reconstruction.

It follows finally that there is no opposition in principle between liberalism as social philosophy and radicalism in action, if by radicalism is signified the adoption of policies that bring about drastic instead of piece-meal social changes. It is all a question of what kind of procedures the intelligent study of changing conditions discloses. These changes have been so tremendous in the last century, yes, in the last forty years, that it looks to me as if radical methods were now necessary. But all that the argument here requires is recognition of the fact that there is nothing in the nature of liberalism that makes it a milk-water doctrine, committed to compromise and minor "reforms." It is worth noting that the earlier liberals were regarded in their day as subversive radicals.

What has been said should make it clear that the question of method in formation and execution of policies is the central thing in liberalism. The method indicated is that of maximum reliance upon intelligence. This fact determines its opposition to those forms of radicalism that place chief dependence upon violent overthrow of existing institutions as the method of effecting desired social change. A genuine liberal will emphasize as crucial the complete correlation between the means used and the consequences that follow. The same principle which makes him aware that the means employed by pseudo-liberalism only perpetuate and multiply the evils of existing conditions, makes him also aware that dependence upon sheer massed force as the means of social change decides the kind of consequences that actually result. Doctrines, whether proceeding from Mussolini or from Marx, which assume that because certain ends are desirable therefore those ends and nothing else will result from the use of force to attain them is but another example of the limitations put upon intelligence by any absolute theory. In the degree in which mere force is resorted to, actual consequences are themselves so compromised that the ends originally in view have in fact to be worked out afterwards by the method of experimental intelligence.

In saying this, I do not wish to be understood as meaning that radicals of the type mentioned have any monopoly of the use of force. The contrary is the case. The reactionaries are in possession of force, in not only the army and police, but in the press and the schools. The only reason they do not advocate the use of force is the fact that they are already in possession of it, so their policy is to cover up its existence with idealistic phrases—of which their present use of individual initiative and liberty is a striking example.

These facts illustrate the essential evil of reliance upon sheer force. Action and reaction are equal and in opposite directions, and force as such is physical. Dependence upon force sooner or later calls out force on the other side. The whole problem of the relation of intelligence to force is much too large to go into here. I can only say that when the forces in possession are so blind and stubborn as to throw all their weight against the use of liberty of inquiry and of communication, of organization to effect social change, they not only encourage the use of force by those who want social change, but they give the latter the most justification they ever have. The emphasis of liberalism upon the method of intelligence does not commit it to unqualified pacificism, but to the unremitting use of every method of intelligence that conditions permit, and to search for all that are possible.

In conclusion, I wish to emphasize one point implied in the early part of the paper. The question of the practical significance of liberty is much wider than that of the relation of government to the individual, to say nothing of the monstrosity of the doctrine that assumes that under all conditions governmental action and individual liberty are found in separate and independent spheres. Government is one factor and an important one. But it comes into the picture only in relation to other matters. At present, these other matters are economic and cultural. It is absurd to conceive liberty as that of the business entrepreneur and ignore the immense regimentation to which workers are subjected, intellectual as well as manual workers. Moreover, full freedom of the human spirit and of individuality can be achieved only as there is effective opportunity to share in the cultural resources of civilization. No economic state of affairs is merely economic. It has a profound effect upon presence or absence of cultural freedom. Any liberalism that does not make full cultural freedom supreme and that does not see the relation between it and genuine industrial freedom as a way of life is a degenerate and delusive liberalism.

6 · Thurman Arnold: *A Philosophy for Politicians*

Thurman Arnold (1891-   ) was a Yale Law School professor when he joined the New Deal in 1933 as a special counsel to the

From Thurman Arnold, *The Symbols of Government* (New York: Harcourt, Brace and World, 1935), pp. 262-271. Reprinted with the permission of the author.

Agricultural Adjustment Administration (AAA). He then became a trial examiner for the Securities Exchange Commission, then Assistant Attorney General in charge of antitrust prosecutions (See Document 20). Both in *The Symbols of Government,* from which the following essay is taken, and in his more famous book *The Folklore of Capitalism* (1937), Arnold came closer than any other writer to an exposition of what has come to be called the "pragmatism" of the New Deal.

. . . Belief in any philosophy, however fantastic, molds a people in the image of that philosophy; and so it is that ancient symbols which are no longer sources of hope become forces which stifle human energy. It is for this reason that in a country as bursting with energy as is America, we can predict the general acceptance of a new and more hopeful philosophy of government to replace the confusion of our present ideals of law and economics. Other depressions have come and gone without altering faith in the economic principles of the past. Yet never before has there existed the present public awareness that the application of those principles is causing a great industrial machine to operate far below its productive capacity.

The fundamental social axiom of the past was that man, by working only for his personal profit, in the long run produced the most ideal social results. Of course this profit motive had to be checked and balanced against its own excesses by law, by ethics, and by religion. But thus curbed it was part of nature's great plan. Attempts to interfere with it led to disaster. Great institutions like the law and the church, representing contradictory ideals, had to be carefully insulated from control of practical affairs by devices like trial by combat. And thus arose a spiritual government scattered between Washington and the various state capitols, and a temporal government scattered between New York and the various state financial centers, the one representing the great ideals and the other the fundamental axioms of social control.

We suggest that the formula of the new social philosophy which is appearing may be the fundamental axiom that man works only for his fellow man; that it is *this* tendency which must be curbed by law, ethics, and common sense, so that there may be incidental room in the system for the man who works only for personal gain, just as there was incidental room in the old economic creed for the humanitarian. Under the profit creed the chief danger was from well-meaning but impractical humanitarians. Under the new creed the chief danger will be from well-meaning but impractical profit takers.

Sometimes in clear outline, sometimes in strange and distorted and destructive forms, the new conception of man as a creature who does not work for himself is appearing all over the world. In Germany and in Italy the normal man is supposed only to work for his fellow countrymen, and the difference between social organization in peace and war has faded. In Russia the normal man is thought of as one who works for the toiling masses of the world. In all of these countries the axiom that the normal man in the long run works only for his own profit is put down as dangerous radicalism. Fanatical devotion to this single ideal is such that it makes human liberty an unimportant value, and even kindness is stifled for purely humanitarian motives. There are explosive dangers to world peace and security in such fanaticism. Nevertheless out of this creed has come a certain morale and order, to take the place of former discouragement and anarchy. For better or for worse, a new abstract economic man who does not work for his own selfish interest, but only for others, has appeared on the mental horizon of the world.

In America this new abstract man is arising out of confusion instead of revolution. He therefore has no fanatical adherents nor any defined logical outlines. He is appearing in institutions not organized for profit and increasing in importance as those institutions expand. A few years ago hospitals and educational institutions were growing into vast and efficient organizations. Their success in violation of the profit creed was explained by the fact that the abstract doctor or professor is a curious freak of such rarefied qualities that he is not motivated as a normal man would be. No inference was permitted that doctors who ran complicated hospitals without possibility of profit could run anything else. Thus distribution of goods to those in want, care of the old or the unemployed, were supposed to be entirely different from distribution of medical supplies to the same people. Charity was a beautiful human quality, which might even be a vocation for those abnormal people not interested in business. It might be an avocation of a great industrial leader who could become interested in unemployed, not as an obligation, but to prove to the people that even such a giant of power and efficiency had his tender moments. But the idea that such activities could be an obligation of business or government, rather than a sentimental interlude, was considered dangerous to those great principles which kept Americans from growing beards and drinking vodka like the Russians.

Today, with amazing speed, what used to be called charity is becoming a recognized obligation of government, and, through it, powers of control over the industrial structure are evolving which is bringing a new class of technicians into power. The movement began with the substitution of community chests for pure largesse in order to get organized efficiency. With the depression, the support of such work was taken over by the Government amid the fear and trembling of all right-thinking people. And now we are startled to observe that the greatest employer of labor in the country is not an industrial baron, but Harry Hopkins, a social worker, operating a growing organization in violation of all the axioms of our former economics. He is constantly confused in his objectives by those who insist that his work is dangerous as an aim in itself, and therefore must be primarily used as a method of priming the economic pump, of stimulating producers' goods, of aiding consumers' goods. He must employ men on useful things to avoid waste, but he must not have them engaged in needed activities because that would be governmental interference with business. Yet in spite of this confusion the work goes on, and a Social Security Bill recognizes the obligation in permanent form.

It is natural that right-thinking men should maintain that what they see going on before their eyes is impossible. Adam Smith, on the basis of the axiom that men work only for profit, predicted that the modern industrial corporation could not develop because no man would work as efficiently for a great organization as he would for himself. In the same way, conservatives today prove with equal conclusiveness that men will never work as efficiently for a government as for a great corporate entity created under the laws of Delaware. Yet it is beginning to be doubtful if such taboos will be strong enough to keep that great class of technicians and experts, interested more in the direct objects of their work than in the symbols of finance, from using their skill to preserve the resources of the nation and distribute its goods. As yet the economic philosophy and social bookkeeping necessary to convince the popular mind that a nation can afford the expense of having all its people hard at work producing and distributing wealth have not been formulated. Sensible and practical plans are still confused with violence, revolution, and the overthrow of an entire class. Yet people are gradually becoming accustomed to the idea, and, as their fear dies, new forms of social bookkeeping gradually appear.

Is it true, as an economic principle, that man works only for his fellow man? The answer is, that it is neither more nor less true than the axiom which gave prestige to a commercial class, that man works only for himself; or the axiom supporting the institution of chivalry, that men work only for the love of pure ladies; or the belief of a medieval priesthood, that men work only for a future life; or the axiom of the law, that men desire only logical justice. Society is composed of all sorts of people and each individual is a whole cast of characters in himself, appearing on the stage of his consciousness in rapid succession. Young men do not think as old men, and even old men do not react alike. "Truth" is irrelevant as a test of an economic philosophy. The value of such a philosophy can only be judged by the value of the governing class whose power it supports. The hope for this new humanitarian economic creed in America must be based on the belief that there exists a huge reservoir of technical skill, capable of running a great productive machine with new energy and efficiency, provided that social ideals can be accepted which permit this reservoir to be tapped.

Will such a philosophy make the world a satisfactory place, and will the radicals cease from troubling and be at rest? Of course not. There can be no conception of social justice without social injustice, since the one idea cannot exist without the other. We must expect the old struggle for prestige and power to go on as strenuously in a world where comforts are adequately distributed as in a world where they are not. There will be radicals under any type of social organization, forming parties of dissent and demanding a new order, so long as men struggle to improve their lot in this world. Such changes in fundamental attitudes and values are a function of life. The world will never see a permanently valid philosophy until science discovers a method of making Time stand still.

Yet, granted that such changes in social ideals and values are a part of social life, there is no reason in the nature of things why they should be accompanied by such violent and painful dislocations. There is no reason why the members of an entire governing class, both good and bad, should be thrown out of power simply because popular ideals have undergone a change. There was a time in the medical profession when new theories had to be denounced because they interfered with the prestige of established physicians. Later, and within the memory of the reader, doctors belonged to the medical party of the homeopaths or the party of the allopaths, and the public had to choose between them. It is no longer true that whole classes of physicians must defeat a new technique or lose face before the public. Without knowing the details of medical theory, the public nevertheless understands the nature of those theories, and the constant search among competent physicians for new hypotheses.

Today, in government, if theories of the class in power are damaged, it reflects on the entire class; and both competent and incompetent members suffer equally. Thus, efficient bankers are compelled to oppose checks on inefficient bankers because of the principle of the change. This is only because the prestige of the entire group is tied up with a set of usages whose continuance is regarded as a matter of fundamental principle which must override all temporary considerations of convenience and common sense. In this way incompetents are maintained in secure positions, and honest men are compelled to come to the defense of the corrupt practices of their fellows. We stand or fall by classes, each with its separate brand of oratorical literature, such as capitalism, socialism, fascism, or communism. Each class is compelled to defend the indefensible practice of its members as necessary incidents to their more ideal aims.

Is it hopeless to attempt to induce the same atmosphere in the conduct of social organizations that we have obtained in medical organizations? Must men always be compelled to line up on different sides and fight for one or the other of two conflicting principles, both of which need representation among the ideals of government? Must the believers in the Constitution combat sensible plans, and the advocates of sensible plans attempt to destroy the Constitution by their bitter realism, to the perpetuation of senseless oratory and high-sounding prejudices and to the end that all change be made as violent as possible? If so, the expert will always be at a disadvantage before the orator who by his fanaticism is able to make ignorance led by prejudice appear as truth led by courage.

There is no reason to believe that the public is not as capable of orienting itself toward governmental theories as toward medical theories. It is not necessarily true that the only choice is between naive faith in principles and cynical denial of the validity of principle. A crowd at a baseball game gets the full emotional value of the game as a symbol of pride in the home town, without making themselves suffer for it in practical affairs. When the same sort of understanding becomes part of our thinking about governmental symbols, we can use the Constitution as a great unifying force without foregoing sensible and practical advantages on its account.

Society shows an uncanny skill in selecting the best technicians once it understands just what those technicians are doing. Efficient ballplayers have an advantage over theatrical ones. Competent physicians have a greater advantage over personalities like Lydia Pinkham as belief in broad general principles and great remedies fades. In the same way we can imagine a condition of public understanding of the function of government as a practical affair which will put orators at a disadvantage before technicians.

There are signs of a new popular orientation about the theories and symbols of government which is arising from a new conception of the function of reason and ideals in the personality of the individual. A new creed called psychiatry is dimly understood by millions of people. Popular magazines are appearing, discussing from an objective point of view problems which used to be considered the exclusive property of the moralist. A conception of an adult personality is bringing a new sense of tolerance and common sense to replace the notion of the great man who lived and died for moral and rational purposes. Under these new attitudes men are becoming free to observe the effects of changing beliefs, without the discomfort of an older generation which swung from complete certainty to utter disillusionment.

Such a conception, once accepted, will in the long run spread to government and social institutions. Governments can act in no other way than in accordance with the popular ideals of what great abstract personalties should do. In medieval times nations were holy and kings led crusades to dramatize that idea. In modern times governments act in the image of great businessmen. The codes to which national conduct attempts to conform are only enlargements of popular ideals of individual codes. When individuals must be logical, consistent, courageous, thrifty, generous, forgiving, implacable, and morally upright, governments dramatize all these values. National policies can only be a confused representation of popular ideals. As the notion of a tolerant adult personality grows in popular comprehension, the opportunity for a scientific attitude toward government will necessarily broaden. Once that conception becomes an unquestioned assumption, the day of the high-class psychopath and fanatic in social control will be over.

It is true that there is little in the present conduct of the governments of the world which can by any stretch of the imagination be called adult. Everywhere we see unnecessary cruelty used to dramatize even humanitarian creeds. Fanatical devotion to principle on the part of the public still compels intelligent leaders to commit themselves, for political reasons, to all sorts of disorderly nonsense. So long as the public holds preconceived faiths about the fundamental principles of government, they will persecute and denounce new ideas in that science, and orators will prevail over technicians. So long as preconceived principles are considered more important than practical results, the practical alleviation of human distress and the distribution of available comforts will be paralyzed. Nevertheless one who desires to be effective in society must be permitted to hope and to work for that hope. The wages of pessimism are futility. The writer has faith that a new public attitude toward the ideals of law and economics is slowly appearing to create an atmosphere where the fanatical alignments between opposing political principles may disappear and a competent, practical, opportunistic governing class may rise to power. . . .

PART TWO

EXPECTATIONS

7 · Franklin D. Roosevelt: *Every Man has a Right to Life*

Of all Franklin D. Roosevelt's campaign speeches of 1932, this one, delivered at the Commonwealth Club in San Francisco, September 23, was the most daring in its exposition of a new economic and social philosophy, contrasting sharply with Herbert Hoover's declarations that the traditional structure of the American economy was still adequate. The speech had been written by Adolf A. Berle, with some assistance from Rexford Guy Tugwell, and Tugwell later wrote that FDR "never saw that speech until he opened it on the lectern." Undoubtedly, it stretched Roosevelt's philosophy to its boldest limits. Later in the campaign, Roosevelt seemed to become more cautious and more conservative; he promised to balance the budget; and clearly he was more concerned about winning the election than about laying down a comprehensive liberal philosophy. But at the Commonwealth Club his words sounded that chord of idealism and fire which, to all later followers of the New Deal, represented the essence of the Roosevelt creed.

I count it a privilege to be invited to address the Commonwealth Club. It has stood in the life of this city and state, and

From *The Public Papers and Addresses of Franklin D. Roosevelt,* ed. Samuel Rosenman, I (New York: Random House, Inc., 1938), 742-756.

it is perhaps accurate to add, the nation, as a group of citizen leaders interested in fundamental problems of government, and chiefly concerned with achievement of progress in government through non-partisan means. The privilege of addressing you, therefore, in the heat of a political campaign, is great. I want to respond to your courtesy in terms consistent with your policy.

I want to speak not of politics but of government. I want to speak not of parties, but of universal principles. They are not political, except in that larger sense in which a great American once expressed a definition of politics, that nothing in all of human life is foreign to the science of politics. . . .

The issue of government has always been whether individual men and women will have to serve some system of government or economics, or whether a system of government and economics exists to serve individual men and women. This question has persistently dominated the discussion of government for many generations. On questions relating to these things men have differed, and for time immemorial it is probable that honest men will continue to differ. . . .

It was in the middle of the 19th century that a new force was released and a new dream created. The force was what is called the industrial revolution, the advance of steam and machinery and the rise of the forerunners of the modern industrial plant. The dream was the dream of an economic machine, able to raise the standard of living for everyone; to bring luxury within the reach of the humblest; to annihilate distance by steam power and later by electricity, and to release everyone from the drudgery of the heaviest manual toil. It was to be expected that this would necessarily affect government. Heretofore, government had merely been called upon to produce conditions within which people could live happily, labor peacefully, and rest secure. Now it was called upon to aid in the consummation of this new dream. There was, however, a shadow over the dream. To be made real, it required use of the talents of men of tremendous will, and tremendous ambition, since by no other force could the problems of financing and engineering and new developments be brought to a consummation.

So manifest were the advantages of the machine age, however, that the United States fearlessly, cheerfully, and, I think, rightly, accepted the bitter with the sweet. It was thought that no price was too high to pay for the advantages which we could draw from a finished industrial system. The history of the last half century is accordingly in large measure a history of a group of financial Titans, whose methods were not scrutinized with too much care, and who were honored in proportion as they produced the results, irrespective of the means they used. The financiers who pushed the railroads to the Pacific were always ruthless, often wasteful, and frequently corrupt; but they did build railroads, and we have them today. It has been estimated that the American investor paid for the American railway system more than three times over in the process; but despite this fact the net advantage was to the United States. As long as we had free land; as long as population was growing by leaps and bounds; as long as our industrial plants were insufficient to supply our own needs, society chose to give the ambitious man free play and unlimited reward provided only that he produced the economic plant so much desired. During this period of expansion, there was equal opportunity for all and the business of government was not to interfere but to assist in the development of industry. This was done at the request of business men themselves. The tariff was originally imposed for the purpose of "fostering our infant industry," a phrase I think the older among you will remember as a political issue not so long ago. The railroads were subsidized, sometimes by grants of money, oftener by grants of land; some of the most valuable oil lands in the United States were granted to assist the financing of the railroad which pushed through the Southwest. A nascent merchant marine was assisted by grants of money, or by mail subsidies, so that our steam shipping might ply the seven seas. Some of my friends tell me that they do not want the Government in business. With this I agree; but I wonder whether they realize the implications of the past. For while it has been American doctrine that the government must not go into business in competition with private enterprises, still it has been traditional particularly in Republican administrations for business urgently to ask the government to put at private disposal all kinds of government assistance. The same man who tells you that he does not want to see the government interfere in business—and he means it, and has plenty of good reasons for saying so—is the first to go to Washington and ask the government for a prohibitory tariff on his product. When things get just bad enough—as they did two years ago—he will go with equal speed to the United States government and ask for a loan; and the Reconstruction Finance Corporation is the outcome of it. Each group has sought protection from the government for its own special interests, without realizing that the function of government must be to favor no small group at the expense of its duty to protect the rights of personal freedom and of private property of all its citizens. . . .

A glance at the situation today only too clearly indicates that equality of opportunity as we have known it no longer exists. Our industrial plant is built; the problem just now is whether under existing conditions it is not overbuilt. Our last frontier has long since been reached, and there is practically no more free land. More than half of our people do not live on the farms or on lands and cannot derive a living by cultivating their own property. There is no safety valve in the form of a Western prairie to which those thrown out of work by the Eastern economic machines can go for a new start. We are not able to invite the immigration from Europe to share our endless plenty. We are now providing a drab living for our own people.

Our system of constantly rising tariffs has at last reacted against us to the point of closing our Canadian frontier on the north, our European markets on the east, many of our Latin

American markets to the south, and a goodly proportion of our Pacific markets on the west, through the retaliatory tariffs of those countries. It has forced many of our great industrial institutions who exported their surplus production to such countries, to establish plants in such countries, within the tariff walls. This has resulted in the reduction of the operation of their American plants, and opportunity for employment.

Just as freedom to farm has ceased, so also the opportunity in business has narrowed. It still is true that men can start small enterprises, trusting to native shrewdness and ability to keep abreast of competitors; but area after area has been pre-empted altogether by the great corporations, and even in the fields which still have no great concerns, the small man starts under a handicap. The unfeeling statistics of the past three decades show that the independent business man is running a losing race. Perhaps he is forced to the wall; perhaps he cannot command credit; perhaps he is "squeezed out," in Mr. Wilson's words, by highly organized corporate competitors, as your corner grocery man can tell you. Recently a careful study was made of the concentration of business in the United States. It showed that our economic life was dominated by some six hundred odd corporations who controlled two-thirds of American industry. Ten million small business men divided the other third. More striking still, it appeared that if the process of concentration goes on at the same rate, at the end of another century we shall have all American industry controlled by a dozen corporations, and run by perhaps a hundred men. But plainly, we are steering a steady course toward economic oligarchy, if we are not there already.

Clearly, all this calls for a re-appraisal of values. A mere builder of more industrial plants, a creator of more railroad systems, an organizer of more corporations, is as likely to be a danger as a help. The day of the great promoter or the financial Titan, to whom we granted everything if only he would build, or develop, is over. Our task now is not discovery, or exploitation of natural resources, or necessarily producing more goods. It is the soberer, less dramatic business of administering resources and plants already in hand, of seeking to reestablish foreign markets for our surplus production, of meeting the problem of underconsumption, of adjusting production to consumption, of distributing wealth and products more equitably, of adapting existing economic organizations to the service of the people. The day of enlightened administration has come.

Just as in older times the central government was first a haven of refuge, and then a threat, so now in a closer economic system the central and ambitious financial unit is no longer a servant of national desire, but a danger. I would draw the parallel one step farther. We did not think because national government had become a threat in the 18th century that therefore we should abandon the principle of national government. Nor today should we abandon the principle of strong economic units called corporations, merely because their power is susceptible of easy abuse. In other times we dealt with the problem of an unduly ambitious central government by modifying it gradually into a constitutional democratic government. So today we are modifying and controlling our economic units.

As I see it, the task of government in its relation to business is to assist the development of an economic declaration of rights, an economic constitutional order. This is the common task of statesman and business man. It is the minimum requirement of a more permanently safe order of things. . . .

Every man has a right to life; and this means that he has also a right to make a comfortable living. He may by sloth or crime decline to exercise that right; but it may not be denied him. We have no actual famine or dearth; our industrial and agricultural mechanism can produce enough and to spare. Our government formal and informal, political and economic, owes to every one an avenue to possess himself of a portion of that plenty sufficient for his needs, through his own work.

Every man has a right to his own property; which means a right to be assured, to the fullest extent attainable, in the safety of his savings. By no other means can men carry the burdens of those parts of life which, in the nature of things, afford no chance of labor; childhood, sickness, old age. In all thought of property, this right is paramount; all other property rights must yield to it. If, in accord with this principle, we must restrict the operations of the speculator, the manipulator, even the financier, I believe we must accept the restriction as needful, not to hamper individualism but to protect it.

These two requirements must be satisfied, in the main, by the individuals who claim and hold control of the great industrial and financial combinations which dominate so large a part of our industrial life. They have undertaken to be, not business men, but princes—princes of property. I am not prepared to say that the system which produces them is wrong. I am very clear that they must fearlessly and competently assume the responsibility which goes with the power. So many enlightened business men know this that the statement would be little more than a platitude, were it not for an added implication.

This implication is, briefly, that the responsible heads of finance and industry instead of acting each for himself, must work together to achieve the common end. They must, where necessary, sacrifice this or that private advantage; and in reciprocal self-denial must seek a general advantage. It is here that formal government—political government, if you choose, comes in. Whenever in the pursuit of this objective the lone wolf, the unethical competitor, the reckless promoter, the Ishmael or Insull[1] whose hand is against every man's, declines to join in achieving an end recognized as being for the public welfare, and threatens to drag the industry back to a state of anarchy,

[1] Samuel Insull was a financier who built a gigantic empire in public utilities through interlocking directorates. The empire collapsed in 1932 and Insull's name became a symbol for ruthless business speculation. [ED.]

the government may properly be asked to apply restraint. Likewise, should the group ever use its collective power contrary to the public welfare, the government must be swift to enter and protect the public interest.

The government should assume the function of economic regulation only as a last resort, to be tried only when private initiative, inspired by high responsibility, with such assistance and balance as government can give, has finally failed. As yet there has been no final failure, because there has been no attempt; and I decline to assume that this nation is unable to meet the situation.

The final term of the high contract was for liberty and the pursuit of happiness. We have learnt a great deal of both in the past century. We know that individual liberty and individual happiness mean nothing unless both are ordered in the sense that one man's meat is not another man's poison. We know that the old "rights of personal competency—the right to read, to think, to speak, to choose and live a mode of life, must be respected at all hazards. We know that liberty to do anything which deprives others of those elemental rights is outside the protection of any compact; and that government in this regard is the maintenance of a balance, within which every individual may have a place if he will take it; in which every individual may find safety if he wishes it; in which every individual may attain such power as his ability permits, consistent with his assuming the accompanying responsibility. . . .

Faith in America, faith in our tradition of personal responsibility, faith in our institutions, faith in ourselves demands that we recognize the new terms of the old social contract. We shall fulfill them, as we fulfilled the obligation of the apparent Utopia which Jefferson imagined for us in 1776, and which Jefferson, Roosevelt and Wilson sought to bring to realization. We must do so, lest a rising tide of misery engendered by our common failure, engulf us all. But failure is not an American habit; and in the strength of great hope we must all shoulder our common load.

8 • Paul H. Douglas: *The Roosevelt Program and Organization of the Weak*

Paul H. Douglas (1892-) was an economics professor at the University of Chicago when Franklin D. Roosevelt came into office. He was especially interested in the problems of wages and social security, and his book *Real Wages in the U. S.* (1930) was an important contribution to economic study. After his election to the United States Senate in 1948, from the state of Illinois, he became one of the leading liberals in Congress. In the early 1930's, he was an outspoken advocate of welfare economics. As this review of New Dealer Rexford Guy Tugwell's book indicates, Douglas was not content with a reform from above unsupervised by the organization of popular movements below.

This well-written volume is deservedly attracting wide attention, not only because of its intrinsic merits but also because of the fact that its author is one of the most trusted advisers of the present Administration and is commonly believed to be influential in the formulation of its economic program. Mr. Tugwell's central thesis is that while machine industry has compelled close and scientific organization within individual plants and companies, there has been almost complete anarchy between these concerns. The economic mechanism as a whole, therefore, works badly. There is overdevelopment of some industries and underdevelopment of others. There is enormous waste in distribution and competition. There are periodic breakdowns in which large sections face virtual starvation in the midst of potential plenty, while there is exploitation of the weak by those in strategic places who can and do take advantage of the common run of workers, investors, and con-

From Paul Douglas, "Rooseveltian Liberalism," a review of *The Industrial Discipline* by Rexford G. Tugwell in *The Nation*, CXXXVI (June 21, 1933), 702-703. Reprinted with the permission of the publisher.

sumers. What Mr. Tugwell in essence proposes is that society should abandon the attitude of laissez faire which the business interests have sought to foster, and which in turn has brought them close to disaster, and that it should instead launch out upon a program of so integrating these plants and industries that they may best serve society as a whole. His book is, in fact, one long appeal to Americans to display social intelligence in mastering those economic mechanisms and institutions which their mechanical ingenuity has brought into being and then allowed to run wild. This, then, is the background which Mr. Tugwell paints with vivid and yet thoughtful strokes, which stamp the author as an artist in his technique as well as an economist.

The specific method of control which is suggested in the foreground is the integration of each industry through a governing board which would make and execute plans for that industry, together with a central body, composed primarily of the associated industries, which would seek to introduce a common policy between industries and coordinate them with each other. These two sets of groups would have, in the main, control over the quantities to be produced, the conditions of competition, the division of markets, wages and working conditions, the pooling of patents, and finally prices. Through the taxation of surpluses reinvested by corporations in their own plants, funds would be forced into the open market, and there would be some control and guidance of how they would ultimately be invested. An excise tax upon industry would furnish the means for building up reserves, rewarding the industries which complied, and subsidizing the unemployment-insurance systems of those States which had such laws.

Although Mr. Tugwell does not develop the points except inferentially it is probable that he would also favor a managed currency with price stabilization as its ultimate goal and have it seen to that the purchasing power of workers, farmers, and the lower middle class should increase at a sufficient rate so that the increased quantity of consumers' goods might be bought without an appreciable fall in prices. He also favors building up organizations of workers, and he would have the government try to protect the consumers by preventing prices from being raised by the cartels to excessive heights.

In short, Mr. Tugwell is proposing a planned and liberalized capitalism as the next step in social development; and such, indeed, seems to be the program of the Roosevelt Administration. In a final and moving passage the author declares:

> Selectivity is still possible; we can experiment now, and we ought to do it before it is too late. Otherwise we are surely committed to revolution. The essential contrast beween the liberal and the radical view of the tasks which lie before us is that liberalism requires this experimenting and that radicalism rejects it for immediate entry on the revolutionary tactic. Liberals would like to rebuild the station while the trains are running; radicals prefer to blow up the station and and forgo service until the new structure is built. Their ultimate objectives may not be so very different. . . . But there is all the difference in the world in the ways of achieving what is hoped for.

No honest person can doubt the sincerity and public spirit with which Mr. Tugwell writes and with which the Roosevelt Administration is proceeding. One can only hope that they may be able to accomplish real reform without revolution. Given the present state of the public mind and the existing balance of power, they can probably take no other course than that which they are following.

The real ultimate difficulty with their program of legalized cartels lies, however, in the assumption that there is a sufficiently strong and independent force outside of capitalism which can control it. At the moment we have a progressive President and an able body of advisers, recruited in the main from the universities, who have no personal axes to grind. Moreover, industry in its despair is uttering words of repentance. But if prosperity should return, capitalism would once again wish to throw off any effective control, and the question would then arise whether Rooseveltian liberalism would be strong enough to check it. We have thus far been unable to regulate our public utilities in the interests of the consumers, and it will be even more difficult to regulate industry as a whole. The owners of industry will struggle for high prices and for low costs and will try to break or discredit anyone who gets in their way. Having control over nearly all of the jobs and most of the surplus income, they tend to be able to coerce most men. For a nation of employees, such as we largely are east of the Mississippi, can hardly be expected to control their employers.

Along with the Rooseveltian program must go, therefore, the organization of those who are at present weak and who need to acquire that which the world respects, namely, power. Trade unions need to be built up and farmers' cooperatives as well. Finally, the urban and rural workers of hand and brain need a strong party of their own. Despite Roosevelt's fine beginning, they cannot permanently depend upon the Democratic Party, which in the East and in some of the Midwest States largely rests upon machines which are in league with the worst forces of the under and the upper world. Unless these things are done, we are likely to find the permanent benefits of Rooseveltian liberalism to be as illusory as were those of the Wilsonian era.

9 • Robert M. MacIver: *The Ambiguity of the New Deal*

Robert M. MacIver (1882-), born in Scotland, was educated at Edinburgh and Oxford Universities, joined the Columbia Uni-

From Robert M. MacIver, "Social Philosophy." Reprinted from *Social Change and the New Deal,* edited by William Ogburn, by permission of The University of Chicago Press.

versity faculty in 1927, and became one of the nation's foremost scholars in the field of social theory. At Columbia he taught political philosophy and sociology and became professor emeritus in 1950. His books *The Modern State* (1926), *Society* (1931), and *The Web of Government* (1947) were distinguished contributions to political science. His essay here, written in 1934, reflects much of the uncertainty with which thoughtful Americans regarded the New Deal during its first year.

It is more than a conjuncture that the year 1933 witnessed both the enactment of the N.R.A. and the repeal of the Eighteenth Amendment. To the prospective vision of most observers each of these events would have seemed, only a few years back, just as impossible as the other. The advance of the state into new areas of economic control, coinciding with its retreat from a domain of moralistic control, represents the growth of a new social philosophy. It may well mark a stage in the passing of an era. The United States has been conspicuous both for its multitudinous laws and for the individualistic temper which these laws nevertheless registered. For the individualistic bias is toward controls which guard the arena of economic and political struggle against the influences which threaten it. Sherman Acts, labor injunctions, laws against gambling, drinking, and Sunday recreations, were all consistent expressions of the same fundamental philosophy, bulwarked as it was in the last resort by the judicial interpretation of the Constitution. And it is the onset of a new philosophy which is attacking them all alike.

The magnitude and the apparent suddenness of the change have taken the world by surprise. When the "new deal" was proclaimed in the summer of 1932, few suspected that the fulfilment of an election promise would be translated into so far-reaching a reorganization of the nation's economic and social structure. No doubt the cumulative effects of the depression had profoundly shaken the philosophy which at first saw in it only a backwash of the inevitable tide of progress and confidently expected that the "natural forces," gaining strength by the interruption, would soon sweep onward through recovery to yet higher levels of what was known as prosperity. But recovery was still the slogan, with the presupposition that, once achieved, the general scheme of life would continue much as before. The significant fusion of the ideas of economic recovery and social reconstruction, so perplexingly exemplified by the N.R.A., had not yet emerged. Under the guise of a recovery program another set of ideas altogether came to the front, the very antithesis of those for which the accredited leaders of the previous decade, such as Coolidge and Hoover and Mellon and Ford, had stood. Recovery, as a technical economic problem, had little enough to do with the abolition of child labor, the recognition of unions, the guarantee of collective bargaining, the legal establishment of minimum wages and maximum hours, the curbing of the stock exchange and the investment house, and the codification of all the industries of the country. The fusion, rather than the reconciliation, of the two principles in a single program creates, as we shall see, one of the most interesting problems for those who would seek to gauge the extent to which a new social philosophy has come to permeate the community.

For the so-called recovery program has in it the potentiality of two quite divergent developments. One is along the lines of a drastic control of capitalist exploitation, involving a socially planned economy in which the depersonalized pursuit of private profit is subject to check at a thousand strategic points. The other is the erection of a system of industrial syndicates, somewhat analogous to the fascist conception of the corporate state but without the unifying discipline which the latter implies. The reversal of the policy of the Sherman Act may lead to this result if certain tendencies of the code-making organizations are allowed free play. For example, if each inclusive industrial association is to acquire an effective power to limit output and raise prices, the competitive struggle is merely resumed under the guidance of the individualistic motive, at a higher level of organization. Competent observers are at present divided as to which of these two tendencies is already victorious. For example, in the *Forum* for January, 1934, an editorial identifying the N.R.A. with the first principle is immediately followed by an article in which it is declared to be the vehicle of the second. The issue will no doubt depend on the quality and strength of the change in attitude which has already replaced the policy of economic laissez-faire by the policy of national economic planning.

The future historian of this epoch may declare, as historians are apt to say of other sudden-seeming changes, that in truth the change in popular attitude from an individualistic to a more collectivistic philosophy was less abrupt and less complete than it seems. I hope the sociologists of today will help the future historian to solve the question, by a careful study of the organs and indexes of opinion during the past few years. That there has been a definite shift in attitudes seems beyond question, though its precise character involves much fuller investigation than it has yet received. It is seen in the fact that the politicians of the opposition shrink, in view of approaching elections, from coming out decisively against the "new deal," that even in republican strongholds such as Pennsylvania the old republican guard are meeting the note of challenge, while some even claim, oblivious of the famous reference to "rugged individualism" which the ex-president made, that the new policy was really inaugurated in the régime of Hoover. It is seen in the lack of resonance to the protests of the relatively few outspoken adherents of the individualistic order, such as Beck and Ogden Mills.[1] It is seen in the loss of popularity

[1] James M. Beck, a Congressman from Pennsylvania, and Ogden Mills, as Secretary of the Treasury, were influential conservative policy-makers during the Hoover Administration. [ED.]

which befell a popular hero—Al Smith—when he took a stand against the government's program. It is seen in the failure of the groups, from chambers of commerce to professors of economics, which have sought to establish resistance points against the new principles. Other groups which might have been expected to lead the attack, such as Wall Street and the orthodox bankers, have been discredited in the popular mind. The present triumph of the program of economic control is finally witnessed to by the resounding popularity of the President himself.

How genuine and how deep-seated the change of mood may be is of course still open to question. Foreign observers have long regarded the tradition of individualism as deeply rooted in the mores of this country. On the other hand it has been pointed out that the basis of this individualism in economic and social conditions has long been undermined. The frontier in American history has disappeared. The alternative of homesteading has no longer any meaning to the city worker. The social mobility of the population has ceased to keep pace with their physical mobility. The proportion of important executive positions which fall to the sons of business men, as compared with those which other groups obtain, has increased—a fact admitted, *malgré eux*, by Taussig and Joslyn in their study of *American Business Leaders*. The reality of class distinctions has become more apparent, even though the study of class has been almost entirely neglected by American sociologists. The range of individualist competition has been lessened by the development of large-scale business in the corporate form, so that by the year 1930 "two hundred big companies controlled 49.2 per cent or nearly half of all non-banking corporate wealth, while the remaining half was owned by the more than 300,000 smaller companies" (Berle and Means, *The Modern Corporation and Private Property*, p. 28). The automatic forces dear to Adam Smith have been increasingly checked in a hundred directions, through controls ranging from those exercised over international trade to those which invaded, in the years prior to 1933, the final citadel of individualist faith, the gold standard itself.

If, then, there was this lag between conditions and attitudes, we cannot conclude from the seeming suddenness of the change that it is transitory or necessarily shallow. Moreover, attitudes tend to be reinforced by the appropriate institutions, and the new administration has in a remarkably short time established a vast system of controls which, even if in part created to meet an emergency, are not likely to disappear with its passing. The experience of other countries has shown, for example, that it would be exceedingly difficult to repeal the kind of social legislation which has been introduced on a national scale under the aegis of the N.R.A. It must also be remembered that it is the traditionally most individualistic sector of the population, the agricultural class, which has been hit most hard by the depression, suffering particularly from the disproportionate burden of indebtedness which grew automatically in proportion to the fall of prices. The A.A.A. is in fact a collectivist experiment of a drastic kind, and in rallying to it the farmers have committed themselves to a whole program of planning quite incompatible with the tenets of individualism.

The deeper meaning of the change in social philosophy has still to be explored. For the trend from individualism to institutionalism may signify something more than a change of front in the pursuit of economic gain—or even of "prosperity." It may be also the expression of a quest for a more satisfying way of life. There have been signs of a growing dissatisfaction with the utilitarian mechanistic *Weltanschauung* which is congenial to economic individualism. The kind of life which fulfils itself in the business, the service club, and the family has narrow cultural horizons, a narrowness portrayed in the recent literature of protest. Moreover, the exploitative character of the individualistic order has been brought home to the consciousness of the average citizen by the revelations of banking scandals and colossal graft. At the present stage the desire for a new orientation of life, for a more co-operative order with larger social aims, has found numerous expressions.

But there are many uncertainties in the situation which must restrain optimistic estimates regarding the inauguration of a period of social and cultural reformation. The experiment of social planning is full of difficulties. The promises which heralded the "new deal" are hard to fulfil. The new economic organizations will probably endure, but the vital question concerns the spirit which will animate them. There has been a growing unrest of labor groups, as shown by the increase of strikes. The codes may be manipulated in favor of the formerly dominant capitalist groups, which will not easily surrender their prerogatives. The consumer—which means the people as a whole—may be disadvantaged by the intrenchment in new lines of industrial dictators. The farmer, unless the situation is safeguarded, may find that the higher prices he receives are outweighed by the higher cost of living, and retreat again to a disgruntled individualism. The idea of economic planning may be tied up to the principle of economic nationalism—a danger of which there have already been significant signs—or even of economic imperialism. The new institutions are here, but the essential point is—Who shall control them?

The answer is important not only for the United States but for the world. The American experiment must be seen against a European background, where far more drastic methods are being tried, involving an abrogation of the essential liberties which have been supposed to be the driving force of Western democracy. But an ideal of national solidarity animates these new movements, gives them a certain dignity and purposefulness, and explains the willingness of large masses to surrender themselves to an order which sacrifices the principle of personal freedom. A book which has some vogue in Europe just now is Jung's *Modern Man in Search of a Soul.* In a way the nations seem to be out on the same elusive quest, seeking some basis of internal unity, some sense of a national mission. Some of them have found, at a price, a kind of mass-soul. Is it necessary to pay this price, to crush cultural divergence as well as to endanger international civilization, for the sake of solidarity? The failure of the American experiment may tempt more men to answer "Yes"; its success would bring succor and example to the many who still wish to answer "No." . . .

10 · Edward A. Filene: *Business Needs the New Deal*

Edward A. Filene (1860-1937), president of William Filene's Sons in Boston, was an early organizer of the U. S. Chamber of Commerce, and a nationally prominent merchant. He was one of a number of businessmen (Russell Leffingwell of the House of Morgan, California banker A. P. Giannini, and Thomas Watson of International Business Machines were others) who supported Franklin D. Roosevelt in the 1932 and 1936 elections. Shortly before Filene wrote this article, conservative businessmen, including leading Democratic Party figures like John J. Raskob, Jouett Shouse, and Irénée du Pont, had formed the American Liberty League, which for several years after 1934 maintained a vigorous opposition to New Deal measures. Businessmen were split in their reaction to Roosevelt, whereas liberals and radicals were by turns encouraged and puzzled. In 1934, expectations of the New Deal were varied, reflecting perhaps that ambiguity of which sociologist Robert MacIver speaks in his essay (See Document 9).

. . . When the so-called New Deal flashed into our nation's thinking, it seemed to be mistaken generally for a new theory

From Edward A. Filene, "What Business Men Think: See the New Deal Through." *The Nation*, CXXXIX (December 9, 1934), 707-709. Reprinted with the permission of the publisher.

of society. Many upheld it as a better social theory than any proposed before, while many viewed it with alarm, calling it a violation of our ancient liberties and a regimentation of life under a political bureaucracy. Still others waited to see what the New Dealers would propose; and the New Dealers proposed a number of measures which these critics did not believe to be economically sound.

It seems to me that the New Deal can never be comprehended from any such approach. The New Deal is not a new solution for old problems. It is a solution for a new problem—a problem arising from the evolution of machine industry and the evolution of American society from an agrarian to an industrial civilization. Nor is the New Deal to be confused with any one of the experimental measures adopted by the Administration in its efforts to get the New Deal going. The New Deal, as I see it, is a movement toward a nation-wide economic constitution, because the time had come when it was no longer possible for industry, agriculture, and trade to function in harmony with our American ideas unless we did evolve an economic constitution. If we want to go on with democracy, and I am sure we do, the New Deal points the way. It is, as I see it, the same way in principle as that by which our infant democracy was protected and nourished—by the nation-wide organization of democracy under an adequate code. I have, therefore, more than business reasons for supporting the New Deal. I have patriotic reasons, humanitarian reasons, even political reasons, for aside from the question of business profits, I loathe absolutism and dictatorship. As a business man, however, I prefer to keep the discussion within the realm of business. To business, the New Deal is imperative. It isn't a question of whether business shall or shall not be operated under a code. Business under any condition must have a code. It is merely a question of whether our big-community business can operate under the old, little-community code, and it has been amply proved that it cannot.

I may seem to speak as if I thought that the needs of business men were paramount; as if the purpose of human life were to keep business prosperous rather than the purpose of business to supply the needs of human life. But that is not the case. I emphasize the business approach to the problem only because I am a business man; nevertheless, if American business does evolve a nation-wide code adequate to the needs of business, there will and can be no opposition from any other element in our society. For whatever the details of such a code may be, its basic principle must be nation-wide planning to enable the masses to purchase the output of modern industry. Idealists may be content with a mere equitable distribution of wealth, but business, if it is to be prosperous, cannot stop at that. It must see that the masses have more and more buying power. There might be an equitable distribution of wealth which would still leave everybody poor, but business can achieve no lasting prosperity now unless the masses enjoy a standard of living which has scarcely yet been thought possible. Only such a standard of living can absorb the products of machine industry, and only such a standard, therefore, can keep the masses employed.

The masses, I know, do not and will not object to that, however much they may have objected to business programs heretofore. In the period when this new industrial machine was in the making, labor and the consuming public were rightfully suspicious of business domination; and business, to win its points, had to smash through these objections with all the strong-arm methods which seemed to suggest themselves. But that period will be over at the moment that American business comprehends the business opportunities inherent in this New Deal. We shall no doubt differ as to methods and measures, but all of us—business men, workers, farmers, professional people—will be consciously working on the same problem, that of getting buying power to the whole people.

Now, as to some of the details of our proposed economic constitution, which so many seem to confuse with the Constitution itself. I am second to none in acknowledging the extraordinary leadership of President Roosevelt, but it has never kept me from questioning a number of those measures. From the very start I could not concur in the suggestion that we must raise prices, and it was hard to understand why almost everybody, including the Administration, seemed to accept price-raising as an immediate objective. I could concede that it might be necessary, as a temporary measure, to raise prices if possible on certain raw materials and farm products. But the great problem, as I saw it, was the problem of enabling the masses to buy more and more, and I argued, and still argue, that people can buy more, other things being equal, if prices are low than they can if they are high.

Mr. Roosevelt himself admitted that he did not know what to do in this new era and promised to find out by fact-finding research and, where necessary, by experiment. The great thing about fact-finding as a method of procedure is that one may start out all wrong and still wind up all right; whereas, if we follow traditional practices instead of facts, we may start all right, but because of changing conditions we may nevertheless wind up all wrong. I could follow Roosevelt, then, with no misgivings. Price-fixing would go out, I was sure, when it became obvious that it could not solve the problem, and if I am not mistaken, it is already going out.

Nor did he try, as many would have liked, to scrap our existing business system and mold one nearer to our utopian ideals. He simply dug up the reasons that our mechanism of trade was not working successfully and proposed action in accordance with these reasons. Some economists, I know, claim that there can be no such nation-wide planning as is now necessary without the destruction of capitalism. But that is unimportant. Capitalism is just a name we give to describe a certain period in economic evolution. If it doesn't fit this new and necessary stage, I think we can find a word to describe the new set-up.

I am for the New Deal, then, because I am a business man. I am for the New Deal because I am an individualist, not a Socialist, and because the Old Deal unnecessarily restricted our individual liberties. I am for the New Deal because I believe in profits, and the New Deal opens up tremendously greater opportunities for legitimate and continuous profits, and opens them up to an incomparably greater number of people.

When the masses were engaged in digging their living directly from the soil, in their little agrarian communities, traders could make huge profits from exploiting them. But only a few, at most, could be exploiters. Business can no longer look to exploitation for its profits because we are all engaged in trading now, and there is no public which business can profitably exploit. The only course which can now be profitable is the doing of things which need to be done and the doing of them by such progressive methods—which in general will be mass production—that the masses can receive the benefits. Since there is no limit to things that need to be done, one may almost say that business opportunities will, under the New Deal, be unlimited.

Business in the old days had a certain fascination, but it lacked some of the elements of good, clean fun. It wasn't fun to hire little children until they were broken by disease or accident, and then bring on a new regiment of children to take their place. Employers, I am sure, didn't like to do that, but business, they were told, was business, and they had to do it because children were less expensive than adults. It wasn't fun to have to engage in misrepresentation. It wasn't fun to browbeat labor, or to corrupt government to secure those special favors which seemed so necessary. The great majority, I know, wanted to be decent, and only acted in ways like this because they did not feel free to act according to more humanitarian principles. In other words, business was regimented, and the meanest chiseler in the trade frequently did the regimenting. When he cut wages, they all cut. When he evolved some particularly sharp practice, others thought it necessary to follow suit.

I am for the New Deal because it liberates business from all that. Because it frees business from the dictatorship of the chiseler, and eliminates only those practices which are not socially helpful. Nation-wide planning, of course, necessitates restrictions, but so does all social order. To achieve service, we must place a taboo on disservice. To achieve wealth, we must place a taboo on waste. We shall not have to apologize for unsocial actions in the future by saying that "business is business," for business won't be that kind of business any longer. Business under the New Deal will be much more fun.

11 · Henry A. Wallace: *We Need A Declaration of Interdependence*

Henry A. Wallace (1888-1965), an Iowa-born expert on farm economics, editor of the widely read periodical *Wallace's Farmer,* left the Republican Party in 1928, campaigned for Roosevelt in 1932, and after FDR's election was appointed Secretary of Agriculture. Wallace was more than an administrator of the various New Deal farm programs; he was an eloquent spokesman for the more idealistic aspirations of the administration. (See Document 35.) Liberals were delighted when in 1940 he ran successfully for Vice-President on the Roosevelt ticket. But he was dropped in 1944 in favor of Harry Truman and in 1948 tried unsuccessfully to mobilize national liberal support behind his race for President on the Progressive Party ticket. After his defeat, he retired from political life. His book *New Frontiers* (1934) was an inspirational, if

From Henry A. Wallace, "America Considers Its Constitution." Reprinted with permission from *The Proceedings of the Academy of Political Science,* XVI, No. 4 (January 1936), 506-523.

often vague, statement for a new approach to government. The essay below may help make clear why Wallace became one of the most popular publicists of New Deal thought.

Men in public office should never make predictions, but it seems desirable this evening to begin with two. The first one is this: Social change will continue in every field of human activity until the end of time. The second one is this: Our institutions—notably our economic and political institutions—will adapt themselves to social change or they will vanish. . . .

Were Madison, Hamilton and their colleagues alive today, it seems to me they would insist upon relating the Constitution to the surrounding environment. It would be characteristic of them to study how best to control and adjust conflicting economic interests. Their objectives, I am sure, would be unchanged. They would still desire above all "to form a more perfect Union," and within that Union to protect diversity, to establish justice and liberty, and to provide for the general welfare. These desires have not changed in any truly fundamental way. They are still the American creed.

They come up for discussion today because the means of achieving them are in doubt. And the doubt is the product of the enormously significant facts of social change since 1787.

It does make a difference, for example, whether our economic and political institutions are to serve a nation of less than four million people clustered chiefly along the Atlantic Seaboard, and with only 3 per cent of them living in cities, or whether they are to serve 120 million people scattered over two billion acres, and with half of them living in cities. It makes a tremendous difference—economic, political, cultural—whether your neighbor or your market is weeks distant or hours distant. It makes a great difference whether political institutions are intended to provide for the growth of a nation with plenty of economic elbow-room, or whether they are to provide for a nation economically mature. It is of considerable moment whether an economic society is young and based on free opportunity for individual enterprises, each relatively self-sustaining, or whether it is mature and made up of a mixture of individual enterprise, vast corporate enterprise, and governmental enterprise, with the economic freedom of the individual greatly reduced. It is a matter of great significance when economic interests change in size and power, and so gain or lose the privilege of dictating the rules of the economic game.

The whole problem has never been better presented than in the report on "Recent Social Trends," prepared under the chairmanship of our distinguished presiding officer of this evening, Dr. Wesley C. Mitchell, and made public in 1932 at the instance of Mr. Hoover.

"Unequal rates of change in economic life, in government, in education, in science and religion," that report observed, "make zones of danger and points of tension. It is almost as if the various functions of the body or the parts of an automobile were operating at unsynchronized speeds."

And then the report gave names and places, revealing how science and invention walked with seven-league boots, and how government crawled; how amazing accomplishments in production were periodically ditched by an equally amazing *lack* of accomplishment in the distribution of income and purchasing power; how attempts to bring the laggards even with the leaders had always to contend against prejudice and ignorance and inordinate greed.

"The result has been that astonishing contrasts in organization and disorganization are to be found side by side in American life: splendid technical proficiency in some incredible skyscraper and monstrous backwardness in some equally incredible slum."

"Social institutions," the report continued, "are not easily adjusted to inventions. . . . There is in our social organizations an institutional inertia, and in our social philosophies a tradition of rigidity. Unless there is a speeding up of social invention or a slowing down of mechanical invention, grave maladjustments are certain to result."

The hopeful thing is that our institutions not only can be changed, but actually are changed from generation to generation. The process of adaptation to social change often goes on almost unnoticed. A prime example is the institution of private property.

In the minds of the men who framed the Constitution it was a fundamental duty of government to protect the institution of private property. Not all agreed on how this was to be done, or even the degree to which it should be done. Apparently it was not the most appealing consideration to such contemporary leaders as Thomas Jefferson. But it was the concept which dominated the Constitutional Convention.

Madison, who spoke very frankly of his fears that a landless proletariat might effect a fusion with other discontented interests and so endanger the "rights" of the minority, declared that, "To secure the public good and private rights against the danger of such a faction and at the same time preserve the spirit and the form of popular government is then the great object to which our inquiries are directed."

Since individual enterprise was the prevailing order of that day, and since with it went a high degree of economic self-sufficiency, the possession of property of course meant complete control of it. The "independent" man, the "self-made" man, and similar expressions had more meaning in that day than they have ever had since. Accordingly the institution of private property was, in the minds of the Founding Fathers, one of the fixed principles of our polity.

Yet in every generation since then, the social trends report observes, "the right of man to do what he will with his own has been curbed by the American people acting through legislators and administrators of their election."

The Proclamation of Emancipation and the 13th Amendment abolished property rights in slaves; the 18th Amendment disregarded property rights in the liquor traffic; in every large city what a man may build on his property is restricted by zoning regulations; the owners and operators of public utilities are subject to public regulations; possessors of income are subject to tax. In all of these cases the people, acting through government, have deliberately curbed the right of a man to do what he will with his own, and have said that contracts must not be contrary to the general welfare.

But government has not been the only modifier, nor even, perhaps, the most significant. Contrast the property rights of a merchant or a farmer in 1787, with the property rights of an investor in one of our huge modern corporations. The investor may draw such dividends as the directors of the corporation see fit, and he may sell his stock when he pleases, but that is the extent of his control over his property. He has nothing to say about the price and production policies governing the products of his property, though his whole welfare may depend on them. There is the further irony that the men who control his property, and who do have a voice in making price and production policies, as often as not have many of the privileges of a property-holder but few of the obligations.

Yet we live in an economic society increasingly dominated by the large corporation, carrying out price and production policies which affect the welfare of all of us. The "invisible hand" may still be operating, but it is not the invisible hand of which Adam Smith wrote. Are our corporate lords and masters, who have so radically altered the institution of private property since 1787, willing to reconsider our political Constitution in the light of their own significant alterations in our economic constitution? Or must we take the unkind view that when vested interests were localized, they wanted a strong central government in order to protect their property from control or regulation by local governments, whereas now that these interests are themselves interstate and strongly centralized, they want a weak central government in order to protect their property from control or regulation by the central government? Justice Holmes once remarked that the 14th Amendment did not, after all, write Herbert Spencer's *Social Statics* into the Constitution.

It was the view of Mr. Hoover's Committee on Social Trends that this problem of unequal social change, of high speed in one field and slow speed in another, can only be met if first of all there is "willingness and determination to undertake important integral changes in the reorganization of social life, including the economic and political orders, rather than the pursuance of a policy of drift." The outstanding problem is to bring powerful individuals and groups to see that interdependence is a fact, and that the old phrase, "No man liveth unto himself," was never more true than it is today.

"In any case, and whatever the approach," the Committee on Social Trends concludes, "it is clear that the type of planning now most urgently required is neither economic planning alone, nor governmental planning alone. The new synthesis must include the scientific, the educational, as well as the economic (including here the industrial and the agricultural) and also the governmental. All these factors are inextricably intertwined in modern life, and it is impossible to make rapid progress under present conditions without drawing them all together. . . . More important than any special type of institution is the attainment of a situation in which economic, governmental, moral and cultural arrangements should not lag too far behind the advance of basic changes."

Since 1932 the word "planning" has become a hissing and a by-word, but in 1932 it was still possible for a group of eminent social scientists to be detached and to talk about planning without fear of offense. Fundamental problems do not get themselves solved in three or four years, no matter how vigorously they may be attacked. And there is always the danger that an improvement in economic conditions will tempt men to assume that all that remains is to repeat some simple slogan until a populace weary of thinking will discover in it the shining, all-embracing truth.

No, the modern emphasis has to be on interdependence and balance. There is as much need today for a Declaration of Interdependence as there was for a Declaration of Independence in 1776. . . .

The modern emphasis has to be on the interdependence not only of individuals, but of large economic groups. . . . Can these modern groups subordinate themselves to the necessity of forming a more perfect union, of securing justice, of providing for the general welfare, of securing the blessings of liberty? Can we, under our Constitution, meet the problem presented by these groups? The answer depends on our willingness and determination to undertake important integral changes in our economic and political institutions, rather than the pursuance of a policy of drift—in brief, we shall have to be as true men as the framers of the Constitution in 1787. . . .

How can we get a powerful pressure group to work toward that objective on behalf of the General Welfare? "Moral suasion" won't do the trick. Powerful parties in foreign countries have been working on the problem, but we do not believe they have the answer for American conditions. Moreover, we don't like the way they define justice, domestic tranquility and liberty. Apparently we have no alternative but to invent the necessary social machinery out of the materials at hand here in America.

We need devices, as I have said, that will require pressure groups to consider the general welfare. When a pressure group obtains governmental powers, such as a tariff or a processing tax, or when it employs such legal devices as the corporation for purposes which have tremendous social consequence, then we must exact of such a group certain reciprocal obligations toward the general welfare. There is such a device written into the Agricultural Adjustment Act, in the form of a price ceiling beyond which the whole mechanism cannot go. Shouldn't other groups using governmental powers be subject to comparable restrictions?

But something more than negative restrictions on pressure groups is required. We need some way of referring the activities and aspirations of all these pressure groups to rational long-time policies. I mean policies that cut across administrations and ignore party lines, policies which will grow out of the answer the people give to certain key problems. . . .

The idea of a Council on the General Welfare is brought forward in the hope that it may be seriously and critically discussed, but with full knowledge that analysis may reveal grave disadvantages. It is a device, as I have said, designed to help us discover, formulate and adhere to intelligent national economic policies. Such a council might be composed of four or five of our most eminent economic statesmen, men of the caliber—if he will forgive me for embarrassing him—of our presiding officer of the evening. The council would obviously have to be non-partisan both in letter and spirit. It could not function if it were composed of dogmatic, doctrinaire economists, of whatever school. It should not function unless it were as revered and trusted as the Supreme Court.

Probably the members should be appointed for overlapping terms, say from 5 to 11 years. Appointment could be by the President with the advice and approval of Congress, but with appointments so arranged that no one President could determine the economic complexion of the council.

It could be the function of this council to consider the enactments of the federal government in the light of the General Welfare, and with specific reference to some such economic objective as that I suggested a few moments ago. If in the mature judgment of the council our national economic objectives were being endangered or violated, it would be the duty of the council to inform the government and the people of this opinion. If, nevertheless, the appropriate branch of the government took no action, and if the council saw no reason for modifying its opinion, it would be its further duty after a proper and ample interval to submit the question to the people. A referendum would then be in order, but only after the people had had opportunity to become thoroughly informed, and to study an impartial presentation of the advantages and disadvantages of the practical alternatives to the existing enactment. The result of the referendum might then serve as a guide to the national government for future policies and acts. . . .

In any event, we may hope that the leaders of today will endeavor to solve our present problems by appealing continually to that spirit of unity in democracy which characterized those brilliant, far-visioned young men who wrote the Constitution. Our environment is greatly changed from theirs, but the spirit of solution should be the same. They sought political balance to protect the property rights of that day. The problem of economic balance was not then so acute. We must now use the political balance which they built to bring about the economic balance which is so essential in a society as dynamic and as complex as ours.

PART THREE

NATIONAL ECONOMIC PLANNING

12 • Franklin D. Roosevelt: *Bold, Persistent Experimentation*

This speech, made to the graduating class of Oglethorpe University, in Atlanta, Georgia, on May 22, 1932, was delivered at a time when there was great uncertainty about whether Franklin D. Roosevelt or Al Smith, whom Roosevelt had nominated at the 1928 Convention, would be the Democratic candidate for president. In his bid for the nomination, Roosevelt was speaking out boldly on broad policies of economic reform. A month before his appearance at Oglethorpe, he had made a radio speech in which he referred to "the forgotten man at the bottom of the economic pyramid," and that phrase, "the forgotten man," became famous. The speech at Oglethorpe was as close as Roosevelt ever came to the implication that some sort of national planning was necessary to make the economic mechanism function with efficiency and justice.

. . . Some of you—I hope not many—are wondering today how and where you will be able to earn your living a few weeks or a few months hence. Much has been written about the hope of youth. I prefer to emphasize another quality. I hope that you who have spent four years in an institution whose funda-

From *The Public Papers of Franklin D. Roosevelt,* I, 639-646.

mental purpose, I take it, is to train us to pursue truths relentlessly and to look at them courageously, will face the unfortunate state of the world about you with greater clarity of vision than many of your elders.

As you have viewed this world of which you are about to become a more active part, I have no doubt that you have been impressed by its chaos, its lack of plan. Perhaps some of you have used stronger language. And stronger language is justified. Even had you been graduating, instead of matriculating, in these rose-colored days of 1928, you would, I believe, have perceived this condition. For beneath all the happy optimism of those days there existed lack of plan and a great waste.

This failure to measure true values and to look ahead extended to almost every industry, every profession, every walk of life. Take, for example, the vocation of higher education itself.

If you had been intending to enter the profession of teaching, you would have found that the universities, the colleges, the normal schools of our country were turning out annually far more trained teachers than the schools of the country could possibly use or absorb. You and I know that the number of teachers needed in the Nation is a relatively stable figure, little affected by the depression and capable of fairly accurate estimate in advance with due consideration for our increase in population. And yet, we have continued to add teaching courses, to accept every young man or young woman in those courses without any thought or regard for the law of supply and demand. In the State of New York alone, for example, there are at least seven thousand qualified teachers who are out of work, unable to earn a livelihood in their chosen profession just because nobody had the wit or the forethought to tell them in their younger days that the profession of teaching was gravely oversupplied.

Take, again, the profession of the law. Our common sense tells us that we have too many lawyers and that thousands of them, thoroughly trained, are either eking out a bare existence or being compelled to work with their hands, or are turning to some other business in order to keep themselves from becoming objects of charity. The universities, the bar, the courts themselves have done little to bring this situation to the knowledge of young men who are considering entering any one of our multitude of law schools. Here again foresight and planning have been notable for their complete absence.

In the same way we cannot review carefully the history of our industrial advance without being struck with its haphazardness, the gigantic waste with which it has been accomplished, the superfluous duplication of productive facilities, the continual scrapping of still useful equipment, the tremendous mortality in industrial and commercial undertakings, the thousands of dead-end trails into which enterprise has been lured, the profligate waste of natural resources. Much of this waste is the inevitable by-product of progress in a society which values individual endeavor and which is susceptible to the changing tastes and customs of the people of which it is composed. But much of it, I believe, could have been prevented by greater foresight and a larger measure of social planning. Such controlling and directive forces as have been developed in recent years reside to a dangerous degree in groups having special interests in our economic order, interests which do not coincide with the interests of the Nation as a whole. I believe that the recent course of our history has demonstrated that, while we may utilize their expert knowledge of certain problems and the special facilities with which they are familiar, we cannot allow our economic life to be controlled by that small group of men whose chief outlook upon the social welfare is tinctured by the fact that they can make huge profits from the lending of money and the marketing of securities—an outlook which deserves the adjectives "selfish" and "opportunist."

You have been struck, I know, by the tragic irony of our economic situation today. We have not been brought to our present state by any natural calamity—by drought or floods or earthquakes or by the destruction of our productive machine or our man power. Indeed, we have a superabundance of raw materials, a more than ample supply of equipment for manufacturing these materials into the goods which we need, and transportation and commercial facilities for making them available to all who need them. But raw materials stand unused, factories stand idle, railroad traffic continues to dwindle, merchants sell less and less, while millions of able-bodied men and women, in dire need, are clamoring for the opportunity to work. This is the awful paradox with which we are confronted, a stinging rebuke that challenges our power to operate the economic machine which we have created.

We are presented with a multitude of views as to how we may again set into motion that economic machine. Some hold to the theory that the periodic slowing down of our economic machine is one of its inherent peculiarities—a peculiarity which we must grin, if we can, and bear because if we attempt to tamper with it we shall cause even worse ailments. According to this theory, as I see it, if we grin and bear long enough, the economic machine will eventually begin to pick up speed and in the course of an indefinite number of years will again attain that maximum number of revolutions which signifies what we have been wont to miscall prosperity, but which, alas, is but a last ostentatious twirl of the economic machine before it again succumbs to that mysterious impulse to slow down again. This attitude toward our economic machine requires not only greater stoicism, but greater faith in immutable economic law and less faith in the ability of man to control what he has created than I, for one, have. Whatever elements of truth lie in it, it is an invitation to sit back and do nothing; and all of us are suffering today, I believe, because this comfortable theory was too thoroughly implanted in the minds of some of our leaders, both in finance and in public affairs.

Other students of economics trace our present difficulties to the ravages of the World War and its bequest of unsolved political and economic and financial problems. Still others trace our difficulties to defects in the world's monetary systems. Whether it be an original cause, an accentuating cause, or an effect, the drastic change in the value of our monetary unit in terms of the commodities is a problem which we must meet straightforwardly. It is self-evident that we must either restore commodities to a level approximating their dollar value of several years ago or else that we must continue the destructive process of reducing, through defaults or through deliberate writing down, obligations assumed at a higher price level.

Possibly because of the urgency and complexity of this phase of our problem some of our economic thinkers have been occupied with it to the exclusion of other phases of as great importance.

Of these other phases, that which seems most important to me in the long run is the problem of controlling by adequate planning the creation and distribution of those products which our vast economic machine is capable of yielding. It is true that capital, whether public or private, is needed in the creation of new enterprise and that such capital gives employment.

But think carefully of the vast sums of capital or credit which in the past decade have been devoted to unjustified enterprises —to the development of unessentials and to the multiplying of many products far beyond the capacity of the Nation to absorb. It is the same story as the thoughtless turning out of too many school teachers and too many lawyers.

Here again, in the field of industry and business many of those whose primary solicitude is confined to the welfare of what they call capital have failed to read the lessons of the past few years and have been moved less by calm analysis of the needs of the Nation as a whole than by a blind determination to preserve their own special stakes in the economic order. I do not mean to intimate that we have come to the end of this period of expansion. We shall continue to need capital for the production of newly-invented devices, for the replacement of equipment worn out or rendered obsolete by our technical progress; we need better housing in many of our cities and we still need in many parts of the country more good roads, canals, parks and other improvements.

But it seems to me probable that our physical economic plant will not expand in the future at the same rate at which it has expanded in the past. We may build more factories, but the fact remains that we have enough now to supply all of our domestic needs, and more, if they are used. With these factories we can now make more shoes, more textiles, more steel, more radios, more automobiles, more of almost everything than we can use.

No, our basic trouble was not an insufficiency of capital. It was an insufficient distribution of buying power coupled with an oversufficient speculation in production. While wages rose in many of our industries, they did not as a whole rise proportionately to the reward to capital, and at the same time the purchasing power of other great groups of our population was permitted to shrink. We accumulated such a superabundance of capital that our great bankers were vying with each other, some of them employing questionable methods, in their efforts to lend this capital at home and abroad.

I believe that we are at the threshold of a fundamental change in our popular economic thought, that in the future we are going to think less about the producer and more about the consumer. Do what we may have to do to inject life into our ailing economic order, we cannot make it endure for long unless we can bring about a wiser, more equitable distribution of the national income.

It is well within the inventive capacity of man, who has built up this great social and economic machine capable of satisfying the wants of all, to insure that all who are willing and able to work receive from it at least the necessities of life. In such a system, the reward for a day's work will have to be greater, on the average, than it has been, and the reward to capital, especially capital which is speculative, will have to be less. But I believe that after the experience of the last three years, the average citizen would rather receive a smaller return upon his savings in return for greater security for the principal, than experience for a moment the thrill or the prospect of being a millionaire only to find the next moment that his fortune, actual or expected, has withered in his hand because the economic machine has again broken down.

It is toward that objective that we must move if we are to profit by our recent experiences. Probably few will disagree that the goal is desirable. Yet many, of faint heart, fearful of change, sitting tightly on the roof-tops in the flood, will sternly resist striking out for it, lest they fail to attain it. Even among those who are ready to attempt the journey there will be violent differences of opinion as to how it should be made. So complex, so widely distributed over our whole society are the problems which confront us that men and women of common aim do not agree upon the method of attacking them. Such disagreement leads to doing nothing, to drifting. Agreement may come too late.

Let us not confuse objectives with methods. Too many so-called leaders of the Nation fail to see the forest because of the trees. Too many of them fail to recognize the vital necessity of planning for definite objectives. True leadership calls for the setting forth of the objectives and the rallying of public opinion in support of these objectives.

Do not confuse objectives with methods. When the Nation becomes substantially united in favor of planning the broad objectives of civilization, then true leadership must unite thought behind definite methods.

The country needs and, unless I mistake its temper, the country demands bold, persistent experimentation. It is common sense to take a method and try it: If it fails, admit it frankly and try another. But above all, try something. The millions who are in want will not stand by silently forever while the things to satisfy their needs are within easy reach.

We need enthusiasm, imagination and the ability to face

facts, even unpleasant ones, bravely. We need to correct, by drastic means if necessary, the faults in our economic system from which we now suffer. We need the courage of the young. . . .

13 · Rexford Guy Tugwell: *Planning Must Replace Laissez Faire*

Rexford Guy Tugwell (1891-   ) was an economics professor at Columbia University when his colleague Raymond Moley of Barnard recruited him as an adviser to Franklin D. Roosevelt in the early days of the administration in 1933. Moley, Tugwell, and Adolf A. Berle, Jr., were three key members in what came to be known as FDR's "Brains Trust." Tugwell served as Assistant Secretary and then Undersecretary in the Department of Agriculture. The most radical of FDR's advisers, he never had as much influence on Roosevelt as did the more conservative Raymond Moley, and in 1936 he resigned. This article, written before Roosevelt took office, offers one of Tugwell's vigorous arguments for national economic planning.

. . . The disasters of recent years have caused us to ask again how the ancient paradox of business—conflict to produce order—can be resolved; the interest of the liberals among us in the institutions of the new Russia of the Soviets, spreading gradually among puzzled business men, has created wide popular

From Rexford Guy Tugwell, "The Principle of Planning and the Institution of Laissez Faire," *American Economic Review*, XXII (Supplement, March 1932), 75-92. Reprinted with the permission of the author. The footnotes have been omitted.

interest in "planning" as a possible refuge from persistent insecurity; by many people it is now regarded as a kind of economic Geneva where all sorts of compromises may be had and where peace and prosperity may be insured.

It is my belief that practically all of this represents an unconsidered adherence to a slogan, or perhaps a withdrawal from the hard lessons of depression years, and that it remains unrelated to a vast background of revision and reorganization among our institutions which would condition its functioning. Most of those who say so easily that this is our way out do not, I am convinced, understand that fundamental changes of attitude, new disciplines, revised legal structures, unaccustomed limitations on activity, are all necessary if we are to plan. This amounts, in fact, to the abandonment, finally, of laissez faire. It amounts, practically, to the abolition of "business."

This is what planning calls for. In spite of its drastic requirements it may be wanted by many people; most of us are not, however, entitled to the contemporary familiarity with which we toss about loaded phrases whose content is altogether unexplored. It is one thing to advocate a social change which is understood and wanted; it is quite another to consent to a movement whose implications are unexplored. These implications may change early consent to later and bitter opposition. This seems nearly certain to happen; the respectful assent which is commanded by the general proposals of the present is not to be counted on when action is required on more particular policies. For these will show quite clearly what sacrifices are required. Those who talk most about this sort of change are not contemplating sacrifice; they are expecting gains. But it would certainly be one of the characteristics of any planned economy that the few who fare so well as things are now, would be required to give up nearly all the exclusive perquisites they have come to consider theirs of right, and that these should be in some sense socialized. In a romantic, risky, adventurous economy the business of managing industry can be treated as a game; the spoils can be thought of as belonging to the victor as spoils have always belonged to victors. But a mature and rational economy which considered its purposes and sought reasonable ways to attain them would certainly not present many of the characteristics of the present—its violent contrasts of well-being, its irrational allotments of individual liberty, its unconsidered exploitation of human and natural resources. It is better that these things be recognized early rather than late. . . .

It is impossible to pursue a discussion of planning beyond the most elementary considerations without raising the question of motive. Most economists, even today, believe that Adam Smith laid his finger on a profound truth when he said that not benevolent feelings but rather self-interest actuated the butchers and bakers of this world; most of them believe, furthermore, that this self-interestedness requires an economy in which profit is the reward for characteristic virtue and lack of it the penalty of sin. This belief must appear, from even an amateurish contact with modern psychology, to be so obviously an instance of wishful borrowing, as to give its persistence something of a stubborn and determined air. For persons with the usual intellectual contacts of our time to go on harboring these views, there has to be some violent rationalization. Surely they must be aware of the growing average size of our industrial organizations; and from this it is a simple conclusion that fewer persons all the time are profit-receivers in any direct sense. Surely they must be aware of the growing separation of ownership and control; and from this it seems a fairly simple inference that since profits go only to owners, control is effectively separated from its assumed motive. As a matter of fact, how many railway men, steel workers, or even central office employees, have any stake in company earnings? We know that there are almost none; and that this is true from workman to superintendent in most industries. Yet in defiance of such well-known and obviously relevant facts we go on treating motives quite as though our knowledge of men and of industry had been derived from a few eighteenth century books rather than from any contemporary knowledge of the world and of men. The truth is that if industry could not run without this incentive it would have stopped running long ago. . . .

If profits are really the actuating motive in modern enterprise, why is it that so great a proportion of them go to those who have no share in the control of operations; and why is it that industry continues to run even when those who run it have no major stake in its gains? But, most important of all, if profits are so important to our system, why do we allow them to be used in such ways as not only to destroy the source of future earnings, but to create unemployment and hardship amongst millions of people whose only contact with them in any form has been through reading about them in the newspapers? . . .

The truth is that profits persuade us to speculate; they induce us to allocate funds where we believe the future price situation will be favorable; they therefore have a considerable effect on the distribution of capital among various enterprises—an effect which seems clearly enough inefficient so that other methods might easily be better; but they have little effect in actually inducing or in supporting productive enterprises. All this appears merely from examination of the evidence available to us as economists; if we look into the evidence from the field of psychology, one of the first things we discover is that this main supporting generalization—that the only effective motive for enterprise is money-getting—appears in the psychologists' works as a standard humorous reference to the psychological ideas of laymen.

A central group of experts charged with the duty of planning the country's economic life, but existing as a suggestive or consultative body only, without power, has been advocated by numerous persons and organizations.[1] It is quite impossible to visualize a genuine Gosplan without power; but, of course, this

[1] Tugwell is referring here to the plan of Gerard Swope, among others. See Document 14. [Ed.]

is not to be a Gosplan. It might lay out suggested courses; it might even timidly advise; but certainly its advice would seldom, if ever, be taken. It would be as unnatural for American businesses, which live by adventures in competition, to abdicate their privileges voluntarily, as it is to expect rival militarists to maintain peace, and for the same reasons. If an institution of this sort could not be used as a mask for competitive purposes or as a weapon to be used against more scrupulous rivals, as the Federal Trade Commission has sometimes been, it would quickly gather about itself a formidable body of enemies armed with tried theoretical objection as well as real power. The chief concern of militarists must always be to maintain the conditions of war; and the chief concern of essentially speculative businesses must always be to maintain the conditions of conflict necessary to their existence. The deadliest and most subtle enemy of speculative profit-making which could be devised would be an implemented scheme for planning production. For such a scheme would quiet conflict and inject into economic affairs an order and regularity which no large speculation could survive. Every depression period wearies us with insecurity; the majority of us seem all to be whipped at once; and what we long for temporarily is safety rather than adventure. Planning seems at first to offer this safety and so gains a good deal of unconsidered support. But when it is discovered that planning for production means planning for consumption too; that something more is involved than simple limitation to amounts which can be sold at any price producers temporarily happen to find best for themselves; that profits must be limited and their uses controlled; that what really is implied is something not unlike an integrated group of enterprises run for its consumers rather than for its owners—when all this gradually appears, there is likely to be a great changing of sides.

Strange as it may seem—directly antithetical to the interests of business and unlikely to be allowed freedom of speech, to say nothing of action—it seems altogether likely that we shall set up, and soon, such a consultative body. When the Chamber of Commerce of the United States is brought to consent, realization cannot be far off. It seems to me quite possible to argue that, in spite of its innocuous nature, the day on which it comes into existence will be a dangerous one for business, just as the founding day of the League of Nations was a dangerous one for nationalism. There may be a long and lingering death, but it must be regarded as inevitable. . . .

The first series of changes will have to do with statutes, with constitutions, and with government. The intention of eighteenth and nineteenth century law was to install and protect the principle of conflict; this, if we begin to plan, we shall be changing once for all, and it will require the laying of rough, unholy hands on many a sacred precedent, doubtless calling on an enlarged and nationalized police power for enforcement. We shall also have to give up a distinction of great consequence, and very dear to many a legalistic heart, but economically quite absurd, between private and public or quasi-public employments. There is no private business, if by that we mean one of no consequence to anyone but its proprietors; and so none exempt from compulsion to serve a planned public interest. Furthermore we shall have to progress sufficiently far in elementary realism to recognize that only the federal area, and often not even that, is large enough to be coextensive with modern industry; and that consequently the states are wholly ineffective instruments for control. All three of these wholesale changes are required by even a limited acceptance of the planning idea. . . .

The next series of changes will have to do with industry itself. It has already been suggested that business will logically be required to disappear. This is not an overstatement for the sake of emphasis; it is literally meant. The essence of business is its free venture for profits in an unregulated economy. Planning implies guidance of capital uses; this would limit entrance into or expansion of operations. Planning also implies adjustment of production to consumption; and there is no way of accomplishing this except through a control of prices and of profit margins. It would never be sufficient to plan production for an estimated demand if that demand were likely to fail for lack of purchasing power. The insurance of adequate buying capacity would be a first and most essential task of any plan which was expected to work. To take away from business its freedom of venture and of expansion, and to limit the profits it may acquire, is to destroy it as business and to make of it something else. That something else has no name; we can only wonder what it may be like and whether all the fearsome predictions concerning it will come true. The traditional incentives, hope of money-making, and fear of money-loss, will be weakened; and a kind of civil-service loyalty and fervor will need to grow gradually into acceptance. New industries will not just happen as the automobile industry did; they will have to be foreseen, to be argued for, to seem probably desirable features of the whole economy before they can be entered upon. . . .

It is, in other words, a logical impossibility to have a planned economy and to have businesses operating its industries, just as it is also impossible to have one within our present constitutional and statutory structure. Modifications in both, so serious as to mean destruction and rebeginning, are required. It is strange, in a way, that we should have come so long a journey to the very threshold of this new economic order with so little change as is yet visible either in our institutions or our intentions. The reason must be that in this, as in so many instances, only the last steps become conscious. We are incorrigibly averse to any estimate of the logic of our acts; and we are also, somewhat paradoxically, fonder of our systems of theory than might be expected, reluctant to expose them to the tests of reality. Consequently we begin with small unnoticed changes and end by not being able to resist vast and spectacular ones—at which time our systems of theory tumble unwept into the grave along with the outworn techniques they accompanied. When this kind of thing follows a relatively unimpeded course there is rapid industrial change such as once happened in England; when politicians, theorists, and vested interests resist too strenuously, there is a revolution on the French model. How rapidly the pressures rise to explosive proportions depends both upon the visibility of a better future and upon the hardships of the present.

There is no denying that the contemporary situation in the United States has explosive possibilities. The future is becoming visible in Russia; the present is bitterly in contrast; politicians, theorists, and vested interests seem to conspire ideally for the provocation to violence of a long-patient people. No one can pretend to know how the release of this pressure is likely to come. Perhaps our statesmen will give way or be more or less gently removed from duty; perhaps our constitutions and statutes will be revised; perhaps our vested interests will submit to control without too violent resistance. It is difficult to believe that any of these will happen; it seems just as incredible that we may have a revolution. Yet the new kind of economic machinery we have in prospect cannot function in our present economy. The contemporary situation is one in which all the choices are hard; yet one of them has to be made.

14 • Gerard Swope: *A Business Approach to Economic Planning*

Gerard Swope (1872-1957) was head of General Electric, but also helped Jane Addams in her social work at Hull House in Chi-

From Gerard Swope "Planning and Economic Organization." Reprinted with permission from *The Proceedings of the Academy of Political Science*, XV, No. 4 (January 1934), 452-457.

cago. He was a businessman who had been involved in the vast industrial mobilization of World War I, and was committed by the time Roosevelt took office to the idea that laissez faire was outmoded. The economy would henceforth have to be planned, Swope felt, and he proceeded to work out his own scheme. The outlines were presented, in the speech reprinted below, at a dinner meeting of the Academy of Political Science of Columbia University. He was at the time, a member of the Industrial Advisory Board of the NRA. To Swope, planning had different implications than for Tugwell. They both seemed to have their own answers to the questions: Who will do the planning; and for whose benefit mainly will it be done? That both Swope and Tugwell supported "planning" indicates the essential ambiguity of the concept of national planning, unless those questions are answered.

. . . Over two years ago, in October 1931, I was requested to appear before the Committee on Manufactures of the United States Senate, which was considering a bill for the establishment of a National Economic Council. I stated then:

I am in entire sympathy with having a National Economic Council, but I need hardly call to the attention of the Committee that this would be creating a new organization in the Government, when already there are several dealing with the subject-matter of the bill in the various departments. . . .

Furthermore, it seems to me that this would be working from the top down, that even if you could get the ablest men, and the scope of the work was not too broad, you would be providing a superstructure resting upon the present chaotic conditions. It therefore would have no stable foundation. It undoubtedly would give much interesting academic information, but it seems to me would lead to no practical results, except, possibly, over a long period of time.

I should think it would be much better to start from the bottom and build up; that is, each industry should study the elements that enter into such an industry, to give the best service to the public, fair treatment to its employees and a reasonable return to its stockholders.

Trade Associations in America are the natural organizations to study the economic elements of each particular industry. Each Trade Association should hold itself responsible for the coordination of production and consumption to stabilize its industry, with the consequent benefits to the employees and to society. The organization and furtherance of the work of Trade Associations should be encouraged.

The Trade Associations, working out their problems in the stabilization of industry, would then be the foundation stones upon which to erect the superstructure of the National Economic Council. This might then be created by bringing together the officers, or duly elected representatives, of these various Trade Associations, to select from their number, or from the outside, a National Economic Council, to study the needs of industry as a whole. Such a Council would consist of men who have come up through the various industries, know those industries and their needs, who would work with others to find a solution to their common problems, and be able to deal with them not only more intelligently but in a more practical and expeditious manner, so that definite, concrete and constructive results might be expected.

In June 1933 the National Industrial Recovery Act was signed. It has often been stated that industry was responsible for the fearful situation in which we find ourselves and might have done much better even before the passage of the Act. It should be recognized that industry was limited by at least two restrictions, now modified by the NRA—namely, the variations in the factory acts in the different states and the anti-trust laws. When the President signed the NRA, he issued a statement containing the following: "It is a challenge to industry which has long insisted that given the right to act in unison, it could do much for the general good, which has hitherto been unlawful. From today, it has that right."

Under the provisions of the National Industrial Recovery Act, commerce and industry are organizing into compact units and drawing up codes of fair competition, under which data will be collected which with intelligent study should lead to a better coördination of production and consumption. My point is that it is here, in each of these trade groups, that this study should start, not at the top of our fearfully large and complicated structure but at its base. . . .

The National Economic Council so constituted of thirty-four members—five government officers; five representing the public, appointed by the President; eight representing labor; and four each from commerce and industry, agriculture, transportation and finance—shall elect its officers. The Council may appoint an economic board of such number as it deems best, either from among its own membership or from outside.

The members of the National Economic Council shall serve without compensation, but their expenses will be borne by the Association which elects them.

A secretarial staff and offices shall be provided in Washington by the National Chamber of Commerce and Industry. The expense of such secretarial staff and offices shall be met by a prorata assessment on the National Chamber of Commerce and Industry, on the banks of the Federal Reserve System and on the agricultural and transportation interests.

Data collected, tabulated and analyzed by these various bodies, namely, commerce and industry, agriculture, labor, transportation and finance, shall be made available to the National Economic Council, with any recommendations these bodies care to make. The National Economic Council may also initiate and ask for any other data and information from these units. The National Economic Council will also study the various data-collecting bureaus of the government, in the effort to unify and simplify this work, and make its recommendations to the President.

It shall be the province of the National Economic Council to study economic changes, advise the President and the Congress in regard to economic trends and make recommendations.

The various units of the Council will direct their work and studies so that the violent upheavals that we have experienced in the past, which have led to so much unemployment and misery, shall be diminished, and also study ways of alleviating the hardships attendant on such cyclical changes as, after the best of human study and experience, will still remain. Other studies tending to provide security and regularity of employment and peace of mind of the workers, shall be undertaken by the Council.

Even if these steps fall short of realizing the high ideal we have set, such correlation, coördination and conscious study should lead us to other steps and nearer to the goal we seek.

15 • Walter Lippmann: *Planning Will Lead to Oligarchy*

Walter Lippmann (1889-), a Socialist of sorts at Harvard, then an editor of the liberal *New Republic* just before World War I, and now a commentator for the New York *Herald Tribune*, has stubbornly resisted ideological classification. One of America's most distinguished journalists, he has avoided rigid dogmas and encompasses a wide range of positions in his political commentaries. His book *A Preface to Morals* (1929) included the declaration that the era of laissez-faire, which he called "the credo of naive capitalism," was outmoded. In an earlier book, *Drift and Mastery* (1914), Lippmann wrote: "Civilization, it seems to me, is just this constant effort to introduce plan where there has been clash, and purpose into the jungles of disordered growth." But he had become disillusioned with the planned society of the socialists, and while watching the Roosevelt experimentation with a combination of

From Walter Lippmann, "Planning in an Economy of Abundance," *The Atlantic Monthly*, CLIX (1937), 39-46.

sympathy and skepticism, he grew more and more convinced that national economic planning had unforeseen dangers. This essay presents his arguments. The conservatism of his later years became evident in *The Good Society* (1937) and *The Public Philosophy* (1955).

Although all the known examples of the species have had their origin in war or hold as their objective the preparation for war, it is widely believed that a collectivist order could be organized for peace and for plenty. 'It is nonsense,' says Mr. George Soule, in *A Planned Society*, 'to say that there is any physical impossibility of doing for peace purposes the sort of thing we actually did for war purposes.' If the state can organize for war, why can it not organize for peace and plenty? If it can mobilize against a foreign enemy, why not against poverty, squalor, and the hideous social evils that attend them?

It is plain enough that a dictated collectivism is necessary if a nation is to exert its maximum military power: very evidently its capital and labor must not be wasted on the making of luxuries; it can tolerate no effective dissent or admit that men have any right to the pursuit of private happiness. No one can dispute that. The waging of war must be authoritarian and collectivist. The question we must now consider is whether a system which is essential to the conduct of war can be adapted to the civilian ideal of peace and plenty. Can this form of organization, historically associated with military purposes and necessities, be used for the general improvement of men's condition? It is a critical question. For in answering it we shall be making up our minds whether the hopes invested in the promises of the collectivists are valid, and therefore entitled to our allegiance. . . .

The question whether an economy can be planned for abundance, for the general welfare, for the improvement of the popular standard of life, comes down . . . to the question of whether concepts of this sort can be translated into orders for particular goods which are as definite as the 'requisitions' of a general staff. An objective like 'the general welfare' has to be defined as specific quantities of specific goods—so many vegetables, so much meat, this number of shoes, neckties, collar buttons, aspirin tablets, frame houses, brick houses, steel buildings. Unless this can be done there will not exist the primary schedule of requirements from which to calculate the plan. The general staff can tell the planner exactly how much food, clothing, ammunition, it needs for each soldier. But in time of peace who shall tell the planners for abundance what they must provide?

The answer given by Mr. Lewis Mumford, in *Technics and Civilization*, is that 'a normal standard of consumption' can be defined by biologists, moralists, and men of cultured taste; that the goods necessary to support it can be 'standardized, weighed, measured'; that they should be supplied to all members of the community. He calls this 'basic communism.' It is not quite clear to me whether he believes that the goods listed in this normal standard are to be furnished as they are to soldiers out of a public commissariat or whether he proposes to guarantee everyone a basic money income sufficient to buy a 'normal' quantity of goods. If he has in mind the providing of rations of standard goods, then, of course, he has considerable confidence in his ability to determine what is good for the people, small respect for their varied tastes, and an implied willingness to make them like what they ought to like. Conceivably this could be done. But I should suppose it could be done only under the compulsion of necessity: that is, if goods were so scarce that the choice lay between the official ration and nothing. On the other hand, if he has in mind a guaranteed minimum income which may be spent freely, then he has no way of knowing whether the consumers will have his own excellent tastes, and go to the stores demanding what he thinks they should demand. But if they do not wish to buy what he would like them to buy, then his planners are bound to find that there is a scarcity of some goods and a glut of others.

The difficulty of planning production to satisfy many choices is the rock on which the whole conception founders. We have seen that in military planning this difficulty does not exist. It is the insurmountable difficulty of civilian planning, and although advocates like Mr. Mumford, Mr. [Stuart] Chase, and Mr. Soule have never, I think, faced it squarely, they are not unaware that it exists. They show that they are troubled because they denounce so vehemently the tastes of the people and the advertising which helps to form those tastes. They insist that the people have foolish and vulgar desires, which may be true enough, and that altogether better standards, simpler, more vital, more æsthetic, and more hygienic, ought to replace them. I agree. But I do not see how the purification of the public taste is to be worked out by a government commission. I can see how and why the general staff can decide how soldiers should live under martial discipline; but I cannot see how any group of officials can decide how a civilian population shall live nobly and abundantly.

For the fundamental characteristic of a rising standard of life is that an increasing portion of each man's income is spent on unessentials; it is applied, in other words, to things in which preference rather than necessity is the criterion. If all income had to be spent on the absolute necessities of life, the goods required would be few in number and their production could readily be standardized into a routine. Now it should be noted that all known examples of planned economy have flourished under conditions of scarcity. In the war economies of 1914-1918, in the collectivist régimes in Russia, Italy, and Germany, the supply of necessary goods has never been equal to the demand. Under such conditions, as during a siege or a famine, the communist principle is not only feasible but necessary. But as productivity rises above the level of necessity the variety of choice is multiplied; and as choice is multiplied the possibility of an overhead calculation of the relation between demand and supply diminishes. . . .

Out of all the possible plans of production some schedule would have to be selected arbitrarily. There is absolutely no objective and universal criterion by which to decide between better houses and more automobiles, between pork and beef, between the radio and the movies. In military planning one criterion exists: to mobilize the most powerful army that national resources will support. That criterion can be defined by the general staff as so many men with such and such equipment, and the economy can be planned accordingly. But civilian planning for a more abundant life has no definable criterion. It can have none. The necessary calculations cannot, therefore, be made, and the concept of a civilian planned economy is not merely administratively impracticable; it is not even theoretically conceivable. The conception is totally devoid of meaning, and there is, speaking literally, nothing in it.

The primary factor which makes civilian planning incalculable is the freedom of the people to spend their income. Planning is theoretically possible only if consumption is rationed. For a plan of production is a plan of consumption. If the authority is to decide what shall be produced, it has already decided what shall be consumed. In military planning that is precisely what takes place: the authorities decide what the army shall consume and what of the national product shall be left for the civilians. No economy can, therefore, be planned for civilians unless there is such scarcity that the necessities of existence can be rationed. As productivity rises above the subsistence level, free spending becomes possible. A planned production to meet a free demand is a contradiction in terms and as meaningless as a square circle.

It follows, too, that a plan of production is incompatible with voluntary labor, with freedom to choose an occupation. A plan of production is not only a plan of consumption, but a plan of how long and where the people shall work, and what they shall work at. By no possible manipulation of wage rates could the planners attract to the various jobs precisely the right number of workers. Under voluntary labor, particularly with consumption rationed and standardized, the unpleasant jobs would be avoided and the good jobs overcrowded. Therefore the inevitable and necessary complement of the rationing of consumption is the conscription of labor, either by overt act of law or by driving workers into the undesirable jobs by offering them starvation as the alternative. This is, of course, exactly what happens in a thoroughly militarized state.

The conscription of labor and the rationing of consumption are not to be regarded as transitional or as accidental devices in a planned economy. They are the very substance of it. To make a five-year plan of what a whole nation shall produce is to determine how it shall labor and what it shall receive. It can receive only what the plan provides. It can obtain what the plan provides only by doing the work which the plan calls for. It must do that work or the plan is a failure; it must accept what the plan yields in the way of goods or it must do without.

All this is perfectly understood in an army or when in wartime a whole nation is in arms. The civilian planner cannot avoid the rationing and the conscription, for they are the very essence of his idea. There is no escape. If the people are free to reject the rations, the plan is frustrated; if they are free to work less or at occupations other than those prescribed, the plan cannot be executed. Therefore their labor and their standards of living have to be dictated by the planning board or by some sovereign power superior to the board. In a militarized society that sovereign power is the general staff.

But who, in a civilian society, is to decide what is to be the specific content of the abundant life? It cannot be the people deciding by referendum or through a majority of their elected representatives. For if the sovereign power to pick the plan is in the people, the power to amend it is there also at all times. A plan subject to change from month to month or even from year to year is not a plan; if the decision has been taken to make ten million cars at $500 and one million suburban houses at $3000, the people cannot change their minds a year later, scrap the machinery to make the cars, abandon the houses when they are partly built, and decide to produce instead sky-scraper apartment houses and underground railroads.

There is, in short, no way by which the objectives of a planned economy can be made to depend upon popular decision. They must be imposed by an oligarchy of some sort, and that oligarchy must, if the plan is to be carried through, be without responsibility in matter of policy. Individual oligarchs might, of course, be held accountable for breaches of the law just as generals can be court-martialed. But their policy can no more be made a matter of continuous accountability to the voters than the strategic arrangements of the generals can be determined by the rank and file. The planning board or their superiors have to determine what the life and labor of the people shall be.

Not only is it impossible for the people to control the plan, but, what is more, the planners must control the people. They must be despots who tolerate no effective challenge to their authority. Therefore civilian planning is compelled to presuppose that somehow the despots who climb to power will be benevolent—that is to say, will know and desire the supreme good of their subjects. This is the implicit premise of all the books which recommended the establishment of a planned economy in a civilian society. They paint an entrancing vision of what a benevolent despotism could do. They ask—never very clearly, to be sure—that somehow the people should surrender the planning of their existence to 'engineers,' 'experts,' and 'technologists,' to leaders, saviors, heroes. This is the political premise of the whole collectivist philosophy: that the dictators will be patriotic or class-conscious, whichever term seems the more eulogistic to the orator. It is the premise, too, of the whole philosophy of regulation by the state, currently regarded as progressivism. Though it is disguised by the illusion that a bureaucracy accountable to a majority of voters, and susceptible to the pressure of organized minorities, is not exercising compulsion, it is evident that the more varied and comprehensive the regulation becomes, the more the state becomes a despotic power as against the individual. For the fragment of control over the government that one man exercises through his vote is in no effective sense proportionate to the authority exercised over him by the government.

Benevolent despots might indeed be found. On the other hand, they might not be. They may appear at one time; they may not appear at another. The people, unless they choose to face the machine guns on the barricades, can take no steps to see to it that benevolent despots are selected and the malevolent cashiered. They cannot select their despots. The despots must select themselves, and, no matter whether they are good or bad, they will continue in office so long as they can suppress rebellion and escape assassination.

Thus, by a kind of tragic irony, the search for security and a rational society, if it seeks salvation through political authority, ends in the most irrational form of government imaginable—in the dictatorship of casual oligarchs, who have no hereditary title, no constitutional origin or responsibility, who cannot be replaced except by violence. The reformers who are staking their hopes on good despots, because they are so eager to plan the future, leave unplanned that on which all their hopes depend. Because a planned society must be one in which the people obey their rulers, there can be no plan to find the planners: the selection of the despots who are to make society so rational and so secure has to be left to the insecurity of irrational chance.

16 · David E. Lilienthal: *Planning Step by Step*

David E. Lilienthal (1899-), a Harvard Law School graduate and member of the public service commission in Wisconsin, was one of three directors appointed by Franklin D. Roosevelt to supervise the operations of the Tennessee Valley Authority, set up in 1933. From the first, the TVA was one of the most controversial of all the New Deal measures. Many viewed it in the way in which Franklin D. Roosevelt had spoken of it, simply as a "yardstick" that would lead private companies to charge more reasonable rates for electric power. Yet, by its comprehensive economic program for the Tennessee Valley—involving the building of dams, the generation of cheap hydroelectric power, the manufacture of fertilizer, soil conservation and reforestation, the control of navigation—the TVA portended, fearfully for some, hopefully for others, some larger scheme of national economic planning. Lilienthal, in the passage below, presents that moderate, piecemeal approach to planning that won out in the Roosevelt administration over the more ambitious schemes of either the radical Tugwell or the conservative Moley. After World War II, Lilienthal served as chairman of the Atomic Energy Commission (1947-49), and in 1964 set down his lifelong experience in government in *The Journals of David Lilienthal.*

TVA is supposed to be a planning agency for this region. Yet nowhere on your organization chart do I find a Department of Social Planning; and when I ask for a copy of the TVA Plan no one can produce it: Some such comment has been made to us many times by friendly and earnest students of TVA.

The reason the TVA Plan is not available is that there is no such document. Nor is there one separate department set off by itself, where planners exercise their brains. To one who has read thus far in this account, it is evident this does not constitute our idea of planning.

The TVA *is* a planning agency, the first of its kind in the United States. The great change going on in this valley is an authentic example of modern democratic planning; this was the expressed intent of Congress, by whose authority we act. But through the years we have deliberately been sparing in the use of the terminology of "plans" and "planning" within TVA and outside, and those terms have hardly appeared thus far in this book. For the term "planning" has come to be used in so many different senses that the nomenclature has almost lost usefulness, has even come to be a source of some confusion. . . .

We have always made plans in America. The question for us is not: Shall we plan? but: *What kind of plans* should we make? What kind of planners? What method of "enforcement of plans"? On these matters what has transpired in the Tennessee Valley, as I have tried to describe it, casts the light of actual experience.

Economic and social planning in America is by no means new and strange, but is indeed as old as the Republic. Generally speaking, planning in this country in the past has been practiced by two great groups: first, by elected public officials, variously called "politicians" or "statesmen"; and, second, by businessmen, variously called "empire builders" or "exploiters of our resources."

Let us look for a moment at some of the instances of planning carried on by public men, selected to represent the economic interests and the social point of view of their constituents. Land planning, for example. By Royal Proclamation in 1763 the colonists were barred from free access to the western lands. Then, by the Ordinance of 1787, the politicians established a different conception of land planning: the opening of the western lands to settlers. The economic and social views of the people of that time called for land planning which would encourage and stimulate the settlement of the West. . . .

Great as were some of the accomplishments of public planners in the past, we know that we suffer today from the consequences of some of those plans. The state of our natural resources has become a national emergency, grave and critical. Some of the public land policies embodied in such planning as the Homestead laws we now realize were short-sighted and costly. Such piecemeal planning for the immediate year-to-year demands of particular groups of constituents we now know was not wise planning. Catastrophic floods, denuded forests, soil exhaustion—these are part of the price we are paying. For a generation now a change in those plans has been urged. . . .

Planning by businessmen, often under some other name, is recognized as necessary to the conduct of private enterprise. It has the virtue of a single and direct objective, one that can be currently measured, that is, the making of a profit. A plan that is impressive in the form of a report but which does not work, as judged by the financial reports of the company, is an unsuccessful plan. It has been just as simple as that. The business planner has rarely felt it necessary to complicate his problem by trying to determine whether the making of profit under his plan benefits the whole of society, or injures it. And, as I have said, it is not often that a single business or even an entire industry is in a position to decide such a question.

This is admittedly a grave defect of planning by the businessman. For his legitimate object, namely a profitable business, is not necessarily consistent with the object of society, that is, a prosperous and happy people. The plans of the A. T. & T. and of the small manufacturer may both be quite effective within those enterprises. But factors affecting the plans of the A. T. & T. and the small manufacturer go far beyond their businesses. Over this multitude of external factors the businessman has no effective control. As this and a thousand valleys demonstrate so tragically, private planning, even when temporarily sound from the viewpoint of a particular enterprise, has often resulted in great injury to many other enterprises, and therefore to the public welfare.

The idea of unified resource development is based upon the premise that by democratic planning the individual's interest, the interest of private undertakings, can increasingly be made one with the interest of all of us, i.e., the community interest. By and large, things are working out that way in the Tennessee Valley. The income of the private business of farming has increased, largely as a result of a program of aiding the region's soil. Sales by private fertilizer companies have increased more rapidly than at any other time in their history as a result of TVA's production and the demonstration of new fertilizer products designed to further the over-all public interest in the land. Promotion of education in forest-fire protection and scientific cutting methods has furthered conservation and at the same time aided the private business of lumbering. Community planning has made towns more attractive and pleasant for everyone, and at the same time increased land values for individual owners. These results and many others I have described have been in the general public interest; all have furthered the interest of particular business enterprises.

Effective planners must understand and believe in people. The average man is constantly in the mind of the effective planning expert. Planners, whether they are technicians or administrators, must recognize that they are not dealing with philosophical abstractions, or mere statistics or engineering data or legal principles, and that planning is not an end in itself.

In the last analysis, in democratic planning it is human beings we are concerned with. Unless plans show an understanding and recognition of the aspirations of men and women, they will fail. Those who lack human understanding and cannot share the emotions of men can hardly forward the objectives of realistic planning. Thurman Arnold, in *The Symbols of Government,* has well described this type of earnest but unrealistic person:

> They usually bungle their brief opportunities in power because they are too much in love with an ideal society to treat the one actually before them with skill and understanding. Their constant and futile cry is reiterated through the ages: "Let us educate the people so that they can understand and appreciate us."

A great Plan, a moral and indeed a religious purpose, deep and fundamental, is democracy's answer both to our own homegrown would-be dictators and foreign anti-democracy alike. In the unified development of resources there is such a Great Plan: the Unity of Nature and Mankind. Under such a Plan in our valley we move forward. True, it is but a step at a time. But we assume responsibility not simply for the little advance we make each day, but for that vast and all-pervasive end and purpose of all our labors, the material well-being of all men and the opportunity for them to build for themselves spiritual strength.

Here is the life principle of democratic planning—an awakening in the whole people of a sense of this common moral purpose. Not one goal, but a direction. Not one plan, once and for all, but the *conscious selection by the people of successive plans.* It was Whitman the democrat who warned that "the goal that was named cannot be countermanded."

If this conception of planning is sound, as I believe, then it is plain that in a democracy we always must rest our plans upon "here and now," upon "things as they are." How many are the bloody casualties of liberal efforts to improve the lot of man, how bitter the lost ground and disillusionment because of failure to understand so simple and yet so vital an issue of human strategy. So frequently have men sought an escape from the long task of education, the often prosaic day-by-day steps to "do something about it," by pressing for a plan—usually in the form of a law—without considering whether the people understand the reason for the law's plan, or how they are to benefit by it.

An unwillingness to start from where you are ranks as a fallacy of historic proportions; present-day planning, anywhere in the world for that matter, will fall into the same pit if it makes the same gigantic error. It is because the lesson of the past seems to me so clear on this score, because the nature of man so definitely confirms it, that there has been this perhaps tiresome repetition throughout this record: the people must be in on the planning; their existing institutions must be made part of it; self-education of the citizenry is more important than specific projects or physical changes.

And it is because of this same conviction that the TVA has never attempted by arbitrary action to "eliminate" or to force reform upon those factors or institutions in the valley's life which are vigorously antagonistic to a plan for unified development.

We move step by step—from where we are. Everyone has heard the story of the man who was asked by a stranger how he could get to Jonesville; after long thought and unsuccessful attempts to explain the several turns that must be made, he said, so the anecdote runs: "My friend, I tell you; if I were you, I wouldn't start from here." Some planning is just like that; it does not start from here; it assumes a "clean slate" that never has and never can exist.

PART FOUR

GIANTISM IN BUSINESS

17 • Ernest Gruening: *Controlling the Giant Corporation*

Adolf A. Berle, Jr., a Columbia University law professor, collaborated with economist Gardiner C. Means shortly before Berle became a member of FDR's "Brains Trust," to produce one of the most influential books of the early New Deal era: *The Modern Corporation and Private Property* (1933). The review in *The Nation* by Ernest Gruening (now U.S. Senator from Alaska) suggests some of the impact of the book on the American public. Berle and Means pointed in their book to the separation of corporate ownership from control. One consequence of this separation, the authors asserted, was the increasing tendency to utilize this control of corporate wealth for irresponsible purposes. They did not explicitly draw the same conclusions from their study as did Gruening: "that in a self-governing democracy the people will proceed from control of the political state, and by means of it, to control also of the now uncontrollable economic super-power. . . ." But many others did. How to deal with the new giant power of the business corporation became, from the start, one of the most puzzling problems of the New Deal.

From Ernest Gruening, "Capitalist Confiscation," a review of *The Modern Corporation and Private Property* by Adolf A. Berle, Jr. and Gardiner C. Means in *The Nation,* CXXXVI (February 1, 1933), 116-117. Reprinted with the permission of the publisher.

Private property is the cornerstone of our economic order. Whether we refer to it as capitalism, the profit system, or the price system, the existing economic structure rests on the sanctity of private ownership. Subject only to the police power of the state, the rights traditionally implicit in personal possession have been deemed inviolate. The profit and enjoyment of what I own, the determination of its usage, belong to me. If I want to shut down my business, halve or double its activity, regardless of the consequences to employees or community—that's *my* business. Such is the concept underlying our contemporary society. Attacks from the "left" designed to stress the superiority of human over property rights have thus far made small impression on the intrenchments erected through the centuries. Neither the theory nor the practice of private ownership has in America yielded appreciably to the assaults of collectivism.

Yet private ownership in America is being destroyed. Paradoxically, the fundamental change in the nature of ownership comes from the citadel of capitalism, has arisen from the ark of acquisitiveness itself. It is the corporation, that creature of our complex society, which is sounding the doom of long-cherished ownership concepts. It is, moreover, the actual implement of destruction. The change has stolen upon us unaware, greatly accelerated in the late era of conservatism. The myth of private ownership with all its appurtenances persists. But the stark fact has become demonstrably otherwise.

This transformation, lucidly exposed in an epoch-making volume by Adolf A. Berle and Gardiner C. Means of Columbia University, is revolutionary. For individual ownership, personal property rights, and economic autonomy "a corporate system has been substituted—as there was once a feudal system," which is still headed toward its zenith.

How did this change come about? It is, first, a product of the industrial revolution. It is, next, the concomitant of great and rapid growth. The joint-stock company became noticeable three hundred years ago for the pursuit of overseas exploration and exploitation. It was still a relatively unimportant and feeble institution one hundred years ago. Ownership of the means of production originally spelled a three-fold relationship—ownership, management, and labor—which persists today only in the case of the small independent farmer. The labor participation was the earliest to disappear. Ownership and management, however, long continued one and inseparable, a status not materially changed by the delegation of management. Management was merely hired—like any employee.

In the corporations of the early nineteenth century, the number of stockholders was small and the structure of the company simple—a division of the capital actually "put up" into one class of shares—so many shares for so many dollars. Ownership determined a company's policies. Such officials as were intrusted with control were in a very true sense both trustees and employees of the capitalists. Little by little the owner has become widely separated from control, and today receives in exchange for his capital a token of dubious value dependent for its worth on factors wholly beyond his power to affect. And whereas the original delegated control was not only supposedly, but actually, functioning in the interests of the owners, ownership and control have through their wide separation become actuated not only by different, but often by radically opposed, interests.

Over three-quarters of all the wealth in the United States today is corporate. Three-quarters of the possessions of the people of the United States are represented today not by tangible goods, but by pieces of paper. And of this, 200 great organizations control 38 per cent. There were in 1929 over 300,000 non-financial corporations in the United States. The largest 200 of these, fewer than .07 per cent of the total, control an amount which is rapidly approaching half the people's corporate wealth. In 1929 this amounted to over $81,000,000,000. At the 1924-25 rate of change they will control 85 per cent of the national wealth by 1950.

The shifting of ownership from the original owner or investor to a "remote control" comprises many steps. Each step has spelled a weakening of the stockholder's position, a lessening of his power to determine the disposition of his property. The "control" of a corporation, exercised by relatively fewer and fewer men, has little by little encroached on the supposed rights of the owner-shareholder and diminished the value of his holdings. The power to issue additional classes of stock is one method of diluting the value of shares already outstanding. Directors may insert class after class of stock with rights prior to those of an earlier investor. Stock-purchase warrants, a recent innovation, carry this process farther. A warrant is an option permitting the holder to purchase one or more shares at a price stated in the warrant. In the event of diminished earnings the warrant is presumably not exercised. But if the prospect is favorable, the additional flotation of stock diminishes proportionately the existing stockholders' equity.

"No-par-value" stock brings about a similar result. In practice it represents a gross discrimination against those who have bought other classes of stock at par. "Blank stock," another recent artifice, is nothing other than a blank check for the directors. Moreover, securities of a corporation may, through the original—or easily amended—charter provisions, become convertible at the option, not of the holder, but of the corporation management. "Paid-in surplus" is available today at the will of the directors for the payment of dividends—a disbursement of the stockholder's potential participation. Other analogous devices exist.

Bookkeeping, developed into a fine art, and court decisions—or the absence of court decisions to prevent unprecedented encroachment—are permitting these changes. The courts have held that a non-cumulative preferred dividend passed need not be made up. A company earning a handsome profit may, at the option of the directors, pay no dividends for years on either preferred or common stock, and then with the accumulation of a vast surplus, begin paying its limited 7 per cent on the preferred, and 50 per cent on the common. The preferred stockholder has no redress. The "control" may manipulate the stock in half a dozen different ways to the detriment of the individual shareholders. It can—despite the much-invoked "due-process" clause of the Fourteenth Amendment—virtually confiscate his property.

Fixing the price at which securities are floated is a right exercised by the inside "control," which in practice often works out to the outside shareholder's disadvantage. If the price was too high, and the stock's value shrinks, he loses. If the price is destined to rise, others closer to the control than he may first drain the potentialities of profit to their own advantage. In theory they are not supposed to do this; in practice they may, can, and do. Into the question of price and salability of the stock certificates—the one visible token of ownership—enters a variety of factors in which the investor is helplessly dependent on the "good faith" of others, whose judgment may first of all be awry and, more important, whose interests do not coincide with his. Brokers' statements, on the basis of which securities are sold at the price fixed, may be truthful as far as they go, but seldom are the whole truth. Accounting manipulation for the purpose of showing abnormal profits is not uncommon practice. Unless direct fraud—deliberate, conscious misstatements—can be demonstrated, the investor has no redress. Abjurations of responsibility and disclaimers of guaranteeing the validity of statements—appearing in small type in the circulars and seldom observed by investors, or, if observed, disregarded by them—give the banking-promoter group a legal loophole.

What has become of the theoretical safeguards of the stockholder? Steadily they have diminished almost to the vanishing-point. The control of the corporation vaguely resides in an inner group which can, with increasing difficulty, be held to effective accountability for mismanagement or erroneous judgment. The control is almost universally exercised, not merely by a minority stock ownership, but increasingly by a fraction so small as to be fantastic when contrasted with the supposed rights of ownership. Even a 1 per cent actual investment is no longer essential for the control of millions, indeed billions, of dollars of other people's money. The proxy system, in theory the opportunity to voice approval or disapproval, has become a snare and a delusion as far as the individual stockholder is concerned. Actually, it has been perverted into a means of perpetuating existing control. Voting trusts produce a similar result. "Pyramiding," the repeated subdivision of controlling stock through a system of superimposed holding companies, is an increasingly common method of securing control of more and more with less and less!

Only 5 per cent of our 200 largest corporations and only 2 per cent of the billions which they represent are today controlled by majority ownership. Against such a set-up the individual stockholder, however aggrieved, is essentially helpless. Seldom does he possess the means to engage successfully in a legal contest with a corporation. Even in those rare cases when he wins a suit, he is apt to be a victor in principle but a victim in fact.

The new power exercised by the "control," originally a purely delegated power, a responsible trusteeship, has become responsible not to ownership but to itself—that is to say, to no one. Existing legal machinery cannot cope with it. "The concentration of economic power separate from ownership has in fact created economic empires and has delivered these empires into the hands of a new form of absolutism, relegating 'owners' to the position of those who supply the means whereby the new princes may exercise their power."

It follows that the shareholder in the modern corporation has "surrendered a set of definite rights for a set of indefinite expectations." How ironical is the conclusion of Messrs. Berle and Means that "the only example of a similar subjection of the economic interests of the individual to those of a group . . . is that contained in the Communist system!" Thus the American property-"owner" has become simply supplier of his savings to an economic super-state. He is hopeful of receiving a wage on that capital. What that wage shall be or whether, indeed, he shall receive any wage at all, is a matter determined wholly by others. He bids fair to be a capital-wage-slave!

Who exercises this startling confiscatory power? Who really controls the wealth of the nation? For whom do 125 millions labor and save? The "control" is centered in fewer than 2,000 individuals, those who dominate the great corporations that in turn dominate American economic life. Actually, this control is far more concentrated than even the number 2,000 implies. The interrelation of great industries, the interdependence, for instance, of the fuel supply—coal, oil, and electric energy—with the utilities and the manufacturing industries, makes for even greater actual concentration of power. The largest corporations are growing the fastest. They are steadily waxing by merger and purchase, engulfing mammoth but lesser units and vesting more power in the individuals at the top.

It is scarcely necessary to cite specific examples of the disastrous consequences of this new irresponsible control. The financial history of the last three years is replete with them. Fill in the names of the "securities" which you "owned," and reconstruct your personal relation to what has happened in America!

The implications in this capitalistic confiscation of property are far-reaching. We may confine ourselves here to the conclusion of those who have with admirable scholarship clarified this trend—Messrs. Berle and Means. With private ownership in process of abolition, the control groups are unwittingly clearing the way for the claims of a group far wider than either the owners or the control. They have placed the community in a position to demand that the modern corporations serve not only the owners or the control but all society. This is a wholly new concept of corporate activity and motivation. But it follows logically.

Sing us no song of property rights! Where have they been

less sacred than in America in the last three years? When has economic security been more ruthlessly trampled under foot? When before in our national life has confiscation been so extensive and intensive? And today, in seeking to recover some measure of stability, the people (not to mention the corporations) look as never before to the state—but to the state merely as an agency for economic resuscitation. How inevitable, therefore, that in a self-governing democracy the people will proceed from control of the political state, and by means of it, to control also of the now uncontrollable economic super-power, a conquest essential if we would make "life, liberty, and the pursuit of happiness" other than a travesty.

18 • William O. Douglas: *How Effective is Securities Regulation?*

William O. Douglas (1898-   ) as a Yale Law professor was a diligent student of the relationship of business to government. The Securities Act, setting up the Securities and Exchange Commission, was passed in 1933 following a sensational investigation of Wall Street malpractices by a committee headed by attorney Ferdinand Pecora. It represented the work of what some historians have called the "Brandeisian" faction of the New Deal. Felix Frankfurter, close to FDR, was a leading exponent of this approach, which went back to Woodrow Wilson's New Freedom, in its emphasis on moderately controlling rather than powerfully directing the activities of big business. In this article, Douglas painstakingly analyzes the specific weaknesses of the Act, as well as its philosophical presumptions. Ironically, soon after he wrote this critique, he was appointed to the Securities and Exchange Commis-

From William O. Douglas, "Protecting the Investor," *The Yale Review*, XXIII (Spring 1934), 521-533. Copyright Yale University Press. Reprinted with the permission of the publisher.

sion, and became its chairman in 1937. President Roosevelt appointed him to the Supreme Court in 1939.

The current battle on the Securities Act is being waged on political lines. The points at issue are not neatly drawn in business or legal terms. The arguments on both sides are often distinguished by their emotional quality rather than by any deep insight into the requirements for protection of investors and for control of the security business. . . .

Therefore, curiously enough, what the Act contains, what it actually does, the soundness of its method of protecting investors are not particularly important. The nature and quality of the arguments mean only that the Act is significant politically. It is symbolic of a shift of political power. That shift is from the bankers to the masses; from the promoter to the investor. It means that the government is taking the side of the helpless, the suckers, the underdogs. It signifies that the money-changers are being driven from the temples. These factors are dominant and controlling. Among other things they mean that it is sheer nonsense to talk of repealing the Securities Act or even of making substantial amendments. To open it up for amendments might end in disastrous emasculation. The Act has been in effect only nine months, and that is too short a period to teach old dogs new tricks. Bankers have not changed miraculously overnight. Their feet should be kept "close to the fire" a while longer. In fact, it might be desirable to move them a bit closer.

What follows is not germane to this political issue. It is not directly addressed to the problem of immediate amendment. It deals with the larger and more difficult problem of protection of investors. It envisages forms of supplementary legislation dealing directly with the forces which must be controlled if high finance, as Mr. Berle would say, is to be the servant not the master of society.

On this broader issue, there are three propositions which seem to me tolerably clear. First, that the Securities Act falls far short of accomplishing its purposes. Second, that in any programme for the protection of investors and in any genuine and permanent correction of the evils of high finance an Act like the Securities Act is of a decidedly secondary character. And, third, that a vigorous enforcement of the Act promises to spell its own defeat because it is so wholly antithetical to the programme of control envisaged in the New Deal and to the whole economy under which we are living. . . .

Thus all that the Securities Act definitely purports to do is wholly secondary in any thoroughgoing and comprehensive programme for social control in this field. In the first place, the Act merely requires the recital of certain facts at one point of time in the life of the security, that is, the date of issue. As has been indicated, this may be a healthy conditioner of the market in the early stages of the life of the security. But its effect will be dissipated very early, in fact, during a period of months rather than years. Soon the statements made will be wholly discounted by a host of other bearish or bullish factors. There is no machinery provided for obtaining subsequent reliable information either in the form of annual reports or otherwise. In the second place, there is nothing in the Act which controls the power of the self-perpetuating management group which has risen to a position of dominance in our industrial organization. There is nothing in the Act which purports to deal with the protection of the rights of minorities. There is nothing which concerns the problem of capital structure, its soundness or unsoundness. There is nothing that deals with the problem of mobilizing the flow of capital to various productive channels. And, finally, there is nothing which deals with the fundamental problem of the increment of power and profit inherent in our present forms of organization.

This may seem to be an unfair criticism of the Act in that it merely states that the Act does not go far enough. In defense one might say that it is but a first step towards greater control of finance. But there is a more serious criticism to be made. The fact is that the Act is fundamentally inconsistent and at variance with the essential characteristics of a more thoroughgoing and comprehensive control in this field.

And this brings me to my last and salient point. The Act is based on an implied assumption that must be dragged to light and carefully examined. This assumption is that we should and must return to a simpler economy; that our large units of production should be pulverized; that business relations and organization should be made more personal; that the investor should be more closely assimilated into the enterprise; that the centrifugal force which has been separating ownership from management should be transformed into a centripetal force which will drive back closer to the business not only the investors but also those in the management who direct policy not detail. In other words, it is Main Street business which the Act envisages and which it desires to see returned. This is evident on every hand. It explains why all directors are held to the same standard of reasonable investigation. It explains why stockholders in many instances are bereft of all defense. It explains the assumption that details of large business enterprises can be readily stated in the registration statement. It explains the great reliance placed on truth about securities, as if the truth could be told to people who could understand it—a supposition which might be justified if little units of business were seeking funds and people were buying shares with the modicum of intelligence with which they are supposed to buy wearing apparel or horses.

So it is that the Act is a nineteenth-century piece of legislation. To understand it we must "turn back the clock" to simpler days. We must unscramble our large forms of organization. We must start anew to bring back into business organization a simplicity and directness consistent more with our beginnings than with our present status. It is sincerely felt by many that this ought to be our course. Such a course would have many obvious advantages. But it is inconceivable to me that it can be our course. We have passed through that phase, and we are now in transition to something different and, I think, something better. Our problem is to perfect a plan for control of our present forms of organization. Such a plan when finally evolved must envisage a wide range—from the increments of profit and control (which are incident to the constitution and form of the organization) to the terms and conditions of the organization, the kind and amount of securities which may be issued, the terms on which they may be issued, and the persons to whom they may be sold. Ultimately this may run to fascism or socialism. Intermediately it means harnessing these instruments of production not only for the ancient purpose of profit but also for the more slowly evolving purpose of service in the sense of the public good. The intermediate control logically seems to take the form of self-government coupled with a slowly increasing and more articulate form of public control to the end that such self-discipline shall not be wholly self-serving.

And so it seems that the Securities Act is antithetical to our more recent developments. Certainly the degree of collectivism present under the N.R.A. and A.A.A. is evidence of a coalescence of present forms of organization into even more stable forms. What the evolution of these new alignments will be is difficult to say. Their direction is clearly towards a more thoroughgoing programme of stabilization. This obviously means, among other things, greater mastery of the forces of competition and monopoly, consumption and production, prices and costs, profits and losses.

Thus the Securities Act struggles against a current that is sweeping business the other way. Its strict enforcement is bound to mean in time its own end, as did the enforcement of the Eighteenth Amendment. It is apparent that the thing industry needs is constructive planning and organization conditioned by the requirements of the public good. When these become articulate, security regulation will be seen to be an integral part of the whole programme of industrial organization and regulation. They need as conspicuous a place in the present codes as labor, prices, and costs. They are inseparably a part of the control over expansion, competition, prices, and related matters which the codes set up. Any comprehensive and consistent control of the type which these parts of the New Deal envisage must inevitably embrace within it control over security issues. That in essence means control over access to the market. That control would be an administrative control lodged in the hands not only of the new self-disciplined business groups but also in the hands of governmental agencies whose function would be to articulate the public interest with the profit motive. . . .

Moreover, it will be unfortunate if we either launch wholeheartedly on a programme of vigorous enforcement of the Securities Act or undertake patchwork amendments to it, without an immediate objective of a more pervasive administrative control. If we do so, we turn our steps to the past, forgetful of the realities of the present; and we merely delay or postpone genuine or permanent control, which eventually will come in one form or another. It is a matter of prudence to fashion that control consistently with the other integral parts of the total programme rather than to resist the relentless tide of events and to seek a return to conditions which have been wiped out in the forward sweep of our economic and social life.

19 • Franklin D. Roosevelt: *Stop Collectivism in Business*

The message that Franklin D. Roosevelt delivered to Congress April 29, 1938, calling for an investigation of monopoly, has been

From *Final Report and Recommendations of the Temporary National Economic Committee* (Washington: Government Printing Office, 1941), pp. 11-20.

called by historian Richard Hofstadter, "one of the most remarkable economic documents that have ever come from the White House." It stated boldly and unequivocally the danger to democracy in the fact that less than a tenth of one per cent of all corporations owned over half the corporate assets in the nation. It called for investigation and action. But it stumbled, finally, on the dilemma that has faced industrial America throughout this century: How can the efficiency of mammoth enterprises be turned to the public good, without attempting the impossible task of grinding them into small economic units, and without either government ownership or rigorous public control? The Temporary National Economic Committee, which was established following Roosevelt's message, was to face this political puzzle through the three years of its investigation.

To the Congress of the United States:

Unhappy events abroad have retaught us two simple truths about the liberty of a democratic people.

The first truth is that the liberty of a democracy is not safe if the people tolerate the growth of private power to a point where it becomes stronger than their democratic state itself. That, in its essence, is fascism—ownership of government by an individual, by a group, or by any other controlling private power.

The second truth is that the liberty of a democracy is not safe, if its business system does not provide employment and produce and distribute goods in such a way as to sustain an acceptable standard of living.

Both lessons hit home.

Among us today a concentration of private power without equal in history is growing.

This concentration is seriously impairing the economic effectiveness of private enterprise as a way of providing employment for labor and capital and as a way of assuring a more equitable distribution of income and earnings among the people of the Nation as a whole.

I. THE GROWING CONCENTRATION OF ECONOMIC POWER

Statistics of the Bureau of Internal Revenue reveal the following amazing figures for 1935:

Ownership of corporate assets: Of all corporations reporting from every part of the Nation, one-tenth of 1 percent of them owned 52 percent of the assets of all of them.

And to clinch the point: Of all corporations reporting, less than 5 per cent of them owned 87 percent of all the assets of all of them.

Income and profits of corporations: Of all the corporations reporting from every part of the country, one-tenth of 1 percent of them earned 50 percent of the net income of all of them.

And to clinch the point: Of all the manufacturing corporations reporting, less than 4 percent of them earned 84 percent of all the net profits of all of them.

The statistical history of modern times proves that in times of depression concentration of business speeds up. Bigger business then has larger opportunity to grow still bigger at the expense of smaller competitors who are weakened by financial adversity.

The danger of this centralization in a handful of huge corporations is not reduced or eliminated, as is sometimes urged, by the wide public distribution of their securities. The mere number of security holders gives little clue to the size of their individual holdings or to their actual ability to have a voice in the management. In fact, the concentration of stock ownership of corporations in the hands of a tiny minority of the population matches the concentration of corporate assets.

The year 1929 was a banner year for distribution of stock ownership.

But in that year three-tenths of 1 percent of our population received 78 percent of the dividends reported by individuals. This has roughly the same effect as if, out of every 300 persons in our population, one person received 78 cents out of every dollar of corporate dividends, while the other 299 persons divided up the other 22 cents between them.

The effect of this concentration is reflected in the distribution of national income.

A recent study by the National Resources Committee shows that in 1935-36—

> Forty-seven percent of all American families and single individuals living alone had incomes of less than $1,000 for the year; and at the other end of the ladder a little less than 1½ percent of the Nation's families received incomes which in dollars and cents reached the same total as the incomes of the 47 percent at the bottom.

Furthermore, to drive the point home, the Bureau of Internal Revenue reports that estate-tax returns in 1936 show that—

> Thirty-three percent of the property which was passed by inheritance was found in only 4 percent of all the reporting estates. (And the figures of concentration would be far more impressive, if we included all the smaller estates which, under the law, do not have to report.)

We believe in a way of living in which political democracy and free private enterprise for profit should serve and protect each other—to insure a maximum of human liberty, not for a few, but for all.

It has been well said that, "The freest government, if it could exist, would not be long acceptable if the tendency of the laws were to create a rapid accumulation of property in few hands and to render the great mass of the population dependent and penniless."

Today many Americans ask the uneasy question: Is the vociferation that our liberties are in danger justified by the facts?

Today's answer on the part of average men and women in every part of the country is far more accurate than it would have been in 1929 for the very simple reason that during the past 9 years we have been doing a lot of common-sense thinking. Their answer is that if there is that danger, it comes from that concentrated private economic power which is struggling so hard to master our democratic government. It will not come, as some (by no means all) of the possessors of that private power would make the people believe—from our democratic government itself.

II. FINANCIAL CONTROL OVER INDUSTRY

Even these statistics I have cited do not measure the actual degree of concentration of control over American industry.

Close financial control, through interlocking spheres of influence over channels of investment and through the use of financial devices like holding companies and strategic minority interests, creates close control of the business policies of enterprises which masquerade as independent units.

That heavy hand of integrated financial and management control lies upon large and strategic areas of American industry. The small businessman is unfortunately being driven into a less and less independent position in American life. You and I must admit that.

Private enterprise is ceasing to be free enterprise and is becoming a cluster of private collectivisms; masking itself as a system of free enterprise after the American model, it is in fact becoming a concealed cartel system after the European model.

We all want efficient industrial growth and the advantages of mass production. No one suggests that we return to the hand loom or hand forge. A series of processes involved in turning out a given manufactured product may well require one or more huge mass-production plants. Modern efficiency may call for this. But modern efficient mass production is not furthered by a central control which destroys competition between industrial plants each capable of efficient mass production while operating as separate units. Industrial efficiency does not have to mean industrial empire building.

And industrial empire building, unfortunately, has evolved into banker control of industry. We oppose that.

Such control does not offer safety for the investing public. Investment judgment requires the disinterested appraisal of other people's management. It becomes blurred and distorted if it is combined with the conflicting duty of controlling the management it is supposed to judge.

Interlocking financial controls have taken from American business much of its traditional virility, independence, adaptability, and daring—without compensating advantages. They have not given the stability they promised.

Business enterprise needs new vitality and the flexibility that comes from the diversified efforts, independent judgments, and vibrant energies of thousands upon thousands of independent businessmen.

The individual must be encouraged to exercise his own judgment and to venture his own small savings, not in stock gambling but in new enterprise investment. Men will dare to compete against men but not against giants.

III. THE DECLINE OF COMPETITION AND ITS EFFECTS ON EMPLOYMENT

In output per man or machine we are the most efficient industrial nation on earth.

In the matter of complete mutual employment of capital and labor we are among the least efficient. . . .

One of the primary causes of our present difficulties lies in the disappearance of price competition in many industrial fields, particularly in basic manufacture where concentrated economic power is most evident—and where rigid prices and fluctuating pay rolls are general. . . .

IV. COMPETITION DOES NOT MEAN EXPLOITATION

Competition, of course, like all other good things, can be carried to excess. Competition should not extend to fields where it has demonstrably bad social and economic consequences. The exploitation of child labor, the chiseling of workers' wages, the stretching of workers' hours, are not necessary, fair, or proper methods of competition. I have consistently urged a Federal wages-and-hours bill to take the minimum decencies of life for the working man and woman out of the field of competition.

It is, of course, necessary to operate the competitive system of free enterprise intelligently. In gaging the market for their wares, businessmen, like farmers, should be given all possible information by government and by their own associations so that they may act with knowledge, and not on impulse. Serious problems of temporary over-production can and should be avoided by disseminating information that will discourage the production of more goods than the current markets can possibly absorb or the accumulation of dangerously large inventories for which there is obvious need.

It is, of course, necessary to encourage rises in the level of those competitive prices, such as agricultural prices, which must rise to put our price structure into more workable balance and make the debt burden more tolerable. Many such competitive prices are now too low.

It may at times be necessary to give special treatment to chronically sick industries which have deteriorated too far for natural revival, especially those which have a public or quasi-public character.

But generally over the field of industry and finance we must revive and strengthen competition if we wish to preserve and make workable our traditional system of free private enterprise.

The justification of private profit is private risk. We cannot safely make America safe for the businessman who does not want to take the burdens and risks of being a businessman.

V. THE CHOICE BEFORE US

Examination of methods of conducting and controlling private enterprise which keep it from furnishing jobs or income or opportunity for one-third of the population is long overdue on the part of those who sincerely want to preserve the system of private enterprise for profit.

No people, least of all a democratic people, will be content to go without work or to accept some standard of living which obviously and woefully falls short of their capacity to produce. No people, least of all a people with our traditions of personal liberty, will endure the slow erosion of opportunity for the common man, the oppressive sense of helplessness under the domination of a few, which are overshadowing our whole economic life.

A discerning magazine of business has editorially pointed out that big-business collectivism in industry compels an ultimate collectivism in government.

The power of a few to manage the economic life of the Nation must be diffused among the many or be transferred to the public and its democratically responsible government. If prices are to be managed and administered, if the Nation's business is to be allotted by plan and not by competition, that power should not be vested in any private group or cartel, however benevolent its professions profess to be.

Those people, in and out of the halls of government, who encourage the growing restriction of competition either by active efforts or by passive resistance to sincere attempts to change the trend, are shouldering a terrific responsibility. Consciously or unconsciously they are working for centralized business and financial control. Consciously or unconsciously they are therefore either working for control of the Government itself by business and finance or the other alternative—a growing concentration of public power in the Government to cope with such concentration of private power.

The enforcement of free competition is the least regulation business can expect.

VI. A PROGRAM

The traditional approach to the problems I have discussed has been through the antitrust laws. That approach we do not propose to abandon. On the contrary, although we must recognize the inadequacies of the existing laws, we seek to enforce them so that the public shall not be deprived of such protection as they afford. To enforce them properly requires thorough investigation not only to discover such violations as may exist but to avoid hit-and-miss prosecutions harmful to business and government alike. To provide for the proper and fair enforcement of the existing antitrust laws I shall submit, through the Budget, recommendations for a deficiency appropriation of $200,000 for the Department of Justice.

But the existing antitrust laws are inadequate—most importantly because of new financial economic conditions with which they are powerless to cope.

The Sherman Act was passed nearly 40 years ago. The Clayton and Federal Trade Commission Acts were passed over 20 years ago. We have had considerable experience under those acts. In the meantime we have had a chance to observe the practical operation of large-scale industry and to learn many things about the competitive system which we did not know in those days.

We have witnessed the merging-out of effective competition in many fields of enterprise. We have learned that the so-called competitive system works differently in an industry where there are many independent units, from the way it works in an industry where a few large producers dominate the market.

We have also learned that a realistic system of business regulation has to reach more than consciously immoral acts. The community is interested in economic results. It must be protected from economic as well as moral wrongs. We must find practical controls over blind economic forces as well as over blindly selfish men.

Government can deal and should deal with blindly selfish men. But that is a comparatively small part—the easier part—of our problem. The larger, more important and more difficult part of our problem is to deal with men who are not selfish and who are good citizens, but who cannot see the social and economic consequences of their actions in a modern economically interdependent community. They fail to grasp the significance of some of our most vital social and economic problems because they see them only in the light of their own personal experience and not in perspective with the experience of other men and other industries. They therefore fail to see these problems for the Nation as a whole.

To meet the situation I have described, there should be a thorough study of the concentration of economic power in American industry and the effect of that concentration upon the decline of competition. There should be an examination of the existing price system and the price policies of industry, to determine their effect upon the general level of trade, upon employment, upon long-term profits, and upon consumption. The study should not be confined to the traditional antitrust field. The effects of tax, patent, and other Government policies cannot be ignored. . . .

No man of good faith will misinterpret these proposals. They derive from the oldest American traditions. Concentration of economic power in the few and the resulting unemployment of labor and capital are inescapable problems for a modern "private enterprise" democracy. I do not believe that we are so lacking in stability that we will lose faith in our own way of living just because we seek to find out how to make that way of living work more effectively.

This program should appeal to the honest common sense of every independent businessman interested primarily in running his own business at a profit rather than in controlling the business of other men.

It is not intended as the beginning of any ill-considered "trust busting" activity which lacks proper consideration for economic results.

It is a program to preserve private enterprise for profit by keeping it free enough to be able to utilize all our resources of capital and labor at a profit.

It is a program whose basic purpose is to stop the progress of collectivism in business and turn business back to the democratic competitive order.

It is a program whose basic thesis is not that the system of free private enterprise for profit has failed in this generation, but that it has not yet been tried.

Once it is realized that business monopoly in America paralyzes the system of free enterprise on which it is grafted, and is as fatal to those who manipulate it as to the people who suffer beneath its impositions, action by the Government to eliminate these artificial restraints will be welcomed by industry throughout the Nation.

For idle factories and idle workers profit no man.

20 · Thurman Arnold: *The Rule of Reason in Antitrust Action*

When Thurman Arnold left his professorship at Yale Law School in March 1938 to accept Roosevelt's appointment as Assistant Attorney General in charge of the Antitrust Division, he faced a dilemma. He had been writing of the fruitlessness of attempting to prosecute the trusts in an age of great industrial combines; yet this was exactly the job now entrusted to him. In the following speech to the Academy of Political Science, Arnold explained the pragmatic formula that would guide his actions: dealing with the problems of "one industry at a time," avoiding "unnecessary dislocation of interests" and not disturbing "efficient size" or "orderly marketing procedures." Under Arnold an enlarged Antitrust Division inaugurated a series of antitrust actions directed particularly against the pricing policies of various industries more extensive than any ever

From Thurman Arnold, "The Policy of Government Toward Big Business." Reprinted with permission from *The Proceedings of the Academy of Political Science*, XVIII, No. 2 (January 1939), 180-187.

taken under the Sherman Act. In the light of the meager results—which Arnold himself had forecast before he took office—his speech below seems a strained attempt to justify a policy doomed to failure from the start.

. . . With respect to the enforcement of the Sherman Act, the policy of government toward business can be reduced to an easy formula on which we all would probably agree. The first part of that formula is this: None of us desire to abandon our traditional attitude of favoring an economy of free and independent business enterprise. I know of no significant movement in the United States which is attempting to depart from that ideal.

As evidence of this it may be noted that our most important investigation, by the Temporary National Economic Committee, is heralded an anti-monopoly investigation, even though the terms of the President's message cover a broad survey of our entire economy. The reason for the particular emphasis on "anti-monopoly" is that the world carries a picture of a state as we would like to see it. This attitude is the first element in forming the policy of government toward big business.

The second element in forming that policy is the fact that it is necessary to compromise between the logical extension of the anti-trust ideal and the fact that modern industrial techniques require large organization. I think no one desires to prevent efficient mass production and distribution. Therefore, wherever size or concerted action is necessary for efficiency in production and distribution, it may usually be supported by the famous rule of reason in the anti-trust law interpretation. There is a second necessary compromise or qualifying principle in the application of our competitive ideal. The complicated machinery of modern distribution requires certain concerted action which must be justified under the principle of orderly marketing. Clearance in the moving picture industry and regulation of the spring surplus of milk are examples. Other illustrations are found in every large industry. A reasonable interpretation of the anti-trust laws must be one that does not wish to disturb either orderly marketing or efficient mass production. In applying these qualifications we must exercise care not to justify any large combinations or any more restraints than are actually necessary. The burden of proof should always be against combinations which give great industrial power to small groups, but when that burden is met the Sherman Act should not be an instrument to promote inefficiency. This, I think, is the rule of reason in the anti-trust laws.

There are certain corollary principles in defining the policy of government toward business under these principles. Once it is decided that enormous concentrations are necessary in the interest of orderly marketing, or in the interest of mass production and distribution, there must be some public responsibility in forming the price policies of such great organizations. In other words, if a monopoly position is an economic necessity, public control of some sort or other must be sought. Competitive freedom from regulation cannot be extended where no actual competition can exist.

I think that if we face this fact, we shall find the areas in which monopolistic positions are necessary to be far more limited than we now suspect. We shall find, moreover, that competition in the great majority of industries is furthered, if we recognize the need of regulating necessary monopoly positions in a few. This idea is as old as our conception of public utilities.

These general formulas, I think, express the background of our tradition. It is almost impossible to define them concretely. Nevertheless, vague though they are, they are the best starting point to solve our economic problems without disturbing American traditions. The question is: How are we going to apply them? My answer is that the only way to do it is to take up one industry at a time. These ideals and principles give us not a chart or a plan, but an attitude and a picture of the society in which we desire to live. Their application to the unlike situations in different industries cannot be by general rule. It is a problem of organization, like the organization of an army. We must not first write the drill regulations and then make the army conform. We must train our companies and our regiments and then mold the drill regulations to their particular necessity. The necessity of taking up one industrial problem at a time is increased because after forty years without adequate antitrust enforcement a number of eggs must be unscrambled. This cannot be done in the abstract. This must be done in such a way as to avoid unnecessary dislocations of interests which have clustered around excessive concentrations of wealth. Each particular industry, in that respect, presents a separate problem. . . .

Our central problem is unused capacity. We have an income level which cannot absorb goods at the price level—65 per cent of the families under $1500 a year; twelve million families facing starvation, and so on. You are all familiar with those figures. I shall not go into them. They mean that business has become wedded to cost accounting systems which have put the prices above the possibilities of purchase under that income level. Distributors are not making any money. Merchants become discouraged. They turn to the chain stores and blame them for their troubles. They seek to tax the chain stores out of existence. Other industries seek to eliminate other competitors whom they call chiselers. States seek to abolish out-of-state competition, turning to their legislatures for aid. There is an epidemic of what amounts to protective tariffs between the states in the United States, not under that name, but under the name of inspection laws, or something equally euphonious. . . .

The conclusion, I think, of this brief talk, because I see my time is up, is simply this: If we are going to be sensible about creating a government which has a minimum of regulation, which is devoted to the ideal of free and independent enterprise, we must remember that organizations are more important than definitions. We will progress by taking up the problems of each organization under the general formula of our ideal, one at a time. It is because the anti-trust law, out of its historical background, offers a method of doing this that I hope it will become the central expression of government policy toward business.

21 • Raymond Moley: *Roosevelt's Refusal to Make a Choice*

In its uncertainty over whether to regulate gently the monster corporations, or to attempt to break them into smaller units, or to force them to behave more responsibly by setting up public corporations like the TVA to compete with them, or by actually nationalizing (which only a few people at the extreme left of the New Deal spectrum advocated), the New Deal revealed a confusion over purpose that was to plague it all through its lifetime. This confusion was criticized by many observers, one of the most knowledgeable of whom was Raymond Moley.

Moley (1886-), a Barnard College professor of public law and a former economic consultant to Governor Alfred E. Smith of New York, was recruited early in 1932 by attorney Samuel Rosenman, a friend of FDR, to become an adviser to Roosevelt in his campaign. After the election, he became an Assistant Secretary of State, and was in the first several years of the Roosevelt Administra-

This extract is from Raymond Moley's *After Seven Years* (New York: Harper & Brothers, 1939), pp. 365-376. Mr. Moley's book was published in 1939. He is now engaged in writing a book, *The First New Deal*, which will be published by Harcourt, Brace & World in 1966. It will go over some of the ground and some of the evaluation of Mr. Roosevelt which appeared in the earlier book.

tion, the most influential member of the "Brains Trust." Essentially a conservative, Moley believed in a strong partnership between government and business to direct the economy. He became more and more distressed with what he felt was a sharp veering to the left of the New Deal, and in mid-1936, he left the administration. As an editor of *Today* and *Newsweek*, he continued to criticize the administration for what he felt was a staggering from policy to policy rather than a coordinated attack on the problems of the nation. In the following excerpt from his book on the New Deal, *After Seven Years*, he relates that larger criticism to the specific problem of Roosevelt's antitrust policies.

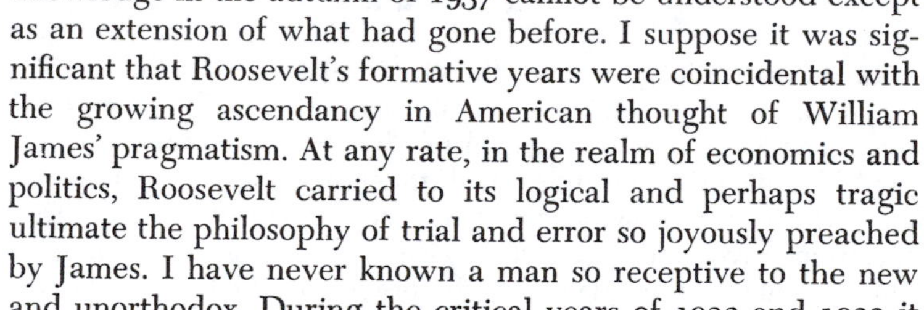

. . . The crisis of indecision that became a matter of public knowledge in the autumn of 1937 cannot be understood except as an extension of what had gone before. I suppose it was significant that Roosevelt's formative years were coincidental with the growing ascendancy in American thought of William James' pragmatism. At any rate, in the realm of economics and politics, Roosevelt carried to its logical and perhaps tragic ultimate the philosophy of trial and error so joyously preached by James. I have never known a man so receptive to the new and unorthodox. During the critical years of 1932 and 1933 it was my most difficult job to see that he took the opportunity to examine skeptically the "plans" and devices that attracted his interest. Even so, the most extraordinary fragments of rejected ideas would remain in his mind to be played with, when time permitted, and, sometimes, as in the case of the "soak-the-rich" scheme, to be suddenly announced as settled policies.

This receptiveness to innovation was not in itself objectionable. On the contrary, it was this very quality in Roosevelt that made it possible for him to root out the economic shibboleths to which most of our best-advertised thinkers had stubbornly clung after 1929. It was this quality that made it possible for him to begin repairing, on a monumental scale, a system which a decade of abuse had left racked and broken.

The hitch came with Roosevelt's failure to follow through. Pragmatism requires the application of the test of utility or workableness or success. And by this Roosevelt refused to abide. He would launch an idea as an experiment, but, once it had been launched, he would not subject it to the pragmatic test. It became, in his mind, an expression of settled conviction, an indispensable element in a great, unified plan.

That Roosevelt could look back over the vast aggregation of policies adopted between March, 1933, and November, 1936, and see it as the result of a single, predetermined plan was a tribute to his imagination. But not to his grasp of economics. One had only to review the heterogeneous origins of the policies he had embraced by the time of his reelection, the varying circumstances, impulses, beliefs that had produced them, to guess at their substantive conflict and contradiction. . . .

If this aggregation of policies springing from circumstances, motives, purposes, and situations so various gave the observer the sense of a certain rugged grandeur, it arose chiefly from the wonder that one man could have been so flexible as to permit himself to believe so many things in so short a time. But to look upon these policies as the result of a unified plan was to believe that the accumulation of stuffed snakes, baseball pictures, school flags, old tennis shoes, carpenter's tools, geometry books, and chemistry sets in a boy's bedroom could have been put there by an interior decorator.

Or, perhaps it would be more apt to say that the unfolding of the New Deal between 1932 and 1937 suggested the sounds that might be produced by an orchestra which started out with part of a score and which, after a time, began to improvise. It might all hang together if there were a clear understanding between the players and the conductor as to the sort of music they intended to produce. But nothing was more obvious than that some of the New Deal players believed that the theme was to be the funeral march of capitalism; others, a Wagnerian conflict between Good and Evil; and still others, the triumphant strains of the *Heldenleben*.

Yet what could be said of the conductor who emerged from such an experience and who announced that he and his orchestra had produced new and beautiful harmonies?

It was Roosevelt's insistence upon the essential unity of his policies that inevitably brought into question his understanding of economics. Except in terms of misunderstanding, there was no way to comprehend such phenomena as an attempt to rehabilitate the soft-coal business which proceeded without reference to simultaneous efforts to encourage the production of electricity through vast water-power projects. There was no other possible explanation for the slow blurring of the distinction between temporary and permanent economic policies, the retention of expedients designed to meet emergency problems, and the justification of such expedients on grounds quite unlike those which had warranted their initial employment. There was no other possible explanation for the two-and-a-half year indifference to the obstacles that thwarted a huge potential demand for additional houses and dammed up a potent force for stable economic recovery. So, too, there would be in 1939 no other possible explanation for the plea that the loss of dollar-devaluation powers would remove "the only check we have on . . . speculative operations" by the same President who, six years before, had announced that he knew of no way governments could check exchange speculation.

Underlying these and a host of other incongruities were two misapprehensions which were basic.

The first centered in a failure to understand what is called, for lack of a better term, business confidence. . . .

In fact, the term "confidence" became, as time went on, the most irritating of all symbols to him. He had the habit of repelling the suggestion that he was impairing confidence by answering that he was restoring the confidence the public had lost in business leadership. No one could deny that, to a degree, this was true. The shortsightedness, selfishness, and downright dishonesty of some business leaders had seriously damaged confidence. Roosevelt's assurances that he intended to cleanse and rehabilitate our economic system did act as a restorative.

But beyond that, what had been done? For one thing, the confusion of the administration's utility, shipping, railroad, and housing policies had discouraged the small individual investor. For another, the administration's taxes on corporate surpluses and capital gains, suggesting, as they did, the belief that a recovery based upon capital investment is unsound, discouraged the expansion of producers' capital equipment. For another, the administration's occasional suggestions that perhaps there was no hope for the reemployment of people except by a share-the-work program struck at a basic assumption in the enterpriser's philosophy. For another, the administration's failure to see the narrow margin of profit on which business success rests —a failure expressed in an emphasis upon prices while the effects of increases in operating costs were overlooked—laid a heavy hand upon business prospects. For another, the calling of names in political speeches and the vague, veiled threats of punitive action all tore the fragile texture of credit and confidence upon which the very existence of business depends. . . .

The second basic fault in the congeries of the administration's economic policies sprang from Roosevelt's refusal to make a choice between the philosophy of Concentration and Control and the philosophy of Enforced Atomization.

It was easy to see that the early New Deal, with its emphasis on agricultural and industrial planning, was dominated by the theory of Concentration and Control—by the beliefs that competition is justified only in so far as it promotes social progress and efficiency; that government should encourage concerted action where that best serves the public and competition where that best serves the public; that business must, under strict supervision, be permitted to grow into units large enough to insure to the consumer the benefits of mass production; that organized labor must likewise be permitted to grow in size but, like business, be held to strict accountability; that government must cooperate with both business and labor to insure the stable and continuous operation of the machinery of production and distribution.

But with the invalidation of the N.I.R.A., there was a shift in emphasis. And this shift took not the form of a complete repudiation of Concentration and Control, but of an endless wavering between it and the philosophy advocated by those Brandeis adherents, like Corcoran, who preached the "curse of bigness," the need for breaking up great corporations on the ground that their growth was the result of the desire for financial control rather than increased efficiency, the desirability of "atomizing" business in order to achieve a completely flexible competitive system which would work without much intervention by government. . . .

Roosevelt obviously clung to the belief that he could *blend* the two philosophies by persuasion and skillful compromise, though the evidence proving that he could merely *mix* them piled up through 1936 and the first half of 1937. And since, in this world, bitterness and distrust are as likely to arise from bewilderment as from inborn propensities, the indecision which had begun in May, 1935, in no small part contributed to the business collapse of 1937.

So the stage was set when the depression struck in September, 1937. And so began the noisy pulling and hauling in Washington between the advocates of budget balancing, the advocates of spending, the believers that the price fixing of monopolies had caused the contraction of business, and the believers that the uncertainty and confusion of administration policy had made impossible those long-term business plans which sustain employment and consumer purchasing power.

The reaction was a steadily deepening indecision.

In November, 1937, the President approved a speech by Secretary Morgenthau intended to reassure business because it committed the administration to stringent budget balancing.

In December, 1937, and January, 1938, the President acquiesced in a campaign launched by Corcoran, Cohen, Ickes, Hopkins, and Robert H. Jackson for the purpose of blaming the depression upon business. Jackson and Ickes at once began an oratorical "trust-busting" offensive—a series of bitter speeches, replete with references to "corporate earls," "corporate tentacles," and "aristocratic anarchy"—planned and partly prepared, according to Alsop and Kintner, by the young lawyers and economists Corcoran had welded into what he called his "well-integrated group" and into what Hugh Johnson characterized as "the janissariat."

On January 3, 1938, Roosevelt spoke, in one breath, of great corporations created "for the sake of securities profits, financial control, the suppression of competition and the ambition for power over others" and, in the next breath, announced, "We ask business and finance . . . to join their government in the enactment of legislation where the ending of abuses and the steady functioning of our economic system calls for government assistance."

On January 4th Roosevelt suggested that he would like to see businessmen and industrialists draw up chairs to a table with government representatives and work out a scheme to adjust production schedules to coincide with demand.

On January 8th the President denounced the "autocratic controls over the industry and finances of the country."

Through February and March the battle over policy, the effort to force a presidential decision dragged.

Governor Eccles of the Federal Reserve Board pleaded for

pump priming and the removal of legislative and administrative constrictions—especially in the fields of labor and housing—that were blocking the normal course of business. Secretary Morgenthau harped on the need for a balanced budget. Jesse Jones of the R.F.C. campaigned for the repeal of the corporate-surplus tax. Donald Richberg urged a resumption of cooperative efforts to plan production. S.E.C. Commissioner John W. Hanes appealed for gestures reassuring to business. The Corcoran-Cohen-Hopkins-Ickes brigade, armed with memoranda provided by Leon Henderson, economic adviser to the W.P.A., and by others of the "well-integrated group," planked day in and day out for a combined spending and anti-monopoly campaign.

There were passionate arguments between many of these advisers, secret meetings in homes and offices to patch up alliances, dashes to Warm Springs where the President was vacationing late in March, importunate telephone calls, desperate and extravagant pleas for action.

It was April, with all business indices plummeting, before Roosevelt agreed, at last, to ask Congress for an investigation of monopolies and for a $3,012,000,000 spending program.

This move was hailed by the "well-integrated group" as the earnest of Roosevelt's complete conversion to their point of view.

In the sense that they had sold to him, together with the emergency program for spending, an elaborate philosophic rationalization of the inevitable, they had won a real victory. The rationalization, of which the most vociferous evangel was David Cushman Coyle, insisted that expenditures which returned dividends only in social benefit or esthetic pleasure were no less "assets" than those which paid dividends in taxable capacity, that a mounting deficit stimulated recovery. Corcoran's susceptibility to this strange and jumbled doctrine seemed to trace back to Brandeis' beliefs, expressed to me in detail in 1933, that private capital investment was virtually at an end because business could no longer find enough attractive opportunities for investment and that government must fill the void thus created. Roosevelt unquestionably embraced the doctrine as a handy way to justify a continuing budget unbalance for which he had excoriated Hoover during the campaign of 1932 and against which he had repeatedly pledged himself, up to January, 1937. But, aside from the reasons for the doctrine's adoption, it became, once adopted, a kind of pansophy—a scheme of universal wisdom. Embellishments appeared. Money must be "shoveled out," Corcoran remarked in private conversation. Roosevelt put it differently. In his budget message of 1939, he said that an indispensable factor in prosperity was government "investment" great enough to lift the national income to a point which would make tax receipts cover the new level of expenditure.

So far, the "conversion" was absolute.

But the claim that Roosevelt was won over to a policy of "antibigness" in April, 1938, did not stand up. True, the President, in a fiery message, prepared with the assistance of Corcoran, Cohen, Jackson, and others of the "well-integrated group," denounced monopoly. Yet he went no further than to ask for a thorough congressional study of "the concentration of economic power in American industry"—a study which was to go on for a year or two.

This request for a study was, certainly, the final expression of Roosevelt's personal indecision about what policy his administration ought to follow in its relations with business. The creation of the "monopoly" committee, or rather the Temporary National Economic Committee, merely relieved Roosevelt, for the moment, from the nagging of subordinates who, whatever the differences in their own economic philosophies, recognized that an administration which was of two minds on this all-important question would contradict itself into disaster.

It merely put off the adoption of a guiding economic philosophy. . . .

22 · Temporary National Economic Committee: *The Concentration of Economic Power*

In response to Roosevelt's message (See Document 19) the Temporary National Economic Committee was set up by joint resolution of Congress in June 1938 as a joint executive and legislative committee with Senator Joseph C. O'Mahoney of Wyoming as chairman. The TNEC held public hearings for eighteen months, produced thirty-one volumes of testimony by more than five hundred witnesses and forty-three monographs written by economists. The report below, by Dewey Anderson, Executive Secretary of the Committee, is a brief summary of those voluminous findings. With such a wealth of powerful data at hand, the final recommendations of the Committee were weak and anticlimactic. They reiterated the Committee's faith in "free enterprise" and condemned the "regimentation of men by government" as well as "by concentrated economic power." The Committee urged "the maintenance of free, competitive enterprise by the effective suppression of the restrictive practices which have always been recognized as evil" and asked for "the vigorous and vigilant enforcement of the antitrust laws. It asked for aid to low-income groups through a food stamp law, low-cost housing, more medical facilities, and "vocational and cultural programs." The Committee suggested changes in the patent laws, legislation forbidding corporations to acquire the assets of large competing corporations, the establishment of national standards for national corporations, and several other proposals. The magnitude of the commit-

From *Final Report and Recommendations of the Temporary National Economic Committee* (Washington: Government Printing Office, 1941), pp. 88-94.

tee's findings contrasted sharply with the feebleness of its recommendations. The continued growth of economic concentration in the years that followed proved that the New Deal had never managed to heed the dictum set forth by President Roosevelt in his message to Congress: "The power of a few to manage the economic life of the Nation must be diffused among the many or be transferred to the public and its democratically responsible government."

MANAGED INDUSTRIAL PRICES

The American system of free enterprise can exist only if industrial markets are free from the manipulations and controls of private groups. Then alone can prices freely perform their function as the regulator and stabilizer of industry. But abundant evidence exists to show that in a vast range of commodities prices, far from being objectively determined in the market, are influenced, administered, or managed by persons of power, so that price competition has disappeared in many industrial fields.

The variety of control elements in industrial markets is legion, depending upon a number of factors such as those inherent in the technology of the industry, and in the size of individual concerns; the type of goods made, whether standardized or made to order; the nature of the demand for the product —whether postponable or non-postponable; and finally, those control elements which vary with what may be called the institutional climate—with the attitude of government and public opinion toward cartels, antitrust activity, patents, controls over radio and press, etc. The techniques of control include, among others, price leadership, basing-point systems, open-price systems which allow each concern to know exactly what its competitors are charging, and uniform cost accounting systems whereby all concerns base their pricing policies upon identical or similar methods of calculations.

Managed industrial prices, by creating disparity in incomes and purchasing power, increase economic maladjustment between freely competitive and managed areas of the economy, accentuate depressions, and retard recovery. In short, the net effect of such change in the purchasing power of any major group of the community must be appraised in relation to its effects upon the volume of spending, of investment, and of hoarding. . . .

The place of the trade association and of the cartel in our economy is of great significance because through this medium control is achieved in fields where firms are numerous and none is dominant. A cartel may be defined as an association of independent enterprises in the same or similar branches of industry, formed for the purpose of increasing the profits of its members by subjecting their competitive activities to some method of common control. The fundamental purposes of trade associations are much the same since, in addition to cooperative research, arbitration, advertising, and publicity, they also frequently establish common cost accounting procedures, operate price reporting plans, interchange patent rights, administer basing-point systems, purchase supplies jointly, and promulgate codes of business ethics. Though membership in both cartels and trade associations is usually voluntary, compulsory cartelization has marked developments in various European countries. . . .

No positive estimate concerning the extent of competition and monopoly in American markets is justified by available evidence. In those industries which appear to be normally competitive, competition is constantly breaking down. Competitors continually seek to limit competition and to obtain for themselves some measure of monopoly power. They enter into agreements governing prices and production. They set up associations to enforce such agreements. They procure the enactment of restrictive legislation. For a time they may succeed in bringing competition under control. But these arrangements, too, are constantly breaking down. Competitors violate the agreements. Associations lack the power to enforce them. New enterprises come into the field. Restrictive statutes are invalidated by the courts or repealed by the legislature. The lines of control are repeatedly broken and reformed. The facts that describe the situation existing in such an industry today may not apply to the one in which it will find itself tomorrow. . . .

It is impossible in small compass to give an overview of the concentration existing in the production of individual commodities. The Commerce study analyzed a cross-section sample of 1,807 manufactured products, selected to present a comprehensive over-all picture of the situation existing in the entire manufacturing segment of the economy. For one-half of the 1,807 products, the leading four manufacturers accounted for 75 percent or more of the total United States output. About a quarter of all the products were found to be extremely concentrated, while low concentration appeared in only about 5 percent of the cases.

In an economy characterized by a high degree of concentration in production the traditional free market is seldom realized. For manufactured products in general, however, concentrated control does not appear to be associated with any unique price and production policy; that is, products manufactured under conditions of both high and low concentration apparently behaved similarly during periods of recession and recovery. . . .

Many of the investment problems of the nation arise out of the concentration of investment funds and their control in a few hands. In 1935-36, about 2 percent of all income receiving units in the United States had incomes over $5,000, while only 1 percent had incomes over $10,000. Nearly 70 percent, on the other hand, received less than $1,500 in that year, and almost a third received less than $750.

In the life insurance business, which controls $28,000,000,000 in assets, there are 308 legal reserve life insurance companies, of which 5 control nearly 55 percent of the total assets of the companies.

There is marked concentration in the size of corporate assets and earning power. For instance, in 1929, 80 percent of all corporation income was received by that 0.3 percent of all corporations whose incomes were over $1,000,000 a year. The deficits incurred during the depression made it difficult to compare earnings of 1934 with the 1929 figure, but it is significant that not until the $1,000,000 income bracket was reached in that year were there any aggregate net earnings.

Concentration of ownership of corporations has been as marked as concentration of size in the corporations themselves. Over half the corporate dividends paid out in recent years have gone to about 2 percent of the total number of families and single individuals in the country. From 1927 to 1937, approximately 35 percent of all corporate net dividend payments went to 25,000 persons, or less than 0.1 percent of the total number of families and single individuals. Furthermore, within the dividend-receiving group, 1/4 of the recipients received more than 3/4 of the dividends paid, and 11 percent received approximately 2/3. . . .

These evidences of ownership, however, are only part of the story. The control of the resources of the country rests in even fewer hands. The dominance of three families over 15 of our 200 largest corporations has already been mentioned. On the boards (in 1937) of the 200 largest non-financial and the 50 largest financial corporations, there were 3,544 directorships, and these posts were held by 2,725 individual directors. Nor was the interlocking brought about primarily by inactive directors, for of the 83 directors holding 4 or more directorates, 59 were active in at least one of the corporations they served.

The piling up of more than $15,000,000,000 in assets by the five largest insurance companies provides an extraordinary chance for domination by a few, because in almost no case does the stockholder or mutual policyholder have a voice in the management of his company, which is carried on almost entirely by a small, self-perpetuating group of managing officers.

CONCENTRATION OF SAVINGS

Individual savings are likewise the property of a very small group at the top of the pyramid. In 1936, the lower two-thirds of the nation's income groups had only negative savings. The bottom third went into the red to the extent of $1,207,000,000, and the middle third to $252,000,000. The top third, on the other hand, saved $7,437,000,000. To put this in another way, if the whole population were divided into equal numerical groups of 2,750,000 families each, the top 10 percent, with incomes over $4,600, saved 86 percent of the total savings made in 1929, while the second group, with incomes ranging from $3,100 to $4,600, saved 12 percent, and the other 2 percent of savings were accounted for by the remaining 80 percent of the population.

Business savings are about two-fifth of the nation's savings. In 1937 less than 0.2 percent of all corporations made 46 percent of all corporate savings, which comprise by far the greater portion of all business savings. These savings are, of course, in large measure controlled by the 200 great corporations, with the consequent management of their use by the extremely small group of men who form their active directorates.

Individual savings are generally transferred from the saver to the investor, by means of such devices as investment trusts, insurance companies, banks, building and loan companies, etc., which means a consequent sacrifice of the management principle by the saver, and an enlargement of the funds in the hands of the management group. . . .

The question of whether taxation can be used to improve the distribution of income depends very largely on whether it is possible to increase the rates of personal income, gifts and estate taxes in the higher brackets. Monograph 20 indicates that there is a large reservoir of untapped funds in the brackets from $5,000 to $50,000, and another in the brackets from $50,000 to $100,000. Although it appears that the topmost brackets are not now being taxed at their point of highest return, it appears that the two sectors just mentioned have been unduly favored.

The thorough examination of fiscal policy and taxation made in the TNEC studies conclusively shows that these broad instruments have not been effectively used to contribute their proper share to a balanced economy. In the critical post-defense period, when every possible aid to economic stability must be utilized, it is inevitable that the tax system must be reformed to contribute its share in the stabilizing process. . . .

PART FIVE

PUBLIC ENTERPRISE

23 • Harry L. Hopkins: *The War on Distress*

Harry L. Hopkins, (1890-1946), for many years a social worker, handled New York State's relief program in 1932 when FDR was Governor. In May 1933 Congress authorized a half-billion dollars for relief, to be channeled through state and local agencies, and Roosevelt chose Hopkins to head the new Federal Emergency Relief Administration. Later, and until FDR's death, he was one of Roosevelt's closest friends and advisers. In 1935, after Congress appropriated an unprecedented five billion dollars for emergency relief, Hopkins took charge of the Works Project Administration, which paid unemployed Americans to build schools, hospitals, playgrounds, paid artists to create murals on public buildings, theater people to produce plays, and writers to do imaginative guidebooks to the different states. By 1937, however, Hopkins noted that the nation was "bored with the poor, the unemployed and the insecure," and in the next few years WPA petered out. In this article, written in the early months of the relief program, Hopkins outlines the extent of the problem and the measures being undertaken by the New Deal to solve it. In the course of this, he gives us a glimpse of the social philosophy behind "the war on distress."

It is difficult to believe, but none the less true, that one sixth of the population of the United States was receiving pub-

From Harry L. Hopkins, "The War on Distress," *Today,* I (December 16, 1933), 8-9, 23.

lic relief in the month of March, 1933. This meant twenty-one million people. It meant four and one-half million families, scattered throughout all of the states of the Union.

These people were receiving an average of fifty cents a day per family, however, a sum which is scarcely adequate to keep body and soul together. The net result of this vast dependency is a collective economic and social tragedy of the first importance. It meant the lowering of the standards of living of one-sixth of the population of the country, and, consequently, the danger of degradation of all sorts. And this great army included many of the solid people of the country—farmers, engineers, architects, bricklayers, clerks—indeed, all of the crafts and trades found in American life.

During the summer a substantial reemployment took place and by October the number receiving relief had dropped to fourteen million persons, which included three million families. The tragedy and the danger, however, were still great.

Even with the most skilled and sympathetic treatment, a trip to a relief office and the disclosure of the most intimate details of one's meager economic situation is a bitter experience for millions of heads of families who have always been able to earn a living for their families. The system by which this has been carried on can be described in no other terms than that of the wholesale degradation of the finest sensibilities of people whose service to industry and the nation certainly deserved a different recompense.

This characterization seems to me to be true in spite of the enormous outpouring of public and private funds and the devoted and sympathetic administration of relief. The difficulty is found in the system of relief itself. It requires an application for relief, a rigid investigation as to need, and the distribution of relief, in amounts and kind, to meet the individual requirements of millions of people.

These relief operations were difficult enough to administer

in 1929, when the number of those unemployed was around two million. They became positively destructive of their primary purposes when additional millions of the best folk in the country had to be aided.

When the story of this depression is finally written, it will be found that it was the social workers who, while struggling to get aid to the unemployed under the relief system, were denouncing its inadequacy. It was they who demanded that these people who were coming to them be lifted out of this system—a system which they, with others, saw was reducing millions to the level of chronic destitution. Those administering relief saw that it was the wrong way to get aid to the millions of unemployed and that it was fraught with grave hazards to all that industrious self-sustaining men and women held sacred. It is to their enduring glory that they demanded that the use of relief for the able-bodied be abolished. To me it is unthinkable that a state or a nation or a people would continue this type of relief a moment longer than is absolutely necessary.

It was out of a sense of what was happening to these people that the Civil Works program was evolved by the President. Our problem was to get men to work at regular jobs at regular wages. We had taken a long step in this direction in some states through providing work-relief, but this did not go far enough. Public Works, on the other hand, being concerned, as it is, with the construction of large units, requires time to plan. Local legal entanglements must be ironed out. While moving with all the speed that could possibly be expected, the Public Works program left a gap to be filled—a plan of direct action. It took less time than it takes to tell for Secretary Ickes to approve the Civil Works project as a Public Works project and to set its machinery in motion.

Once the problem is thought of in terms of unemployment, so far as it concerns the able bodied, the aged and the unemployable, we approach the means with which to meet it very simply. There are two major considerations. First, we must confer on the able bodied unemployed some tangible and material benefits. One would readily admit that this can best be done by means of a job; a job at fair rates of pay under conditions of work that provide the right of collective bargaining, American standards of living and, for the farmer, an adequate price for that which he brings to the market so that he, also, may purchase a decent American standard of living. In short, it means the right to work for wages for those millions who have been tramping the streets for months since 1929 with no opportunity for work. The second consideration is that whatever is done shall add to the social well-being and the economic stability of the nation.

At this writing two weeks have elapsed since the launching of the Civil Works program, and reports from the three thousand counties of the nation show upwards of two million men employed. I confidently expect that the grand total of four million will have been employed by December 15. The rapidity with which it operates is a tribute to the ability and devotion of the men and women who constitute the Civil Works Administration. Through the efforts of these administrators, men were certified by the thousands, over night, to Civil Works projects. Through the United States Employment Service other thousands are now daily being certified to new projects.

The crux of the fear about the whole undertaking centered in the doubt that genuinely worthwhile projects could be found on which these millions could be employed. We see now this was groundless. Fine projects of enduring benefits to the communities, states and the nation have been found everywhere.

In Texas one city is extending its sewer system for several miles; in Kansas the long neglected and much used market roads are being widened and bridges are being built. In Alabama dilapidated houses, unfit for human habitation, are being torn down and cleaned out. In all parts of the nation projects of a sanitary character are being conducted, such as malaria control, sanitary toilet construction and tick eradication. The rural school houses of entire states are being repaired and rebuilt.

Water supply systems are being built, streets repaired and constructed, swimming pools and playgrounds constructed, and extensive tree-planting, highway beautification, airport building, traffic surveys and fire-hazard surveys are being carried on.

Federal projects have been organized. These include sealing abandoned coal mines that contaminate water supplies; coast and geodetic surveys, prevention of soil erosion on important watersheds, rural sanitation, improvement of Federal agricultural experiment stations and many types of research.

The Civil Works Administration was created to provide immediate employment for four million persons on just these types of projects. This is being done; these men and women are at work on thousands of national, state and local projects which are necessary and useful to the nation and the community.

This action was taken not to indicate a permanent policy of employing four million men, but to meet an emergency. And yet, in its broad outlines, it does offer an opportunity, and at any rate a partial answer to the age-old problem of how America shall care for her unemployed.

It is far too early to appraise the effectiveness of the Civil Works program. It is hardly more than launched. Its administrators have found myriads of problems to solve. Only time and the meeting of many minds and interests can work out many of these, if indeed some of them can ever be solved. Some things, however, seem clear even now. Most important, is the fact that unemployed people want to work for what they get. They resent being asked to be a party to any subterfuge of a job as a means of getting relief. And for my part, I glory in their refusal and resentment of all such subterfuges.

The direct benefits of giving of jobs have been immediate. In a northern tier of states where formerly 130,000 men were employed on work-relief, there were, on November 16th,

425,000 men and women employed on Civil Works projects. Nor are we limiting the jobs to persons on relief rolls. We have reserved two million of the four million jobs for those who were not receiving relief. This will give the opportunity of work to those who have stuck it out, who have at times, even mistakenly so, elected to suffer and see their children suffer rather than receive aid in a form that violated their self-respect and their right to earn what they receive. Even though one may differ with such men, one cannot help but admire them and take every measure to see that they get their fair share of whatever opportunity to work is available.

Again it is clear, and has been for years, that towns, villages, cities and rural areas are in need of the elemental things that the army of unemployed can construct and provide. It is a commonly known fact that there is a vast lag between what we know of how to make the communities of the nation good places in which to live, and what we have done about it. We know how to make cities safe, healthy and pleasant places. We know how to make parks and recreation centers and areas that would serve city and rural folks alike. We know how to wipe out those drab and tragic areas of our large cities. We know that vast amounts of our national wealth are being filched by the ravaging of virgin forests. We have worked out these ways and means of making life for the average man, woman and child, healthy, safe, joyous, and some day we will close the gap between knowledge and doing.

What is equally clear is that those who make up the ranks of unemployed are equal to the task of putting into effect the knowledge which we possess.

The possibilities that lie at hand in this field are enormous.

The rebuilding of whole sections of our great cities, the development of our national forests, the reforestation of the land and the building of great recreational centers offer an ideal opportunity for providing employment indefinitely. These projects would be those which are not encompassed under the profit system. We know from past experience, for example, that individuals will not put capital into the development of our national forests for, in point of fact, most that has been done by private industry in the past has been of a character to destroy our national forests.

Our recreational facilities on publicly owned land are still totally inadequate. It is quite possible to provide opportunities for all workers in the country to take vacations at inexpensive rates on state and federal owned park reservations. The project of this nature projected on a long time plan will in the long run be self-liquidating and represent a contribution of the unemployed themselves of enormous social value to the nation.

Control of malaria and great drainage projects will never be accomplished in this country except through the support of state funds. If we are to be guided by past experience, we know that even such an elemental thing as providing houses in which the people can live decently has not been attained. It is said on competent authority that we need at least eight hundred thousand additional homes for workers, and there are over a million sub-standard homes which need to be repaired. This project too, over a long period of time, would be self-liquidating in theory and in fact.

The Conservation Corps with its three hundred thousand men is an ideal example of the use of the unemployed on national and state projects. This instrument could be extended far beyond its present limits. But in addition to a project of this character, it would be essential to have work opportunities near the homes of heads of families.

And, finally, no program of this kind could be successful which does not include work opportunities for women.

Any plan to absorb the unemployed would of necessity have to be capable of using large numbers of men at times when industry could not absorb them, and capable at other times of using a lesser number of men. Therefore any plan must be flexible. In general, the projects should be such as confer essential benefits upon the nation and such as would not be undertaken by private initiative. The recovery program is working. Four million men have gone back to their regular jobs since March 4. The dynamics of the President's program and his personality have galvanized the people into action. To me, the New Deal is NEW. It is the effort of a free people to achieve under democratic form of government the blessings of a highly organized industrial order. Recovery connotes to me a policy of reconstruction in which the social order will be amended to include the right of people to work and an assurance of benefits for the workers that are not based on the whims of the individual but are grounded in the fabric of social justice.

24 • Nathan Straus: *End the Slums*

Nathan Straus (1889-), a journalist, and then a member of the New York State legislature, was appointed by Roosevelt to head the United States Housing Authority in 1937, a post he held until 1942. Unlike FDR's first appointments in this field, Straus was a vigorous advocate of public housing and ably administered the disbursement of loans to municipalities for the building of low-income housing projects. He knew very well that not enough money was being appropriated, that real estate interests were a powerful force preventing a much more ambitious program of slum-clearance, but he continued to carry out the New Deal program with the resources at his disposal. In this speech, delivered November 18, 1937, to a conference of the United States Chamber of Commerce, he de-

From Nathan Straus, "End the Slums" *Vital Speeches of the Day,* IV (January 1, 1938), 182-184.

scribes the New Deal housing program as projected in the new Wagner-Steagall Act.

Whether we like to face it or not, the fact remains that the United States is the most backward country in the civilized world in providing decent housing for our people. We have piled up an appalling number of slums; we are today confronted by one of the gravest housing shortages in our history. Moreover, the building industry still lags behind; residential construction this year has been far less than our current needs. All business suffers the double burden of a lag in the durable goods industries and the consequent public expense of an irreducible army of unemployed. The wise projection of a housing program offers almost unlimited possibilities, in quickening the rate and widening the scope of general economic recovery. Contrasted with relief, public housing is better for business, cheaper for the taxpayer, and infinitely more rehabilitating to those who need help.

Private funds and private industry must take care of the bulk of the demand for residential construction. My task is to care for that sector which offers no inducement of profit to individual effort. My concern is with rehousing the dwellers in the slums.

What is a slum? Under the Act which I am administering, a slum is defined as "any area where dwellings predominate which, by reason of dilapidation, over-crowding, faulty arrangement or design, lack of ventilation, light or sanitation facilities, or any combination of these factors, are detrimental to safety, health or morals."

Many of you, I am sure, have seen as I have the inside of a slum tenement. You will know what it means for the father of a slum family to try to bring up his children with the manners and morals of a civilized society. You who know the slums realize the hopeless plight of a mother trying perhaps to nurse a sick child in a room without light, without air, without running water, and without adequate heat. There is no need to elaborate that picture. Perhaps Jacob Riis—the pioneer in the housing movement in this country—summed it up best when he said a generation ago: "The most pitiful victim of city life is not the slum child who dies, but the slum child who lives. Every time a child dies the nation loses a prospective citizen, but in every slum the nation has a probable consumptive and a possible criminal. You cannot let people live like pigs and expect them to be good citizens."

Let us assume that all of you have personal knowledge of life in a city slum. If you have, there is not a doubt in the world but that your heart and your head alike tell you that the slums must go. Your heart tells you in plain human sympathy. Your head tells you in the language of hard business sense. It tells you that a nation built on human misery at the bottom is unstable for those at the top. Your hard business sense tells you that crime, disease and revolt against society is bred in the slums. President Lincoln well said, "I believe this Government cannot endure half slave and half free." It is perhaps equally true that a nation cannot endure if two-thirds live in comfort and cleanliness while one-third exists in misery and filth. Enlightened self-interest demands that we declare our determination to end the slums.

A decent home for every American family would be a stout bulwark indeed for our democratic form of government and our free institutions. The slums must go or the society that tolerates them will. It is the unescapable logic of that argument that has been the propelling force back of the great government rehousing program of Holland, Switzerland, Sweden, France and Great Britain.

Now if we agree that we want to end the slums, how do we go about it? Why not let private industry do it? There is only one answer. Because it cannot.

The figures are very simple. You do not have to go into building costs or complex calculations.

Families living in the slums of the cities pay rentals of from $4 per room, per month, to $7 per room, per month. These are, of course, mostly cold-water flats. The figure varies from city to city and from district to district, but it is a safe generalization that slum families pay from $15 per apartment, or house, to $25 per apartment, or house, in rent. They do not pay more because they cannot afford any more.

Let's look at the other side of the ledger. The actual cost of operation of a large-scale project, if properly maintained, and if heating is included in the cost, runs from $5 to $6 per room per month, depending on local conditions.

From the experience gained in the Federal projects now in operation we know that the actual cost of operating decent housing, with no allowance for taxes, interest or amortization, is about equal to the rent slum families can afford to pay. The bare cost of upkeep and maintenance is equivalent to the rent paid in the slums. That picture is not attractive and the figures are not pleasant. But I can assure you that they are essentially accurate.

So private industry cannot today profitably rehouse slum dwellers in decent homes. The fact that slums do exist in our country in alarming proportions is evidence in itself that private industry cannot profitably eliminate them and provide good low-rent housing in their place. If this were possible, self-interest would long ago have wiped out our slums and provided good accommodations in their place. Society as a measure of self-preservation must destroy the slums, and the rehousing of the slum dwellers must be done with governmental aid, if it is to be done at all.

How? Many plans have been suggested. Many have been tried abroad. A few have been tried here.

The Wagner-Steagall Act is based on careful study of governmental housing programs in the various countries of Europe and it embodies the essential principles of the most successful of them.

I believe it is a practicable and workable law.

The Act provides two alternative forms of financial assistance to housing projects. The one which has aroused the greater interest at the present time is that which provides for an annual subsidy to achieve low rents.

The United States Housing Authority Act provides in essence that low-cost housing projects for rehousing slum dwellers should be initiated, constructed and managed by local authorities. A local authority may be a city, county, or state government. More often, in fact, it is a municipal housing authority set up under a State enabling act.

Capital funds for rehousing slum dwellers are to be made available jointly by the United States Housing Authority and the local authorities. The United States Housing Authority may loan up to 90 per cent of the cost of a project at not less than the going Federal rate of interest, plus one-half of one per cent. At least ten per cent of the capital funds must be provided by the local authority. The rent per room necessary to pay all operating costs and also to repay the Federal loan with interest (in not more than 60 years) is determined. The rent which the slum dwellers in that city can afford to pay is determined. The difference between these two figures is then made up by an annual contribution or annual subsidy from the United States Housing Authority and from the city or state or other local authority. The Housing Act provides that the local authority shall contribute in annual subsidy at least $1 for every $5 contributed by the United States Housing Authority. The local authority's share may be in the form of cash or tax exemption. In any event, only so much may be paid as an annual contribution by the United States Housing Authority as is necessary to achieve low rents. Thus the annual subsidies to bring rents in the new projects down to the figures slum dwellers can afford to pay, will become a joint responsibility of the Federal and local governments. Although I can touch only on major provisions of the Act, there are, however, three matters of policy which are sufficiently important to be stated:

(1) Construction costs—excluding land—are limited to $1,000 per room in cities of less than half a million population and $1,250 per room in larger cities.

(2) A number of slum dwelling units must be eliminated equivalent to the number of new dwellings constructed under the Act in any locality—although this may be postponed in case of a housing shortage or emergency.

(3) Apartments in the new buildings may be rented only to the lowest income families.

Those are the broad outlines of the Wagner-Steagall Housing Act creating the United States Housing Authority.

Investments in homes have always been considered prime, by savings banks and insurance companies as well as by private investors. The investment of the United States Government, under the United States Housing Authority Act, is an investment in mortgages on low rental homes. Five hundred million dollars, over a period of three years, is provided in the law for that.

You may have been concerned about the effects of the Housing Act on business. Two questions may have come to your mind.

First, you may have felt that the United States Housing Authority would compete for the rent payer's dollar with the private building industry. Second, you have thought about the National Budget and the expenses involved in this program.

Let me assure you that no competition with private industry is contemplated by me or, if I read the law right, is even possible under the Act. Figures compiled by the United States Chamber of Commerce indicate that the average home building in this country in the years from 1920 to 1929 was 677,000 dwelling units per year. Your own Committee report on Revival of Residential Construction, approved at the Chamber's annual meeting last year, fixed a minimum of 400,000 living units as being needed annually in our cities to meet current need.

Contrasted with this enormous need the funds provided under the Act will produce a maximum of 40,000 units per year, or only 10 per cent of our national needs. To this quantitative factor there must be added a qualitative consideration —namely, that public housing will serve only those very low income groups who are not in the market at all for private home-building.

English experience has demonstrated the non-competitive character of public housing. In the seven years just elapsed, England with a population only one-third of ours has constructed 403,000 dwelling units of public housing, or on a population basis about 4½ times as much annually as we contemplate under the Wagner-Steagall Act. But despite this—in fact *because* of it, in the view of competent economists, England has built 1,447,000 homes, or 3½ times as many, by private enterprise during the same period. This, I believe, is a convincing demonstration of the fact that an adequate public housing program does not impede the expansion of private building. On the contrary, I believe that by raising the standards of demand it actually stimulates private construction.

If I have read the mandate of the Congress aright, I am directed by the Act to build to minimum standards of decency. Let me assure you with all the solemnity of which I am capable that I intend to discharge my duty in full compliance with that mandate. The housing built under the Wagner-Steagall Act will be minimal housing—homes that are clean and decent and sunny—but homes built to standards set at the minimum compatible with decency and comfort. We want to use our funds not to house a few families in ideal homes, but to house as many slum dwellers as possible in decent homes.

If you have wondered about the drain on the National budget involved in the housing program you may be reassured by the figures of the total subsidy or grant provided in the bill.

During the first year the United States Authority may make commitments for annual contributions up to $5,000,000 per year. It may make commitments for an additional $7,500,000 per year in each of the following two years, and none after that without further authority from the Congress. The maximum annual burden upon the Treasury and the taxpayer for subsidies under the housing law is thus $20,000,000 per year, once the program is in full swing and assuming a program much larger than the $500,000,000 lent by the Federal Government. To maintain one-half a billion dollars' worth of such housing will be a burden on our annual budget of less than $18,000,000 per year.

To protect further the United States Government investment in the low-cost housing, the law provides that the annual contribution or subsidy shall be applied by the local authority first to service of the United States mortgage loan, thus making it doubly certain that the financing loans shall ultimately cost the taxpayer nothing.

The law seems to me to be sound in theory. It is based on the best European experience. I feel confident that it will prove practicable and workable.

With the inauguration of the Government low-cost housing program under the Wagner-Steagall Act, the United States of America for the first time will take its place among those nations of the world which have resolved, as a measure of national self-respect, to end the slums. This is not a temporary program. It is not an emergency program. It is not even an unemployment relief program—although it will be a great stimulus to employment. The Wagner-Steagall Act constitutes the charter of a rehousing program. Under it, we will be able to provide, I hope, decent homes for at least 100,000 families of minimum income. If we can do even that in the next three years, we will have taken one step—and not a small one—toward making America a better place to live tomorrow.

25 • Lewis Mumford: *The Government Should Support Art*

Lewis Mumford (1895-) has been one of the most prolific and most acute social critics of our time; among his many books are *Technics and Civilization* (1934), *The Culture of Cities* (1938), and *The City in History* (1961). A close student of public housing and city planning, he wrote often in the 1930's about the need for massive public enterprise to house, with efficiency and beauty, the people of the nation. He was gratified at the New Deal's support for a Federal Theater, a Federal Writers' Project, a Federal Art Program, and when it seemed that the latter was about to be abandoned by the administration, he addressed the following urgent plea to President Roosevelt.

Mr. President:

Every author knows that there are thoughts, upon which he has spent his utmost effort, that turn out to be less significant when published than he had fancied. And then there are other words, sometimes uttered lightly or written carelessly, as casually as Lincoln wrote the Gettysburg Address, which contain,

From Lewis Mumford, "A Letter to the President," *The New Republic*, (December 30, 1936), pp. 263-265. Reprinted with the permission of the author.

unperceived at the moment they are uttered, the writer's finest achievement. Often the writer himself is ready to disclaim these important thoughts. He is fortunate if an editor or an admirer is at hand who will appraise them correctly and keep them from being discarded or forgotten.

I wish to address you, Mr. President, about an achievement of your administration that seems to many of us, though not apparently to yourself, to be one of the three most significant things you have accomplished. And I address you in haste—and in this public fashion—because you have permitted orders to go out which will turn this great achievement into a ruin, a ruin far more teasing and ironical, because of what the foundations have promised, than was the Washington Monument during those long years when its unfinished state was a reproach to the nation. The work I refer to is that which has been done under the WPA to support the artist as a working member of the community and to give the arts a permanent habitation in America. Through these efforts, the salvage of individuals, undertaken through this relief agency, has unexpectedly become the salvation of the arts; and it is as a historical and critical interpreter of the arts in America that I now make bold to appeal to you.

Other national matters have deservedly had your graver attention and your more vigorous effort; but the arts projects, like the writer's fortunate thought, have brought in perhaps the greatest return. I cannot believe that you yet recognize the importance of what has been done through these agencies, quite apart from their immediate aid in rehabilitating the starving and the destitute. For I believe that if you saw the values that have already been built up here, you would not undo the work, and would be ready to ensure its permanence and push it even farther. I wish to persuade you that indifference to the arts projects of the WPA would not merely be unjust to the artists themselves, who have worked with a zeal and a devotion of which we must all be proud; but it would be an outright betrayal of a unique opportunity that will not come back again, even if the blunder be perceived, without duplicating wastefully much of the effort that has so far been expended.

The excellence of the work done to further American art under the WPA may well surprise you: indeed, the most hopeful observer could hardly have predicted it. Public art has usually been another name for standardized mediocrity: the questions of selection, patronage and control are problems of such delicacy that countries with a long tradition in the arts have not always successfully solved them. And in our country, with its mixed population, its great diversity of regional and social characteristics, one might well have feared in advance the limitations of those convenient stereotypes which make life easier for the administrator at the expense of the purposes which he administers. By a happy stroke, those who were put in charge of the arts projects have understood both the nature of the arts and that of our country: they have worked out a combination of national, state and local initiative that, so far from creating a single arbitrary stereotype, has resulted in a great diversity of efforts, vividly shot through with the colors of the local region and the local community. These projects have given the artist a home; and they have planted the seed of the fine arts, hitherto raised under glass in a few metropolitan hothouses, in every village and byway in the country, renovating soils that have become sour with neglect, and opening up new areas for cultivation.

My own attention has been concentrated mainly on the work that has been done in the plastic and graphic arts, as well as in the factual exploration of the American scene being done for the first time through the Writers' Project for the American Guidebook; but I know that those who are interested in music and the dance and the theatre share my enthusiasm in equal degree for the work done in these departments: so I plead for the arts as a whole, even though I choose examples from the field with which I am closely in contact. The actual achievement has been astounding, not less in quality than in volume. A great mass of talent, some of it the best our generation has produced, has for the first time been put regularly to work in the service of the community. The older artists have been rejuvenated by these new opportunities; many have produced their best work in this public capacity. And many younger artists, never before exhibited, have been discovered: a whole school of vigorous young painters has, for example, appeared in the Middle West. Both groups have been rescued from frustration and despair. Work has been found, appropriate work, for the most diverse capacities and for the most individual visions of life; and while the clumsy hand of esthetic dictatorship has not fallen on these projects, there has been a firm subtle pressure in the direction of what is strongest and finest in our inheritance in the arts.

The artists who have been engaged in these WPA projects have been given something more precious than their daily bread: they have at last achieved the liberty to perform an essential function of life, in the knowledge that their work had a destination in their community. The spread of this art, through new public agencies, is not less significant than its production. Through local museums and art galleries and special schools, many of which, like the museums in the South, are now serving communities that had been hitherto destitute of the fine arts, the artist has been brought into working relations with his fellow citizens. That contact has been beneficial in both directions. The easel paintings and prints and murals now spread on the walls of schoolhouses, town halls, hospitals and other public buildings bring new meanings, as well as new joys, into the life of the ordinary citizen. Industry does not supply these needs; it never has and, since the motive of profit is lacking, it never will. Private philanthropy is too puny to endow them. Nothing short of the collective resources of our country as a whole has proved competent to bring the fine arts into the lives of everyday Americans. When pianos were first shipped into the frontier towns of the West, Emerson hailed the enterprise: "The more piano," he observed, "the less wolf." One may well, without invidious intention, refer in similar terms to the moralizing and civilizing work of the WPA arts projects.

The production of paintings, prints and sculptures, though central to this grand work of re-laying the foundations of our popular American culture, is nevertheless only a part of it. No less significant, in their several ways, are the survey of historic buildings and the extraordinary work that has been started on the Index of American Design. None of this work is yet finished; in the nature of things it will demand continuous effort over many years: the historic-building survey, for example, does not in general carry beyond 1850; and it still has before it the vast and important documentation of American architecture beyond that point, when it began to make its more specifically American contribution. One may safely say that on the cultural side the history of the arts in America will never be adequately written until the material collected in these surveys is carried further and completed. Need I dwell on the importance of this fact? Need I stress the service the WPA projects have so far performed in deepening our regional foundations and making a permanent home for the spirit in our land?

To dismiss the workers on the arts projects and dismantle the projects themselves will not "release" a large body of people for commercial or industrial employment. There has never been a place in our present industrial system for the artist, except as a flatterer of the rich and idle, or as a mere servant of business enterprise. If the artist is effectually to serve his community, he cannot depend upon the private patron. Now that the community itself has devised appropriate ways for patronizing and encouraging the arts and giving them a permanent public home, it is time that art be taken for what it is—a realm like education which requires active and constant public support. The discovery of art as a vital factor in contemporary American culture was not, of course, the original intention of the WPA art projects. But the fact is that the discovery has now been made; and it would be blind, perhaps even perverse, to ignore its implications.

Broadly speaking, the experiment made by the WPA arts projects has been so sucessful that it urgently merits continuation—quite apart from the wisdom or charity of thrusting the artists now so usefully engaged back into the hopeless ranks of the permanently unemployed and destitute. Art has proved to be one of our relatively untouched public resources: a true form of wealth, whose wise and conservative exploitation under the guidance that has so far been given by the government will increase the happiness of the whole community. Can it be said of us that we could afford art when we were, as a nation, in dire need, and that we were ready to make art an outcast and a hanger-on as soon as the income of the country began to rise again? That is too bitter a paradox for a generous intelligence to accept.

For this reason, Mr. President, I respectfully urge you to revise—and that means reverse—the policy that is now apparently under way, of diminishing and finally cutting off the various agencies devoted to the employment of the artist and the spread of the arts in our country. In the WPA arts projects you and your administrators have, I believe, done better than you realize: you have created a solid public platform for American art and you have furthered a great civilizing influence, capable of solving, as no commercially supported arts can solve, the problem of how to use our collective wealth and our individual leisure with dignity and sanity and permanent delight. All this is to your credit and honor; the historian will note the achievement here. But to withdraw support at this moment would not merely strip away part of the value of the work already done: it would be to defraud future generations of the heritage that is justly theirs.

Like most representative Americans, Mr. President, you have shown that you still have the pioneer's gift for swift improvisation: the courage to meet a new situation with whatever resources lie at hand and the willingness to prove all things. But if to "prove all things" is a wise Baconian motto, one must not forget the second injunction: "Hold fast to what is good!" Without that discrimination and resolution even the virtues of the pioneer cannot endure. The worth of the WPA arts projects has been proved: a magnificent achievement. Now is the time, not to tear down the scantling, but to build the permanent structure.

26 · Hallie Flanagan: *The Drama of the Federal Theater Project*

Hallie Flanagan (1890-) was the head of the Experimental Theatre at Vassar College when Harry Hopkins named her to take charge of the Federal Theater Project under the WPA. The first American woman to win a Guggenheim Fellowship, she was one of the pioneering figures in the American theater and brought the same willingness to innovate to the Federal Theater. Aside from giving employment to actors, directors, and technicians of all sorts, the Federal Theater's greatest achievement was bringing the world of the theater to those who had never been able to afford to see a play. In four years, the various performing groups in the project played to about thirty million people. In June of 1939, with Congress beginning to dismantle a number of New Deal programs, the Federal Theater Project was quietly dropped. This article gives

From Hallie Flanagan, "Papa's Got a Job," *The Virginia Quarterly Review,* XV (April 1939), 249-258. Reprinted with the permission of the publisher.

some sense of both the personality and the idealism that Hallie Flanagan and others brought to the Federal Theater Project.

One of the scenes of a new Federal Theater revue, "Sing for Your Supper," comes to its climax in a number called "Papa's Got a Job." A cast of about one hundred and seventy-five actors, dancers, and vaudeville performers, who know what those words mean, make of the scene a funny, exciting, and profoundly moving celebration which is at once a comment on the technique of the Federal Theater and on the economic situation which brought that theater into existence.

For in 1935 papa didn't have a job. He didn't have a job in heavy construction, he didn't have a job in engineering, he didn't have a job in the professions, he didn't have a job in the arts or in the theater. New York critics were complaining that the stage was in a decline, theaters were dark across the United States, the road company was history, and in the summer of 1935 the relief rolls of American cities showed that thousands of unemployed theater professionals, affected not only by the economic depression but by the rapid rise of cinema and radio, were destitute.

At this point, Mr. Harry Hopkins, then Works Progress Administrator, made a momentous decision. He decided that unemployed theater professionals and their fellow musicians, painters, and writers could get as hungry as unemployed engineers. He further decided—and this was much more revolutionary—that their skills were as worthy of conservation. He also believed that these unemployed artists wanted to work and that their work would be of value to millions of people, many of them in small villages or city slums, American citizens who had not hitherto been able to afford music, painting, or the theater.

So the government of the United States, upon the recommendation of Congress, gave papa a job. The result was an unprecedented outpouring of music, painting, writing, acting, some of it brilliant, some of it indifferent, but all of it together, while probably impossible for us to evaluate at present, significant in the pattern of contemporary American culture. For these actors, directors, designers, writers, dancers, musicians, receiving only the small security wage set by Congress, with no stellar billings and with a press and public at first hostile or skeptical, leaped to meet their chance, becoming, almost overnight, performers in a drama more exciting than any which has yet reached our stage. The bare statistics of Federal Theater are in themselves a drama: some nine-thousand theater workers employed in forty theaters in twenty states, playing within three years before audiences totaling twenty-five million. It is not only the drama of theater successes in what is probably the world's most critical theater center, plays such as "'. . . one-third of a nation . . .'" "Prologue to Glory," "Haiti," and "Big Blow," together with earlier New York successes: "Murder in the Cathedral," "Dr. Faustus," "Macbeth," "Chalk Dust," "Battle Hymn," "Triple-A Plowed Under," "Power," "Class of '29," "The Sun and I," "Emperor's New Clothes," "Processional," "Professor Mamlock." It is also the drama of the Caravan Theaters in city parks, Shakespeare on a hillside, Gilbert and Sullivan on a lagoon, the circus under canvas, opera on a truck. It is the drama of a theater for the children of the steel mills in Gary, and for other children in Cleveland, New York, New Orleans, Newark, Los Angeles. It is the drama of a theater for the blind in Oklahoma; of a repertory theater, presenting Shaw, Shakespeare, O'Neill, Fitch, and Toller, on Long Island. It is the drama of "Created Equal" in Boston, of "Let Freedom Ring" in Detroit, of "Altars of Steels" in Atlanta, of "The Man in the Tree" in Miami, of "The Lonely Man" in Chicago, of the "International Cycle" in Los Angeles, the "Northwest Cycle" in Portland, Seattle, Denver, and San Francisco.

It is the drama of the Florida Wheel, a traveling Federal Theater carrying classical repertory over the turpentine circuit to regions so remote that people came in by oxcart, came in barefoot with lanterns to see "Twelfth Night." It is the drama of twenty-one simultaneous openings of Sinclair Lewis's "It Can't Happen Here" and of the cycles of George Bernard Shaw and Eugene O'Neill. It is the drama of Federal Theater radio, reaching, through the hospitality of great radio stations, vast audiences with such productions as James Truslow Adams's "Epic of America," and Paul de Kruif's "Men against Death." It is the drama of vaudeville companies playing before amazing audiences in schools, playgrounds, camps, prisons, reformatories, asylums, hospitals. It is the drama of our National Service Bureau sending out scripts and theater research to twenty thousand schools, farm granges, and 4-H clubs in rural areas. It is the drama of ambitious youth experimenting in the fields of light, direction, design, writing, and radio, experimenting to such effect that their work is being rewarded by scholarships from universities and foundations, and by good jobs with commercial managers.

Fifteen hundred people returned to jobs in private industry are a part of the Federal Theater drama, as are nine thousand who remain, working with increased imagination in forty theaters in twenty states, lacing the intervening countryside with local and regional tours.

The drama of Federal Theater is the drama also of its audience, a vast exciting new audience of twenty-five millions of rich and poor, old and young; students in colleges, housewives in small towns, lumberjacks in Oregon, sharecroppers in the South. Federal Theater is the drama of a hundred thousand children who never saw a play before. . . .

. . . When our productions are poor, as they often are, it is because we have lacked power or imagination; or because we have let ourselves be hurried, by people who still think of the theater in terms of a stock company, into the ridiculous scramble to do half a dozen inferior shows instead of one good one; or because of other reasons which makes us as Federal Theater directors no less fallible in judging material than any other theater director. But failures should not be blamed on either the human material at our disposal or the governmental framework in which we operate; nor should our failures be blamed on the fact that nine out of ten of our people must come from relief rolls and nine out of every ten dollars go for wages, leaving only one dollar out of ten for scenery, costumes, royalties, theater rentals, advertising, and all other theater expenses. These are the constants in the equation which it is our job to solve.

Let me further illustrate the relation between art and necessity, a relationship which lies at the root of Federal Theater—a relationship which I believe is developing on our project not only a new technique of theater direction, but a new intensity of performance. In Los Angeles I listened to one of our orchestras rehearsing music composed on the project for Shaw's "Cæsar and Cleopatra." Afterward I said to the composer: "The flute motif is unusually beautiful—so fleeting that you always want more." He said: "In composing the score I had to take account of the fact that while my flutist is very gifted he has a tremor which makes it impossible for him to sustain for more than one bar at a time." It is the job of those of us directing Federal Theater to compose for every production in such a way that the tremors developed through years of unemployment, privation, and despair, become, in the final theater product, not liabilities but assets.

Our exploration of the dramatic medium is not only thematic but geographic. Ours is not a national theater in the sense that we are called upon to decide what themes, actors, or methods of production are representative of our vast country and our diverse population. Federal Theater is rather, as the name implies, a federation of many theaters, each responsible for exploring its own dramatic possibilities, yet each seeing its activities as a part of a nationwide pattern.

Such variety of types of production, talent, and communities to be served requires centralized planning, and in this planning, which must become increasingly broad, imaginative, and exploratory, lies the future of Federal Theater. Neither Washington nor New York should dictate arbitrarily to New Orleans, Denver, or Detroit; therefore the policy board of the Federal Theater includes the directors of each region: the East, the West, the Midwest, the South, together with the directors of the three large city projects, New York, Los Angeles, and Chicago, and the directors of radio and the National Service Bureau. This board meets every four months, deciding on the program for the ensuing four months. At this time each director brings in the plan he has worked out with the various directors of companies in his region, the plays he wants to do, how he wants to do them, and each plan is considered in its relation to the whole national picture.

Out of this centralized yet geographically conscious planning, great regional theaters are developing, each with its own types of production and its own local celebrations. For example, in the South we have theaters in cities as diverse as Oklahoma City, New Orleans, Atlanta, Miami, Tampa, Jacksonville, and Roanoke Island. Each has its own theater, its own program. Jacksonville has a touring company, traveling by bus to high schools throughout the northern part of the state with a classical repertory which last year consisted of a Plautus comedy, "Everyman," "Twelfth Night," "She Stoops to Conquer," and "Girl of the Golden West." The high schools, believing this activity to be a valuable part of the school curriculum, pay transportation and other-than-labor expenses. The part this traveling company plays in the lives of the audience is perhaps indicated by the fact that when our company returns after a month's absence the children in the street call the actors by their play names—"Hello, Malvolio," "Hello, Olivia," "Hello, Sir Toby Belch." . . .

The Midwest is making a contribution in giving us plays of authentic American material such as "Big White Fog," a strong Negro play written by Theodore Ward, a Negro on our Chicago project; "Frankie and Johnnie," a spectacular dance drama directed by Ruth Page; and "Spirochete," the Living Newspaper on the fight against syphilis, written by Arnold Sundgaard, another young dramatist on our Chicago project, and produced in cooperation with the Chicago Health Department.

Federal Theater has from the first liked particularly plays of pioneer America: John Brown in "Battle Hymn" by Michael Blankfort and Michael Gold; Hoffman Hays's "Davy Crockett"; "John Henry" by Frank Wells—these are only a few of the historic or legendary figures seen upon our stages. Sometimes it is not a character, but a whole phase of history, such as that created for Arkansas in "America Sings"; for the Indian period in Lynn Rigg's "Cherokee Night"; for the Dunkards in Pennsylvania in Archibald's "Feet on the Ground"; for the Southwest in Myra Kinch's "American Exodus"; for the Midwest in Virgil Geddes's "Native Ground."

Perhaps this kinship with the pioneer is due to the fact that our Federal Theater is a pioneer theater. Our companies go through pioneer hardships; they play the turpentine circuit in Florida; they play the C. C. C. camps in the dead of winter in the remote Northern woods. They played the devastated areas in the wake of the flood, acting on improvised stages before thousands of homeless flood victims. We underestimate the quality called patriotism if we think it does not bring to any Federal Theater troupe a thrill of pride to portray the early days of a country which has recently, through Congressional action, given a new lease of life to the theater.

In a larger sense, also, the Federal Theater is a pioneer theater because it is part of a tremendous rethinking, redreaming, and rebuilding of America. Being a part of a great nationwide work project, our actors are one, not only with the musicians playing symphonies in Federal orchestras; with writers recreating the American scene; with artists compiling from the rich and almost forgotten past the Index of American Design; but they are also one with thousands of men building roads and bridges and sewers; one with doctors and nurses giving clinical aid to a million destitute men, women, and children; one with workers carrying traveling libraries into desolate areas; one with scientists studying mosquito control and reforestation and swamp drainage and soil erosion.

What has all this to do with the theater?

It has never had much to do with the theater in America before, and that may be one thing that has been the matter with that "fabulous invalid." But it has everything to do with the Federal Theater. For these activities represent the present frontier in America, a frontier against disease, dirt, poverty, illiteracy, unemployment, despair, and at the same time against selfishness, special privilege, and social apathy. The struggles along this frontier are not political in any narrow sense. They would exist under any administration. Taken collectively they illustrate what William James meant when he talked about a moral equivalent for war. In this struggle our actors know what they are talking about. In this larger drama they are themselves performers. Hence the Federal Theater, being their theater, becomes not merely a decoration or a luxury, but a vital force in our democracy. For the Federal Theater (and perhaps it is worth asking if this is not always true of any theater) will be worth no more and no less in its final evaluation as an art form than it is worth as a life force. Whatever it may be or may become, its deep and not-to-be-forgotten immediate significance for American life is that papa's got a job.

27 • Max Lerner: *A TVA "Yardstick" for the Opinion Industries*

Max Lerner (1902-), a prolific writer, social critic, and newspaper columnist, has lectured and taught at various American universities. In the 1930's he was one of the more eloquent younger

From Max Lerner, "Propaganda's Golden Age," *The Nation*, CXLIX (November 11, 1939), 522-524.

spokesmen for economic and political change who saw in the New Deal elements that, if pursued, might result in a thoroughgoing attack on poverty and privilege in the nation. From his *Ideas for the Ice Age* (1941) to the ambitious *America as a Civilization* (1957), Lerner's radicalism seemed to have thawed.

Liberalism fights for its dogmas inch by inch before it yields them. The doctrine of the final triumph of the idea—that the truth, even though unaided, must prevail—died a hard death, if indeed it may be said to have died at all. But even more tenacious is the linked notion that there exists anything like a competitive system for ideas. To say that because I can get up and spout on a soap-box in Union Square or write in *The Nation* or start a newspaper in competition with Mr. Hearst or Mr. Howard I have a freedom of opinion comparable to theirs is fantastic. I speak with the voice of one, Mr. Howard with the voice of millions. It is not because he is a better man than I, or because his ideas are truer or sounder, or because they represent more authentically the humanist tradition. It is because he has a major control in the opinion industry and I have not. My freedom to start a newspaper in competition with him is as real as my freedom to enter the field against the United States Steel Corporation. The fact in each instance is that it is hollow to talk of "freedom," whether economic freedom or freedom of opinion, except where there is equality or at least a framework of governmental control to reduce inequality.

Freedom is not laissez faire. We have come by this time to recognize that in the area of our economic life, but in the area of opinion we still cling to the belief that it is. It has taken us decades of social blundering to understand that economic freedom in the sense of the unregulated decisions of an irresponsible capitalism is no longer possible. We had better face the fact that the opinion industries are as much "affected with a public interest" as any others. A nation that has decided on a program of democratic control of the rest of its industrial area endangers the entire structure of control by allowing the corporate interests to shape public opinion at will. It is very well for liberals to speak of making a weapon of liberalism; but to make a fetish of the principle is far different from wielding the weapon.

But all ideas have their uses. There has been much discussion among liberals of the problem of means and ends. We tend to forget that here, as elsewhere, absolutes are arid, and that ends and means are interrelated. Freedom is an end with respect to economic security; a culture that does not give scope to diversity of opinion is an unfree culture no matter how economically secure it may be, and the whole economic life of that culture is truncated. But freedom is also a means with respect to economic security, majority rule, cultural creativeness. To have an abstract freedom of opinion in a culture that is so organized that freedom—or, better, laissez faire—of opinion plays into the hands of economic scarcity and economic tyranny is but sand in our mouths—not nourishing but a matter for gritting of teeth. And that is actually the case with us. Freedom of opinion is precious in itself, yet it is also self-defeating if it is not used to insure the free building up of majority opinion, the orderly replacement of one majority by another, the refashioning of economic institutions to achieve the maximum security for all. Freedom has little meaning except in the context of equality, just as economic equality has only a stunted meaning except in a free society.

We must organize our freedom of opinion in such a way as to make it usable and not academic. But how do it? It is not an easy task, and it has its risks. The first step is to face the problem and face it in a tough-minded way. The question of means can then be tackled. My own preference is to extend the principles of the TVA "yardstick" and the SEC "truth in securities" into the opinion industries.

We must avoid a government-operated radio as in Great

Britain, and we must avoid a government-monopolized press as in Germany, Italy, Russia. I propose the TVA principle in our radio system: in addition to, and side by side with, the great private broadcasting chains, let us have two major airways reserved for the government and run for it not by its bureaucrats but by the guild of radio artists. That it can be done has been demonstrated with brilliant success by the Federal Theater, which has prodded the creative forces of the theater from their slumber. Why should not a similar Federal Radio chain, run non-competitively and without advertising, serve to set a standard for the other chains to live up to, and serve to broadcast the merciless truth about our social conditions when the other chains fear to? The radio is inherently a better mechanism to use in the competition of ideas than is the press. To begin with, the air already belongs to the nation and there can be no question raised legitimately of confiscation. The radio chains have their present position on sufferance. It would be only a step forward to use two of these strategic airways directly for public purposes and turn them over to the technicians, just as the actual teaching in our school and university system is in the hands of technicians.

With respect to the movies, the TVA principle would have to be different: it would have to be a private TVA. But why should not socially conscious money enter the movie industry, and set up great producing units that would put out the sort of film toward which Hollywood is only now beginning to make some feeble gestures? And why should not an RFC that finances all sorts of schemes be used to finance culturally productive enterprise of this sort? This would involve tackling the problem of distribution outlets as well; and there is much to be said for a framework of governmental controls over these outlets. It would involve also using the new film consumer organizations to give utterance to protests against the cowardly and the shoddy and to shape the supply in relation to the demand.

As for the press, the only solution is the long and hard road of creating competition by the deliberate and large-scale process of creating new competitors. There is no inherent economic law toward gigantism among newspapers. We could do with a good many more newspapers, even though it meant that none of them could be leviathans. Here, too, in every locality where there is no competition of ideas in the press, socially conscious money must enter to create competition—and it would be a legitimate function of the government to subsidize individuals and cooperatives that want to start such newspapers, much as we subsidize new housing. In the end, in the hands of good working newspaper men and women, they would pay for themselves financially and more than pay for themselves in cultural enrichment. Alexander Meiklejohn has suggested that our press be socialized like our universities. We could do much worse and we are doing much worse. But there is another possibility: to use the government power and the whole liberal tradition to bring about competition of ideas in a press that remains free from government control; which is, in the best sense, to socialize the press.

Given the reorganized opinion industries, one can turn to the problem of the control of outright propaganda with some hope of success. The problems of the internal organization of the opinion industries are problems of power; the propaganda problem is one of truth. The first involves the adequate representation of diverse points of view, equality of bargaining power in opinion, the accessibility of adequate information for the common man; the second involves a ban on flagrantly distorted information, intended deliberately as a poison for the public mind. The first involves the break-up of the opinion monopolies and the creation of a positive framework for competition in ideas; the second involves the regulation of cutthroat competition and fraudulent practices in opinion. Of these the first is most important in the long run if we are ever to have a genuine market for ideas; but the second is more urgent in the short run as a matter of sheer democratic survival.

In meeting the propaganda danger, something like the SEC

pattern would be the most effective procedure. We have a Truth in Securities Act to make sure that there is no rigging of the stock market, no false prospectuses, no unethical practices in the marketing of stocks and bonds. Yet we allow rigging the opinion market, unethical practices in the marketing of ideas. Are our securities more precious to us than our security, our stocks more delicate plants than our ideas, our investors more in need of protection than our common people? We have a Wheeler-Lea act against false advertising of drugs and cosmetics; are we to have nothing to protect us against the infinitely more dangerous advertising of anti-labor, anti-democratic, anti-Semitic lies?

I know that liberals will immediately say: Why could not a Truth in Opinion Act be used against the left as well as the right? The answer is that it is already in use against the left. Anti-alien and anti-radical measures are already being passed in Congress and in virtually every state legislature. Have any of the corporate heads or any of their legal aids protested against them? The Dies committee is already smearing the left with its so-called investigations; has it done anything substantial to investigate corporate fascism and regional fascism in America? We know perfectly well that before the legislation was enacted to control business, labor was already hemmed in by a de facto regulation. There was always a danger that the regulatory structure imposed upon business would be turned against labor as well; and, indeed, the Supreme Court tried its best to do so. Yet the total effect has been on the whole to carry through the original legislative intentions. The liberals and the left need not fear the creation of precedents that may be used against them. When a time of crisis comes, it will not be past precedents that count; new precedents, as Hitler has shown in Germany, can easily be created in the interests of ruthless power. What must be feared is not precedents but the sort of social breakdown that will make all precedents, good and bad, equally irrelevant.

To avoid this social breakdown we must move in the direction of a clear economic program, calling for democratic control of industry, and at the same time in the direction of regulation of anti-social propaganda. Individuals of the highest caliber would be required to man a board such as I have suggested. There come to my mind men like Lloyd Garrison, Alexander Meiklejohn, Alvin Johnson, William Allen White—men wise and tolerant in the way of words but so tenacious of the ethics of the thinking craft that they could recognize the spurious and dishonest. The task of such a board would be to require complete information about the provenience and financing of political statements, to see that all inflammatory radio statements are backed up by a bill of particulars, to allow for the answering of controversial material—and, if necessary, to ban material that is poisonous and spurious. The decisions of this board would be, of course, reviewable by the courts under the rule of law. With any sort of good direction the task of the board would become that of monitor rather than censor; and as one of the consequences the press and radio would in the long run set up their own code of ethics. Such a law would be hard to write. Yet surely it would be no more difficult than the drafting of the SEC.

This would not proceed on the principle that there need be no tolerance for the intolerant. I think that is an unnecessarily dangerous principle. To pick the intolerant would be a subjective matter; to hound them, an all too easy absolutism. What we want to create for all is a set of rules within which tolerance and intolerance shall operate.

What chance has such a program of becoming a reality? In the immediate future, very little. The confusion between laissez faire and genuine freedom in the opinion industries is unlikely to be dissipated easily, and as long as it remains in the popular mind, any attempt, however prayerful and innocuous, to restore competition in ideas will lead to anguished howls from the monopolists—and the howls will be echoed through the entire country. Nevertheless, we must continue our attempts to clarify our thinking in this area. One of the crucial reasons for the failure of progressive movements in the past has been their unwillingness or inability to operate in this area, with the result that the mass mind has been turned against them and they have been doomed to a melancholy soliloquy.

American history is the story of the attempts of the minority will to suppress the democratic consciousness. It is the story, therefore, of successive upsurges of democratic strength, each of which has threatened to break the minority power. In 1932 there was such an upsurge. There will be another. When it comes, the progressives must understand that unless they can restore freedom in the opinion industries, they are again doomed to a brief flurry of excitement and reformism and then to a frustrated soliloquy.

28 • Alvin Hansen: *The Need for Long-Range Public Investment*

Alvin Hansen (1887-), a professor of economics at Harvard University, was one of the most influential spokesmen in the United States for what came to be called the theory of "the mature economy." Drawing upon the ideas of John Maynard Keynes, the British economist, Hansen related them more specifically to the American economy, and particularly to the conditions of economic crisis that the United States faced in the depression years. The implications for public policy were clear: the United States government must play a larger role in the economy and it must be willing to spend great

From *Hearings, Temporary National Economic Committee,* 76th Congress, VII-IX, 3497-3557.

sums of money to make up for deficiencies in capital investment that private business could not undertake. But in the very years when Hansen and others were presenting such ideas more and more boldly, the New Deal was pulling back on large-scale spending, its original thrust blunted by a measure of well-being. The conservative opposition began to show more determination to restrict than FDR and his circle did to expand the public sector of the national economy. When Professor Hansen gave the testimony below to the Temporary National Economic Committee, the die seemed already cast; his approach would not be followed, and the only large-scale government spending to come would be for World War II.

We are completing this year a decade of unemployment on a scale never before known in our history. This decade of unemployment was interrupted by a partial recovery which culminated in 1937. This depression is of a magnitude and duration which has eclipsed all others, not excepting even the deep and prolonged depressions of the seventies and nineties. It is a unique phenomenon. It cannot be explained in terms of ordinary business-cycle analysis. For the time being at least we are experiencing a chronic maladjustment, a failure of adequate outlets for capital expenditures for a society geared to a high savings, high investment level. We are caught in the midst of powerful forces in the evolution of our economy which we but dimly understand. Something has gone wrong with the forces making for expansion. We are undergoing a fundamental change in the structure of our economic life.

In every historical epoch it has always been difficult for the generation then living to understand what is going on. It is extraordinarily difficult to get a proper perspective on current drifts and tendencies. Forces slowly accumulating over a long period of time have suddenly converged to give us a decade of unparalleled unemployment. Change is indeed the law of life, but change has come in recent years with accelerated speed.

It is not difficult to see that the economic system of tomorrow will be very unlike the economic system of the past. We are living in a period of transition. Yet in this period men's thinking is still dominated by frozen patterns of the past into which people try to mold the facts of the present.

The economic order of the western world is undergoing in this generation, it seems to me, a structural change no less basic and profound in character than the industrial revolution beginning 150 years ago and extending deep into the nineteenth century. That revolution transformed the western world from a primitive, rural economy into a highly industrialized machine economy. In this generation we are passing over a divide which separates the great era of the growth and expansion of the nineteenth century from an era which we cannot as yet characterize with clarity and precision. . . .

The history of the last 200 years affords no basis for the assumption that the rise of new industries proceeds at a steady pace. But beyond the immediate effect upon the so-called business cycle is the larger problem of the effect of the presence or the lack of new industries upon the vigor of investment booms. In periods when great new industries are rising to maturity over several decades, it is likely that booms will be very vigorous and carried to high points, and depressions will be short-lived. And similarly in periods when great new industries have reached their maturity and ceased to grow, and equally important new industries have failed to take their place, it is likely that booms will be less vigorous, prosperity relatively short-lived, and depressions deep and prolonged.

Thus, throughout the nineteenth century the emergence, development, and growth of giant new industries has played an enormous role not only in the cycle movement itself, but also in the vigor and intensity of America's booms, and the depth, severity, and length of depression periods. It is my view that the deep and prolonged depression of the nineties relates to the cessation of growth of the railroad industry. There was a temporary lull before the electrical and automobile industries emerged, and similarly in the decade of the thirties, in which we are now living, we are having a similar experience. The great automobile industry has risen to maturity, and no comparable new industry has appeared to fill the gap. It is my growing conviction that the combined effect of the declining population growth, together with the failure of any really important innovations of a magnitude sufficient to absorb large capital outlays, weigh very heavily as an explanation of the failure of the recent recovery to reach full employment. Other factors are certainly important, particularly our failure to grapple effectively with certain specific situations, such as those presented by the railroads or by the public utilities, or building construction. . . .

Hoarded savings cause unemployment in the capital-goods industries, thereby reducing consumption expenditures, which in turn further reduces capital outlays, and so the national income falls. Conversely, to get full employment and a full national income it is necessary to make large capital outlays in plant expansion. These put to active use the flow of savings, give employment in the capital goods industries, and this employment in turn raises the level of consumption expenditures which again stimulates further capital outlays on plant expansion.

If we can get adequate capital outlays on plant expansion we shall easily reach full employment on a full-income level, but it is extremely important to keep firmly in mind the fact that we cannot maintain full employment unless there is continuously going on a sufficient volume of plant and equipment expansion over and above replacement and renewals to absorb the full flow of savings. Savings do us good or harm according as they find or do not find investment outlets in productive expansion of plant and equipment and durable goods, including residential building and public works. . . .

Considering the current investment outlet deficiencies compared with the decade of the twenties to which I have referred, it appears very doubtful that we can solve our problem of full employment by relying exclusively on private investment. Private investment, it seems to me will have to be supplemented and, indeed, stimulated by public investment on a considerable scale. Public investment could furnish an outlet for a part of our flow of savings and thus put them to active use, raising income and employment above the current chronic stagnation level. . . .

There is danger, however, that we stress too much the merit of self-liquidating public projects and loans. There are many potentialities for public investment in areas that are of the greatest social and economic significance, but which are not self-liquidating. They may, nevertheless, be extremely necessary and useful and even highly productive in an indirect manner. Expenditures on the conservation and development of energy and natural resources may indirectly raise the national income by very much more than the annual amortization and interest charges incurred. Insofar as this is the case, such public investments are in fact profitable in a financial sense, even though they are not strictly self-liquidating.

Public investment in the conservation and increased efficiency of our human resources can, if wisely expended, be equally productive. Outlays for hospitalization, public health, pollution abatement, sewerage projects, public low-cost housing may be no less productive in an indirect sense than outlays on national resources. . . .

We cannot afford to engage in irresponsible public spending. On the other side, we cannot afford to be niggardly with respect to public investment projects which are either directly or indirectly productive, and which serve to raise the standard of living and thereby contribute to private business expansion, and especially is this the case when we have huge unused and idle resources. . . .

Intelligent debate begins with the question of borrowing for non-self-liquidating projects. It is certainly true that the volume of such borrowing ought to be scrutinized in terms of its relation to taxable income and taxable capacity, but we need here also to look very carefully into what a balanced budget really means. I think it is clear that the ordinary run of governmental expenditures, the operating expenditures, which in modern times must include social service relief and welfare expenditures, should be balanced by tax receipts over an entire business cycle.

But when public investments are made in long term durable projects, it falls well within the limits of a wisely conceived financial plan to borrow for such capital expenditures if provision is made for amortization and interest charges within the lifetime of such durable projects. When an individual builds a house and borrows the funds to defray part of the cost, his personal budget cannot be said to be out of balance if his income is adequate to cover interest and amortization charges on the debt incurred.

Indeed, the borrowing and amortization plan is nothing more or less than a means whereby he may pay for the services of the house, so to speak, on an installment basis. A similar procedure has always been regarded as legitimate and appropriate for State and local bodies. Peculiarly under the conditions of a more slowly expanding economy there are sound reasons for the Federal Government embarking on a longer volume of public investments, on the basis of a borrowing and amortization plan. It is true that if the Federal Government financed all such improvements from such tax receipts the community would escape the interest burden, but it is not clear to me that the payment of interest is not quite as legitimate a charge for public investment services as it is in the field of private enterprise.

And insofar as the borrowing, interest and amortization mechanism may facilitate the employment of resources that would otherwise be idle and make possible the construction of community capital projects, the benefits of which would otherwise be unavailable, the interest charge is all the more legitimate. If tax revenues are provided amply to cover amortization and interest charges, the budget is in fact balanced. . . . If it is deemed desirable, a part of the public investment could quite well be paid from taxation, provided the taxes are so levied as to fall on savings and not on consumption—in that case there would not be an offsetting deduction. . . .

Then . . . let me sum up very briefly. Our tax structure bears heavily on consumption and for the so-called middle income brackets, from $2,500 to $50,000, relatively lightly on savings. We have in recent years been collecting large sums for social security but we have paid very little out into benefits. Our ratio of savings to income continues to be relatively high. We need, therefore, above all to find adequate markets for our flow of savings into plant expansion and new construction if we are to avoid a depressed income level and chronic unemployment. To this end we should encourage private plant expansion wherever and by whatever means it is possible and reasonable to do so. We can get a great deal of private plant and equipment expansion. It will require consolidation, stabilization, and improvement in reforms already made.

It will require modification in our social security program, it will require reform in our tax structure, it will require stable and responsible labor relations, it will require adjustment of prices to the lower costs springing from technical improvements in order to tap potential demand and thus secure larger output, and thereby also larger private capital plant and equipment expansion.

After all these things have been done, it is my view, and on this there may be honest difference of opinion, that it will be necessary after all these things have been done with respect to private investment to supplement private plant expansion and equipment expansion with a reasonable amount and volume of public investment. There should be no irresponsible spending. There are too many things urgently needed and useful on their own account. There is a sensible middle course which we ought to be able to agree upon as reasonable in view of the economic situation currently confronting us. No policy could be more wasteful at a time when there are large unused resources of both capital and manpower than to forego useful public outlays of a sort for which we will have something to show in the form of durable improvements and in the conservation and increased productivity of human and natural resources.

PART SIX

ORGANIZING LABOR

29 · The Wagner Act: *Unions of Their Own Choosing*

The New Deal created a new era for American labor. The action and reaction of two events helped produce the change: the organization of the new mass industries from 1935 to 1938 by the Congress of Industrial Organizations; and the passage of the National Labor Relations Act in 1935 under the leadership of Senator Robert F. Wagner of New York. The Wagner Act did not get FDR's support until it was passed by the Senate and reported out of committee in the House of Representatives. But then he suddenly threw his weight behind it, and the bill became law. The Wagner Act firmly established the legal right of labor to organize and to represent employees in collective bargaining. Under these provisions, unionization grew rapidly through the New Deal period. The terms of the Act, below, constitute more than a legal document; they represent a new philosophy toward labor by government.

AN ACT

To diminish the causes of labor disputes burdening or obstructing interstate and foreign commerce, to create a National Labor Relations Board, and for other purposes.

U.S. Statutes at Large, XLIX, 449.

Be it enacted by the Senate and House of Representatives of the United States of America in Congress assembled,

FINDINGS AND POLICY

SEC. 1. The denial by employers of the right of employees to organize and the refusal by employers to accept the procedure of collective bargaining lead to strikes and other forms of industrial strife or unrest, which have the intent or the necessary effect of burdening or obstructing commerce by (a) impairing the efficiency, safety, or operation of the instrumentalities of commerce; (b) occurring in the current of commerce; (c) materially affecting, restraining, or controlling the flow of raw materials or manufactured or processed goods from or into the channels of commerce; or the prices of such materials or goods in commerce; or (d) causing diminution of employment and wages in such volume as substantially to impair or disrupt the market for goods flowing from or into the channels of commerce.

The inequality of bargaining power between employees who do not possess full freedom of association or actual liberty of contract, and employers who are organized in the corporate or other forms of ownership association substantially burdens and affects the flow of commerce, and tends to aggravate recurrent business depressions, by depression wage rates and the purchasing power of wage earners in industry and by preventing the stabilization of competitive wage rates and working conditions within and between industries.

Experience has proved that protection by law of the right of employees to organize and bargain collectively safeguards commerce from injury, impairment, or interruption, and promotes the flow of commerce by removing certain recognized sources of industrial strife and unrest, by encouraging practices fundamental to the friendly adjustment of industrial disputes arising out of differences as to wages, hours, or other working conditions, and by restoring equality of bargaining power between employers and employees.

It is hereby declared to be the policy of the United States to eliminate the causes of certain substantial obstructions to the free flow of commerce and to mitigate and eliminate these obstructions when they have occurred by encouraging the practice and procedure of collective bargaining and by protecting the exercise by workers of full freedom of association, self-organization, and designation of representatives of their own choosing, for the purpose of negotiating the terms and conditions of their employment or other mutual aid or protection. . . .

SEC. 7. Employees shall have the right to self-organization, to form, join, or assist labor organizations, to bargain collectively through representatives of their own choosing, and to engage in concerted activities, for the purpose of collective bargaining or other mutual aid or protection.

SEC. 8. It shall be an unfair labor practice for an employer—

(1) To interfere with, restrain, or coerce employees in the exercise of the rights guaranteed in Section 7.

(2) To dominate or interfere with the formation or administration of any labor organization or contribute financial or other support to it: *Provided,* That subject to rules and regulations made and published by the Board pursuant to Section 6(a), an employer shall not be prohibited from permitting employees to confer with him during working hours without loss of time or pay.

(3) By discrimination in regard to hire or tenure of employment or any term or condition of employment to encourage or discourage membership in any labor organization: *Provided,* That nothing in this Act, . . . or in any other statute of the United States, shall preclude an employer from making an agreement with a labor organization (not established, maintained, or assisted by any action defined in this Act as an unfair labor practice) to require as a condition of employment membership therein, if such labor organization is the representative of the employees as provided in Section 9(a), in the appropriate collective bargaining unit covered by such agreement when made.

(4) To discharge or otherwise discriminate against an employee because he has filed charges or given testimony under this Act.

(5) To refuse to bargain collectively with the representatives of his employees, subject to the provisions of Section 9(a).

REPRESENTATIVES AND ELECTIONS

SEC. 9. (a) Representatives designated or selected for the purposes of collective bargaining by the majority of the employees in a unit appropriate for such purposes, shall be the exclusive representatives of all the employees in such unit for the purposes of collective bargaining in respect to rates of pay, wages, hours of employment, or other conditions of employment: *Provided,* That any individual employee or a group of employees shall have the right at any time to present grievances to their employer. . . .

SEC. 10. (a) The Board is empowered, as hereinafter provided, to prevent any person from engaging in any unfair labor practice (listed in section 8) affecting commerce. This power shall be exclusive, and shall not be affected by any other means of adjustment or prevention that has been or may be established by agreement, code, law, or otherwise. . . .

(e) The Board shall have power to petition any circuit court of appeals of the United States . . . , or if all the circuit courts of appeals to which application may be made are in vacation, any district court of the United States . . . , within any circuit or district, respectively, wherein the unfair labor practice in question occurred or wherein such person resides or transacts business, for the enforcement of such order and for appropriate temporary relief or restraining order, and shall certify and file in the court a transcript of the entire record in the proceeding, including the pleadings and testimony upon which order was entered and the findings and order of the Board. Upon such filing, the court shall cause notice thereof to be served upon such person, and thereupon shall have jurisdiction of the proceeding and of the question determined therein, and shall have power to grant such temporary relief or restraining order as it deems just and proper, and to make and enter upon the pleadings, testimony, and proceedings set forth in such transcript a decree enforcing, modifying, and enforcing as so modified, or setting aside in whole or in part the order of the Board. No objection that has not been urged before the Board, its member, agent, or agency, shall be considered by the court, unless the failure or neglect to urge such objection shall be excused because of extraordinary circumstances. The findings of the Board as to the facts, if supported by evidence, shall be conclusive. . . .

The Board may modify its findings as to the facts, or make new findings, by reason of additional evidence . . . taken and filed, and it shall file such modified or new findings, which, if supported by evidence, shall be conclusive, and shall file its recommendations, if any, for the modification or setting aside of its original order. The jurisdiction of the court shall be exclusive and its judgment and decree shall be final, except that the same shall be subject to review by the appropriate circuit court of appeals if application was made to the district court as hereinabove provided, and by the Supreme Court of the United States upon writ of certiorari or certification. . . .

(f) Any person aggrieved by a final order of the Board granting or denying in whole or in part the relief sought may obtain a review of such order in any circuit court of appeals of the United States in the circuit wherein the unfair labor practice in question was alleged to have been engaged in or wherein such person resides or transacts business. . . .

INVESTIGATORY POWERS

SEC. 11. For the purpose of all hearings and investigations, . . .

(1) The Board, or its duly authorized agents or agencies, shall at all reasonable times have access to, for the purpose of examination, and the right to copy any evidence of any person

being investigated or proceeded against that relates to any matter under investigation or in question. Any member of the Board shall have power to issue subpenas requiring the attendance and testimony of witnesses and the production of any evidence that relates to any matter under investigation or in question, before the Board, its member, agent, or agency conducting the hearing or investigation. . . .

SEC. 12. Any person who shall wilfully resist, prevent, impede, or interfere with any member of the Board or any of its agents or agencies in the performance of duties pursuant to this Act shall be punished by a fine of not more than $5,000 or by imprisonment for not more than one year or both.

LIMITATIONS

SEC. 13. Nothing in this Act shall be construed so as to interfere with or impede or diminish in any way the right to strike.

30 · Heywood Broun: *Why Exclude Domestic Workers?*

Heywood Broun (1888-1939) was a Harvard graduate, a sports writer and drama critic for the *New York Tribune*, a war correspondent during World War I, and then a columnist for the *New York World*. His column "It Seems To Me" was pungent, personal, witty. A Socialist and pacifist, he once resigned, once was fired by the *World*, but when it was absorbed into the *World Telegram*, his column was resumed. His pro-labor sympathies led him to become a founder and president of the American Newspaper Guild, a union

From Heywood Broun, "Like One of the Family," *The Nation*, CXL (May 29, 1935), 631. Reprinted with the permission of the publisher.

of newspapermen, which became part of the CIO. In this article, Broun criticizes one of the important gaps in the Wagner Act. The article reveals the mood of many who were part of the wider New Deal circle, yet critical of the Roosevelt administration for not going far enough in social reform.

In a day and age when organization is beginning to push into industries where it was unknown before it seems strange that no very serious attempt has been made to unionize domestic servants. The necessary first step, of course, would be to change the name to "houseworkers." The difficulties of successful organization are obvious enough, but they should not stand in the way, for the need is very great. Housework is probably one of the very few industries in which there is absolutely no standard of hours. Pay is generally low, and working conditions run the gamut from good to abominable.

As yet no encouragement has been held out to houseworkers by Washington. General Johnson had at least one request that a code be written, and replied that he was considering the matter. That was the end of the movement. The Wagner labor-disputes bill, which has just been passed by the Senate, excludes domestic servants from its prohibition of "unfair practices" on the part of the employer. It is axiomatic that strong unions get more out of legislation than weak ones and as yet the government has held that it is no part of its function actually to go into the task of organizing labor. In order to gain relief houseworkers will probably have to achieve at least a skeleton organization on their own momentum.

Even though it may be granted that forming an organization would be difficult, it is by no means impossible, nor is it true that no proper standards of wages and hours can possibly be set. The houseworker is under the disability of the same tradition which affects newspaper reporters and doctors. A very large body of public opinion holds that their work is never done. When the attempt is made to organize houseworkers, we shall hear the scornful question whether it is reasonable to have the butler put on his coat and go home at his appointed quitting time even if the guests still linger over their salad. The answer is that pay or additional time off for overtime might be established.

Undoubtedly opposition will be bitter against any kind of organization. There will be the usual silly sort of talk about, "No cook is going to tell me what kind of vegetables I am going to have for dinner." And undoubtedly we shall be informed that a man's house is his castle and that the sanctity of the home must be preserved. All this should be brushed aside in considering the fact that the turnover in housework is whimsical and prodigious. The servant who happens to offend the most crotchety of employers may find herself virtually blacklisted by the refusal of a reference. It is by no means uncommon for a houseworker to pay an employment office a fee for a job which is snatched away within twenty-four hours.

In all differences between employer and employee the employer sits in the driver's seat, but this is peculiarly true of the domestic servant. Some article around the house is mislaid or missing, and a servant is dismissed under a cloud. Is there any other job in which an employee may have to submit to the indignity of having her belongings ransacked before she is allowed to leave? I do not know whether this practice is legal but it is certainly done on many occasions.

Housewives are fond of saying that the lot of the servant is singularly easy because she gets her board and lodging for nothing and maybe some of her clothes. These are the very factors which degrade the worker. The business of "living in" virtually puts the houseworker on call twenty-four hours a day. It robs him or her of any possible privacy and association with friends and family. Forty years ago one day a month off was the traditional allowance. This has grown to once a week or once every other week, but it is difficult for the houseworker to plan ahead in regard to her spare time since in many households the day off is subject to last-minute change at the will of the employer.

The labor of the domestic servant is certainly a commodity in that it is bought by many in the cheapest possible market. I distinctly recall the complaint of a well-to-do woman that relief made it impossible for her to obtain servants for less than $6 a week. The so-called security of the houseworker in times of depression is wholly fictional. Domestic servants are the first to feel hard times. Our newspapers are filled in bleak periods with the stories of the heroism of Mr. and Mrs. K who have gone to live in a little farmhouse and abandoned their great estate.

But aside from hours and wages, the whole tradition of master and servant in our democracy is tainted with anachronism. A worker who has a perfectly dignified and legitimate service to sell finds herself under the necessity of being called by her Christian name and bawled out by someone who is an utter stranger. Office workers may think their lot a hard one, but even in the most hard-boiled office the employee is rarely spoken to in the terms which people often use toward servants. Any kind of organization would lend dignity to a calling which is essentially wholly honorable and necessary. There lingers an unconscious assumption that a houseworker is a serf or a bound servant.

Such progress as has been made in the last few years to a better standard is for the most part due to the attitude of Negro houseworkers. In New York, at least, colored maids and cooks are loath to "live in." In spite of Harlem's high rents they are generally insistent upon going home when the day's work is done. Save in the case of children's nurses it seems to me that this is a reform which should be fostered. In a subtle way it alters the whole relationship for the better. It gives the houseworker a sense of being upon the same footing as other employees. It marks the limitations of the job.

Many a touching novel or play has been written about the devotion of the old servitor. In the melodramas he used to turn up in the last act and lift the mortgage with his own savings. Indeed, the whole tradition of fiction is to sentimentalize the task. But the day is at hand when the houseworker will no longer be content to be treated "like one of the family." He has a right to demand something better than that.

31 • John L. Lewis: *Industrial Democracy in Steel*

John L. Lewis (1880-) was a miner who rose through union ranks to become president of the United Mine Workers, in the American Federation of Labor. He was head of the AFL's Committee for Industrial Organization, and came into continually sharper conflict with William Green and other established AFL leaders on the question of organization of unskilled workers in the auto, steel, rubber, and other mass-production industries. In 1935, under Lewis' leadership, a number of AFL unions broke away and formed the Congress of Industrial Organizations, which proceeded, through a militant program of strike action, to organize, one by one, the great corporations of the mass industries. Lewis had been a Republican all his life, but in 1936, he backed FDR. (In 1940, he returned to the Republican fold.) This speech, delivered by Lewis in the midst of the bitter and bloody battle to organize the steel industry, reflects some of the militancy that marked the labor movement in the days of the New Deal.

I salute the hosts of labor who listen. I greet my fellow Americans. My voice tonight will be the voice of millions of

From John L. Lewis, "Industrial Democracy in Steel," a radio address delivered July 6, 1936.

men and women employed in America's industries, heretofore unorganized, economically exploited and inarticulate. I speak for the Committee for Industrial Organization, which has honored me with its chairmanship and with which are associated twelve great National and International Unions. These unions have a membership in excess of one million persons, who to a greater or lesser degree enjoy the privileges of self-organization and collective bargaining.

They reflect adequately the sentiment, hopes and aspirations of those thirty million additional Americans employed in the complex processes of our domestic economy who heretofore have been denied by industry and finance the privilege of collective organization and collective participation in the arbitrary fixation of their economic status.

Let him doubt who will that tonight I portray the ceaseless yearning of their hearts and the ambitions of their minds. Let him who will, be he economic tyrant or sordid mercenary, pit his strength against this mighty upsurge of human sentiment now being crystallized in the hearts of thirty millions of workers who clamor for the establishment of industrial democracy and for participation in its tangible fruits. **He is a mad man or a fool who believes that this river of human sentiment, flowing as it does from the hearts of these thirty millions, who with their dependents constitute two-thirds of the population of the United States of America, can be dammed or impounded by the erection of arbitrary barriers of restraint. Such barriers, whether they be instrumentalities of corporate control, financial intrigue or judicial interdict, will burst asunder and inevitably destroy the pernicious forces which attempt to create them.**

I salute the members of my own union as they listen tonight in every mining community on this continent. From the Warrier

River in the southland up through the great Appalachian range to the island of Cape Breton, they listen. Across our parched mid-western plains to the slopes of the Rockies and the Cascades, and to the far province of Saskatchewan, they are at attention. To them, whose servant I am, I express my pride in their courage and loyalty. They are the household troops of the great movement for industrial democracy and from their collective sentiment and crystallized power I derive my strength.

In their daily calling the mine workers toil with the spectre death ever at their side, and the women of the mining camps share their Spartan fortitude. Enduring hardship, inured to danger, contemptuous of death, breathing the air of freedom, is there anyone who believes that the men of the mines will flinch in the face of the battle for industrial democracy which now impends in America? . . .

The American Iron and Steel Institute boasts that it includes ninety-five per cent of the steel production of the country and represents an associate corporate investment of $5,000,000,000. This gigantic financial and industrial combination announces that its members "are ready to employ their resources to the full" to prevent the independent organization of their employees. It contravenes the law!

It may be admitted that the corporations associated in this Institute speak with one voice. In the so-called competitive bidding of these combinations on government contracts, it has repeatedly appeared that prices submitted were uniform even to the third decimal. The press has stated that the rejection of bids and readvertising brought the same unanimity on submitted prices. And now the Institute has undertaken to voice for its members a common policy in dealing with all the workers in this industry.

It is idle to moralize over the abstract relations between an employer and his employee. This is an issue between an industry clearly organized on its management side and the 500,000 men upon whose toil the whole structure depends. The question is whether these men shall have freedom of organization for the purpose of protecting their interest in this colossal economic organism. . . .

Interference and coercion of employees trying to organize, comes from the economic advantages held by the employer. In the steel industry it is manifested in an elaborate system of spies, and in a studied discharge of those who advocate any form of organization displeasing to the management. It is shown by confining all yearning for organization to make-believe company unions, controlled and dominated by the management itself. This coercion is finally shown in the implied threat of a blacklist which attends the announcement of a joint and common policy for all the steel corporations of this country.

Why shouldn't organized labor throw its influence into this unequal situation? What chance have the steel workers to form a free and independent organization without the aid of organized labor? What opportunity will they have to bargain collectively through representatives of their own choosing except by the formation of an organization free from management control? . . .

Although the industry has produced thousands of millionaires, and hundreds of multi-millionaires among bankers, promoters, so-called financiers, and steel executives, it has never throughout the past 35 years paid a bare subsistence wage, not to mention a living wage, to the great mass of its workers.

The industry has constantly sought to give the impression that it pays exceptionally high wages, and so far reaching and efficient are its means of publicity that this idea is widely accepted.

Actually, there is no basis for this belief. When comparisons are made between the earnings of workers in the steel industry and the earnings of workers in other industries of a comparable character, the standing of the steel industry is at best no more than mediocre and at worst no less than disgraceful. . . .

The wages paid its common unskilled workers is a good test of the liberality of an industry's wage policy. Put to this test, the steel industry makes an extremely bad showing. This is made clear by the fact that the steel industry, with hourly earnings of 47.9 cents in March, 1936, ranks no higher than fourteenth, and in the matter of weekly earnings, with $16.77 occupies twentieth place out of the possible list of 21 industries for which returns are given by the National Industrial Conference Board. . . .

On the other hand, the profits of the industry have been relatively as enormous as its wage payments have been small. Greater payments have not been made to wage and salary workers because the large monopoly earnings realized have been used to pay dividends on fictitious capital stock, to add physical values in the way of plant extensions, and to multiply the machines that displace human labor.

Under the wildest flight of imagination, what greater injury could be done to steel workers by labor unions or any other legitimate agency than is evidenced by this financial exploitation by private bankers and promoters! . . .

No greater truth, of present day significance, was ever stated by a President of the United States, than the declaration made by President Roosevelt in his speech at Franklin Field to the effect that America was really ruled by an economic dictatorship which must be eliminated before the democratic and economic welfare of all classes of our people can be fully realized.

Along with the evolution and dominance in the economic affairs of the country of large corporate units engaged in the production and distribution of raw materials and manufacturing products on a national scale such as those corporations of the steel industry today, there has also concurrently developed a highly concentrated control over the money, banking, and credit facilities of the country. Its power, as the result of exhaustive congressional investigations, has been shown to rest in the hands "of a small, inner group" of New York private bankers and financiers symbolized and dominated by the New York banking house of J. P. Morgan & Company.

By acting as fiscal agents for our large, national corporations, this group has been able to place its own representatives on their boards of directors and to determine, as in the case of the U. S. Steel Corporation, their financial and operating policies. Our basic financial, manufacturing, mining, transportation and utility interests have thus been brought under domination of this financial cabal.

In its earlier manifestations—from the beginning of the century to the World War—this financial dictatorship was named by those who vainly but gallantly fought against it—Congressman Lindbergh, the elder La Follette, President Theodore Roosevelt, Justice Brandeis, President Wilson, Senator Norris, and a score of other crusaders for democracy and humanity—as the "Money Trust," or "The Invisible Government."

Profiteering during the World War greatly augmented the sources and power of this group. Its corporate and political control was also greatly extended by the speculative excesses of the so-called "New Era" of 1923-1929.

In his inaugural address of March 4, 1933, President Roosevelt, in reviewing essential reforms, referred to the fundamental significance of this group by the declaration that "The Money-Changers must be driven from the Temple." The Banking and Currency Committee of the United States Senate after several years of careful investigation later reported, during the summer of 1934, that during the post-war decade this financial oligarchy had usurped "the wealth stream of the nation to its very capillaries."

An economic dictatorship has thus become firmly established in America which at the present time is focussing its efforts upon retaining the old system of finance-capitalism which was in operation before the depression and thus preventing the attainment of political and industrial democracy by the people.

Organized labor in America accepts the challenge of the omnipresent overlords of steel to fight for the prize of economic freedom and industrial democracy. The issue involves the security of every man or woman who works for a living by hand or by brain. The issue cuts across every major economic, social and political problem now pressing with incalculable weight upon the 130 millions of people of this nation. It is an issue of whether the working population of this country shall have a voice in determining their destiny or whether they shall serve as indentured servants for a financial and economic dictatorship which would shamelessly exploit our natural resources and debase the soul and destroy the pride of a free people. On such an issue there can be no compromise for labor or for a thoughtful citizenship.

I call upon the workers in the iron and steel industry who are listening to me tonight to throw off their shackles of servitude and join the union of their industry. I call upon the workers in the textile, lumber, rubber, automotive and other unorganized industries to join with their comrades in the steel

industry and forge for themselves the modern instruments of labor wherewith to demand and secure participation in the increased wealth and increased productive efficiency of modern industrial America.

The more than a million members of the twelve great National and International Unions associated with the Committee for Industrial Organization will counsel you and aid you in your individual and collective efforts to establish yourselves as free men and women in every economic, social and political sense. I unhesitatingly place the values represented by thirty million human beings engaged in industry and their sixty million dependents as being above and superior in every moral consideration to the five billions of inanimate dollars represented by the resources of the American Iron and Steel Institute or to the additional billions of inanimate dollars that perforce may be allied with the empire of steel in the impending struggle which the Institute, in the brutality of its arrogance, seeks to make inevitable.

32 · *Liberals Disagree on the Sit-Down Strikes*

The sit-down strike, a new and daring tactic in the arsenal of the American labor movement, was first used in late 1936 by General Motors workers in Flint, Michigan, organized by the CIO United Automobile Workers Union. Instead of leaving the plant, strikers stayed and occupied it for six weeks. The issue divided officials. Governor Frank Murphy of Michigan, a New Dealer, refused to send troops to remove the sit-down strikers and was clearly

From Robert Morss Lovett, "A G.M. Stockholder Visits Flint," *The Nation*, CXLIV (January 30, 1937), 123-124. Reprinted with the permission of the publisher.

sympathetic with their aims. On the other hand, Vice-President John L. Garner was displeased with Roosevelt's decision not to intervene on behalf of property rights against the sit-down strikers. In the following exchange, Robert Morss Lovett (1870-1956), a prominent New Deal supporter, and Oswald Garrison Villard (1872-1949), editor of *The Nation,* reveal one of the points at which consensus of agreement was broken among followers of the New Deal. The "open letter," page 218, is Villard's.

As the owner of a few shares of the General Motors Corporation I became somewhat alarmed when I learned that the workers were sitting down in my plants at Flint, Fisher Body No. 1 and Fisher Body No. 2, preventing the company from finishing and shipping cars and threatening to interrupt the orderly flow of dividends. Accordingly I took Sunday for a visit of investigation. Arriving at Flint I went to Fisher 2, and on introducing myself as their employer was cordially received by some 400 men occupying the plant. I must admit that I was fortunate in having as my companion Adolf Germer, who is on the board of strategy directing the strike.

My first anxiety was for the condition of my property, and I was relieved to find it well cared for. Springs and cushions were being used for beds, it is true, sometimes laid side by side as in a dormitory, sometimes isolated in cubicles between bales of goods. I was glad to see certain marks of domesticity—a clothes tree, an alarm clock, a whisk broom. The boys had made themselves pretty comfortable. I asked who was responsible for cleanliness, order, and protection of property, and learned that the government was what might be described, except for its unfortunate connotation, as a soviet. Mass assemblies were called at frequent intervals at which everything of importance was discussed. Court was held every morning. I asked what crimes were committed and was told that bringing in liquor and circulating rumors were the usual offenses. Those found guilty of the charges against them were put out.

After a hearty Sunday dinner of roast chicken and ice cream, I was preparing to go over to Fisher 1 when I noticed several round holes in the great glass windows, and inspecting more closely some of the foetus-like bodies of cars on the tracks, awaiting their delayed birth, I saw similar holes in the glass and dents in the metal sides. I thought these indicated wanton violence against my property, and asked how it occured. Gun fire by the police, was the answer. I knew that there had been fighting on the Monday before in the street outside, but these disasters were on the second floor. It was obvious that there had been firing from a distance into the plant, endangering the lives of my employees, whom I was beginning to like though they were on strike, and damaging my property. Accordingly I asked for particulars, and as I have seen no clear account of the affair in any newspaper, despite the columns of newsprint that have been given to the strike, I will set down the facts as they were related to me by at least eight participants and eyewitnesses.

The sitdown strike involving 1,500 to 2,000 workers started at Fisher 1, when it appeared that the management was loading dies and special machinery into box cars to be shifted to other cities. Our company is fortunate in having factories scattered over the country; so that by transferring equipment a strike in Flint, Michigan, can be broken by workers in Atlanta, Georgia. Incidentally, that is why the workers demand the industrial form of organization and insist on dealing with General Motors as a whole instead of with the component companies.

The sitdown strike spread to Fisher Body 2, where from 400 to 600 men were involved. Relations were harmonious with the company police, who agreed to let the outer door stand open for food to be brought in. Attempts were made from time to time to shut off heat, light, and water, but workers with a mechanical turn of mind turned them on again.

On Monday afternoon the city police under Chief James Wills undertook to block both ends of the street in front of Fisher 2, to prevent food from being brought in. Later the police made an attack in force with tear gas and gun fire, to enter the plant. The strikers from inside countered the tear gas with streams of water, and the bullets with heavy hinges and other missiles. Some twenty-eight persons were injured, fourteen so seriously as to be taken to the hospital, which, I was told, had received warning beforehand to have an emergency ward ready. The defeat of the forces of law and order is referred to as Bulls' Run. The company police of Fisher 2 apparently took no part in the battle, and were found next morning in a ladies' rest room, where they had stood all night at attention, lacking room to sit down. They were released without acrimony by the workers in the factory.

Leaving Fisher 2, I went over to Fisher 1. After the battle, through Governor Murphy's efforts, the strikers and the management of General Motors had been brought to an agreement to go into conference on Monday, January 18, the workers to evacuate the Fisher plants on the promise that the company would not move machinery or dies. They were to march out of Fisher 1 at one-thirty, and a big crowd was collecting outside to see the evacuation. In the long facade of Fisher 1, which stretched away, it seemed, for half a mile into the foggy distance, no door was open, and I had to go in by a window; but once inside I found the boys very good-natured and, when they realized that I was their employer, flatteringly eager for my autograph. Suddenly a loud-speaker blared forth. It seemed that the General Motors management had agreed to negotiate also with the Flint Alliance, and this was regarded as a breach of faith by the board of strategy of the United Automobile Workers of America, since the question whether the U. A. W. A. should be the sole bargaining agency was one of the points to be negotiated. Accordingly orders were given to hold the plant, the sit-down strike to continue until negotiations were finally complete. The crowd surged back to Fisher 1, where an impromptu outdoor meeting was held to protest the action of the company.

The agreement of the company officials to admit the Flint Alliance to the discussion was a highly provocative action and was deprecated as such by Governor Murphy. It looked like an attempt of the company to get out of the negotiation into which it had been persuaded. The Flint Alliance is an anti-strike organization mainly of white-collar workers and their families and various beneficiaries of General Motors, directed by George Boysen, ex-mayor of Flint and a former paymaster of the Buick Company. It is in no sense a labor union and is detested by the workers. It represents rather the political forces of Flint, which are aligned with General Motors—mayor, police, courts. On that Sunday in Flint there was meeting the Michigan Conference for the Protection of Civil Rights, at which it was forcibly pointed out to the workers that they had only to use their ballots to turn out the whole nest of unclean birds at the next election—defeat the mayor, move the impeachment of Judge Black for his action in granting a sweeping injunction against the union and in favor of a corporation, General Motors, in which he has substantial holdings, and force the removal of Chief of Police Wills for invoking violence both savage and futile.

The General Motors strike of 1937 may prove to be historic inasmuch as it has acclimated the sitdown strike in this country as a weapon of industrial conflict. The right of non-working employees to occupy the plant can hardly be classed among civil liberties. It is rather one of the industrial liberties which are on the way to becoming legally recognized. A little over a century ago it was illegal for workers to combine to refuse work for less than a certain sum. Quite recently it was against the law to picket a struck plant. Today picketing is among the civil rights. Already intelligent governors are applying the rule of reason and common sense to situations which law has not reached in its majestic progress. Governor Earle of Pennsylvania has refused to order the state troops to dispossess the bootleg miners, who are taking coal from seams which are their natural source of livelihood, which the legal owners refuse to work. Governor Murphy has refused to use his militia to throw out the sitdown strikers in the General Motors plants, and has ordered the company to cease the effort to cut off heat, light, and water.

The sitdown is the most effective form of strike. It permits the strikers to remain in comfort, even if somewhat bored, instead of trampling about on the picket line in heat, cold, wind, and wet. It obviates the most unpleasant and demoralizing feature of a strike, the use of strike-breakers. It eliminates violence, or at least places responsibility for it squarely on the police. It promotes the morale of the strikers. Above all it is a forcible reminder to workers, to management, to shareholders, and to the public that legal title is not the final answer to the question of *possession*. Who has the better human and natural right to call the Fisher plant his—I, whose connection with General Motors is determined by the price recorded on the New York Stock Exchange, or the worker whose life and livelihood are bound up in the operation of making cars? I bought my shares at long odds and probably have already collected the purchase price in dividends. When I place a winning bet in a horse race I do not claim a share in ownership of the horse. I know from my political economy that my position is the result of labor and sacrifice. Whose? Not mine. Obviously the enormous mass of wealth represented by the capitalization of General Motors, repeatedly enlarged by split-ups and stock dividends, is the surplus resulting from the toil of millions of workers over many years. Obviously they have not shared fairly in the wealth they have produced.

Some years ago I gave in the *New Republic* an account of the effort to mobilize the stockholders of the textile mills of New Bedford in support of the strikes against a wage cut. The strikers drew up a powerful plea to the stockholders arguing that the plight of the companies was due largely to the graft and nepotism of managers, who were in effect double-crossing both owners and workers. It would be a less hopeful effort to bring any considerable number of the holders of General Motors stock to intervene in behalf of the workers against the immensely successful management of the company, but nevertheless an appeal from the U.A.W.U. board of strategy to the shareholders, broadcast through the press, would have some effect. We should be informed of the fact that since the settlement arranged by President Roosevelt three years ago there has been constant chiseling by some of our employees to the disadvantage of others. In the Chevrolet plant men are dismissed for wearing badges, for speaking of the union in the lunch hour. At the A. C. spark-plug works girls are entitled to pay increases based on the length of their employment, but they are dismissed when they rise too high in the scale. They may be taken back after a time as beginners.

It is absurd to pretend that either the company or the government under whose auspices the agreements were made has provided any practicable means of rectifying these grievances of the workers. The managers to whom we pay grotesquely huge salaries act the part of ownership, and their behavior is an insult to the intelligence and humanity of those to whom they are legally responsible. They interpose objection to dealing with the U. A. W. U. on the ground that it does not represent all the workers. I should judge that at Flint it was pretty nearly their unanimous choice. In any case it does represent the only effective form of labor organization applicable to a gigantic and far-flung industrial aggregation such as General Motors, and the only practicable method of forcing the elimination of unfair practices under which the workers suffer. As such it deserves the support of the public and especially of that not inconsiderable number who hold the legal responsibility of ownership of the corporation.

JOHN SMITH, PAINTED POST, NEW YORK

DEAR SIR:

Your letter of June 10 is one of many hundreds inquiring about my position in regard to certain recent labor happenings. I have chosen to reply to it because you also ask if Arthur Krock of the New York *Times* is justified in saying that my silence on these questions is "a studied policy," and you ask, "a studied policy of what?" I take this opportunity to set you and Mr. Krock right and to tell you and everybody else just where I stand on some recent anxiety-creating developments in the labor situation.

Let me say at once that I am entirely opposed to lawlessness on either side in labor disputes. I hold it criminal for employers to use force to break strikes, to hire professional thugs from those abominations the so-called "strike-breaking agencies," to stir up trouble where there was none. I hold it equally reprehensible and still stupider for labor to use force to achieve greater rewards and better living conditions. I well know that labor often says, "We must meet force with force; we must defend ourselves against the brutalities of employer-owned police by similar tactics." I deny that absolutely. I go farther. I believe that whatever may seem to be the justification for reprisals, every time labor violates the law or seeks to take it into its own hands, it does itself tremendous harm. It alienates supporters, sloughs off friends, and strengthens those employers who resort to corruption and trickery, to brass knuckles, clubs, and tear gas. Both sides become anti-social, hostile to an orderly public life, when they declare that the end justifies the means. Neither side has the right to violate the law. Neither side can assert that two wrongs make a right. Within the framework of the law we can adjust our differences. If the laws favor one side or the other we can alter them promptly, just as we have made many, many new laws and altered many old ones since I became

From Oswald Garrison Villard, "Issues and Men: A Letter F.D.R. Ought to Write," *The Nation*, CXLIV (June 26, 1937), 729. Reprinted with the permission of the publisher.

President. But at bottom we must maintain respect for our courts and the civil authority. Without that we are well on the way to the chaos of utter lawlessness.

No one will accuse me, I am sure, of being unfriendly to labor or indifferent to its needs and aims. Under no other Administration has labor made such strides. Never before has collective bargaining been written upon our statute books. Never before has so great an advance been made for labor as that which is embodied in the Wagner Labor Act, the Social Security Act, and other legislation to which I have affixed my name. I have the right, therefore, to criticize labor when in my judgment it deserves it. I do so now. I say that picketing which by force keeps out of factories people who have the right to enter them is not picketing but violent blockading. As such it is entirely beyond the law governing picketing. I am opposed to sitdown strikes because the sitdown is the forcible taking over of other people's property without their consent.

And when labor or capital seeks to prevent the United States mails from being delivered, it is guilty, in my judgment, of a criminal conspiracy. You also ask my opinion of the withholding of mail by the Post Office from blockaded and besieged factories. I regret that this has happened, and I have made it clear to the Post Office Department that because it has lacked courage it has appeared to take sides and that that *must not be.* A department which boasts that neither heat, nor cold, nor rain, nor snow deters it from delivering its mail cannot afford to be frightened off by picket lines. The next time this happens we shall resort to armored trucks and, if need be, United States guards. Neither labor nor capital has the right to suspend the legitimate functions of this government, and neither will be permitted to do so as long as I am in the White House.

Perhaps you will wonder why I have not said these things before. Frankly I had hoped that it would not be necessary for me to speak out. I have recognized the extraordinary character of the present labor crisis. Labor is readjusting itself to new conditions and is naturally aroused when it comes into head-on collision with reactionary employers determined not to yield their hitherto complete economic supremacy. I had hoped that its new leaders would not permit their men to get out of hand and that the men themselves would exercise self-control, be conscious of their responsibility to their leaders, their cause, and the public. But this has not always happened. Indefensible local strikes have been called; pulling the switches which threw a whole valley into darkness was treason to workers everywhere. In no fewer than 195 communities industries were crippled, homes and hospitals deprived of electricity, essential services stopped. I should like to say to the misguided men who thus abused their power, just *after* they had won a remarkable victory over their employers, that that action did an injury to the cause of the workers from one end of the country to the other, everywhere strengthening the forces of reaction; especially as there was no grievance whatever to palliate the act.

When this happened, it was, needless to say, impossible for me to remain silent. I could not lay myself open to the charge of playing politics or of cowardice in order to gain a political advantage.

FRANKLIN D. ROOSEVELT

33 • Philip Murray: *How the NLRB Changed "Little Siberia"*

In 1937, in a long series of hearings, the Senate Committee on Education and Labor, chaired by Robert LaFollette, Jr., of Wisconsin, produced many volumes of testimony revealing violence and intimidation used against labor organizers by employers. Two years later, Philip Murray (1886-1952), whom John L. Lewis had chosen

From *Hearings on Bills to Amend the National Labor Relations Act,* Senate Committee on Education and Labor, 76th Congress, 1st Session, pp. 4657-4661, 4638-4639.

to head the Steel Workers Organizing Committee (SWOC) for the CIO (and who later succeeded Lewis as CIO president), testified before the same committee on the change in conditions produced by the legislation of collective bargaining under the Wagner Act, in Aliquippa, Pennsylvania, home of the Jones & Laughlin Steel Corporation.

Little Siberia they called it, and with good reason. The AFL organizers were not even permitted to enter Aliquippa (then called Woodlawn) during the great steel strike in 1919. Friends or relatives of its inhabitants were not allowed to stop for an unauthorized visit. Roads were barred and every stranger alighting from the train was questioned, and, if he could not render a good account of himself and his business, hustled into jail overnight and then back to whence he came. When the great steel strike was called in September 1919 the cordon sanitaire proved its effectiveness; not a man walked out of the Jones & Laughlin Aliquippa mills.

This control was not limited to emergency occasions. It was ever-present, all pervasive. Of the 30,000 people living in the town, 12,000 were employed in the Jones & Laughlin mills, thus leaving only a very small percentage of the adults to carry on the necessary activities of the town. The corporation owned the street railway system (now abolished), the motor-coach system, the water supply system, and approximately 700 homes occupied by its workers. It dominated the municipal government and financial institutions of the town. In short, it was the undisputed overlord. . . .

1933 brought forth the New Deal, the National Industrial Recovery Act, and Section 7(a) thereof. That section ostensibly guaranteed the right freely to organize for purposes of collective bargaining. In order to forestall genuine organization, Jones & Laughlin, along with hundreds of other companies, set up an employee representation plan in June 1933. The plan, usually referred to as the ERP, provided for the election of officers by the employees, and machinery for the settlement of grievances. It was never submitted to the employees for approval; they were simply told to elect representatives. This was done on company time and plant property. The men were paid for the time they lost in voting. The plan consisted of some 30 delegates elected from the various departments once a year. A representative did no work in the mill. He was paid at his regular job rate for whatever time he handed in.

Company union representatives more than once asked for and received 27 hours' pay for work performed within a single day. William Turner, last chairman of the plan, boasted that his job paid him $14,000 a year. . . . Periodic meetings were held with the management's representative, Mr. John Mitchell. Nothing could be done without his consent, and he made it rather clear in the beginning just what he would approve. He would agree to have a fountain installed here or a guard rail put up there. . . . Many of the first grievances settled by the union were these same points vainly raised in the ERP. . . .

Captains Mauk and Harris, of the J. & L. police, considered the Aliquippa police department merely as an adjunct of the mill police. The borough police were given specific duties to perform and, according to sworn testimony, they more than carried out their orders. In cooperating with the company in its effort to stamp out unionism in Aliquippa, the city police acted with the fury of the Inquisition. Statements like the following can be multiplied many times:

"In 1934 I was arrested for some kind of disturbance. . . . My landlord, Ignuts Ianacich, told me that while I was away a city cop and Kelley of the J. & L. police broke into my room and searched it. They went through the trunk and found my union cards and took them away with them. Later in the same day two city police called at my home and said that Burgess Sohn [a local administrative official] wanted to see me. At headquarters, Chief Ambrose had me searched and took the union cards which were in my coat pocket.

"The next day I was again called into the police headquarters by Chief Ambrose. He showed me my union cards and asked me what they were. I said that they were union pledge cards and then he slapped me twice on my face.

"The following day I was again taken to the office of Chief Ambrose and was handcuffed. A minute or two later, Kelley and Captain Harris, of the J. & L. police, forced me into the room. Ambrose looked at my handcuffs and said 'Not tight enough. We better squeeze them a little more.' He did so, causing me great pain. The pain caused me to shake, and Captain Harris looked at me and said, 'What's the matter? Got a cold?' Then he said, 'How do you like the union now?' I was then put back in my cell. When my case came up . . . I was acquitted of assault and was freed."

The borough police were likewise part of the company's spy system. . . . An affidavit made of a former Aliquippa policeman states that: . . .

"Whenever a man was sent to cover a meeting his job was to take down everything that the speakers said, and after the meeting was over he was to make out a written report for Captain Harris. Every meeting of the CIO was covered. This was started in June 1936. Sometimes Costlow, sometimes Pastine, sometimes myself, and sometimes some other policeman would be assigned to the job. Chief Ambrose would occasionally visit the meeting himself. Mass meetings . . . were covered with a police car armed with tear gas and riot clubs.

"Full monthly police reports were made out, and given by Chief Ambrose to a patrolman to be taken to the superintendent of the J. & L. police, H. G. Mauk.

"At every meeting of the CIO Lieutenant Kelley, of the J. & L. police, or one of his stool pigeons would take the license number of every car parked near the hall. He would turn over this list to Chief Ambrose, who would detail a patrolman to check up on the names of the car owners. Chief Ambrose would then turn over this list of names to the J. & L. police. One time, when I covered a CIO meeting in my own car for the J. & L.

under the instructions of Chief Ambrose, my license number was included with the rest and my name was on the list.

"About the time of the J. & L. strike, Borough Secretary McElhany gave me a package to deliver to E. K. Miller, assistant general manager of J. & L. He told me to be careful with it as it contained tear gas. I delivered it to No. 4 headquarters."

By May 1937 a distinct majority of Aliquippa's steel workers had become members of the SWOC. In addition, a majority of the Jones & Laughlin Steel Corporation's twelve-thousand-odd employees in its Pittsburgh Works had also become members of the SWOC. On behalf of these members the SWOC requested a conference with the corporation's officials early in May. The United States Steel Corporation had already recognized SWOC and signed a collective-bargaining contract with it. The same form of recognition was requested from Jones & Laughlin, which hesitated to grant it. Instead, Jones & Laughlin rushed plans to convert its company union, or employee representative plan, into a so-called independent union to compete with the SWOC. This brought negotiations to a head, and in self-defense Jones & Laughlin workers went on strike. The strike, at once, was successful; in fact, it was 100 percent. When the Jones & Laughlin officials saw their works completely closed down for the first time in their history, they reentered negotiations with the SWOC. The corporation officials told me and my associates that they would sign a contract similar to the one between the SWOC and U.S. Steel, provided we could show that a majority of Jones & Laughlin's workers were SWOC members. . . .

Happily for the workers and the corporation, the National Labor Relations Board was in existence. Because of the existence of the Board, the Jones & Laughlin strike was one of the shortest on record, involving approximately 25,000 workers. It lasted just thirty-six hours.

In the past there would have been no other way out than a

long-drawn-out battle, but here under the Wagner Act there was a definite, sane, constitutional, and democratic way of settling our differences. The company said we did not really represent its men. SWOC insisted that it did. The obvious way to settle it, therefore, was to hold an election.

The National Labor Relations Board provided the machinery for this, and the strike was settled with an agreement that the terms of the U.S. Steel contract would be in effect until an election was held by the National Labor Relations Board within 10 days to determine whether or not the Steel Workers Organizing Committee represented a majority of the Jones & Laughlin employees. The result was a smashing victory—17,208 for the union and 7,207 against the union.

The Jones & Laughlin Steel Corporation thereupon signed a collective-bargaining contract with the SWOC, recognizing it as the sole bargaining agency for all of its production and maintenance workers. This contract was the beginning of the extension of democratic principles and procedures into the operation of the Jones & Laughlin works. Twenty-five thousand workers who had been governed for years by the dictatorial rules that management arbitrarily promulgated elected their own representatives. These representatives sat around the conference table with management and negotiated fair democratic rules to govern the operations of the Jones & Laughlin mills. Here was an overt experiment in democratic ways. . . .

The Jones & Laughlin election is one of the largest conducted by the National Labor Relations Board. It represents a great victory of reason over strife in American industrial life. The Congress is to be congratulated for the enactment of the National Labor Relations Act, which has made this great achievement of democracy over autocracy possible.

PART SEVEN

THE FARMER

34 · Fiorello LaGuardia: *Urban Support for the Farmer*

Even in the supposedly prosperous 1920's, the farmer in the United States was in constant economic difficulty. Surpluses grew and prices fell, but the payments the farmer had to make to the banker, the railroader, and the middleman remained high. During the depression, the farmer's situation deteriorated rapidly. Banks failed; homes and farms were foreclosed; products piled high in the storage bins. Throughout the 1920's Congressional attempts to give federal aid to the farmer had been resisted. By early 1933, a new President and a new Congress created a new mood. Fiorello LaGuardia (1882-1947), who had fought all through the 1920's for aid to the poor in cities and on the farms, and who represented a slum district in East Harlem (1923-1933), spoke on the floor of the House for a new philosophy to control relations between the government and the farmer. In 1933, LaGuardia became mayor of New York and held that office until 1945.

. . . I say that there are two conflicting schools of economic thought, and the issue was clearly drawn during the last presi-

From the *Congressional Record*, January 10, 1933, pp. 1489-1493.

dential election. President Hoover courageously raised the issue in his speech at Madison Square Garden on October 31, 1932. In the language of Mr. Hoover:

> This campaign is more than a contest between two men. It is more than a contest between two parties. It is a contest between two philosophies of government.

That is absolutely correct, and the contest has been decided. . . .

We can no longer talk of the individual or depend upon "rugged individualism" or resort to the maxims of 150 years ago. We can not abandon the individual when economic and industrial conditions have stripped all semblance of individuality from the citizen. If industry has regimented men, we must necessarily legislate for them under such conditions. If the farmer has lost his individuality by reason of new methods of transportation, distribution, control, and world-wide price fixing of his products by forces beyond his control, we must necessarily have to consider the farmers as a class and protect them as such. The only semblance of individuality that is left is the affliction, the misery, and the poverty that surround the individual when he loses his place in the ranks of his industrial regiment and the farmer when his unit is destroyed by the ticker tape and the adding machine. . . .

The American farmer to-day is becoming a tenant peasant. They are being dispossessed of their farms by the thousands. Gentlemen, they are resisting, with pardonable disregard of the law, the power of the State in enforcing the mandates of the courts. It is a condition that we can not ignore. Suppose, you will say, the price of commodities increases; what will your workers in the city do? We are prepared for that. We will demand increased wages. That is the other half of the answer. Yes; it can be done, and will be done. "Where will it come from?" I hear some one remark; and I will answer that in just a moment. Why, banks, industries, and railroads have come to Congress for aid. Why not the farmer? Is not the chief trouble with industry and the railroads the inability to meet so-called fixed charges? We know that these fixed charges are the interest charges on blunders or plunders of the past, together with an unreasonable expectation of returns on investment. Once we squeeze out the water and wash out unwarranted charges and reduce interest charges, it will be easy to meet increased wages. That and bringing agriculture to a parity with industry by fixing prices according to the actual cost of production will establish in this country a new era of prosperity, enjoyed not by a small class but by all the real producers of wealth. That is the objective. . . .

What chance has the farmer to-day when we leave him to the mercy of what once was the law of supply and demand? When the farmer took his product to town to sell to the consumers waiting for it, and they had no other source of supply, then, indeed, it might have been applicable. But what chance has the farmer when the demand is controlled by manicured-finger men in Chicago and New York dealing in agriculture by means of the ticker tape and control the prices of the farmer's commodities? What chance has the farmer got, under a system of supply and demand, with elevators, storage houses, and refrigerators where food can be garnered and held so as to control the market price? The farmer can not store his product. He has not the facility, and besides he needs immediate cash. This bill will go a long way to remove existing evils. . . .

Personally, I should prefer to avoid all circumvention and provide for straight price fixing for all surplus agricultural commodities. Eventually we will come to that. The habit of thinking along certain constitutional lines makes many timid, and there is an honest difference of opinion whether we could constitutionally do so.

It is my belief that in the face of the existing emergency,

with the complete nation-wide bankruptcy of the farmers of the country, that we could do so. When a farmer sells his products at less than it cost him to produce, and that is what he is doing every day, and unable to exchange his products for the necessaries of life and for the commodities which he needs to raise his products, he is not selling at such prices of his own free will. He is selling under duress. He is forced and coerced to sell the products for less than it cost to produce, because he has no means to withhold his product, and he is being forced by commitments of taxes, crop mortgages, interest on farm mortgages, and the perishable nature of his products to make the sale. It is not a free sale or a free act in any sense of the word. The party buying at such prices or the other part of the contract is taking advantage of the situation. There is no privity between the cotton exchange of Liverpool, England, and the cotton grower of the South. Yet no one will deny that the price of raw cotton is fixed at Liverpool. There is no privity between the producers and the commodity exchanges of Chicago, and yet no one can deny that the prices are fixed by these exchanges. What constitutional provision, therefore, would we violate if as a matter of public policy we authorize an agency of the Government to fix prices of agricultural commodities based upon average cost of production. Certainly, the production of food for the Nation is a matter of national concern. If to-morrow we were to be stricken with drouth, pestilence, or other destructive causes and the Nation were confronted with famine, the Government would have to step in and provide relief for the people of the country. Yet here we are with the farmers universally bankrupt; and if foreclosures continue, there will be no individual ownership of land. Then what? Can insurance companies and savings banks till the soil and produce food for the Nation? . . .

Whether governmental control for future production or planning in the hands of industry or agriculture, it will have to be

Government supervision and control. We can not leave it entirely to industry, because they could take advantage of the situation and perhaps ignore the public requirements and interest in the matter. Future production planning under proper governmental supervision is one of the necessary factors in an economic readjustment that some of us are shaping. . . .

We have not overproduction to the extent that it is generally believed; when the people of this country will have sufficient to eat and wear and be able to live up to the American standard of living, we will be better able to tell just what the domestic requirements are. Only after all of the people of the country are properly and sufficiently fed, the remainder, if any, can be called a surplus. With industrial productive planning, it will be necessary to bring down the hours of labor and the working days of the week. I will not enter into that phase of our economic changes at this time.

No one can deny that this increased return to the farmer will result in an increased purchasing power. The American farmer is the best market to-day for American industry. He has been so impoverished that 99 per cent of the farmers of this country have not bought clothes for the last two years. The farmers are so impoverished that their farms are going to wrack and ruin; and the minute they get an increased revenue, they will be able to buy the material necessary to make repairs on the farms and will be able to replenish the farms with machinery and put new clothes on the backs of their children. . . . Mr. Roosevelt speaks of the forgotten man. He understates the condition. It is the exploited masses that now require the attention of Congress, and in this great army of exploited masses is to be included the farmer. We must legislate for all of the American people and not for the benefit of those who control the wealth, who control property, and I am sorry to say, who for long have controlled Government. This is the first step in a fundamental economic readjustment.

35 • Henry A. Wallace: *A Defense of the New Deal Farm Program*

One of the first major pieces of legislation passed after FDR took office was the Agricultural Adjustment Act of May 1933. The AAA sought to raise the income of the farmer by a set of contracts in which farmers voluntarily curtailed production of certain commodities, and in return received government subsidies financed by taxes on mills and other processing agencies. This use of the tax power led the Supreme Court to void the act in 1936, but the fundamental idea of curtailing production and subsidizing the farmer was maintained in the Soil Conservation Act of 1936 and the new Agricultural Adjustment Act of 1938.

This speech, delivered by Secretary of Agriculture Henry A. Wallace shortly after the passage of the 1938 act, offers a clear exposition of its provisions and a defense of the New Deal's underlying approach to the farm problem.

Tonight I want to talk about the new farm Act, and its meaning for farm and city people.

In the next few minutes I want to make very clear to every one three points:

First, the new Agricultural Adjustment Act provides for a simple and straightforward farm program.

Next, the Act provides for a farm program of abundance. It lays the basis for a workable Ever Normal Granary, and in this way means better living for farm people and for city people.

Finally, the new Act applies the principles of Democracy

From Henry A. Wallace, "The New Farm Act. Balanced Abundance for Farm and City," a radio address delivered March 7, 1938. Reprinted in *Vital Speeches of the Day*, IV (March 15, 1938), 338-340.

directly to the most serious problems that farmers have to face. Democracy and abundance are the strong team that the new farm bill is hitched to. It tries in practical ways to bring balanced abundance to the people. Congress has every reason to be proud of this work.

The new Act has been called complicated, but actually it is just as simple as, and perhaps simpler than the old Adjustment Act. In the farming communities it will be carried out by county and community committees of farmers, just like the old Act was. I believe that within a month most of the county committees will understand very well how the new Act applies in their own communities. The chief reason it sounds complicated is that Congress decided to write into law many details that used to be covered by general provisions. Not perhaps in legal language, but certainly in terms of action, this Act in its main outlines is simple and clear.

You who are listening—whether you live in the city or on the farm—want to know what those outlines are. Let me tell briefly about them.

First of all, the new Act continues and strengthens the work of the Triple A on soil conservation. Farmers everywhere in the United States may take part in the program regardless of what crop they grow. So we may think of one part of the Act as making soil conservation an important and enduring framework for the whole program.

Then there is another part of the Act. This part makes available certain supplemental measures for the producers of five commodities listed in the Act. These commodities are corn, wheat, cotton, tobacco and rice. Let me enumerate three of the supplemental measures. First, national acreage allotments, divided up among the farms, with acreages big enough to produce plenty of domestic and export markets and in addition for larger than average carry-overs. Second, storage loans, to put a plank under prices when threatened by a slump and also to finance farmers in holding surplus supplies until they are needed and will bring a living price. Third, marketing quotas which can be used when the Ever Normal Granary overflows, provided always the farmers are so unitedly in favor that at least two-thirds of those taking part in a referendum vote to put the quotas into effect. These new provisions are to be dovetailed into the AAA soil conservation work. All payments are to be conditioned on soil conservation. . . .

This new Act comes to grips with a big and practical question. That question is how to protect both food supplies and farm income against extreme swings due to tricky weather.

Since 1930, the farmers and consumers have paid the terrible cost of these excessive fluctuations, which helped nobody except a few lucky speculators. In 1932, an extreme upswing in supplies coincided with an extreme downswing in prices. That was one kind of a disaster. The farmers' buying power disappeared. What farmer could buy shoes or an overcoat or an automobile with 30-cent wheat rotting on the ground and 12-cent corn being burned for fuel? The elevators were bursting with wheat, but the breadlines grew longer and longer. The vital element of balance between producing power and consuming power was gone. Factories without customers shut down. The nation learned that under our economic system abundance without balance means misery.

This country does not want to go through the 1932 experience again.

In 1934 and 1936, we had the opposite kind of a disaster. Those were the years of the two greatest droughts in our recorded history. The hot sun of those summers blasted the wheat and burned up the corn. Livestock died for want of water. Once again farmers and city people realized that they had strong interests in common. As farmers fought against the effects of drought, city people were hurt by steeply rising prices. . . .

We need a practical method to maintain balance, because that is the only way to have and to keep real abundance.

That way is to use our surpluses to balance our shortages. This is the purpose of the Ever Normal Granary plan of the new Act. It proposes to level off the peaks into the valleys of supply, so as to create and keep on hand larger reserves of food and feed for agriculture and the nation.

Specifically, the new Act is expected to result in doubling the average annual carryovers of both corn and wheat.

I want to emphasize how the parts that encourage abundance work. The program is tied tightly to good land use. Surpluses one year and shortages the next go hand in hand with waste and destruction of soil fertility. The land is the real source of prosperity. If farmers are forced by ruthless competition to exhaust the soil there can be no enduring abundance. The place of soil conservation in this program is vital.

The national acreage goals provide for balanced abundance. They encourage planting enough for all domestic, export and carry-over needs, but not so much as to bring back the excesses of 1932. Parceled out among the individual farms, these goals encourage good land use, instead of waste and depletion of the soil.

The commodity loans are available on corn, wheat and cotton whenever large supplies threaten farmers with price collapse. The loans are to be high enough to make impossible a return of prices like those of 1932, but not so high as in any ordinary situation will prevent free movement of export crops into foreign markets. The loans will advance farmers the money that they need to hold supplies off the market in times of unusually large production.

Marketing quotas can be used. But for food and feed, they are available only in emergency. Let me tell just what that means. When supplies mount higher and higher, and the Ever Normal Granary overflows; when any government investment in loans is threatened; and when the future of the farm program is endangered, then the quotas can be placed in effect. But remember that always there is one more important condition. The quotas can never be used unless they are approved by two-thirds of the producers voting in a referendum. If the quotas are opposed by more than one-third of those voting, there will be no quotas and the government will not offer loans.

Crop insurance for wheat, beginning with the 1939 crop, will offer wheat farmers protection at cost against losses of yield due to drought, flood, hail, insects or disease. The premiums will be held in storage in the form of wheat. They will go into the Ever Normal Granary reserve supply and be used to pay farmers for losses in bad years. . . .

The new Farm Act means greater abundance also for city consumers. The people in the cities may not know it but they are victims of freakish weather and its effects on farm supplies. The maintenance of larger reserves of wheat and corn under this Act will do more to stabilize prices of bread and meat than any farm plan that has ever been enacted or proposed. This Act will reduce the wild fluctuations of corn supplies and prices of pork and beef. I expect never again to see meat prices as high relative to consumer income as they were in the first nine months of 1937. Hogs at \$3 are not good for farmers. Hogs at \$13 are not good for consumers. Hogs at \$8 are much better for both. . . .

Leaving far behind the scarcity of 1932, this program of abundance can, and, I am convinced, will be carried out in the spirit and letter of democracy.

Farmers today are feeling the impact of powerful economic forces. They have to seek better protection for themselves against these forces, or else suffer results that we know from experience are very severe. The farmers are 6,000,000 competing units in a world of corporate organization and increasing industrial controls. Their export markets have been reduced by tariffs and embargoes. They have felt the shock of rapid technological changes in both agriculture and industry. This generation has seen the closing of the frontier and the end of the free land that once absorbed jobless labor. Failure to let farmers build good defenses against these forces finally plunged agriculture into the great depression.

The task of democracy in our day is to help people meet problems like these. If democracy is to survive it must serve this function. With the free lands gone, export markets shrunken, and corporations dominant, the great problems that now confront the farmer are economic problems. Once we had to fight for political freedom. But now the battle is for economic freedom—freedom from the menace of depression and insecurity. The time has come when democracy must be applied in the economic affairs of the people, or else we can have no democracy that is worthy of the name.

Economic democracy in agriculture will face one test five days from now. Next Saturday the first referendum will be held under the new Act. In these referendums, the growers of cotton and of flue-cured and the dark tobaccos will vote by secret ballot for or against the use of marketing quotas this year for their crops. The quotas, as I have said, will not be put into effect unless their use is favored by two-thirds of the producers voting.

To me, the referendum method set forth in the Farm Act is economic democracy. But now is a good time to face directly the question whether it *is* economic democracy or government regimentation. I saw an argument the other day that the referendum is not democratic because the vote is taken only among farmers and does not include non-farming groups. But the referendums are only a step in carrying out a democratic process which began with enactment of the law by Congress representing all groups of the people. Referendums are provided for because Congress wisely saw that they are a practical and necessary step in carrying out a part of the farm program which depends for its success upon having the overwhelming support of the farmers concerned. Congress representing the whole people has defined the conditions under which referendums of producers are in the general welfare, therefore, putting the issue of marketing quotas right up to the farmers themselves looks fair and democratic. . . .

That is economic democracy. Democracy means respect for minority rights but not frustration by the minority of all progress. Democracy does not condemn to waste of soil and destruction of income vast numbers of farmers who want to cooperate to save themselves and their lands.

Democracy and anarchy are two different things. Anarchy means complete personal license to do as you please without regard to the general welfare. But in a democracy personal freedom is balanced by personal responsibility for the rights of all. When the majority in a democracy puts up traffic lights so as to keep going ahead, it is understood that the minority as well as the majority should respect the signals.

Let me sum it all up this way. There are two vital things about the Farm Act.

One thing is its provision for abundance. In 1937 agriculture produced a superabundance of food and fiber for the nation (and right here, let me say parenthetically that the "scarcity" charge against the new Farm Act is the worst misrepresentation I ever heard)—and for the future the Act provides ways of maintaining the abundance that now exists.

The other vital thing is the Act's reliance upon the democratic process. In my opinion, the new farm program is economic democracy in action.

With these two things, abundance and democracy, agriculture has a plan which is a challenge to industry. It is a challenge to industry to reverse present declines of production so as to balance with large output of factory goods the existing abundance of farm commodities. If industry follows the trail blazed by agriculture, both farm and city people will make more rapid gains. Agriculture is going to do its share. Its program serves farm welfare and the general welfare.

I believe the new Farm Act will make history.

36 · William R. Amberson: *Damn the Whole Tenant System*

The New Deal's major farm program, the first and second AAA, was designed mainly to help the commercial farmer who grew a crop for the market. It gave the most help to those who needed it least, the biggest producers among the nation's six million farm families, those two million families who received 75 per cent of the total income from the sale of commercial crops. The rural poor, those two million families who received less than 10 per cent of the total income, received the least aid from the Act. The following article, focusing on the plight of poor farmers in the southern "Cotton Belt" indicates why a large part of the farm population felt they were, as one writer put it, "stepchildren of the New Deal."

The social outlook of the Secretary of Agriculture is well known, and there can be no doubt that the higher administration of the department is genuinely interested in building a better life for all classes in our farm population. Thus the authors of the 1934-35 Cotton Acreage Reduction Contract, foreseeing the possibility of economic and social disorder in connection with the operation of their program, wrote into the document a section which was presumed to be a sufficient

From William R. Amberson, "The New Deal for Sharecroppers," *The Nation*, CXL (February 13, 1935), 185-187. Reprinted with the permission of the publisher.

charter for the defense and protection of the rights of agricultural laborers. Section 7 of the contract reads as follows:

> [The producer shall] endeavor in good faith to bring about the reduction of acreage contemplated in this contract in such a manner as to cause the least possible amount of labor, eonomic, and social disturbance, and to this end, in so far as possible, he shall effect the acreage reduction as nearly ratably as practicable among tenants on this farm; shall, in so far as possible, maintain on this farm the normal number of tenants and other employees; shall permit all tenants to continue in the occupancy of their houses on this farm, rent free, for the years 1934 and 1935 (unless any such tenant shall so conduct himself as to become a nuisance or a menace to the welfare of the producer); during such years shall afford such tenants or employees, without cost, access for fuel to such woods belonging to this farm as he may designate; shall permit such tenants the use of an adequate portion of the rented acres to grow food and feed crops for home consumption and for pasturage of domestically used live stock; and for such use of the rented acres shall permit the reasonable use of work animals and equipment in exchange for labor.

The general intent of this section to protect cotton farm tenants and croppers from displacement is surely clear. A critical examination, however, reveals the essential weakness of its phraseology. The producer is not pledged "to bring about reduction" but only to "endeavor . . . to bring about reduction." "In so far as possible," twice repeated, and "as nearly ratably as practicable" further weaken the section, which now becomes scarcely more than a gesture of benevolence. As the section proceeds, however, it becomes stronger, permitting "all tenants to continue in . . . occupancy," and then guaranteeing access to rented acres and woods land without qualification other than the "nuisance or a menace" phrase.

The right of tenants and croppers to share in the benefit payments is guaranteed by Section 10. Here it is found that the ordinary cropper, working on a fifty-fifty basis, without tools or teams of his own, is allowed ½ cent a pound for cotton not grown in 1934 as his share of the "parity payment"; whereas the owner receives all of the "rent," 3½ cents a pound, and ½ cent of the parity payment. Concerning this curious eight-to-one division of the government benefits there has been much discussion. The croppers have aptly called their share the "poverty payment." Dr. Paul W. Bruton, formerly of the AAA legal staff, has written:

> The contract should have been drawn so that the benefit payments would have been made directly to landlords and tenants in proportion to their respective interests in the crop. . . . Under the 1934 and 1935 contract the landlord has everything to gain and the cropper everything to lose. . . .

There is reason to believe, however, that much may yet be accomplished if a more adequate machinery of inspection and enforcement be set up. Let the Secretary of Agriculture create a National Agricultural Labor Board, responsible directly to him, with regional offices and a representative in at least each Congressional district. This board should have power to enforce the labor provisions of all AAA contracts and should concern itself not merely with hearing complaints but with making appropriate surveys to prevent abuses from arising. In the cotton country croppers have been driven from pillar to post for so long and have sunk so low in the human scale that they cannot imagine any other type of life, and do not know how to resist exploitation. They react by developing an irresponsible and antagonistic attitude. For half a century now the 40 per cent annual labor turnover has, at each year's end, filled Southern roads with miserable families seeking a new home. With a federal reduction program in operation, new opportunities have almost vanished. The plight of these people thus becomes in a peculiar sense a national responsibility.

For enforcing its contracts the Department of Agriculture holds a much stronger position than the governmental agencies which preside over Section 7-a of the industrial codes, since it controls important financial benefits the withholding of which can throw many a plantation into bankruptcy. It must, however, clarify its mind as to its attitude toward the various classes of our farm population. In the cotton country its present program is greatly aiding the 30 per cent of owners and higher types of tenants, but it has been of no aid to most of the 70 per cent of croppers and day laborers, many of whom are worse off than ever before. Under its program the older habits of exploitation persist, merely moving in new channels and assuming new forms. The department has not yet come to grips with the basic problems. The creation of a more effective agency for the adjustment of labor disputes under present contracts is only a step in the larger program which is needed. The following concrete suggestions are offered:

1. When new contracts are drawn, the labor clauses must have the binding force of law, without quibble or equivocation, and the full protection of the department must be extended to every man, regardless of race, color, or union affiliation, who has honestly performed his labor.

2. The right of agricultural laborers to organize and bargain collectively should be proclaimed and recognition of this right written into all contracts.

3. Tenants and share-croppers should be given representation upon all boards and local committees set up to administer the AAA program.

4. The labor of children under fourteen years of age in the fields should be forbidden by national statute. Many children now begin to pick cotton at the age of five and to "chop" at ten, at wages as low as 3 cents an hour.

Ultimately the plantation system must be liquidated. Dr. J. H. Dillard is quite justified when he writes: "Damn the whole tenant system. There can be no decent civilization until it is abolished." We must do away with the whole antiquated scheme of landlord-tenant arrangements, to which there must always cling many of the worst features of chattel slavery without its benefits.

Forces are already working to accomplish this liquidation. Universal bankruptcy has threatened and will threaten again, as cotton prices fluctuate and interest and taxes pyramid. Official Washington is by no means entirely oblivious to the present situation; the basic difficulty is the lack of a unified program. The rural rehabilitation program of the FERA is establishing thousands of destitute families on a new and more independent basis, which may represent the entering wedge of a force that will ultimately transform the present system. The urgent need for a change has now been recognized by the PWA Mississippi Valley Committee, which in its report to Secretary Ickes advocates a federal program which will enable all tenants to acquire ownership of land. The alternative method of large-scale cooperative farms must also be tested. If tenure is absolutely guaranteed, without power to sell or mortgage, possibly on long-term leases from the government under a Federal Loan Authority, it will free a whole people from their present shackles and make possible the education of a more responsible and effective generation than the South has ever known.

The solution of the human and economic problems of the Cotton Belt is not to be found within the South alone. No purely regional program will suffice. Its special products must be properly utilized in a national and, ultimately, an international scheme, planned for the use of all.

37 • John Steinbeck: *The Torment of Migrant Workers in California*

Migrant farm workers, their ranks swelled by the farmers forced off their own land, were probably the most destitute of all agri-

From John Steinbeck, "Dubious Battle in California," *The Nation*, CXLIII (September 12, 1936), 302-304. Reprinted with the permission of the publisher.

cultural workers. When John Steinbeck (1902-   ) wrote the following article, his famous novel about migrant workers, *The Grapes of Wrath* (1939), had not yet been published, although he had written a novel about union organizing, *In Dubious Battle* (1936). This account of the plight of migrants in California during the depression documents the problems such workers are still facing long after the New Deal years.

In sixty years a complete revolution has taken place in California agriculture. Once its principal products were hay and cattle. Today fruits and vegetables are its most profitable crops. With the change in the nature of farming there has come a parallel change in the nature and amount of the labor necessary to carry it on. Truck gardens, while they give a heavy yield per acre, require much more labor and equipment than the raising of hay and livestock. At the same time these crops are seasonal, which means that they are largely handled by migratory workers. Along with the intensification of farming made necessary by truck gardening has come another important development. The number of large-scale farms, involving the investment of thousands of dollars, has increased; so has the number of very small farms of from five to ten acres. But the middle farm, of from 100 to 300 acres is in process of elimination.

There are in California, therefore, two distinct classes of farmers widely separated in standard of living, desires, needs, and sympathies: the very small farmer who more often than not takes the side of the workers in disputes, and the speculative farmer, like A. J. Chandler, publisher of the Los Angeles *Times*, or like Herbert Hoover and William Randolph Hearst, absentee owners who possess huge sections of land. Allied with these large individual growers have been the big incorporated farms, owned by their stockholders and farmed by instructed managers, and a large number of bank farms, acquired by foreclosure and operated by superintendents whose labor policy is dictated by the bank. For example, the Bank of America is very nearly the largest farm owner and operator in the state of California.

These two classes have little or no common ground; while the small farmer is likely to belong to the grange, the speculative farmer belongs to some such organization as the Associated Farmers of California, which is closely tied to the state Chamber of Commerce. This group has as its major activity resistance to any attempt of farm labor to organize. Its avowed purpose has been the distribution of news reports and leaflets tending to show that every attempt to organize agricultural workers was the work of red agitators and that every organization was Communist inspired.

The completion of the transcontinental railroads left in the country many thousands of Chinese and some Hindus who had been imported for the work. At about the same time the increase of fruit crops, with their heavy seasonal need for pickers, created a demand for this mass of cheap labor. These people, however, did not long remain on the land. They migrated to the cities, rented small plots of land there, and, worst of all, organized in the so-called "tongs," which were able to direct their efforts as a group. Soon the whites were inflamed to race hatred, riots broke out against the Chinese, and repressive activities were undertaken all over the state, until these people, who had been a tractable and cheap source of labor, were driven from the fields.

To take the place of the Chinese, the Japanese were encouraged to come into California; and they, even more than the Chinese, showed an ability not only to obtain land for their subsistence but to organize. The "Yellow Peril" agitation was the result. Then, soon after the turn of the century Mexicans were imported in great numbers. For a while they were industrious workers, until the process of importing twice as many as were needed in order to depress wages made their earnings drop below any conceivable living standard. In such conditions they did what the others had done; they began to organize. The large growers immediately opened fire on them. The newspapers were full of the radicalism of the Mexican unions. Riots become common in the Imperial Valley and in the grape country in and adjacent to Kern County. Another wave of importations was arranged, from the Philippine Islands, and the cycle was repeated—wage depression due to abundant labor, organization, and the inevitable race hatred and riots.

This brings us almost to the present. The drought in the Middle West has very recently made available an enormous amount of cheap labor. Workers have been coming to California in nondescript cars from Oklahoma, Nebraska, Texas, and other states, parts of which have been rendered uninhabitable by drought. Poverty-stricken after the destruction of their farms, their last reserves used up in making the trip, they have arrived so beaten and destitute that they have been willing at first to work under any conditions and for any wages offered. This migration started on a considerable scale about two years ago and is increasing all the time.

For a time it looked as though the present cycle would be identical with the earlier ones, but there are several factors in this influx which differentiate it from the others. In the first place, the migrants are undeniably American and not deportable. In the second place, they were not lured to California by a promise of good wages, but are refugees as surely as though they had fled from destruction by an invader. In the third place, they are not drawn from a peon class, but have either owned small farms or been farm hands in the early American sense, in which the "hand" is a member of the employing family. They have one fixed idea, and that is to acquire land and settle on it. Probably the most important difference is that they are not easily intimidated. They are courageous, intelligent, and resourceful. Having gone through the horrors of the drought and with immense effort having escaped from it, they cannot be herded, attacked, starved, or frightened as all the others were.

Let us see what the emigrants from the dust bowl find when they arrive in California. The ranks of permanent and settled labor are filled. In most cases all resources have been spent in making the trip from the dust bowl. Unlike the Chinese and Filipinos, the men rarely come alone. They bring wives and children, now and then a few chickens and their pitiful household goods, though in most cases these have been sold to buy gasoline for the trip. It is quite usual for a man, his wife, and from three to eight children to arrive in California with no possessions but the rattletrap car they travel in and the ragged clothes on their bodies. They often lack bedding and cooking utensils.

During the spring, summer, and part of the fall the man may find some kind of agricultural work. The top pay for a successful year will not be over $400, and if he has any trouble or is not agile, strong, and quick it may well be only $150. It will be seen that rent is out of the question. Clothes cannot be bought. Every available cent must go for food and a reserve to move the car from harvest to harvest. The migrant will stop in one of two federal camps, in a state camp, in houses put up by the large or small farmers, or in the notorious squatters' camps. In the state and federal camps he will find sanitary arrangements and a place to pitch his tent. The camps maintained by the large farmers are of two classes—houses which are rented to the workers at what are called nominal prices, $4 to $8 a month, and camp grounds which are little if any better than the squatters' camps. Since rent is such a problem, let us see how the houses are fitted. Ordinarily there is one room, no running water; one toilet and one bathroom are provided for two or three hundred persons. Indeed, one larger farmer was accused in a Growers' Association meeting of being "kind of communistic" because he advocated separate toilets for men and women. Some of the large ranches maintain what are called model workers' houses. One such ranch, run by a very prominent man, has neat single-room houses built of whitewashed adobe. They are said to have cost $500 apiece. They are rented for $5 a month. This ranch pays twenty cents an hour as opposed to the thirty cents paid at other ranches and indorsed by the grange in the community. Since this rugged individual is saving 33⅓ per cent of his labor cost and still charging $5 a month rent for his houses, it will be readily seen that he is getting a very fair return on his money besides being generally praised as a philanthropist. The reputation of this ranch, however, is that the migrants stay only long enough to get money to buy gasoline with, and then move on.

The small farmers are not able to maintain camps of any comfort or with any sanitary facilities except one or two holes dug for toilets. The final resource is the squatters' camp, usually located on the bank of some watercourse. The people pack into them. They use the watercourse for drinking, bathing, washing their clothes, and to receive their refuse, with the result that epidemics start easily and are difficult to check. Stanislaus County, for example, has a nice culture of hookworm in the mud by its squatters' camp. The people in these camps, because of long-continued privation, are in no shape to fight illness. It is often said that no one starves in the United States, yet in Santa Clara County last year five babies were certified by the local coroner to have died of "malnutrition," the modern word for starvation, and the less shocking word, although in its connotation it is perhaps more horrible since it indicates that the suffering has been long drawn out.

In these squatters' camps the migrant will find squalor beyond anything he has yet had to experience and intimidation almost unchecked. At one camp it is the custom of deputy sheriffs, who are also employees of a great ranch nearby, to drive by the camp for hours at a time, staring into the tents as though trying to memorize faces. The communities in which these camps exist want migratory workers to come for the month required to pick the harvest, and to move on when it is over. If they do not move on, they are urged to with guns.

These are some of the conditions California offers the refugees from the dust bowl. But the refugees are even less content with the starvation wages and the rural slums than were the Chinese, the Filipinos, and the Mexicans. Having their families with them, they are not so mobile as the earlier immigrants were. If starvation sets in, the whole family starves, instead of just one man. Therefore they have been quick to see that they must organize for their own safety.

Attempts to organize have been met with a savagery from the large growers beyond anything yet attempted. In Kern County a short time ago a group met to organize under the A. F. of L. They made out their form and petition for a charter and put it in the mail for Washington. That night a representative of Associated Farmers wired Washington for information concerning a charter granted to these workers. The Washington office naturally replied that it had no knowledge of such a charter. In the Bakersfield papers the next day appeared a story that the A. F. of L. denied the affiliation; consequently the proposed union must be of Communist origin.

But the use of the term communism as a bugbear has nearly lost its sting. An official of a speculative-farmer group, when asked what he meant by a Communist, replied: "Why, he's the guy that wants twenty-five cents an hour when we're paying twenty." This realistic and cynical definition has finally been understood by the workers, so that the term is no longer the frightening thing it was. And when a county judge said, "California agriculture demands that we create and maintain a peonage," the future of unorganized agricultural labor was made clear to every man in the field.

The usual repressive measures have been used against these migrants: shooting by deputy sheriffs in "self-defense," jailing without charge, refusal of trial by jury, torture and beating by night riders. But even in the short time that these American migrants have been out here there has been a change. It is understood that they are being attacked not because they want higher wages, not because they are Communists, but simply because they want to organize. And to the men, since this defines the thing not to be allowed, it also defines the thing that is completely necessary to the safety of the workers.

This season has seen the beginning of a new form of intimidation not used before. It is the whispering campaign which proved so successful among business rivals. As in business, it is particularly deadly here because its source cannot be traced and because it is easily spread. One of the items of this campaign is the rumor that in the event of labor troubles the deputy sheriffs inducted to break up picket lines will be armed not with tear gas but with poison gas. The second is aimed at the women and marks a new low in tactics. It is to the effect that in the event of labor troubles the water supply used by strikers will be infected with typhoid germs. The fact that these bits of information are current over a good part of the state indicates that they have been widely planted.

The effect has been far from that desired. There is now in California anger instead of fear. The stupidity of the large grower has changed terror into defensive fury. The granges, working close to the soil and to the men, and knowing the temper of the men of this new race, have tried to put through wages that will allow a living, however small. But the large growers, who have been shown to be the only group making a considerable profit from agriculture, are devoting their money to tear gas and rifle ammunition. The men will organize and the large growers will meet organization with force. It is easy to prophesy this. In Kern County the grange has voted $1 a hundred pounds for cotton pickers for the first picking. The Associated Farmers have not yielded from seventy-five cents. There is tension in the valley, and fear for the future.

It is fervently to be hoped that the great group of migrant workers so necessary to the harvesting of California's crops may be given the right to live decently, that they may not be so badgered, tormented, and hurt that in the end they become avengers of the hundreds of thousands who have been tortured and starved before them.

38 • Carey McWilliams: *Farm Workers and "Dirt Farmers" Need Power*

Because the AAA helped mainly the independent commercial farmer, an insistent demand developed for attention to the farm laborer, the sharecropper, the migrant. In 1935, the Resettlement Administration was set up under Rexford Guy Tugwell to grant loans to distressed farmers, helping them move to better land. Two years later, this was replaced by the Farm Security Administration, which embarked on a series of programs designed to help the poor farmer. The FSA loaned money to farmers who wanted to improve their techniques, made loans also to tenants who wanted to buy family-size farms of their own, operated camps to house and care for migratory workers, and established several experimental cooperative farming communities. With all this, however, its scale of operations was far too small to do more than attack the edge of the huge problem of rural poverty. In addition, it incurred the hostility of the American Farm Bureau Federation, came under powerful attack in 1941, and gradually expired for lack of money and support. Carey McWilliams (1905-   ), Commissioner of Immigration and Housing in California, social critic, and writer (now, editor of *The Nation*), had reported in *Factories in the Field* (1939) on the

From Carey McWilliams, *Ill Fares the Land* (Boston: Little, Brown and Company, 1942), pp. 352-390. Reprinted with the permission of the author.

plight of the farm laborer in California. In this selection, written in the early 1940's, he finds farm poverty prevalent, despite all the efforts of the New Deal, and argues that more than superficial remedies are needed.

. . . Less is known about farm laborers than is known about any important labor group in America. It has only been within the last few years that we have even begun to learn a little about where and how the farm worker lives. But today we do know that the problem of farm labor is not confined to a few commercial truck and fruit-growing areas; that it is nationwide in scope and that it has ramifications reaching into every aspect of our national economy. . . . It is important, therefore, to get a general notion of the size, composition, and status of the farm-labor group in America. . . .

Counting sharecroppers, there are about 1,500,000 farm-labor *households* in the United States. It has been estimated that there are 6,000,000 members of farm laborers' families. Wage workers, as such, constitute 26 per cent of the total working farm population. . . .

In July of 1935, 184,000 farms (those employing three or more laborers) were employing 1,156,000 hired workers, or about 43 per cent of the total number of hired workers. Only two fifths of the farms of the nation reported an expenditure for labor in 1929. Women and children make up a large percentage of the unpaid labor group. . . . No one knows the number of migratory agricultural workers. The FSA, in a release of May 11, 1940, estimates that there are at least 500,000 migratory workers in agriculture and that, when their families are counted, they number in excess of 1,500,000 people. There is every reason to believe that this estimate is conservative.

If regular hired hands are excepted, this group today is the most thoroughly underprivileged group in American life. We know that about 50 per cent of all agricultural labor is seasonally employed; that agricultural labor has few, if any, opportunities to accept other types of employment; that it has little nonagricultural income; and that, even in 1929, farm workers "earned far too little to meet the costs of any accepted American standard of living." According to a survey in ten counties in eight states in different sections of the country, the average annual earnings of farm laborers ranged between $125 and $347 for the crop year 1935-1936. We know that in the Southern states the net cash earnings of hired workers, whether sharecroppers or wage hands, only occasionally exceed $100 per worker per year, and that even when goods for home use and perquisites are added the total net income per workers seldom exceeds $150. . . . We know, as Carl C. Taylor has said, that many farm laborers "cannot, or do not, even send their children to school. They do not know the stability and security of being a real, integral part of a community, and therefore enjoy almost no social participation of any kind. They are a socially isolated, sometimes shifting, sometimes stagnant group, without anchor, without keel, and without direction." Many of them are homeless, jobless, and voteless. They live in the worst housing in America. Of the million and a half houses occupied by sharecroppers and farm laborers, reports Mr. Hamilton, "the great majority are below the standard of health and decency." We know that, as Mr. Hamilton also points out, "unlike the poor man in the city, the farm laborer who lives in an isolated rural area does not have easy access to such institutions and services as hospitals, schools, libraries, doctors, and organized welfare services." He finds it, therefore, difficult to help himself. We know that few farm laborers own subsistence livestock, such as cows, pigs, or chickens; and that few of them have a chance to grow garden produce. Yet many of them work in the most productive farming areas in America. We know, also, "that the prospect of eventual land ownership is scarcely within the realm of possibility" for the vast majority of these workers. And this is the worst phase of the entire problem, for, as Carlyle once said, "It is not to die or even to die of hunger that makes a man wretched. Many men have died. But it is to live miserably and know not why, to work more and yet gain nothing, to be heartworn, weary, yet isolated and unrelated."

The agricultural worker is a pariah, a social outcast. He not only lacks the protection of social legislation, but in the matter of public assistance, of social services, of institutional aid, of vocational guidance, he is either ignored or discriminated against. He goes round and round, like a dog chasing its tail, unable to break through the set of vicious circumstances to which he has been born. He is in the most bottomless rut imaginable. And once a system of this kind has been set up, it is extremely difficult to change. Speaking at a conference of agricultural workers in March 1936, Mr. Henry Wallace said: "The situation with regard to agricultural labor is the most baffling in our whole economic structure. It is a no-man's land —I feel the situation is a little bit loaded with dynamite." . . .

The first thing to do, therefore, to aid this group is to remove the disabilities under which they now suffer. While some qualifications might be noted for absolute accuracy, nevertheless it can be said generally that agricultural labor has no legislative protection at present in this country. Farm workers are "exempt" from our entire scheme of social legislation, state and federal. Historically several reasons were urged to establish the precedent for exempting agriculture from social legislation. It was said that agricultural labor did not need this protection; that the industrial revolution had not arrived in agriculture; that farmers were subject to special hazards, such as weather conditions, which made them a legitimate object of legislative favoritism. But the "real reasons for the exemption of farm laborers," as Professor Willard C. Fisher pointed out in 1917, "are political, nothing else. Farm laborers are not organized into unions, nor have they other means of bringing their wishes to the attention of legislators." Most of our social legislation, in fact, has been enacted as the result of a political "deal" between organized labor and the farm groups. The basis of this deal has always been: we, the farm representatives, will not object to this legislation, if you, the representatives of organized labor, will agree to exempt agricultural employees. . . .

To improve the status of farm labor we should proceed immediately to eliminate the exemption of agricultural labor wherever that exemption appears in our social legislation, state and federal. This means bringing agricultural labor within the protection of the National Labor Relations Act; of State Labor Relations Acts; of Workmen's Compensation Laws; of the wage-and-hours legislation; of the Social Security Act. Wherever the phrase "agricultural labor is exempt" appears, it should be removed. . . .

It is all very well to point out what is desirable in order to deal with the problem of rural migration. But one of the major causes of the present problem consists in the fact that farm-labor and farm-migrant groups are not adequately represented, either functionally or politically, in our scheme of things. "Economic half-castes," these millions of American citizens are faced with many political handicaps: the poll tax; isolation; mobility. Because they are not represented, our legislation tends to become lopsided and undemocratic. California presents a typical illustration of this point. Farm laborers constitute perhaps 53 per cent of the total farm population of the state. Yet a small group of farmers, so called, constituting not more than 3 per cent of the entire farm population, dominate agricultural legislation in California. They are able to force through the legislature almost any type of legislation they desire; they can obtain, from the Department of Agriculture in the state government and also from the Department of Agriculture in Washington, and from the University of California, almost any free service that they desire. In manifold ways, their operations are heavily subsidized, by both state and federal government. But farm laborers, because they are not organized, can obtain no legislative consideration. Nor can migrant farm families.

In large measure this situation can be explained by the fact that farmers themselves are not effectively organized. The Grange and the Farmers' Union do, for the most part, really represent farmers. But the powerful American Farm Bureau might fairly be characterized as a "company union" of farmers. The initial funds for the formation of the Farm Bureau came from the Lackawanna Railroad, the Chicago Board of Trade, and similar organizations. The Farm Bureau was created, in fact, for the express purpose of keeping down farm unrest. The officials of the organization have, on many occasions, sold the elaborate propaganda apparatus of the Farm Bureau to various special-interest groups. It is a common experience nowadays to see "farm" organizations rush to Washington to defend the chain stores; to defend the sugar-beet refiners; to lobby for the most outrageous special-interest legislation. The fact is that most farm organizations, as Mr. Tugwell has pointed out, "represent those farmers who would be least likely to recognize any common interest with workers." In actual fact, the real dirt farmer has a "more serious quarrel with his banker, his furnish-merchant, and his seed, feed, and fertilizer dealers than he has with his workers." Because of the character of the major farm organizations, a large part of our agricultural legislation is thoroughly undemocratic in the sense that it is intended to benefit merely the top tier of farmers.

Today, as the gulf widens between the "upper half" (it should be called the upper 10 per cent of farmers) and the "lower half," a farmer-labor alliance becomes politically feasible. Farm workers cannot be effectively organized unless "dirt farmers" are also organized. Together they would represent a powerful social group and, fundamentally, their basic economic interests are identical. Whatever the small farmer can do to improve the position of farm labor redounds to his own advantage. If farm labor were brought within the scope of our existing social legislation, it could be organized; and this same extension, insofar as it affects the right of self-organization, should be granted the small farmer. The court records in California are full of cases clearly indicating how small farmers have been victimized and discriminated against when they attempted to organize for the protection of their own interests. Once farm labor and the small farmers were organized effectively, they would soon be given the ear of Congress, and the democratic process would have a chance to function in American agriculture.

The close correlation between the index of industrial production and the price of farm commodities now makes possible a still broader alliance: between the "under half" of American agriculture and organized labor. Such an alliance would represent the most powerful democratic force conceivable in our society. . . .

No amount of "expert testimony" before Congressional committees can possibly result in remedial legislative action on the problem of agricultural migration, unless effective political power can be mobilized in support of the various proposals made. For what has happened, essentially, to American agriculture is that it has become tied to the "chariot of industrial dominion." Before the basic causes can be dealt with effectively, this "industrial dominion" must itself be subjected to democratic processes; it must become democratized. Every proposal made before the La Follette and the Tolan Committees could be enacted tomorrow and the problem of agricultural migration would not be "solved." Some of the more urgent pressures making for migration would be relieved; the immediate welfare of thousands of farm families would be improved. But until this colossus of industrial dominion, and the processes which created it and the relationships upon which it is predicated, are brought under adequate social controls, then the basic causes of dislocation in American agriculture will not have been corrected. In many respects, therefore, the problem is essentially political in character. . . .

For the problem of agricultural migration is merely part of

the total industrial problem in the United States. The migrants are "messengers": they are visible evidence of breakdown, of maladjustment. . . . There will be no peace for these people, no security in their lives, until our entire industrial system is thoroughly democratized and made to serve the interests of the people themselves.

There was a time in American history when people did have an organic relation to the land upon which they lived, and worked, and built their homes. They were as much a part of that land, of that landscape, as the trees and rocks, the streams and the grass. It was the most beautiful land, the most varied land, the richest land in the world. It stretched westward in seeming inexhaustibility. There were always more free land, additional frontiers, greener pastures. Even after the passing of the frontier was mournfully noted in our chronicles, there remained still more land: new frontiers reclaimed from the desert, new agricultural empires created by drainage and reclamation projects. The frontier experience so profoundly affected American thought that people still imagine there is a home for them somewhere else; that, in some distant land, they can once again recapture that heritage of peace, of security, of useful, honest, and productive work which once was theirs. Thousands of American farm families have set out to find that treasured land where, under new skies, they might once more become "giants of the earth," rooted deeply to the soil. But something has happened, not to the people, but to the relationship that once obtained between them and the land. It is as though the soil itself had become poisoned. And the thousands who are on the road today are but the precursors of those who will set out on the highways tomorrow. . . .

. . . There is nothing to be gained technically, nor, in the long run, socially, by attempting to break up large holdings and to return to a concept of farming which prevailed a century ago. But the burdens of this transition should not be borne exclusively by the group in agriculture least capable of sustaining any additional burden—the lower half, the emerging agricultural proletariat. Industrialized agriculture, like industry generally, should be made to assume a measure of social responsibility for the well-being of those whom it employs. Today industrialized agriculture not only escapes that responsibility, but is actually subsidized in manifold ways. If the subsidies are to continue, they should be conditioned, in each instance, upon the maintenance of decent labor standards and working conditions. This is the immediate objective—the obvious next step.

As to the future, it is rather idle to speculate at the moment about ideal patterns of rural social relationships or idyllic rural utopias. If such patterns were worked out and put into effect on an experimental basis, they would probably be destroyed, or perverted in their purpose, within a brief period of time. Likewise, to debate the merits of the various "types of farms"—industrial, commercial, subsistence—is also a rather idle form of speculation. We could establish large-scale co-operative farms within the existing framework of society, but they, too, would very likely wither up and die. To date the Farm Security Administration has established precisely four such farms in the United States. Important as these farms are, from an experimental point of view, it seems unlikely that they could be expanded rapidly enough to be of much practical value. There is, in fact, no "solution" of this problem (although its effects can and should be mitigated by means such as I have suggested) so long as we permit this "chariot of industrial dominion"—the whole complex of our industrial order—to be exploited by a small section of the population to the distinct disadvantage of the great masses of people in this country. Never, to paraphrase Winston Churchill, did so many owe so little to so few.

. . . The question is not whether we want the family-sized farm or the farm factory; it is not even a question of which is the more efficient. The question is: what kind of society do we want? For our economic order is a unity, with its own rules, its own logic, its own psychology. The rifts between the various groups in agriculture—the conflicts between country and town, industry and agriculture—are merely reflections of the unequal position which obtains between social classes engaged in production. Naturally any means calculated to improve the economic position of working farmers in relation to the groups who now exploit them are valuable instrumentalities and should be fully utilized. They may even result in a limited measure of success; they may grow into or become the nuclei of important units of co-operative effort. Too frequently we insist upon categorical affirmations limited in scope and application: one must be either for or against the family-sized farm; one must either advocate or oppose collectivization in agriculture. Actually this is not the issue. . . .

The basic fault that currently obtains in the relationships between the various groups engaged in agricultural production is that they are undemocratic. Some groups have far too much power—economic, social, and political—in relation to other groups and this discrepancy feeds upon itself and tends to grow greater. Until this power is broken, controlled, or counterbalanced in some manner, the basic cause of the present-day paradox of scarcity in the midst of abundance, of technical advance making for riches to one group and poverty to another, of expanding agricultural production and increasing rural retrogression, cannot be squarely met. For the inequality in the economic field is reflected in the political field. Legislation, even when ostensibly intended for the benefit of the disadvantaged groups in agriculture, usually ends up by benefiting the already successful commercial farmers. Some of the very means taken under our agricultural program to protect sharecroppers and tenants, as I have shown, only made matters worse for them, because those who were exploiting them merely changed the form of exploitation and actually used the legislation to further their own ends. They were able to do so because they still retain the economic controls. Until the masses of the people actually get possession of the reins of power, both economic and political, they will not be able to create a democratic non-exploitative economic order.

To deal with the basic causes of migration, we can no longer think in terms of rehabilitating a few thousand individual farm families, of makeshift work programs, of improvised welfare projects, of social legislation to protect farm workers (valuable as these proposals are to attain immediate objectives). These measures will not, and cannot, suffice. We must think in bolder terms; we must plan on a much larger scale. The general direction which our thinking and planning should take is clearly indicated. Democracy is not only a means but it is the goal toward the attainment of which our efforts should be directed. The findings of the La Follette Committee, of the Tolan Committee, of the Temporary National Economic Committee, all point to the conclusion that our industrial and economic order in all its phases—industrial, agricultural, and financial—is not democratic. It is neither owned nor administered nor directed democratically. It functions in an autocratic manner. It is at variance with our social and political ideals. Its prime objective seems to be the concentration of wealth and power in the hands of a constantly decreasing number of individuals. It breeds poverty and want, scarcity and insecurity, not by accident, but by necessity. It can no more eliminate unemployment, short of the emergency created by war (and then only temporarily), than an engine can run without fuel. We need to refashion this economic order to a more democratic pattern by democratic means and for democratic objectives. If we fail to do so the shadows are likely to lengthen across the land.

PART EIGHT

MINIMUM SECURITY

39 • Hugo Black: *For a Thirty-Hour Work Week*

Hugo L. Black (1886-), named to the Supreme Court by FDR in 1937, was a Senator from Alabama in 1932. Shortly after Roosevelt's victory in November, he introduced a bill to set a limit of thirty hours work a week in plants producing articles for interstate commerce. Such a move, he felt, would create millions of jobs by spreading employment more widely over the population. The Black bill passed the Senate but Roosevelt was cool to it, and it never got farther than that. However, it did prod FDR into action to find another recovery measure; the result was the drafting of the National Recovery Act in the spring of 1933. Section 7A of that Act stipulated that the codes to be adopted in various industries should contain minimum-wage and maximum-hour provisions. The voiding of the NRA by the Supreme Court in 1935 left the nation without any minimum-wage provisions, and it was not until 1938 that such legislation was passed. Black's argument for his proposal, made on the floor of the Senate, was inspired by the urgency of the unemployment situation in early 1933. But it also reflected a general sentiment among many American progressives for federal guarantees of minimum security to the economically underprivileged.

From the *Congressional Record,* April 3, 1933, pp. 1115, 1127.

I call attention . . . to the fact that this bill, and our right to pass this bill, rest squarely upon section 8, article I of the Constitution, which, insofar as it is pertinent, reads as follows:

> The Congress shall have power * * * to regulate commerce with foreign nations, and among the several States.

It is not out of place . . . to call attention to the fact that recent years have developed a judicial tendency to emphasize human relationships and social necessities in the application of legal principles. Many people have looked upon this gradual evolution of the judicial mind as indicating an awakened consciousness to the wants and needs of human beings in a highly complex commercial civilization. Legalistic formulas invented in past centuries to fit past conditions and theories have in recent years been exposed to public and judicial criticism as a people faced by new problems and modern dangers seek a way to release themselves from human inequalities produced and fostered by a reverence for these antiquated formulas.

Even the great Supreme Court of this Nation has written judicial interpretations of the Constitution, persuaded by briefs containing a few pages of legal principles and hundreds of pages of facts compiled from an examination of social statistics relating to health, morals, and human happiness. Without sacrificing any of those principles of honesty and good faith that have since the foundation of this Government protected the right of ownership of property honestly acquired and fairly used, the tendency of today is to give a new and exalted emphasis to the more sacred right of human beings to enjoy health, happiness, and security justly theirs in proportion to their industry, frugality, energy, and honesty. My reference is to the growing hostility to permitting a blind and extravagant worship of property rights to smother, submerge, and take away fundamental and inherent human rights.

In our system of checks and balances each right and privilege has its place. In the very infancy of this Government, however, a great southerner said that "the spirit of commerce is the spirit of greed." While this indictment cannot stand against all individuals engaged in commerce, it is unfortunately too true with reference to many. I attribute the modern emphasis upon social rights, now frequently and happily reflected in our judicial decisions, as an effort to curb this spirit of avarice, and preserve for our people the beneficent advantages that a fair trade and commerce can afford a nation. . . .

. . . Now, at this very time, with more than 12,000,000 people helpless and hopeless in the grip of unemployment, starvation, hunger, misery, and want, we find people in every State of this Nation, men and women, sitting there with the constant whir of machinery dinning into their ears, working from 10 to 16 hours a day in order to earn a mere pittance to keep themselves from starving to death.

Do you tell me that this problem is not national? Do you tell me that the time has not come for bold and courageous action if we are to meet it?

"Oh," they say, "you will breed idleness." No; we do not breed idleness. Throughout all the years the excuse for machinery has been that it would relieve human beings from the drudgery and slavery of long hours of constant toil. That relief has been promised them since the advent of the machine. The time has come now when with the use of machinery and efficiency we can produce with a 30-hour week more than we can sell at home and abroad.

What do we find? We find that instead of the advantages of improved machinery going to consumers and the men who work, it has gone to increase the tolls of those who own the plants; and they have built them and overbuilt them until they find themselves crucified on their cross of greed and unable to sell their product because they have robbed the laborer of the ability to purchase.

Mr. President, they tell us that this proposal will breed idleness. Well, what is the difference? Are not 12,000,000 wholly idle today? Are they not idle without hope? Do they not have despair in their hearts and fear that those whom they love will not be able to live because of the lack of food? Have we not taken away from them the security that comes from honest work and honest toil and an honest job? And are we not at the same time destroying our unemployed people by permitting others to work long hours and depriving them of the legitimate opportunities of leisure which should be theirs?

I do not subscribe to this doctrine, this propaganda which has been industriously circulated mainly by the writings of people who were never compelled to listen to the whir of machinery 12 or 13 hours a day, who never went down into the recesses of the earth to dig coal, but who have talked about the "exaltation" of constant, laborious drudgery. I have never heard, in that beautiful story that appears in Holy Writ, that anybody was excluded from the Garden of Eden because of the fact that work was a blessing and not a curse.

I welcome the coming of earned leisure to people when I think of the minds dwarfed by constant toil, when I think of the intellects that perhaps might have soared to great heights in the thought and genius of this Nation that have been deprived of their opportunity by reason of the fact that they must sit and listen to the grinding whir of machinery hour after hour until their energy is sapped, their life practically is taken, and the very blood is drained from their faces. I think, what may we have lost in some of those people?

I think of that man who strolled around in a little country churchyard in England. He could have strolled in a million more all over this Nation where machinery has taken its toll of life; and he could have said, in each one:

> Some mute inglorious Milton here may rest,
> Some Cromwell guiltless of his country's blood.

I do not anticipate leisure with any apprehension or any horror. I welcome it. I am glad that the day has come when, in our land that we love, we can, if we are bold enough and courageous enough, give to the men who toil that which is theirs—the benefit of that leisure which comes from machinery and efficiency. Where should it go? Where is it going today? It is not going to the 12,000,000 men who are unemployed. It is not even going to the people who are working 16 hours a day. No, Mr. President; the avarice and greed of commerce has seen to that. Now that their spokesmen see the time coming when there is an enlightened public sentiment all over this land, manifested in the Senate, manifested in the House, manifested in the White House, manifested in the Supreme Court—when they see that the time is ripe for recognizing the fact that people, human beings, are the things that need to be protected in this country—no wonder they come forward at this late hour and say, "If you will just let us alone, we will reduce the hours of labor."

Mr. President, I am not willing to depend upon them now. They come too late. Quick action is imperative. I introduced this bill in the belief that, if passed, it will mark a milestone in the way of human progress. I believe it will immediately put millions to work. I hope that it may be passed, and may establish throughout this country a normal working day of 6 hours. If we can produce what we need in that time, why work any more? Do people love laborious work so much? Those who have written about the great glories of tiring and wearisome labor have usually done so from a safe place occupied by them where they knew they would never be dependent upon their hands to earn their daily bread.

Mr. President, I speak here today for the 12,000,000 who have lost their jobs. I speak for 25,000,000 more who have partially lost their jobs. I speak for the whole 48,000,000 who are walking the streets today not knowing whether they will have a job tomorrow or not. I speak for the unorganized millions who must support the unemployed with billions of taxes. And then you tell me that Congress, which has the right to regulate interstate commerce, has no power to say that these poisoned goods shall not infest the currents and streams of interstate commerce, destroying the commerce itself, sapping the lifeblood of the individuals and the Nation! You tell me that Congress is here with hands held out impotently, saying, "We would like to do this, but the Constitution is in the way"!

That Constitution was never written to be an obstacle to human progress. It has never been so held. It is expansive; it is elastic to meet conditions as they are. I do not believe that that great document, which was written in order to protect human liberty and human government, can be safely interposed in order to block this great forward movement upon which America is bound to embark.

My friends, in conclusion let me say this:

I do not know what your action will be with reference to this bill; but mark my words: All over this Nation the people are watching Congress, and the people know that they have not been getting a square deal. Up in that little town in New Jersey that was testified about, where 40 per cent of the people are working, some of them 16 hours per day, as these jobless people see the overwork forced upon the others we cannot take out of their minds the fact that there is something wrong. We cannot sit here and continue to pour out the money and credit of the United States to sustain failing business enterprises and at the same time ignore the men and women upon whom the safety of this Republic depends. When enough of them are out of jobs, and when enough of them lose hope, when they see legislation fail to pass that they knew would relieve conditions, do not be deceived. The people are the same in every age and in every country—patient, long-suffering, kind, you may say—but the kindness is taken out of the human heart when its owner sees the factory working 12, 13, 14, 15, 16 hours a day, with underpaid labor, as the unemployed hold out their hands in distress in order to get the very necessities of life for themselves and their children.

I present this bill as a real step forward on the part of the people of this country. It is not a complete remedy for existing conditions. We shall have to go farther, and we might just as well recognize the fact. . . .

40 · Stuart Chase: *The Consumer Must be Permitted to Consume*

Stuart Chase represents that group of New Deal thinkers who wanted to use the crisis of the 1930's to effect permanent structural changes in the American economy. In the many books and articles that he wrote in the 1930's, Chase stressed that the nation was in a new era, with abundance on the one hand and waste on the other. The imperative need, he said, was for a rational and just distribution of goods to consumers. (See Document 4.)

"In the last resort," said Thorstein Veblen, "the economic moralities wait on the economic necessities." No single one of the economic moralities is held in more tender regard among Western peoples than that carried in the phrase: "In the sweat of thy brow shalt thou eat thy bread." To secure useful goods, one must give useful labor. This is, to date, axiomatic. Useful labor, moreover, has taken on a moral dignity, almost a divinity, which would have shocked Plato or Pericles, who held common labor to be menial and degrading.

It is true that the modern rule has one important exception. It is not applicable to that 2 per cent or so of the population which Veblen has characterized as the kept classes. Those who live by virtue of the absentee ownership of profitable invest-

From Stuart Chase, "Eating without Working: A Moral Disquisition," *The Nation*, CXXXVII, (July 26, 1933), 93-94. Reprinted with the permission of the publisher.

ment, whether in lands, buildings, royalties, or stocks and bonds, are totally exempt from its compulsions. It is manifest that in so far as they live on the usufruct of their portfolios they eat without working. Fortunately the classical economists have been at some pains to rationalize this breach of a great moral principle. It appears that the kept classes consume without producing *now*, because *in the past* they have produced without consuming. They are justly entitled to a "reward for abstinence." This would be news to many young people and ladies in exclusive finishing schools; it would be news to every fortunate gambler in real estate and stocks; news to all the recipients of engraved certificates of esteem from the house of Morgan; it would be news to Mr. Charlie Mitchell and the million-dollar bonus boys—corporate, not khaki—but so the classic apologia goes. And certainly no group in the community is more alert to the moral virtue of diligence, application, and industry, on the part of others, than the kept classes. "Satan finds some mischief still for idle hands to do." Even child labor is defended on the grounds that it keeps children out of mischief. Indeed a perspicacious psychologist might amuse himself with the theory that lack of useful work in a given group is compensated by their profound regard for the necessity of useful work at other points in the social structure.

The economic morality of work stands, then, for 98 per cent, more or less, of the population, charmingly and persuasively encouraged by the remaining 2 per cent. Impinging upon this principle, however, comes a thoroughly unmoral economic reality. Its pressure is already immense, and day by day grows stronger. Raw natural energy, harnessed in a prime mover and yoked in an operating machine, is destroying human work. The curve of technical invention is cumulative and tends to grow, according to Dr. William F. Ogburn, at a geometrical rate. It is perhaps the strongest economic force in the modern world; nor can it be stopped short of scrapping what is known as Western civilization, and retreating to the handicraft of the Middle Ages.

The economic reality of the automatic process and quantity production has a steadily declining use for human labor, particularly manual labor. What it does demand is efficient consumption of its fabulous output. Unless its serialized machines and processes are run at approximate capacity on the "balanced load" principle, it cannot properly function—as in the present depression. It demands efficient functioning at the cost of wrecking the whole economic structure. To function it must have millions and millions of the sturdiest sort of consumers; consumers with admirable digestive tracts and great powers for depreciating personal equipment. Slowly, under this imperative, consumption is becoming, as a matter of economic reality, more important than work; purchasing power more important than man hours.

Slowly, reluctantly, even kicking and screaming, industrial nations are being driven to the hitherto abhorrent notion that the consumer must be furnished with purchasing power whether he works or not. Two years ago in this republic the word "dole" carried rather more opprobrium than the word "racketeer." Yet the dole marches on, five hundred millions of it in the last Congress.

It is touching to watch the tortures of the moralists caught on the horns of this dilemma; one school of them seriously proposes that the output, rather than be allowed to fall into the hands of the consumer, should be destroyed. A billion pounds of coffee, millions of bushels of wheat, thousands of bales of cotton, uncounted gallons of milk have recently been subjected to holocaust and destruction, thus preserving the economic morality of the wayfaring citizen. He has not worked, so he must be prevented from consuming. This censorship, however, like another recent noble experiment in prohibiting consumption, has not served economic realities, however much it may have served the cause of beautiful morals. The jam in the industrial mechanism is not relieved by even such monumental measures of deliberate waste.

The consumer must be permitted to consume. There is no

other final outcome to the pressure of the technical arts. The 98 per cent must absorb, with or without working, even as the 2 per cent have done hitherto. That this will reduce the relative advantages of conspicuous consumption on the part of the 2 per cent is regrettable, perhaps, but inevitable.

A few business men and a few college professors saw the handwriting on the wall as early as 1922. Mr. Henry Ford saw it even earlier. They began the now familiar talk about the "economy of high wages," furnishing the worker with power to buy back what, with his declining assistance, the machine process could make. This movement never progressed much beyond talk, but it was the thin entering wedge.

From a broader point of view, of course, the consumer is not without moral claims of his own. The output of modern industry rests on five fundamental factors: (1) Natural resources available; (2) skilled and unskilled labor (a declining factor but still very important); (3) technical management (an increasingly important factor); (4) non-human forms of energy (from coal, oil, water power); (5) the cultural heritage of the technical arts.

If the consumer can find a job to aid production in factor 2, well and good; that gives him a direct if modest claim on the output, as has long been recognized. But increasingly he will be denied a job as technological unemployment gains. Either that, or the work demanded of him will be startlingly reduced by a shorter working week. In either case, toil will decline, and with it those claims founded on useful work.

Technical management has a sound and growing claim on the output; but as there are probably not more than 200,000 families headed by active technicians in the United States, this is far too small a group to be of any appreciable help in carrying off the product. There are 30,000,000 families in the country.

The other three factors—natural resources, energy, and the technical arts—are, or should be, the common inheritance of the whole community, which is the same as saying the common inheritance of the consumer. His common property provides the factors which are most important in the whole productive mechanism. He has, accordingly, from this broader point of view, a reasonably good moral right to the usufruct of his property. Now this may or may not be good moral doctrine; certainly economic realities are on the road to making it a practicable doctrine. To establish the right of the consumer to consume, will take time—it may, indeed, take a revolution or two. But if I read the march of history aright, it will not be gainsaid.

While history will undoubtedly solve this problem in her own brusque and hidden ways, it may not be out of place to speculate upon the methods which she may conceivably pursue. In the serried vanguard of the opposition which now blocks the free flow of consumption stand the private banking system and the debt structure. It is probable that both must be liquidated to a percentum of their present grandeur, a percentum which it would be rash to estimate, save for the reservation that it will be extremely small.

The creation of money, the allotment of purchasing power, is a social function of the first importance and should be restored to the federal government, in whose hands the Constitution placed it. It is forever impossible for the private banker, working for private gain, adequately to finance the consumer. It wounds his moral sensibilities, for one thing. By reducing his time-honored toll and that of his stockholders, it would condemn itself to him as "unsound." If recent history does not demonstrate the incompatibility of private banking and effective consumption, mathematics can prove it readily. The consumer, therefore, cannot adequately consume until the private banker, as the chief executor of the nation's credit, is lifted gently but firmly out of the picture. It is unfortunate that Mr. Roosevelt did not seize the unparalleled opportunity to lift him out, to the applause of a grateful nation, on March 4 last.

The liquidation of the debt structure promises to be an even more drastic and shocking business. History may handle this problem by inflation, by devaluation of the dollar, by deliberate scaling down, by a hit or miss tumbling down, after the fashion of the walls of Jericho. It is to be noted, however, that the walls of Jericho were solid stone and mortar, not notes and paper.

As for the methods whereby the consumer will ultimately be financed, history has a wide choice. She may select minimum subsistence payments per capita or per family; she may choose consumers' dividends, or a straight rationing of prime necessities, or an enormously shortened work week with undiminished wages—thus keeping all able-bodied consumers nominally employed; or a guaranteed job, more or less of a nominal character, in the public-works division; or a combination of these methods.

Somehow, somewhere—but in the not too distant future—mass consumption must move up to the technical requirements of mass production, at the cost of whatever moralities and financial dream castles lie in the way. No realist will even consider retreating to the economy of the Middle Ages. Yet this retreat, painful and disorderly as it would be, is the sole alternative to deliberate and purposeful mass consumption. All men cannot at present work. All men must eat.

41 · Frances Perkins: *The Principles of Social Security*

Frances Perkins (1882-1965), Roosevelt's Secretary of Labor, was the first woman cabinet member in American history. She had been a social worker at Hull House in Chicago and came to Washington

From Frances Perkins, "The Social Security Act," a radio address delivered September 2, 1935, reprinted in *Vital Speeches of the Day*, I (1934-1935), 792-794.

with a strong belief in federal action to alleviate distress. In June 1934, President Roosevelt asked her to head a cabinet Committee on Economic Security. The relief programs of the New Deal's first years could take care of only three million of the more than ten million unemployed, and there was a growing demand that the United States follow the lead of those countries in Western Europe that had adopted systems of old-age and unemployment insurance. In addition, the movement among the aged led by Dr. Francis Townsend in 1933 and 1934 was exerting strong pressure for a pension to give $200-a-month financed by a sales tax for all persons over 60. The plan finally proposed by Secretary Perkins' committee was introduced in the Senate by Robert F. Wagner, the immigrant son of a German janitor, and in the House by David Lewis of Maryland, a former miner. In August 1935 the Social Security Act was passed, and several weeks later, Francis Perkins outlined its principles in the radio address reprinted below.

People who work for a living in the United States of America can join with all other good citizens on this forty-eighth anniversary of Labor Day in satisfaction that the Congress has passed the Social Security Act. This act establishes unemployment insurance as a substitute for haphazard methods of assistance in periods when men and women willing and able to work are without jobs. It provides for old-age pensions which mark great progress over the measures upon which we have hitherto depended in caring for those who have been unable to provide for the years when they no longer can work. It also provides security for dependent and crippled children, mothers, the indigent disabled and the blind.

Old people who are in need, unemployables, children, mothers and the sightless, will find systematic regular provisions for needs. The Act limits the Federal aid to not more than $15 per month for the individual, provided the State in which he resides appropriates a like amount. There is nothing to prevent a State from contributing more than $15 per month in special cases and there is no requirement to allow as much as $15 from either State or Federal funds when a particular case has some personal provision and needs less than the total allowed.

Following essentially the same procedure, the Act as passed provides for Federal assistance to the States in caring for the blind, a contribution by the State of up to $15 a month to be matched in turn by a like contribution by the Federal Government. The Act also contains provision for assistance to the States in providing payments to dependent children under sixteen years of age. There also is provision in the Act for cooperation with medical and health organizations charged with rehabilitation of physically handicapped children. The necessity for adequate service in the fields of public and maternal health and child welfare calls for the extension of these services to meet individual community needs.

Consider for a moment those portions of the Act which, while they will not be effective this present year, yet will exert a profound and far-reaching effect upon millions of citizens. I refer to the provision for a system of old-age benefits supported by the contributions of employer and employees, and to the section which sets up the initial machinery for unemployment insurance.

Old-age benefits in the form of monthly payments are to be paid to individuals who have worked and contributed to the insurance fund in direct proportion to the total wages earned by such individuals in the course of their employment subsequent to 1936. The minimum monthly payment is to be $10, the maximum $85. These payments will begin in the year 1942 and will be to those who have worked and contributed.

Because of difficulty of administration not all employments are covered in this plan at this time so that the law is not entirely complete in coverage, but it is sufficiently broad to cover all normally employed industrial workers. . . .

This vast system of old-age benefits requires contributions

both by employer and employee, each to contribute 3% of the total wage paid to the employee. This tax, collected by the Bureau of Internal Revenue, will be graduated, ranging from 1% in 1937 to the maximum 3% in 1939 and thereafter. That is, on this man's average income of $100 a month he will pay to the usual fund $3 a month and his employer will also pay the same amount over his working years.

In conjunction with the system of old-age benefits, the Act recognizes that unemployment insurance is an integral part of any plan for the economic security of millions of gainfully employed workers. It provides for a plan of cooperative Federal-State action by which a State may enact an insurance system, compatible with Federal requirements and best suited to its individual needs.

The Federal Government attempts to promote and effectuate these State systems, by levying a uniform Federal pay-roll tax of 3% on employers employing eight or more workers, with the proviso that an employer who contributes to a State unemployment compensation system will receive a credit of 90% of this Federal tax. After 1937, additional credit is also allowable to any employer who, because of favorable employment experience or adequate reserves, is permitted by the State to reduce his payments.

In addition, the Act provides that after the current fiscal year the Federal Government allocate annually to the States $49,000,000 solely for the administration of their respective insurance systems, thus assuring that all money paid for State unemployment compensation will be reserved for the purpose of compensation to the worker. It has been necessary, at the present time, to eliminate essentially the same groups from participation under the unemployment insurance plan as in the old-age benefit plan, though it is possible that at some future time a more complete coverage will be formulated.

The State of New York, at the present time, has a system of unemployment compensation which might well illustrate the salient factors desired in such a plan; in the event of unemployment, the worker is paid 50% of his wages weekly for a period not exceeding 16 weeks in any 52 weeks. This payment begins within three weeks after the advent of actual unemployment. California, Washington, Utah and New Hampshire have passed unemployment insurance laws in recent months and Wisconsin's law is already in effect. Thirty-five States have old-age pension statutes and mothers' pension acts are in force in all but three States.

With the States rests now the responsibility of devising and enacting measures which will result in the maximum benefits to the American workman in the field of unemployment compensation. I am confident that impending State action will not fail to take cognizance of this responsibility. The people of the different States favor the program designed to bring them security in the future and their legislatures will speedily pass appropriate laws so that all may help to promote the general welfare.

Federal legislation was framed in the thought that the attack upon the problems of insecurity should be a cooperative venture participated in by both the Federal and State Governments, preserving the benefits of local administration and national leadership. It was thought unwise to have the Federal Government decide all questions of policy and dictate completely what the States should do. Only very necessary minimum standards are included in the Federal measure leaving wide latitude to the States.

While the different State laws on unemployment insurance must make all contributions compulsory, the States, in addition to deciding how these contributions shall be levied, have freedom in determining their own waiting periods, benefit rates, maximum benefit periods and the like. Care should be taken that these laws do not contain benefit provisions in excess of collections. While unemployment varies greatly in different States, there is no certainty that States which have had less normal unemployment heretofore will in the future have a more favorable experience than the average for the country.

It is obvious that in the best interests of the worker, industry and society, there must be a certain uniformity of standards. It is obvious, too, that we must prevent the penalizing of competitive industry in any State which plans the early adoption of a sound system of unemployment insurance, and provide effective guarantees against the possibility of industry in one State having an advantage over that of another. This the uniform Federal tax does, as it costs the employer the same whether he pays the levy to the Federal Government or makes a contribution to a State unemployment insurance fund. The amount of the tax itself is a relative assurance that benefits will be standardized in all States, since under the law the entire collection must be spent on benefits to unemployed.

The social security measure looks primarily to the future and is only a part of the administration's plan to promote sound and stable economic life. We cannot think of it as disassociated from the Government's program to save the homes, the farms, the businesses and banks of the Nation, and especially must we consider it a companion measure to the Works Relief Act which does undertake to provide immediate increase in employment and corresponding stimulation to private industry by purchase of supplies.

While it is not anticipated as a complete remedy for the abnormal conditions confronting us at the present time, it is designed to afford protection for the individual against future major economic vicissitudes. It is a sound and reasonable plan and framed with due regard for the present state of economic recovery. It does not represent a complete solution of the problems of economic security, but it does represent a substantial, necessary beginning. It has been developed after careful and intelligent consideration of all the facts and all of the programs that have been suggested or applied anywhere.

Few legislative proposals have had as careful study, as thorough and conscientious deliberation, as that which went into the preparation of the social security programs. It is embodied in perhaps the most useful and fundamental single piece of

Federal legislation in the interest of wage earners in the United States. As President Roosevelt said when he signed the measure: "If the Senate and House of Representatives in their long and arduous session had done nothing more than pass this bill, the session would be regarded as historic for all time."

This is truly legislation in the interest of the national welfare. We must recognize that if we are to maintain a healthy economy and thriving production, we need to maintain the standard of living of the lower income groups of our population who constitute ninety per cent of our purchasing power. The President's Committee on Economic Security, of which I had the honor to be chairman, in drawing up the plan, was convinced that its enactment into law would not only carry us a long way toward the goal of economic security for the individual, but also a long way toward the promotion and stabilization of mass purchasing power without which the present economic system cannot endure.

That this intimate connection between the maintenance of mass purchasing power through a system of protection of the individual against major economic hazards is not theoretical is evidenced by the fact that England has been able to withstand the effects of the world-wide depression, even though her prosperity depends so largely upon foreign trade. English economists agree with employers and workers that this ability to weather adverse conditions has been due in no small part to social insurance benefits and regular payments which have served to maintain necessary purchasing power.

Our social security program will be a vital force working against the recurrence of severe depressions in the future. We can, as the principle of sustained purchasing power in hard times makes itself felt in every shop, store and mill, grow old without being haunted by the spectre of a poverty-ridden old age or of being a burden on our children.

The costs of unemployment compensation and old-age insurance are not actually additional costs. In some degree they have long been borne by the people, but irregularly, the burden falling much more heavily on some than on others, and none of such provisions offering an orderly or systematic assurance to those in need. The years of depression have brought home to all of us that unemployment entails huge costs to government, industry and the public alike.

Unemployment insurance will within a short time considerably lighten the public burden of caring for those unemployed. It will materially reduce relief costs in future years. In essence, it is a method by which reserves are built up during periods of employment from which compensation is paid to the unemployed in periods when work is lacking.

The passage of this act with so few dissenting votes and with so much intelligent public support is deeply significant of the progress which the American people have made in thought in the social field and awareness of methods of using cooperation through government to overcome social hazards against which the individual alone is inadequate.

During the fifteen years I have been advocating such legislation as this I have learned that the American people want such security as the law provides. It will make this great Republic a better and a happier place in which to live—for us, our children and our children's children. . . .

42 • Henry Ellenbogen: *The Social Security Act is Only a Beginning*

Conservatives attacked the Social Security Act as a violation of what they called the traditional American spirit of self-help. Senator

From the *Congressional Record*, August 19, 1935, pp. 13675-13677.

A. Harry Moore of New Jersey said it would "take all the romance out of life." To many liberals, however, it was a poor compromise with conservative tradition, and did not go far enough. In this speech on the floor of the House of Representatives, Congressman Henry Ellenbogen of Pennsylvania (1900-) pointed to some of the flaws in the Social Security Act, although he welcomed it as a step forward.

What should the citizens of a country, who have contributed to that country's progress and growth, expect from it in return?

The answer to that question is the answer to the problem of social security. In the past it was a job in good times, the bread line in bad. The answer is changed now. We now say: You have a right to expect protection against the effects of bad times, as well as a job in good times. You have a right to live decently, to be brought into the world decently, to have safeguards set up for you against the destitution you may encounter if you lose your job or health, and when you reach old age.

These are the obligations which are rightfully the Government's, and which it finally has assumed. If only it had assumed them sooner! We might not have had to go through these 5 bitter years. If we had been sensible enough to realize that, good years or bad, the great mass of wage earners in this country have never received more than bare subsistence incomes, and could, under no circumstances, set aside anything more than a few pennies, if that, for the inevitable hard bumps of life.

In 1929, 5,899,000 or nearly 6,000,000 families, 21½ percent of the total number of families, had a yearly income from nothing up to a maximum of $1,000.

Eleven million six hundred and fifty-three thousand, or nearly 12,000,000 families, 42½ percent of the total number of families, had incomes of less than $1,500 per year.

Nineteen million five hundred and fifty-eight thousand, or nearly 20,000,000 families, 71 percent of all families in the United States, had incomes of less than $2,500 per year. And that was in the year 1929, the year of prosperity.

And now let us look at the number of families with large incomes.

Sixty-three thousand families, 0.230 percent of the total number of families, had incomes of more than $50,000.

Four thousand families, 0.015 percent of the number of families, had incomes of $500,000 and over per year.

Members of families with an income of less than $1,000 a year can, of course, save very little toward meeting the cost of unemployment, old age, sickness, or accidents.

In the year 1929, 10,500,000 families had an income of $1,000 to $2,000 a year. These on an average, saved the magnificent sum of $80 a year. These families and the millions of families with a still lower income are the builders of America. They have dug its ditches, paved its roads, operated its machines, constructed its buildings, and produced its abundant wealth. We repay a debt when we make a start toward giving them some measure of decency in living. We merely turn back to them a part of what they have given us.

It is no longer necessary to sell the idea of old-age pensions in this country. The idea has been sold, for which we can be truly thankful, for it was hard sledding at first.

In 1934 we had in the United States about 7,200,000 persons who were 65 years of age or older. Even if we base our calculations upon the relatively prosperous years of 1920 to 1929, and disregard for the moment the terrible need which the current depression has brought to the aged, we shall find that out of these 7,200,000 at least 2,400,000 were in need.

The depression increased the number of needy among the aged far beyond 2,400,000. . . .

However, old-age pensions, as provided for in the Social Security Act, are but the foundation for a real set-up of old-age security in America.

To my mind, these provisions of the act should be, and I hope in time will be, much more liberal and generous than they are now. . . .

In a country where the advances of the machine age burn people out at 50 and 55, the limit of 65 is far too high.

That age limit, among other things, is my criticism of the national act. Here is what the Government will do under the Social Security Act. The Government says to the State, "I'll match you; for every dollar you give for old-age pensions, I'll give a dollar. However, my maximum will be $15 a month; if you want to pay more than that, you can." I regret that under this arrangement the aged will receive $30 or less in most of the States. This is far too low to permit a decent standard of living for our old people. It is far too low to give them the security which they should have.

No State will receive any money from the Federal Government toward the payment of old-age pensions, unless the State has or will pass an old-age pension law, satisfactory to the Federal Social Security Board and which complies with the minimum standards fixed in the act of Congress. . . .

And finally, the 65-year limit in the Federal bill must go. It is entirely too high. After all, this is supposed to be a pension for old age, not a graveyard pension. Most people who are 60 years of age are old—the years ahead of them hold no prospect of jobs or gainful occupation. They have every right to live their last years in comfort, in economic peace and security.

Of course, there is nothing in the act to prevent States granting pensions to those under 65, but States simply will not do it, unless the Federal grant is extended to those under 65.

These are my objections. They show serious flaws in the

set-up. But it is better than what we had previously. We have started something, surely, and from these beginnings we go forward.

There has been some confusion, in connection with the Social Security Act, between old-age pensions and old-age insurance. The two have been used interchangeably, which is not correct.

Briefly, the difference lies in the fact that for old-age pensions the beneficiary does not pay; for old-age insurance he does. The Social Security Act makes appropriations to States for the payment of old-age pensions. But it does not stop there. It also sets up an old-age insurance system, which is designed to supersede the pension system, and which on January 1, 1942, will begin the payment of benefits to those 65 years of age or older.

This system will be administered directly by the Federal Government. The States will have no part in it. It will be purely a Federal matter. The funds for this insurance system, as distinguished from the pension system, will be raised by compelling employers and employees to make equal contributions to a common insurance fund.

There is one defect in this old-age insurance system as set up in the act of Congress, a vital, a fundamental defect. The Federal Government does not contribute to it.

The Federal Government, as in many European countries, should contribute one-third of the total fund.

Where will it get the money? I do not want to use this speech as a springboard for a dissertation on the maldistribution of wealth and income in this country, but I will venture to state that in a country where 87 percent of its wealth is owned by 4 percent of its population, inheritance and income taxes could well be increased for this purpose. . . .

An interesting, and perhaps disturbing fact, is that two large classes of wage earners will not benefit by this insurance. They are agricultural workers and domestics. It is deplorable that they often lose out when social and economic advances are made. All in all, almost 26,000,000 workers are expected to come under the bill's provisions.

The monthly benefits to be paid from the fund will vary from $10 to $85, depending both on the average monthly wage or salary formerly received by the aged and on the number of years when he was employed and contributed to the insurance fund.

The most important thing to keep in mind, in considering the unemployment "insurance" provisions of the new Social Security Act, is that there is no such thing as unemployment insurance. The term itself is a convenient misnomer for unemployment compensation—an income to be received during periods of idleness. Unemployment compensation is not intended and cannot insure employment. It does not prevent unemployment—as life insurance does not prevent death. The purpose of unemployment-compensation laws is to assure the employee a fixed proportion of his working income during a period of enforced idleness. . . .

Does the Social Security Act provide for unemployment compensation? It does not, at least not directly. In fact, this is the weakest part of the Social Security Act. It presents an unsatisfactory attempt to tackle one of our greatest economic problems.

The act does not establish direct unemployment compensation for the worker. It does this: It levies a tax on all employers of eight or more employees, the tax rising annually from 1 percent in 1937 to a maximum of 3 percent in 1939. Employers of about 26,000,000 employees are to be covered by the tax. There is the same deplorable exclusion of domestic and farm labor as prevails under the old-age insurance set-up. . . .

I believe the entire method of approach is fundamentally wrong. Unemployment insurance must be considered on a national, and not a State basis. Industry knows no State boundaries. Employees and industries move from State to State. Only a national system can provide adequate protection for the employees, as well as equal competitive conditions for employers. With 48 State laws we may have almost that many widely varying systems, just as we have wide divergence in the various State workmen's compensation laws.

That is the grave defect in the social-security bill, insofar as unemployment compensation is concerned. I pointed this out in hearings on the bill before the House Ways and Means Committee. At the very least, if we cannot at once have a national system, the social-security bill should have laid down certain definite minimum standards for the State system. This it has not done; there are few specific requirements as to what the State laws should contain. The States are given carte blanche, as it were, in writing their laws.

What should have been demanded of the States? First, minimum standards as to amounts of compensation. Second, the maximum waiting period, before benefits are paid should have been definitely fixed. Third, schedules of the minimum duration of benefit payments to idle employees should have been laid down. Fourth, the so-called "Wisconsin plan," which is in no sense of the word social insurance and provides little protection for the worker, should have been outlawed. Fifth, the most important, the bill should have definitely barred the States from forcing employees to contribute to unemployment compensation funds.

Without such standards, I do not see that we are going to get very far in setting up decent unemployment compensation systems.

Keen will be the disappointment of those who are now jobless. They are not included in the contemplated scheme for unemployment compensation, unless they first secure a substantial amount of private employment.

Under the program of the administration the jobless who can work, are to be taken off relief and to be employed on work-relief projects. Whether they will be, only the future can tell—I am very doubtful. The jobless will be the group most disappointed in the Social Security Act—and justly so.

One cannot conclude a discussion of the unemployment-compensation features of the Social Security Act without re-examining, if only briefly, its chief feature—the financing of unemployment compensation by a tax on pay rolls. This tax will largely be shifted upon the consumer in the form of higher prices. Therefore, this is in reality a tax upon consumption to be paid for by the broad masses of the people.

Frankly, I am very much disturbed at this method of setting up of an unemployment-compensation system. In the final analysis, the reason we must have unemployment compensation, old-age pensions, old-age insurance, and the like is because our national wealth and income have been so badly distributed. Very few people will deny this any longer.

But I fail to see where a more equitable distribution will be obtained by gigantic pay-roll taxes. The money will be taken from the worker, perhaps in lowered wages, more certainly in higher prices for what he buys. The latter condition will also apply to consumers generally.

Where, then, is the gain? We will be taking the buying money, the money that should be in circulation, out of it, pile it up in reserves, decrease purchasing power, and, in short, continue the old vicious cycle.

Higher taxes on inheritances, gifts, tremendously large incomes—from those sources and not from the pay roll and consumers' taxes, should come a large part of the money for the payment of social-security benefits. From huge fortunes should come at least a part of the money needed for the payment of these expenditures.

In addition to these three chief provisions—old-age pensions, old-age insurance, and unemployment compensation—the Social Security Act recognizes a number of other social problems, and makes some contribution toward alleviating them.

I like particularly the recognition of the child problem, especially during this depression period. Perhaps it is not generally known that, although children under 16 comprise only 28 percent of the population, of those on relief 40 percent are in this age group—9,000,000 children.

The act appropriates $24,750,000 for dependent children, children in families where the support of the father, through death or otherwise, has been lost.

Under the Federal act, the Government will pay one-third, the State one-third, and the county one-third.

For maternal and child health an appropriation of $3,800,000 is allotted. Particular attention is to be centered on maternity and infant welfare in rural and farm areas, and in localities where economic distress is especially severe. In this connection, it is distressing to know that the maternal-mortality rate in the United States is higher than that of almost any other progressive country.

Another appropriation of $2,850,000 is made for hospital and later care of crippled children. In this country there are between 350,000 and 400,000 crippled children, many of them victims of infantile paralysis, and if treatment is extended early enough, the condition of a larger number could be greatly improved.

The act allots $1,500,000 to enable the Children's Bureau of the Department of Labor to cooperate with State public-welfare agencies in establishing and extending help to the half million or more neglected and dependent children, and those who come before the juvenile courts. These are injured and harmed lives, and far greater sums could be expended to repair them and reestablish them in society.

Finally, the act makes greater provision, through an appropriation of $8,000,000 for more extended participation by the Government in public-health services. These services have unfortunately, been drastically curtailed during the depression—a period when they are most necessary. Out of more than

4,000 counties in the country, only 528 have full-time health officers.

Admitted, each of these appropriations is small—any one of them might well be increased tenfold. But likewise, they are all splendid stimulants to carry on and forward fields of work which have been sadly neglected and often ignored.

As you analyze the new Social Security Act and study its provisions and limitations, you are forcibly impressed with the fact that the Federal Government, itself, occupies a secondary role in the set-up. In the main, responsibility for immediate action rests on the States. The financial burden is largely placed upon the employers, the employees, and through increased prices on the consumer. The balance of the cost is divided between the States and the Federal Government. Important, however, is the fact that the Federal Government admits a responsibility in providing for the unemployed, the aged, the indigent, and the physically handicapped. . . .

This principle of State action and separate and distinct State laws will cause a great deal of difficulty. Particularly it is likely to prevent real unemployment insurance in many of the States. Our industries are built along national and not along State lines. Unemployment reserve systems should also be built along national and not along State lines. At least, the Federal act should have fixed minimum standards which every State law must observe.

I am not satisfied with the provisions of the Social Security Act. I am not satisfied with its provision for old-age pensions, for unemployment compensation, or for child welfare. But the principle which this act of Congress establishes, the decent, humane, and social philosophy upon which it is based, is far more important than its specific provisions. We now have the foundation; we can improve and enlarge from time to time the building which we construct upon that foundation.

To me, anything offered in this specific measure, and anything which will be added as time goes on are way stations on a long road we have to travel. Ahead of us lies a great ideal.

The idea will be security of the individual from birth to death. Maternity and infant care will look after him when he is born. Social security would in every sense protect the child—protect him from sickness and want, and make every possible effort to halt both sickness and want should they emerge. It would provide immediate hospitalization for crippled children, curing those who could be cured, and leading those who are physically handicapped into avenues of usefulness. Vocational training, the use of arts and crafts—these would be available.

Health insurance would protect individuals and families in periods of extended illness, and proper care would be forthcoming immediately in sickness, now so often neglected because of lack of financial resources.

And finally, there would be true protection against the hazards of unemployment, and the misery and uncertainty of insecure old age.

I will not conclude by saying that these are Utopian wishes. I believe that such a program is but the minimum for a decent and secure economic existence, and it would be tragic to contend that the wealthiest and most powerful Nation on earth cannot achieve it.

43 · Franklin D. Roosevelt: *A Fair Day's Pay for a Fair Day's Work*

The wage-hour provisions in the NRA codes had fallen when the Supreme Court declared in 1935 that the NRA was unconstitutional. In 1937, Senator Hugo Black introduced a federal wage-hour law,

From *The Public Papers of Roosevelt,* VI, 122-123.

based on the constitutional doctrine that the national government could regulate conditions in industries involved in interstate commerce. The message below was sent to Congress by FDR on May 24, 1937, and inaugurated what turned out to be a long struggle for wage-hour legislation. There was powerful opposition from Southerners, who saw it as an attempt to put Southern industry, which had very low wage scales, at a disadvantage. Conservative business interests in the North also opposed the bill. Neither the American Federation of Labor nor the Congress of Industrial Organizations gave the bill enthusiastic support. But in 1938, after a long, hard fight in both houses of Congress, the Fair Labor Standards Act passed. It was a weak bill, with only a 25 cent-an-hour minimum wage, which would rise to 40 cents after two years; and many categories of labor were exempted. But it did include a provision barring child labor in the production of goods for interstate commerce. Most of all, it was the beginning of an important new function of American government.

The time has arrived for us to take further action to extend the frontiers of social progress. Such further action initiated by the legislative branch of the government, administered by the executive, and sustained by the judicial, is within the common sense framework and purpose of our Constitution and receives beyond doubt the approval of our electorate.

The overwhelming majority of our population earns its daily bread either in agriculture or in industry. One third of our population, the overwhelming majority of which is in agriculture or industry, is ill-nourished, ill-clad and ill-housed.

The overwhelming majority of this Nation has little patience with that small minority which vociferates today that prosperity has returned, that wages are good, that crop prices are high, and that government should take a holiday. . . .

Today, you and I are pledged to take further steps to reduce the lag in the purchasing power of industrial workers and to strengthen and stabilize the markets for the farmers' products. The two go hand in hand. Each depends for its effectiveness upon the other. Both working simultaneously will open new outlets for productive capital. Our Nation so richly endowed with natural resources and with a capable and industrious population should be able to devise ways and means of insuring to all our able-bodied working men and women a fair day's pay for a fair day's work. A self-supporting and self-respecting democracy can plead no justification for the existence of child labor, no economic reason for chiseling workers' wages or stretching workers' hours.

Enlightened business is learning that competition ought not to cause bad social consequences which inevitably react upon the profits of business itself. All but the hopelessly reactionary will agree that to conserve our primary resources of man power, government must have some control over maximum hours, minimum wages, the evil of child labor and the exploitation of unorganized labor.

Nearly twenty years ago in his dissenting opinion in Hammer v. Dagenhart, Mr. Justice Holmes expressed his views as to the power of the Congress to prohibit the shipment in interstate or foreign commerce of the product of the labor of children in factories below what Congress then deemed to be civilized social standards. Surely the experience of the last twenty years has only served to reinforce the wisdom and the rightness of his views. And, surely if he was right about the power of the Congress over the work of children in factories, it is equally right that the Congress has the power over decent wages and hours in those same factories.

> "I had thought that the propriety of the exercise of a power admitted to exist in some cases was for the consideration of Congress alone and that this Court had always disavowed the right to intrude its judgment upon questions of policy or morals. It is not for this Court to pronounce when prohibition is necessary to regulation if it ever may be necessary—to say that it is permissible as against strong drink but not as against the product of ruined lives. . . ."

But although Mr. Justice Holmes spoke for a *minority* of the Supreme Court he spoke for a *majority* of the American people.

One of the primary purposes of the formation of our federal

union was to do away with the trade barriers between the states. To the Congress and not to the states was given the power to regulate commerce among the several states. Congress cannot interfere in local affairs but when goods pass through the channels of commerce from one state to another they become subject to the power of the Congress, and the Congress may exercise that power to recognize and protect the fundamental interests of free labor.

And so to protect the fundamental interests of free labor and a free people we propose that only goods which have been produced under conditions which meet the minimum standards of free labor shall be admitted to interstate commerce. Goods produced under conditions which do not meet rudimentary standards of decency should be regarded as contraband and ought not to be allowed to pollute the channels of interstate trade. . . .

Our problem is to work out in practice those labor standards which will permit the maximum but prudent employment of our human resources to bring within the reach of the average man and woman a maximum of goods and of services conducive to the fulfillment of the promise of American life.

Legislation can, I hope, be passed at this session of the Congress further to help those who toil in factory and on farm. We have promised it. We cannot stand still.

44 • Samuel Lubell and Walter Everett: *The Breakdown of Relief*

In 1937-1938 recession swelled the numbers of unemployed by four million. Although in the spring Roosevelt persuaded Congress

From Samuel Lubell and Walter Everett, "The Breakdown of Relief," *The Nation*, CXLVII (August 20, 1938), 171-174. Reprinted with the permission of the publisher.

to vote over three and a half billion dollars for WPA, public works, housing, and other New Deal activities, this was not enough to take care of everyone in need. Journalists Samuel Lubell and Walter Everett described economic conditions they found in a tour of the midwest, offering a fundamental criticism of the New Deal approach to poverty.

Relief in a good part of the United States is crumbling under the impact of the recession like a town rocked by a series of earthquakes. In some cities relief agencies have already slammed their doors against thousands in dire need. Akron's reliefers must keep body and soul together on twelve cents a person for a day's food. Cleveland's poor are still begging from door to door and foraging in garbage cans. Detroit's jobless sick must trust to God or nature if their illnesses require any but the cheapest drugs. Evictions have became a daily routine in Chicago. Distress and suffering are spreading like the plague.

For five weeks we have been touring industrial cities in western Pennsylvania, Ohio, Indiana, Michigan, and Illinois—places where the recession hit the hardest. Everywhere unemployment is almost as great as during the blackest days of the depression, and relief loads are even heavier. One out of every six families in Pittsburgh either is receiving direct relief or is on the WPA; one out of five in Chicago; one out of four in Akron; more than one out of four in Detroit; one out of three in Cleveland; one out of two in Flint. Most of the cities and some of the states have plunged neck-deep into debt to provide even miserable handouts. Many communities are on the brink of default. Virtually none have funds to last longer than the next few months.

Food, clothing, and shelter budgets for families receiving direct relief have been lopped so drastically and so generally that it is impossible to measure the results in human suffering.

After the first few days of traveling through "dole slums," we came to expect that children six, seven, and eight years old would have legs as spindly as the starving Armenians for whom we used to contribute our pennies. Regional WPA officials estimate that in Ohio, Indiana, Michigan, and Illinois budgets have been slashed on the average 20 to 50 per cent. And that cut has been made since the start of the recession, when "economy" had already lowered relief standards below the level of adequacy set by private charities.

Wilfred S. Reynolds, director of the Council of Social Agencies in Chicago, estimates the city's standard relief budget to be 15 per cent below his agency's definition of adequacy. In the last six months that already inadequate budget has been reduced by something like half. Even now, with fresh funds appropriated by the special session of the legislature in May, there is no allotment for electricity or gas. Food allotments have been maintained at "par," but those getting aid must do their purchasing in daily dribbles, for ice is not included. Medical care is furnished "when required," half-rent "when necessary." The "when required" generally means in an emergency; the "when necessary" could be translated "when evicted."

Chicago, like many other cities, has adopted the intriguing policy of letting rent payments run behind until the landlord's patience is exhausted and the family evicted. Only when the client comes into the district office with a court order to move in forty-eight hours will relief authorities give him a month's rent for a new flat. Housing conditions of relief families are indescribable. Some landlords refuse to rent to persons without a job. Those who accept them generally offer lodgings that no regular rent-payer would take. Joel D. Hunter, head of Chicago's United Charities, told us of one house into which sixteen Negro families had moved. Separated by beaverboards, sixty persons lived in that one-family dwelling, some of the smaller children sleeping in wardrobe drawers.

Leo Hart, an organizer for the Steel Workers' Organizing

Committee in South Chicago, said hardly a day passed without some union member being put out on the street. As many non-unionists must be behind in rent. Hart took us to see Louis Carillo, a steel worker, who had been evicted a week before with his eight children. The Carillos had found temporary lodgings in a friend's home. We entered through a smelly alley and a yard formed of cinder dumpings and rubbish. The Illinois Central tracks ran beside the house; across the tracks was a bookie establishment. Carillo's furniture was still in the truck. In the driver's seat, sprawled over two pillows, without sheets, was one of the Carillo children. That driver's seat was the boy's bed at night.

Carillo is a Mexican who came to Chicago in 1924. We found him wearing a battered hat, soiled shirt, torn trousers, and suspenders with one snapper gone. He hadn't shaved for two days, and the graying tips of his whiskers stood out against his dark skin. He spoke with an accent. "I jus' found myself a shack. I'll move later today. I bin stayin' here as long as I could get away with it. This my first time bin evicted. My girl got sick in 1936—her lungs," he went on. "We took her to the hospital. It did her good! Then, they told me they didn't have enough money to keep her. We had to take her home. It was cold in our house. She got worse." Carillo's thirteen-year-old daughter was spared the ordeal of the eviction, though. She died last May.

It is a mistake to think that the Illinois legislature solved Chicago's relief ills. It is even more of an error to speak of the relief crises of cities like Cleveland, Toledo, Dayton, and Columbus in the past tense. The law passed by the Ohio Assembly will go about as far in meeting the relief problems of these and other Ohio cities as a cup of coffee and a flop for the night would go in making a new man out of a panhandler. These cities already are several million dollars in red. All the new law does is allow them to go deeper into debt by mortgaging tax receipts for the next three years. When we left Cleveland late in June enough money had been scraped together for food orders for ten days. Last week a relief worker whom we had befriended there wrote us in Chicago. "Things remain in the same general state as in June. The city has borrowed some money from the bankers. Four-day orders are being issued but only for the most urgent cases. The others beg and forage as they did in the spring."

Relief Administrator Frank E. Bubna described conditions in Cleveland as "about the same as in the worst part of the depression, if anything a little worse." Cleveland's movie houses are crowded; its ball park is packed. But for weeks the authorities were unable even to provide milk for needy children, and the WPA's supplies of skimmed milk, dried beans, flour, and vegetables were all the poor had to eat. It was the Federal Surplus Commodities Corporation that made good Mayor Harold Burton's promise that "no one will starve." The WPA has stretched its definition of "employable" so that every man who can so much as hold a tool and sign a time-sheet has been certified. WPA rolls have leaped from 20,000 last fall to almost 75,000 in mid-July. Only about 18,000 families are on direct relief, fewer than the city has cared for at any other time since the crash. Cleveland's total industrial pay roll has been estimated as around $2,600,000 a week. The WPA is spending upward of $1,250,000 weekly. . . .

Unemployment and relief obviously are permanent problems. But still state legislatures won't admit it. The Ohio General Assembly, dominated by the rural members, has persistently refused to allot relief funds for more than six months in advance. Rural prejudices have been fanned by Governor Martin L. Davey and a powerful business lobby, the Inter-Organization Conference. Ohio's cities can solve their relief problems only by obtaining the power to raise funds through taxes. The sole purpose of the Inter-Organization Conference has been to defeat any and all tax proposals. Since 1935, when the conference was set up, no new tax laws have been enacted. The

Illinois Manufacturers' Association, which has fought relief appropriations as consistently, seems animated by the same type of reasoning. At a conference called by Governor Henry Horner to discuss the need for a special session last spring, a representative of the association heatedly argued: "We can't keep feeding these bums forever."

Nine years of depression and widespread unemployment, five years of relief administration by government agencies, and still there isn't a city in this entire area that has anything resembling a sound relief policy! The mental bankruptcy of public officials is evidenced by their frantic "purges." Cleveland hired a private agency to make "credit investigations" of sample relief clients at $3 a head, only to net "savings" that weren't sufficient to meet the investigators' bills. In Cincinnati relief authorities abruptly dropped all clients and had them reapply. Perhaps they hoped some of the needy would lose the address of relief headquarters in the shuffle.

Illinois is administering its relief program in truly medieval fashion through townships. The townships raise their own funds, set their own standards. There are more than 1,400 of them—townships and standards. Relief taxes are levied on real property, which means that the richer townships can do without state assistance, while the poorer communities, where the need is greatest, collect so little that even with state aid essential items have to be restricted.

Illinois, Michigan, and Ohio have no income tax. Instead of financing their relief programs in this way, they have resorted to sales taxes—levies which take their toll even out of relief checks.

Millions of dollars are being spent on relief—expenditures have soared to a new high and and still are mounting—but to no one's satisfaction: not to those on relief, who are getting barely enough to keep alive; not to officials administering relief, who are powerless to stop the deterioration, physical, mental, and moral, that is going on among relief clients; not to the taxpayer, who wonders where it will all end and what lasting good is being accomplished. And all because the country refuses to recognize that relief is a permanent problem, that bare subsistence handouts cannot take the place of rehabilitation.

45 • Henry E. Sigerist: *Government Should Also Protect "The Right to Health"*

Henry E. Siegerist (1891-1957), a physician and a medical historian at Johns Hopkins University, was an ardent advocate of a national government system of health insurance. Although the Social Security Act did appropriate some money for public health, the basic problem of medical care for the nation's poor was left untouched. In the heated discussion of the government's role in the economy that accompanied the Social Security and Wage-Hour laws, it seemed natural to some to extend the principle of the welfare state even further. In this article, Dr. Sigerist summarizes the argument for "socialized medicine."

In a report published last year by the American Foundation, a professor of medicine in a grade A medical school in the Middle West, member of the Association of American Physicians, wrote: "I do not believe that a patient is entitled to free medical service any more than he is entitled to free housing, free clothing, and free feeding." In other words: if a society is unable to provide work for all its members, it is perfectly

From Henry E. Sigerist, "Socialized Medicine," *The Yale Review*, XXVII (Spring 1938), 463-481.

normal for the unemployed to be evicted from his home and to run around naked, sick, and starving. Such a view is not only barbaric but it is utterly foolish. Nobody seriously believes that any group of unemployed American workers would sit down quietly and wait for death to relieve them. They would kick before they starved, and any government that shared the professor's view would be overthrown at the first major economic crisis.

If our professor's statement represented the general view of American society, there would be no reason for discussing our present system of medical care. Medical service then would be a commodity sold on the market to whoever could afford to purchase it. American society, however, like any other civilized society feels differently in the matter. It has come to realize that a highly specialized modern industrial nation cannot function normally if its members are sick and that it is a wasteful burden to carry a large number of sick and half sick people. The propertied class, moreover, knows very well that a diseased working class is a menace to its own health. Tuberculosis to-day is largely confined to the low income groups, but venereal diseases have not yet learned to respect class barriers.

Most people agree that it is in the interest of society to fight disease and to provide medical care for the whole population regardless of the economic status of the individual. This is, to begin with, a purely practical and utilitarian consideration. Our attitude, however, is also influenced by humanitarian motives. After all, some of the humanitarian ideals of the nineteenth century are still alive. Every society has many thousands of perfectly useless members, mostly feeble-minded and mentally diseased people who will never be able to work and will never contribute anything to society. And yet we do not destroy them. We consider them unfortunate fellow citizens. We feed them, nurse them, try to provide tolerable living conditions for them, hoping that science, some day, will give us sufficient data to allow us to reduce their number.

There are people to-day—their number is increasing—who think that man has a right to health. The chief cause of disease is poverty. If we are unable to provide work for everybody and to guarantee a decent standard of living to every individual willing to work, whatever his intelligence may be, we are collectively responsible for the chief cause of disease. The least we can do is to make provisions for the protection and restoration of the people's health. They have an undeniable right to such provisions.

Once we accept the principle that medical care must be available to all, we must examine whether the people actually receive the services they need, under the present system. There are still doctors who pretend quite ingenuously that there is not one man in the United States who could not get medical care in case of illness if he took the trouble to ask for it. They point out proudly that our hospitals have charity wards and that the medical profession, conscious of its humanitarian traditions, has always been ready to help the poor without remuneration.

Nobody will deny the good will and idealism of the medical profession. It has made desperate efforts to remain a liberal profession and has refused steadily but in vain to be dragged into business, into a competitive world that is ruled by iron economic necessities. The doctors are not responsible for the fact that the social and economic structure of society has changed. They did the best they could and kept to the job under increasingly adverse conditions. Their good will and idealism are still wanted, more than ever before; not for charity services, however, but to enable them to face the present conditions with an open mind and courageously, and to co-operate in their readjustment.

Long before the depression, it was felt that medicine had infinitely more to give than the people actually received. At the height of prosperity, in 1928, the Committee on the Costs of Medical Care was appointed to survey conditions. Whoever looked around without prejudice saw people, many people, who had not sufficient medical care. We all knew families whose budget was wrecked by a sudden illness, and we all had friends who hesitated to enter a hospital or to undergo certain treatments because they could not afford them. The many reports of the Committee on the Costs of Medical Care gave us facts and figures for what we vaguely knew, and demonstrated unmistakably that large sections of our population lacked adequate medical care.

If any doubts are left, they will be dispelled by the results of the National Health Survey that was undertaken by the United States Public Health Service as a W.P.A. project. From preliminary reports we already know that the lower a family's income is, the higher is the incidence of disease and the smaller the volume of medical care received. We know that hundreds of thousands of cases of illness are needless and could have been prevented, that many thousands of people die prematurely; and we also know that one-third of the population of this wealthy country is not only ill-fed, ill-housed, and ill-clothed, but also ill-cared for in sickness.

The facts that have become known as a result of the various surveys are so overwhelming that even the American Medical Association could not ignore them and had to admit recently that "a varying number of people may at times be insufficiently supplied with medical service."

The present conditions are not only most depressing and harmful to society but also unnecessary and stupid in a country that has such splendid medical equipment. No country in the world has a better standard of physicians, public health officers, nurses, and social workers; no country has better hospital or laboratory facilities. It is almost a miracle how the United States in less than half a century caught up with European medicine and surpassed it in many respects. Accumulated wealth and the wisdom of a group of medical leaders made it possible. And yet, one-third of the population has no medical service or not enough, and great possibilities of preventive medicine have not even been considered yet. . . .

In other words, it is not only difficult for the indigent to secure for himself adequate medical care, but for all families of moderate means, all those whose income does not exceed $3,000 or even more. This, however, means more than three-quarters of the entire population. The fee-for-service system may have worked—I doubt if it ever did—as long as medicine had little to give. To-day it is impossible to protect the people's health effectively under any such system because there is too wide a gap between the scientific status of medicine and the economic status of the population. Therefore, if we think that the people's health is a major concern of society, we must necessarily devise some other system. . . .

I know what the traditional objections to socialized medicine are. We frequently hear that such a system would lead to "regimentation," while the word that applies to it is "organization." Why should anybody feel regimented by having the possibility to budget the cost of illness and by having the privilege to receive all the medical care he needs? We do not feel regimented when we send our children to school, or when we appeal to a court to protect our rights and our honor, or when we call on a minister of the church for advice without paying him a fee. Nobody would be compelled to seek treatment, and if a man particularly enjoyed his arthritis he would retain the liberty of having it. Conditions are different in the case of communicable diseases where a sick man is a direct menace to his environment. This has been recognized long ago, and society has made provisions to isolate as much as possible the contaminated individual. In several countries, the spreading of venereal diseases is considered a criminal offense and is prosecuted by law. There is a duty to health because the sick man is useless to society and often a burden, but it is a moral, not a legal obligation. Gradually we come to recognize that health is much more than the absence of disease, that it is something positive, a joyful attitude towards life.

Another objection frequently heard is that doctors, if they were salaried and had not the incentive of making money, would neglect their duties. I think that such an assumption is an insult to the medical profession, and it is very queer that this objection is frequently made by medical organizations. The Code of Ethics of the American Medical Association explicitly states that "a profession has for its prime object the service it can render to humanity; reward or financial gain should be a subordinate consideration." Can a doctor wish for more than to be given complete social security and to be able to devote all his time and all his energy to his patients without being obstructed by economic barriers? I have not been in practice for a long time, but for seventeen years I have helped to train physicians and I have kept in close touch with many of my former students, who are now practising in cities and in rural districts. More than once they have come to see me in despair because they were unable to practise the type of medicine they had been taught. Economic considerations compelled them to lower their standards and to compromise. Every young doctor knows of such conflicts, and many of the best minds go into public service because they refuse to be dragged into business. If a man's ambition is to become rich, he should not enter the medical career—one of the most harassing professions, in which very few people ever became wealthy. Thousands of doctors work on salaries at present, and nobody can deny that they are doing a good job. And whenever a position is vacant, hundreds apply for it, so that the idea of being salaried cannot be quite unattractive. Under socialized medicine, there would be plenty of incentive for the doctor. He could rise to positions of greater responsibility, and his income would increase accordingly.

Many people are afraid that under socialized medicine the free choice of a physician would be somewhat limited. They insist that everybody should be able to select the one doctor in whom he has greatest confidence. There can be no doubt that confidence is an essential factor in the relation of doctor to patient. The elder Seneca said: 'Nihil magis aegris prodest quam ab eo curari a quo volunt"—Nothing is more advantageous to invalids than to be cared for by the person they wish. We must not forget, however, that our present system allows only very few people to choose their own doctor. The dispensary patient has to accept whatever doctor happens to be there. In most rural districts, only one or possibly two physicians are available so that the patient has practically no choice; and even those patients who in the cities could make a wide selection very often call on the neighborhood doctor whoever he may be. It is very difficult for a layman to pass judgment on the competence of a physician. If medicine were socialized, the free choice of a doctor would possibly be somewhat more limited than it is to-day, but the physicians being members of an organization would be under a certain control. They would have ample opportunities for post-graduate training, and incompetent elements could be eliminated—which is practically impossible to-day. Medical science, moreover, has progressed so much and has developed so many objective methods of examination, and the general standard of the medical profession, on the other hand, has been raised so considerably in the last decades that a man need not be a genius to be a competent doctor.

Everybody agrees that the personal relationship between physician and patient must be preserved. The patient does not want to consult a committee when he is in trouble, nor can medicine be practised by a corporation. The patient will always call on one doctor and open up his heart to him, but the fact that this doctor is a member of an organized group from which he can seek help and advice does not spoil the relationship. What spoils it to-day is that the doctor has to charge a fee for each individual service and that the patient has to pay the bill. Once the money question is removed, the relationship between physician and patient becomes purely human. The value of a commodity can be estimated pretty accurately, while it is humanly impossible to estimate the value of a medical service in dollars and cents. Advice given by a doctor in a half hour's conversation may have tremendous repercussions in a man's life, while a major operation may be entirely worthless. If we remove the doctor from the economic struggle, we set him free and allow him to practise what medical science has taught him. . . .

PART NINE

THE NEGRO

46 • Guy B. Johnson: *Does the South Owe the Negro a New Deal?*

In June 1938, President Roosevelt asked the National Emergency Council, which had been set up in 1933 to bring cabinet members and agency heads together to solve economic problems, to prepare a report on the needs of the South. This meeting led to a Conference on Economic Conditions in the South, which convened the following month, and to which Roosevelt said: "It is my conviction that the South presents right now the nation's no. 1 economic problem." The result of the Conference was a *Report on Economic Conditions of the South,* which examined in detail the low standards of living. That the plight of the Negro was the number one social problem in the South was left unsaid, however.

Guy Johnson (1901-), was a sociologist at the University of North Carolina. His article gives a clear picture of the situation faced by Negroes in the South while the New Deal was grappling with the over-all problem of economic crisis.

For these seventy years since emancipation, the South has pursued a policy of repression toward the black fourth of its

From Guy B. Johnson, "Does the South Owe the Negro a New Deal?" *Social Forces,* XIII (October 1934), 100-103. Reprinted with the permission of The University of North Carolina Press, publisher of *Social Forces.*

population, and few voices from within have been raised to protest the folly and the futility of that policy.

The assumption upon which the South has been proceeding is that this policy of exclusion and repression is the only way whereby she may insure white supremacy, racial peace, and social progress. White supremacy, whatever that means, has been maintained; racial peace has been maintained after a fashion; but social and economic progress has proceeded at snail's pace. The South, with its vast resources and unlimited potentialities, continues to be a region of deficiencies and inadequacies. It should be apparent to any thinking person that the South has been so preoccupied with keeping the Negro in the ditch that she has had neither the time nor the strength to pull herself out of the ditch. Veritably she has paid dearly for whatever satisfaction she has got from "keeping the Negro in his place."

Let us examine some of the ways in which the South has stacked the cards against the Negro and estimate the consequences for the progress of the Negro and of the South as a whole.

The economic position of the Negro is so insecure that the masses of the race are but a step removed from poverty. This condition is in large measure due to the fact that the white South has continued to apply the philosophy and the folkways of slavery to the Negro. Differentials in wages, hours, kinds of work, and conditions of work operate to keep the Negro from getting ahead.

Except in the upper South where his position has always been relatively advantaged, the Negro farmer has made little progress up the ladder of ownership. Eighty per cent of the Negro farm operators in the South are still tenants. They are victims of a vicious system of farming which has been perpetuated partly for the purpose of keeping them in subjection and controlling their labor. "It is not good for a Negro to own property," or "He is too prosperous for a Negro"—how often such statements are made and how well they express the folkways of the white South! As if we did not know that a wholesome farming economy calls for ownership and self-support.

The Negro laborer moves in a sphere which for the most part is restricted to menial and low-paying types of work. He is generally excluded from the labor unions, and is thus denied what little leverage the union movement affords in the struggle for economic security. If white men decide that they can do "Negro work," the Negro's traditional occupations slip from his helpless grasp. If he masters a skilled trade in spite of all obstructions, he must work for less than white men or lose the work to them. If he is employed by the state to teach in the Negro schools, his salary is a third to a half of the salary of white teachers doing similar work—a striking confirmation of folkways by stateways.

Even in the administration of federal relief, the Civil Works program, the A.A.A., etc., there has been, particularly in the lower South, a tendency to perpetuate the existing inequalities. Negro tenants received pitifully little of the crop reduction money last fall. Landlords quite generally took charge of the checks and applied them to back debts of the tenants. Furthermore, many landlords are known to have "understandings" with local relief administrators to prevent the "demoralization" of their Negro labor, and it is reported that some go as far as to charge to their tenants' accounts all food and other supplies furnished by the relief office. The director of relief in a southern seaboard city remarked not long ago, "I don't like this fixing of a wage scale for work relief. Why, the niggers in this town are getting so spoiled working on these relief jobs at thirty cents an hour that they won't work on the docks for fifty cents a day like they did last year." In allotting C.W.A. jobs, re-employment offices throughout the South ignored the Negro skilled worker almost as effectively as if he did not exist. In one tobacco center, for example, 13 per cent of the white C.W.A. workers received the skilled rates of pay, while only 1.2 per cent of the Negro workers received such pay. In another industrial city,

15 per cent of the whites on C.W.A. pay rolls received skilled rates, but not one Negro did so. If skilled Negroes worked, they worked at the unskilled rates.

Whether the South's economic policy has been conscious or unconscious, deliberate or unintentional, its effect has been to retard the advance of the Negro up the ladder of economic competence. Has the South profited thereby? No, on the contrary it has jeopardized its own progress, for the economic progress of the Negro is one of the conditions without which the South cannot hope to attain its fullest development as a major region. Every advance of the Negro means something in cold dollars and cents to business in the South. Suppose that the buying power of the South's 9,361,000 Negroes were doubled or tripled, so that instead of being about two billions of dollars per year it would be from four to six billions. Does that suggest anything in terms of the South's progress toward economic independence? Does it suggest anything in terms of better homes, better health, better living, cultural development, and human adequacy for both races in the South? Veritably, the Negro is the South's greatest undeveloped human resource. The South has all to gain and nothing to lose by a policy of fairness and justice in the economic sphere.

It is in the realm of political and civic affairs that the South has most effectively stacked the cards against the Negro. Let us not argue about the historical basis of the "keep-the-Negro-out-of-politics" philosophy. Let us even grant with the older generation that Reconstruction was neither well-meant nor well-done and that the South had good reason to take drastic steps to restore white control. But, we may ask, how long shall Negro exclusion be continued? What has it done and what is it doing to the Negro and to the South?

It would probably not be exaggerating to say that in literacy, educational attainments, and in character, the average Negro today is better qualified to discharge the duties of citizenship than were the masses of white men when they were granted free suffrage. Yet there are few places in the South today where Negroes register and vote freely and without fear for the candidates for public office. In all the South, with the exception of two or three all-Negro communities, there is not a Negro in an elective office. Negroes as jurors are in most parts of the South unheard of, and in other parts so rare as to be the subject of extensive comment in the press. In only seventeen southern cities are Negro policemen used to assist in law enforcement, although there are 3,000,000 urban Negroes in the South. On the various policy-making boards and councils which affect their lives, Negroes are almost entirely lacking in representation. Even their schools are controlled by white boards, and any power which Negroes exercise is through the indirect or "back-door" method.

What does all this mean in terms of the behavior of Negroes and functioning of the Negro community? Let us look at a few actual situations.

(1) A southern town receives a grant from C.W.A. to improve its streets. A plan is drawn up and agreed upon after some wrangling. The wrangling is exclusively white, since no one even suggests that any of the streets in the Negro section be paved. It is announced that only those streets which have previously been curbed can be paved. Are any of the Negro streets eligible? No, they have not been curbed. The work is done, the C.W.A. money is spent, but white people whose streets are not paved grumble until the town council decides that it can pave uncurbed streets and that it might as well raise the tax rate fifteen cents on the hundred dollars and thereby give everybody paved streets—that is, everybody except the Negroes. Negroes own property in the town assessed at $250,000, and the increased tax rate will add $375.00 to their taxes. So far their protests have not reached the public consciousness.

(2) A Negro school building is to be located. The white school board meets, asks the advice of one or two Negro citizens, then chooses the site to suit itself. The school is placed

far out beyond the Negro residence section on an unsightly eroded knoll which a certain white man is glad to be rid of. The Negroes are disappointed and resentful, but they do not make any effective protest for fear of losing white friends who helped them get the new building.

(3) A Negro teacher is being chosen for a rural school. The school board elects a certain young woman sight unseen upon the advice of the colored principal. The young woman holds a certificate, it is true, but she cannot spell simple words, cannot write a simple letter understandably. How could the school board know that the principal was merely paying off an obligation to the young woman's family?

(4) A bond issue is voted in a certain city for the construction of a municipal auditorium. A magnificent building is erected, but the only place Negroes can sit during entertainments and public functions is in a gallery where it is very difficult to see and hear. Many of them feel that they have been as effectively "left out" as if no provision whatever had been made for them. Negroes are 30 per cent of the population, and they pay 10 per cent of the taxes on real and personal property.

(5) A new federal building is erected in a well-known city. In the old building two Negro janitors took care of all the work. The new building calls for twelve janitors. Negroes are jubilant, thinking they will surely have these jobs which their race has considered more or less its own. But only the two Negro janitors get jobs. Ten white men are put in. Negroes protest to the postmaster, to their congressmen, to the Postmaster-General, but several months have passed and the white men are still working.

Such instances might be continued indefinitely. What of the "public" playground which the Negro may not use? What of the "public" hospital which denies him entrance or treats him like a pauper? What of the "public" library which he may not use freely?

By deliberate design in some cases and by pure thoughtlessness in others, the interests and needs of the Negro citizen are thwarted or neglected. It is clear that there is a connection between the Negro's political impotence and his inability to command a decent share of the services and benefits of government. Thus the folkways of white supremacy hold a double check upon the progress of the Negro community. Is it not asking too much of a people so situated to be cheerful, contented, patriotic? To be diligent and efficient in their daily work? To be deeply concerned over law observance and the general welfare of the community?

It is a serious thing to block the path of reasonable hope for any group. Despair lies at the bottom of much of the disorganization and unwholesomeness in the lower stratum of Negro life. Where there is no opportunity there is no vision of the future, no guiding principle to organize and integrate the pattern of behavior.

The South pays dearly for the economic bondage and the political impotence of its black folk. For, in one way or another—in inefficiency, in waste, in poor health, in low moral standards, in excessive rates of dependency and delinquency—the Negro has levied a tax on the South just as surely as if the states themselves had levied it.

And there is another sense in which the South pays. Edgar Gardner Murphy, in *The Basis of Ascendancy,* has expressed it as follows:

> The processes by which we have taken an oblique advantage of the black man, whether in the exercise of the suffrage, or in the support of the public schools, or in the practice of the courts . . ., are processes by which white men have quickly learned to take oblique advantage of one another. And we also know that what we do is an offense against ourselves, that we do not like it, and that—from man to man—we say so. For we know that the process by which men have sometimes cheated the Negro out of his legitimate privileges, as these privileges are written in our settled precedents and our established laws, is a process by which they have cheated themselves, not infrequently, out of their consciences and their peace.

The same policy which has kept the Negro from participation

in the duties and benefits of social control has begotten in the race a militant school of leadership which has waged and will continue to wage a battle for the recognition of the legal rights of the Negro. The existence of that militant group is a reflection on the southern white man's sense of justice and fair play. Negroes have been patient, forbearing, and peaceful in their struggle for rights, but there is no guarantee that they shall always remain so.

Can the South afford to continue the old policy toward the Negro? Does it wish to alienate the Negro until, embittered and resentful, he turns to radicalism as his helpmate in his struggle for rights? Or does it prefer to embark willingly and courageously upon a policy which shall take the inequalities out of the bi-racial system and usher its Negro citizens peacefully into a larger participation in the life of the region? Self-interest, simple justice, and common sense demand that the South give the Negro a new deal.

47 · John P. Davis: *The New Deal: Slogans for the Same Raw Deal*

Particularly in the early days of the New Deal, before the benefits of New Deal welfare measures began trickling into Negro homes, leaving a warm feeling for Roosevelt and the Democrats, the Negro press was sharply critical of the administration. In this article, Negro writer John P. Davis, referred to by the NAACP magazine, *The Crisis,* as "Bad Boy Administration Critic," spells out the reasons for this criticism.

From John P. Davis, "A Black Inventory of the New Deal," *The Crisis,* XLII (May 1935), 141-142, 154. Reprinted with the permission of the publisher.

It is highly important for the Negro citizen of America to take inventory of the gains and losses which have come to him under the "New Deal." The Roosevelt administration has now had two years in which to unfold itself. Its portents are reasonably clear to anyone who seriously studies the varied activities of its recovery program. We can now state with reasonable certainty what the "New Deal" means for the Negro.

At once the most striking and irrefutable indication of the effect of the New Deal on the Negro can be gleaned from relief figures furnished by the government itself. In October, 1933, six months after the present administration took office, 2,117,000 Negroes were in families receiving relief in the United States. These represented 17.8 per cent of the total Negro population as of the 1930 census. In January, 1935, after nearly two years of *recovery measures,* 3,500,000 Negroes were in families receiving relief, or 29 per cent of our 1930 population. Certainly only a slight portion of the large increase in the number of impoverished Negro families can be explained away by the charitable, on the grounds that relief administration has become more humane. As a matter of fact federal relief officials themselves admit that grave abuses exist in the administration of rural relief to Negroes. And this is reliably borne out by the disproportionate increase in the number of urban Negro families on relief to the number of rural Negro families on relief. Thus the increase in the number of Negroes in relief families is an accurate indication of the deepening of the economic crisis for black America.

The promise of NRA to bring higher wages and increased employment to industrial workers has glimmered away. In the code-making process occupational and geographical differentials at first were used as devices to exclude from the operation of minimum wages and maximum hours the bulk of the Negro workers. Later, clauses basing code wage rates on the previously existing wage differential between Negro and white workers tended to continue the inferior status of the Negro. For the particular firms, for whom none of these devices served as an effective means of keeping down Negro wages, there is an easy way out through the securing of an exemption specifically relating to the *Negro* worker in the plant. Such exemptions are becoming more numerous as time goes on. Thus from the beginning relatively few Negro workers were even theoretically covered by NRA labor provisions.

But the employers did not have to rely on the code-making process. The Negro worker not already discriminated against through code provisions had many other gauntlets to run. The question of importance to him as to all workers was, "as a result of all of NRA's maneuvers will I be able to buy more?" The answer has been "No." A worker cannot eat a wage rate. To determine what this wage rate means to him we must determine a number of other factors. Thus rates for longshoremen seem relatively high. But when we realize that the average amount of work a longshoreman receives during the year is from ten to fifteen weeks, the wage rate loses much of its significance. When we add to that fact the increase in the cost of living—as high as 40 per cent in many cases—the wage rate becomes even more chimerical. For other groups of industrial workers increases in cost of living, coupled with the part time and irregular nature of the work, make the results of NRA negligible. In highly mechanized industries speed-up and stretch-out nullify the promised result of NRA to bring increased employment through shorter hours. For the workers are now producing more in their shorter work periods than in the longer periods before NRA. There is less employment. The first sufferer from fewer jobs is the Negro worker. Finally the complete break-down of compliance machinery in the South has cancelled the last minute advantage to Negro workers which NRA's enthusiasts may have claimed.

The Agricultural Adjustment Administration has used cruder methods in enforcing poverty on the Negro farm population. It has made violations of the rights of tenants under crop reduction contracts easy; it has rendered enforcement of these rights impossible. The reduction of the acreage under cultivation through the government rental agreement rendered unnecessary large numbers of tenants and farm laborers. Although the contract with the government provided that the land owner should not reduce the number of his tenants, he did so. The federal courts have now refused to allow tenants to enjoin such evictions. Faced with this Dred Scott decision against farm tenants, the AAA has remained discreetly silent. Farm laborers are now jobless by the hundreds of thousands, the conservative government estimate of the decline in agricultural employment for the year 1934 alone being a quarter of a million. The larger portion of these are unskilled Negro agricultural workers—now without income and unable to secure work or relief.

But the unemployment and tenant evictions occasioned by the crop reduction policies of the AAA is not all. For the tenants and sharecroppers who were retained on the plantations the government's agricultural program meant reduced income. Wholesale fraud on tenants in the payment of parity checks occurred. Tenants complaining to the Department of Agriculture in Washington have their letters referred back to the locality in which they live and trouble of serious nature often results. Even when this does not happen, the tenant fails to get his check. The remainder of the land he tills on shares with his landlord brings him only the most meagre necessities during the crop season varying from three to five months. The rest of the period for him and his family is one of "root hog or die."

The past year has seen an extension of poverty even to the small percentage (a little more than 20 per cent) of Negro farmers who own their own land. For them compulsory reduction of acreage for cotton and tobacco crops, with the quantum of such reduction controlled and regulated by local boards on which they have no representation, has meant drastic reduction of their already low income. Wholesale confiscation of the income of the Negro cotton and tobacco farmer is being made by prejudiced local boards in the South under the very nose of the federal government. In the wake of such confiscation has come a tremendous increase in land tenantry as a result of foreclosures on Negro-owned farm properties.

Nor has the vast public works program, designed to give increased employment to workers in the building trades, been free from prejudice. State officials in the South are in many cases in open rebellion against the ruling of PWA that the same wage scales must be paid to Negro and white labor. Compliance with this paper ruling is enforced in only rare cases. The majority of the instances of violation of this rule are unremedied. Only unskilled work is given Negroes on public works projects in most instances. And even here discrimination in employment is notorious. Such is bound to be the case when we realize that there are only a handful of investigators available to seek enforcement.

Recently a move has been made by Negro officials in the administration to effect larger employment of Negro skilled and unskilled workers on public works projects by specifying that failure of a contractor to pay a certain percentage of his payroll to Negro artisans will be evidence of racial discrimination. Without doubting the good intentions of the sponsors of this ingenious scheme, it must nevertheless be pointed out that it fails to meet the problem in a number of vital particulars. It has yet to face a test in the courts, even if one is willing to suppose that PWA high officials will bring it to a test. Percentages thus far experimented with are far too low and the number of such experiments far too few to make an effective dent in the unemployment conditions of Negro construction industry workers. Moreover the scheme gives aid and comfort to employer-advocates of strike-breaking and the open shop; and, while offering, perhaps, some temporary relief to a few hundred Negro workers, it establishes a dangerous precedent which throws back the labor movement and the organization of Negro workers to a considerable degree. The scheme, whatever its Negro sponsors may hope to contrary, becomes therefor only another excuse for their white superiors maintaining a "do-nothing" policy with regard to discrimination against Negroes in the Public Works Administration.

The Negro has no pleasanter outlook in the long term social planning ventures of the new administration. Planning for subsistence homesteads for industrially stranded workers has been muddled enough even without consideration of the problem of integrating Negroes into such plans. Subsistence Homesteads projects are overburdened with profiteering prices for the homesteads and foredoomed to failure by the lack of planning for adequate and permanent incomes for prospective homesteaders.

In callous disregard of the interdiction in the Constitution of the United States against use of federal funds for projects which discriminate against applicants solely on the ground of color, subsistence homesteads have been planned on a strictly "lily-white" basis. The more than 200 Negro applicants for the first project at Arthurdale, West Virginia, were not even considered, Mr. Bushrod Grimes (then in charge of the project) announcing that the project was to be open only to "native white stock." As far north as Dayton, Ohio, where state laws prohibit any type of segregation against Negroes, the federal government has extended its "lily-white" policy. Recently it has established two Jim-Crow projects for Negroes. Thus the new administration seeks in its program of social planning to perpetuate ghettoes of Negroes for fifty years to come.

An even more blatant example of this policy of "lily-white" reconstruction is apparent in the planning of the model town of Norris, Tennessee, by the Tennessee Valley Authority. This town of 450 model homes is intended for the permanent workers on Norris Dam. The homes are rented by the federal government, which at all times maintains title to the land and dwellings and has complete control of the town management. Yet officials at TVA openly admit that no Negroes are allowed at Norris.

TVA has other objectionable features. While Negro employment now approaches an equitable proportion of total employment; the payroll of Negro workers remains disproportionately lower than that of whites. While the government has maintained a trade school to train workers on the project, no Negro trainees have been admitted. Nor have any meaningful plans matured for the future of the several thousand Negro workers who in another year or so will be left without employment, following completion of work on the dams being built by TVA.

None of the officials of TVA seems to have the remotest idea of how Negroes in the Tennessee Valley will be able to buy the cheap electricity which TVA is designed to produce. They admit that standards of living of the Negro population are low, that the introduction of industry into the Valley is at present only a nebulous dream, that even if this eventuates there is no assurance that Negro employment will result. The fairest summary that can be made of TVA is that for a year or so it has furnished bread to a few thousand Negro workers. Beyond that everything is conjecture which is most unpleasant because of the utter planlessness of those in charge of the project.

Recovery legislation of the present session of Congress reveals the same fatal flaws which have been noted in the operation of previous recovery ventures. Thus, for example, instead of genuine unemployment insurance we have the leaders of the administration proposing to exclude from their plans domestic and agricultural workers, in which classes are to be found 15 out of every 23 Negro workers. On every hand the New Deal has used slogans for the same raw deal.

The sharpening of the crisis for Negroes has not found them unresponsive. Two years of increasing hardship has seen strange movement among the masses. In Chicago, New York, Washington and Baltimore the struggle for jobs has given rise to action on the part of a number of groups seeking to boycott white employers who refuse to employ Negroes. "Don't Buy Where You Can't Work" campaigns are springing up everywhere. The crisis has furnished renewed vigor to the Garvey Movement.[1] And proposals for a 49th State are being seriously considered by various groups.

In sharp contrast with these strictly racial approaches to the problem, have been a number of interracial approaches. Increasing numbers of unemployed groups have been organized under radical leadership and have picketed relief stations for bread. Sharecroppers unions, under Socialist leadership in Arkansas, have shaken America into a consciousness of the growing resentment of southern farm tenants and the joint determination of the Negro and white tenants to do something about their intolerable condition.

In every major strike in this country Negro union members have fought with their white fellow workers in a struggle for economic survival. The bodies of ten Negro strikers killed in such strike struggles offer mute testimony to this fact. Even the vicious policies of the leaders of the A. F. of L. in discrimination against Negro workers is breaking down under the pressure for solidarity from the ranks of whites.

This heightening of spirit among all elements of black America and the seriousness of the crisis for them make doubly necessary the consideration of the social and economic condition of the Negro at this time. It was a realization of these conditions which gave rise to the proposal to hold a national conference on the economic status of Negroes under the New Deal

1 A Negro nationalist movement led by Marcus Garvey, a West Indian, between 1914 and 1925. [ED.]

at Howard University in Washington, D. C., on May 18, 19 and 20. At this conference, sponsored by the Social Science Division of Howard University and the Joint Committee on National Recovery, a candid and intelligent survey of the social and economic condition of the Negro will be made. Unlike most conferences it will not be a talk-fest. For months nationally known economists and other technicians have been working on papers to be presented. Unlike other conferences it will not be a one-sided affair. Ample opportunity will be afforded for high government officials to present their views of the "New Deal." Others not connected with the government, including representatives of radical political parties, will also appear to present their conclusions. Not the least important phase will be the appearance on the platform of Negro workers and farmers themselves to offer their own experience under the New Deal. Out of such a conference can and will come a clear-cut analysis of the problems faced by Negroes and the nation.

48 • Robert C. Weaver: *The New Deal is for the Negro*

There were unmistakable overtures by the New Deal to the Negro. Eleanor Roosevelt made her sympathies clear. Secretary of the Interior Harold Ickes appointed Negroes to important posts in his department. Most important, millions of poverty-stricken Negroes benefited from the relief program, WPA, TVA, public housing, and other welfare measures of the New Deal, and as a result they

From Robert C. Weaver, "The New Deal and the Negro. A Look at the Facts," *Opportunity: Journal of Negro Life*, XIII, No. 7 (July 1935), 200-203. Reprinted with the permission of the National Urban League.

turned, for the first time in American history, toward the Democratic Party. FDR himself was clearly sympathetic toward the Negro, although he never gave the problem of civil rights the same high priority that he gave to economic recovery. Not one civil rights law was passed while he was president.

Robert C. Weaver (1907-), an adviser in Negro Affairs in the Department of Interior under Ickes, was one of a number of Negroes appointed to important posts in the Roosevelt Administration. These were sometimes said to constitute a "Black Cabinet" in the New Deal. Weaver, to counter the arguments of critics like John Davis, presents here the positive picture of New Deal accomplishment for the Negro. Weaver remained in government and in the Johnson administration became head of the new department of Urban Affairs.

It is impossible to discuss intelligently the New Deal and the Negro without considering the status of the Negro prior to the advent of the Recovery Program. The present economic position of the colored citizen was not created by recent legislation alone. Rather, it is the result of the impact of a new program upon an economic and social situation.

Much has been said recently about the occupational distribution of Negroes. Over a half of the gainfully employed colored Americans are concentrated in domestic service and farming. The workers in these two pursuits are the most casual and unstable in the modern economic world. This follows from the fact that neither of them requires any great capital outlay to buy necessary equipment. Thus when there is a decline in trade, the unemployment of workers in these fields does not necessitate idle plants, large depreciation costs, or mounting overhead charges. In such a situation, the employer has every incentive to dismiss his workers; thus, these two classes are fired early in a depression.

The domestic worker has loomed large among the unemployed since the beginning of the current trade decline. This situation has persisted throughout the depression and is reflected in the relief figures for urban communities where 20 per cent of the employables on relief were formerly attached to personal and domestic service. Among Negroes the relative number of domestics and servants on relief is even greater.

In selected cities, 43.4 per cent of the Negroes on relief May 1, 1934, were usually employed as domestics. The demand for servants is a derived one; it is dependent upon the income and employment of other persons in the community. Thus, domestics are among the last rehired in a period of recovery.

The new works program of the Federal Government will attack this problem of the domestic worker from two angles. Insofar as it accelerates recovery by restoring incomes, it will tend to increase the demand for servants. More important, however, will be its creation of direct employment opportunities for all occupational classes of those on relief.

Although it is regrettable that the economic depression has led to the unemployment of so many Negroes and has threatened the creation of a large segment of the Negro population as a chronic relief load, one is forced to admit that Federal relief has been a godsend to the unemployed. The number of unemployed in this country was growing in 1933. According to the statistics of the American Federation of Labor, the number of unemployed increased from 3,216,000 in January 1930 to 13,689,000 in March 1933. In November 1934 the number was about 10,500,000 and although there are no comparable current data available, estimates indicate that current unemployment is less than that of last November. Local relief monies were shrinking; and need and starvation were facing those unable to find an opportunity to work. A Federal relief program was the only possible aid in this situation. Insofar as the Negro was greatly victimized by the economic developments, he was in a position to benefit from a program which provided adequate funds for relief.

It is admitted that there were many abuses under the relief set-up. Such situations should be brought to light and fought. In the case of Negroes, these abuses undoubtedly existed and do exist. We should extend every effort to uncover and correct them. We can admit that we have gained from the relief program and still fight to receive greater and more equitable benefits from it.

The recent depression has been extremely severe in its effects upon the South. The rural Negro—poor before the period of trade decline—was rendered even more needy after 1929. Many tenants found it impossible to obtain a contract for a crop, and scores of Negro farm owners lost their properties. The displacement of Negro tenants (as was the case for whites) began before, and grew throughout the depression. Thus, at the time of the announcement of the New Deal, there were many families without arrangements for a crop—an appreciable number without shelter. The following summary of conditions in one county of a southern state will serve as an illustration. In Greene County, North Carolina (where the population in 1930 was 18,656 divided almost equally between whites and Negroes) the FERA survey reported data as of January 1934 relative to the period of displacement of families. This material shows that for this county, displacement of tenants was most severe in 1931-1932.

The problems facing the Negro farmer of the South are not new. They have been accentuated by the crop reduction program. They are, for the most part, problems of a system and their resistance to reform is as old as the system. This was well illustrated by the abuses in the administration of the Federal feed, seed, and fertilizer laws in 1928-1929. These abuses were of the same nature as those which confront the AAA in its dealings with Negro tenants.

The southern farm tenant is in such a position that he cannot receive any appreciable gains from a program until steps are taken to change his position of absolute economic dependence upon the landlord. Until some effective measure for rehabilitating him is discovered, there is no hope. The new program for land utilization, rural rehabilitation, and spreading land ownership may be able to effect such a change. Insofar as it takes a step in that direction, it will be advantageous to the Negro farmer. The degree to which it aids him will depend upon the temper of its administration and the extent to which it is able to break away from the *status quo*.

In listing some of the gains which have accrued to Negroes under the New Deal, there will be a dicussion of three lines of activity: housing, employment, and emergency education. These are chosen for discussion because each is significant in itself, and all represent a definite break from the *status quo* in governmental activity, method, and policy. They do not give a complete picture; but rather, supply interesting examples of what is, and can be, done for Negroes.

The Housing Division of the Federal Emergency Administration of Public Works has planned 60 Federal housing projects to be under construction by December 31, 1935. Of these, 28 are to be developed in Negro slum areas and will be tenanted predominantly or wholly by Negroes. Eight additional projects will provide for an appreciable degree of Negro occupancy. These 36 projects will afford approximately 74,664 rooms and should offer accommodations for about 23,000 low income colored families. The estimated total cost of these housing developments will be $64,428,000, and they represent about 29 per cent of the funds devoted to Federal slum clearance developments under the present allotments.

Projects in Negro areas have been announced in seven cities: Atlanta, Cleveland, Detroit, Indianapolis, Montgomery, Chicago, and Nashville. These will cost about $33,232,000 and will contain about 20,000 rooms. Two of these projects, the University development at Atlanta, and the Thurman Street development in Montgomery, are under construction. These are among the earliest Federal housing projects to be initiated by the PWA.

After a series of conferences and a period of experience under the PWA, it was decided to include a clause in PWA housing contracts requiring the payment to Negro mechanics of a given percentage of the payroll going to skilled workers. The first project to be affected by such a contractural clause was the Techwood development in Atlanta, Georgia. On this project, most of the labor employed on demolition was composed of unskilled Negro workers. About 90 per cent of the unskilled workers employed laying the foundation for the Techwood project were Negroes, and, for the first two-month construction period, February and March, 12.7 per cent of the wages paid skilled workers was earned by Negro artisans. . . .

Under the educational program of the FERA, out of a total of 17,879 teachers employed in 13 southern states, 5,476 or 30.6 per cent were Negro. Out of a total of 570,794 enrolled in emergency classes, 217,000 or 38 per cent were Negro. Out of a total of $886,300 expended in a month (either February or March 1935) for the program, Negroes received $231,320 or 26.1 per cent. These southern states in which 26.1 per cent of all emergency salaries were paid to Negro teachers, ordinarily allot only 11.7 per cent of all public school salaries to Negro teachers. The situation may be summarized as follows: Six of the 13 states are spending for Negro salaries a proportion of their emergency education funds larger than the percentage of Negroes in those states. The area as a whole is spending for Negro salaries a proportion of its funds slightly in excess of the percentage of Negroes in the population. This development is an example of Government activity breaking away from the *status quo* in race relations.

There is one Government expenditure in education in reference to which there has been general agreement that equity has been established. That is the FERA college scholarship program. Each college or university not operated for profit, received $20 monthly per student as aid for 12 per cent of its college enrollment. Negro and white institutions have benefited alike under this program.

In the execution of some phases of the Recovery Program, there have been difficulties, and the maximum results have not been received by the Negroes. But, given the economic situation of 1932, the New Deal has been more helpful than harmful to Negroes. We had unemployment in 1932. Jobs were being lost by Negroes, and they were in need. Many would have starved had there been no Federal relief program. As undesirable as is the large relief load among Negroes, the FERA has meant much to them. In most of the New Deal setups, there has been some Negro representation by competent Negroes. The Department of the Interior and the PWA have appointed some fifteen Negroes to jobs of responsibility which pay good salaries. These persons have secretarial and clerical staffs attached to their offices. In addition to these new jobs, there are the colored messengers, who number around 100, and the elevator operators for the Government buildings, of whom there are several hundred. This is not, of course, adequate representation; but it represents a step in the desired direction and is greater recognition than has been given Negroes in the Federal Government during the last 20 years. Or again, in the Nashville housing project, a Negro architectural firm is a consultant; for the Southwest Side housing project in Chicago, a Negro is an associate architect. One of the proposed projects will have two Negro principal architects, a Negro consultant architect, and a technical staff of about six Negro technicians. In other cities competent colored architects will be used to design housing projects.

This analysis is intended to indicate some advantages accruing to the Negro under the Recovery Program, and to point out that the New Deal, insofar as it represents an extension of governmental activity into the economic sphere, is a departure which can do much to reach the Negro citizens. In many instances it has availed itself of these opportunities. An intelligent appraisal of its operation is necessary to assure greater benefits to colored citizens.

49 • Walter White: *U. S. Department of (White) Justice*

Lynchings and other atrocities committed against Negroes reached a peak in the early years of the twentieth century and continued into the 1920's and early 1930's. In 1933 the National Association for the Advancement of Colored People drafted a federal antilynching bill. This was introduced in Congress year after year by Senators Edward Costigan of Colorado and Robert F. Wagner of New York, but failed to overcome a powerful opposition consisting of Southern Democrats and anti-Negro Republicans like William E. Borah. Though Roosevelt spoke out against lynching, he never gave full support to the antilynching bill, fearful perhaps that those Southerners who ruled important committees in Congress would then withdraw support for his economic measures. The Department of Justice did not take any significant action to enforce Reconstruction-era civil rights laws that might have been used to protect Negroes against violence. In 1939, under the liberal Attorney General Frank Murphy, a Civil Rights Section was set up in the Criminal Division of the Department of Justice, but it was small and incapable of taking action on more than a few of the approximately 10,000 complaints it received annually. In the article below, Walter White (1893–1955), for many years Secretary of the NAACP, conveys some of the bitterness Negroes felt because of the lack of federal action to protect their lives and liberties.

From Walter White, "U.S. Department of (White) Justice," *The Crisis*, XLII (October 1935), 309-310. Reprinted with the permission of the publisher.

The Department of Justice in Washington may lay claim to a 100 per cent performance in at least one branch of its activities—the evasion of cases involving burning questions of Negro rights. It sidestepped the issue of the exclusion of Negroes from southern elections on the ground that it was loaded with political dynamite. Other legalistic reasons were later added but the first orders to "Go Slow" were placed on purely political grounds. On the lynching issue the department has set a new record for its ability to dodge from one excuse to another.

On June 6, 1933, a white girl was murdered near Tuscaloosa, Alabama, and shortly thereafter three Negro boys were thrown in jail on suspicion of the murder. On August 12, 1933, the sheriff of Tuscaloosa county unlawfully under color of authority took it upon himself to order their removal from Tuscaloosa to Birmingham "for safekeeping." The sheriff's deputies started at night for Birmingham in two automobiles: two deputies and the boys in the leading car, and a car full of deputies trailing behind. The sheriff ordered the convoy to take a back road because, as the deputies later testified, he did not want to risk the convoy being overtaken by a mob on the highway. When the convoy reached the Tuscaloosa county line, the trailing car turned back, leaving the first car with the boys in it to make the rest of the journey alone. Two miles across the county line the car with the boys in it was *met,* not overtaken, by other cars full of masked men. The boys were taken out, riddled with bullets, and two of them killed. The Southern Association for the Prevention of Lynching made an investigation which found the sheriff culpable.

A delegation made up of representatives from several national organizations on August 24 called at the Department of Justice pursuant to appointment made with William Stanley, executive assistant to Attorney General Homer S. Cummings, who had promised to receive it in the absence of the attorney general, to request the department to investigate the lynching and prosecute the offending sheriff under Revised Statutes 5510 which makes it a federal offense to deprive an inhabitant of any state of any rights, privileges or immunities secured or protected by the federal Constitution under color of law or custom. But although Stanley had made the appointment himself, when the delegation arrived at the department, Stanley was not present, had sent no excuse for his absence, and investigation disclosed that he had not even entered the appointment on his calendar pad.

The delegation was so indignant that the officials of the department four hours later carried them in to see the attorney general himself. The attorney general was suave; he would make no commitment; he called for a brief. Accordingly a thorough brief was filed with the department October 13, 1933, and Stanley stated that he would let the delegation know the decision of the department by November 1. Actually he kept the delegation in suspense until March 5, 1934, although months before both he and the attorney general had told Roger N. Baldwin of the American Civil Liberties Union that the department did not intend to take any action in the case.

In the meanwhile a bill amending the original Lindbergh kidnaping law of 1932 had been introduced in Congress. The 1932 act had made kidnaping a federal offense where the kidnaped person was knowingly transported in interstate or foreign commerce and "held for ransom or reward." The amendment to the 1932 act proposed to broaden the scope of federal jurisdiction and make kidnaping a federal offense when the person kidnaped was knowingly transported in interstate or foreign commerce and "held for ransom or reward *or otherwise*" (italics ours). It also proposed that there should be a prima facie presumption that the person kidnaped had been carried across the state line unless released within three days.

While the bill was before the Senate judiciary committee the attorney general submitted a memorandum to the committee in support of the amendment as follows:

"This amendment adds thereto (to the Lindbergh Act of 1932) the word 'otherwise'. . . The object of the word 'otherwise' is to extend the jurisdiction of this act to persons who have been kidnaped and held, not only for reward *but for any other reason.*

"In addition this bill adds a proviso to the Lindbergh Act that in the absence of the return of the person kidnaped . . . during a period of three days *the presumption arises* that such person has been transported in interstate or foreign commerce, but such presumption is not conclusive.

"I believe that this is a sound amendment which will clear up border line cases, justifying federal investigation in most of such cases and assuring the validity of federal prosecution in numerous instances in which such prosecution would be questionable under the present form of this act." (Italics ours.)

In other words, at this stage the attorney general placed the Department of Justice squarely behind the amendment, giving to its provisions the broadest possible interpretation. But as soon as questions of lynching were raised, the attorney general abandoned his broad construction and began hopping from one position to another to avoid taking jurisdiction.

The bill passed Congress and became enacted into law June 22, 1934, with all the provisions of the amendment adopted except that the time within which a kidnaped person had to be held for presumption of an interstate transportation to arise was increased from three days to seven; and certain other changes not here material.

On October 4, 1934, one Curtis James' house was broken into near Darien, Georgia, about fifty miles from the Florida line, and James, a Negro, shot and abducted by a mob. In spite of an intensive search he was not found. After waiting more than the seven days provided by the amended Lindbergh law, the National Association for the Advancement of Colored

People on October 15 wrote the Department of Justice asking whether the abductors of James could not be prosecuted under the amended Lindbergh law. Under date of October 20 the department replied:

". . . there is nothing to indicate that the person alleged to have been kidnaped was transported in interstate commerce and was held for ransom, reward or otherwise. In the absence of these facts establishing these elements it would seem that the matter would be one entirely for the authorities of the State of Georgia. . ."

It is interesting that in the James case the Department of Justice recognized that a lynching case might be covered under the words "or otherwise" of the amended Lindbergh act, but it dodged jurisdiction by repudiating the presumption. In short the department deliberately ignored the fact that not returning James within seven days created a presumption that there had been an interstate kidnaping, and thereby gave the federal government jurisdiction over the crime. It demanded that the N.A.A.C.P. substitute itself for the department's own Bureau of Investigation and produce the *facts* establishing an interstate kidnaping.

Then on October 26, 1934, a Negro named Claude Neal was kidnaped from the jail in Brewton, Alabama, by a mob which came to the scene in automobiles bearing Florida licenses. Neal was transported across the Alabama line into Florida, held for fifteen hours and then murdered after unspeakable barbarities near Marianna, Florida. The N.A.A.C.P. felt that at last it had a perfect case for federal prosecution, but before it could even get a letter to the Department of Justice requesting an investigation, the department had issued a public statement that the words "or otherwise" in the amended Lindbergh law did not cover the case of lynching. Faced by the indisputable fact of an interstate kidnaping, the department was forced to the position that the amendment Lindbergh law covered kidnaping for purposes of gain, but not for purposes of murder.

With loud fan-fare and carefully staged publicity, on November 7, 1934, the attorney general announced to the country a National Crime Conference called by him in Washington, December 10-13, 1934, "to give broad and practical consideration to the problem of crime" including causes and prevention of crime; investigation; detection and apprehension of crime and criminals. A comprehensive and distinguished list of delegates, including bar associations, was invited; but no Negro associations. On November 9 the N.A.A.C.P. wrote the attorney general asking whether lynching would be placed on the conference agendum. On November 16 the department replied:

". . . the program for the conference has not as yet been completed, obviously it will be impossible to cover all the phases of the crime problem in the short space of three days. No definite decision has been made with reference to the subject of lynching. I wish to thank you, however, for bringing this matter to our attention."

The crime of lynching was not even within the range of the department's vision.

No word came from the department concerning its decision whether to place lynching on the conference agendum, so on November 22 the N.A.A.C.P. wired the attorney general inquiring whether the decision had been made, and what. The department replied November 27 that "it was not probable that the subject of lynching will be given place on program of Crime Conference." Repeated efforts were made by local representatives of N.A.A.C.P. to see the Department of Justice in an attempt to obtain a reconsideration of the decision not to place lynching on the agendum, but the department remained unmoved.

Finally on the opening night of the conference when President Roosevelt made his key-note speech and roundly denounced lynching as one of the major crimes confronting this country, another wire was sent the attorney general asking in view of the President's pronouncement whether he would not at that date place lynching on the agendum. No reply was received the following morning, so at 12:30 P. M. that day the District of Columbia branch of the N.A.A.C.P. began to picket the Crime Conference.

The pickets were arrested almost as soon as they appeared and charged with violation of the District of Columbia sign law and parading without a permit. But that afternoon at 2:25 P. M. the branch received a telegram from the attorney general stating that although there was no room for a discussion of lynching on the formal agendum of the conference, there was a discussion period after each session and that if a discussion period were free, he hoped that the subject of lynching would be taken up on the floor. He further invited a delegation consisting of representatives of the local colored bar association to membership in the conference.

In spite of this action by the attorney general however, the chairman of the conference announced that the discussion period would be limited to the papers read on the formal agendum at the particular session. Under the circumstances the District of Columbia branch of the N.A.A.C.P. decided to resume the picketing.

On the last day of the conference, December 13, just before the morning session adjourned, about sixty pickets suddenly appeared on the sidewalk in front of the convention hall, and silently took up pre-arranged stations about ten feet apart, stretching all the way from the entrance of the hall about three squares along the street the delegates had to use in leaving the conference. To avoid the sign law which prohibited signs twelve inches or over, the pickets carried signs across their breasts eleven inches wide. Ropes were looped around their necks to symbolize lynching. To avoid the charge of parading, each picket remained silent and stationary. The police were taken completely by surprise. To add to the confusion of the police the pickets were provided with a mimeographed sheet of instructions, one of which read that if anybody bothered them they were to call on the police for protection, as the police would not arrest them if they were not violating any law, since to do so would subject the police to an action for damages. The police fumed; an attorney for the Department of Justice hurriedly left to consult the law and find grounds for arresting the pickets, but never returned. That afternoon the conference, smoked out beyond the point of endurance, adopted a completely inane and harmless resolution condemning the use of illegal means in disposing of matters arousing racial antagonisms. The attorney general held both his peace and his hand.

Finally March 12, 1935, a Negro, Ab Young, was lynched near Slayden, Mississippi, allegedly for shooting a white man. Young had been seized in Tennessee, and taken across the line into Mississippi for the ceremonies. Memphis news reporters were on hand either by accident or previous notice.

The N.A.A.C.P. telegraphed both the attorney general and the President of the United States asking for investigation and prosecution under the amended Lindbergh law. To date it is still awaiting a reply. The coroner's jury returned a verdict that Young had died at the hands of parties unknown.

The attorney general continues his offensive against crime—except crimes involving the deprivation of life and liberty and citizenship to Negroes.

50 • Harold L. Ickes: *Not "Special Consideration" but a "New Social Order for All"*

Harold L. Ickes (1874-1952), a colorful and rambunctious figure in the Roosevelt Administration, was also its most forthright spokes-

From Harold Ickes, "The Negro as a Citizen," *The Crisis*, XLIII (August 1936), 230-231, 242. Reprinted with the permission of the publisher.

man for Negro rights. He was a former head of the Chicago branch of the NAACP, and when he took office under the New Deal, he was responsible for appointing a number of Negroes to key offices in his Department. In addressing the twenty-seventh annual conference of the NAACP in Baltimore, Ickes developed the characteristic New Deal position that "under our new conception of democracy, the Negro will be given the chance to which he is entitled—not because he will be singled out for special consideration but because he preeminently belongs to the class that the new democracy is designed especially to aid."

I am happy to be here tonight to address the 27th anniversary of the National Association for the Advancement of Colored People. In addition to my natural appreciation of the privilege of addressing you, I feel at home here. The things for which you stand and the broad purposes to which your Association has been dedicated have been among my life-long interests. I have always been sensitive about justice and fair play for those who were without a friend at court. More than once I have stood in the line of battle against those who would exploit the weak and persecute the helpless.

For the past 27 years your Association has been waging this kind of a battle. As a lifeguard you have patroled the beach to safeguard the civic and personal liberties of members of the Negro race. You have fought disfranchisement, segregation, and lynching. Through mass protests, by appeal to the courts, and by arousing public opinion, you have rendered a significant service not alone to Negroes, but to the country as a whole. In cultivating a disposition to accord Negroes their full rights as citizens, you have helped all of us to remember the fundamental principles upon which the Nation is founded. . . .

Under our new conception of democracy, the Negro will be given the chance to which he is entitled—not because he will be singled out for special consideration, but because he preeminently belongs to the class that the new democracy is designed especially to aid. It is to the advantage of Negroes, therefore, that they thoroughly familiarize themselves with the modified social and economic foundation upon which the new democracy is being built. This requires knowledge and understanding of the new forces brought into being by science and technology, and of the various social and political elements which are emerging as a result of greater understanding among men. In order to throw their moral strength and the weight of their influence on the side of the new liberalism and progressivism that is emerging from the welter of our political life, they must have sufficient intelligence and training to make a wise choice among social values. Unfortunately, we know too well that the educational opportunities enjoyed by Negroes are too meager and even in many cases too antiquated for them to develop the type of intelligence required for effective functioning in our keenly competitive democratic society. This makes it all the more important to develop a sound leadership such as this organization can supply.

I have said that the Negro has been probably the greatest sufferer during the period of our development when exploitation was the general rule. I wish to elaborate on this.

In the economic realm, the Negro has lived for generations on the very fringes. He has been required to work at jobs of the lowest grades, for long hours, at small pay. There has been slight opportunity or encouragement for him to break into the higher levels of employment or into new fields. As a rule, organized labor has refused to enroll him in its ranks. This discrimination has frequently resulted in his use as a "scab" for strike breaking purposes. The general lack of educational facilities has been most acute in the vocational and economic realms. There has been neither proper vocational training, adapted to occupational needs, nor instruction in those important economic and social principles which should be the stock-in-trade of every worker. In some cases where, by means of apprenticeship or otherwise, he has become skilled in certain trades he has been refused a license to engage in that trade.

In the exercise of the suffrage that is guaranteed him by the Constitution the Negro has met with many abuses and obstacles. In some localities he is callously disfranchised; in other places, for generations, he has been exploited by corrupt politicians, who have bought his vote or have made him promises which were never expected to be kept. And, finally, he has been the victim of taxation without representation.

Educationally the Negro on the average lags far below the accepted standards in those communities where separate schools for the Negro and white races are maintained. Studies made in the Office of Education of the Department of the Interior show (1) a lack of availability of educational facilities for Negroes; (2) inadequate financial support; (3) poorly prepared, poorly paid, and improperly selected teachers; and (4) ill-adapted educational programs. Here we have a sad commentary on our democratic principle of equal opportunity, especially when we realize the importance of education in our scheme of life and that Negroes are required to meet the same standards as other citizens.

The general social and civic status of Negroes reveals a picture quite as unsatisfactory as those which portray the economic and educational phases of their lives. Their high morbidity, their crime rate, their infant mortality and their short life span may be attributed very largely to conditions of their environment. Their homes, for which they are charged exorbitant prices both as buyers and renters, are located in the poorest and most insanitary sections of the community, without adequate streets, pavements, water supply, lighting, sewerage, drainage, or fire and police protection. In addition to malnutrition, due to the sub-marginal existence that so many of them lead, there is a lack of medical and hospital care, of pre-natal and maternal care, as well as a general absence of counter-balancing influences such as recreational, welfare, and educational agencies and facilities.

When the extent to which Negroes have been the victims of prejudice, passion, ignorance, and discrimination is realized and the degree to which they have met with frustrations in their legitimate efforts to improve themselves and their race, their achievements merit our admiration. A race possessing less fortitude and faith would have fallen by the wayside.

I congratulate you on your patience, and on the fact that you have worked while you waited. I believe that your cheerful disposition, your faith, your loyalty and your lack of resentment are some of the qualities that have brought you the success that already is yours. May I admonish you as a sincere friend to "keep the Faith!" In spite of the wrongs that have been committed against you, do not become bitter. Hatred is a venom which poisons the blood and incapacitates the person who generates it. Resist wrong stanchly, fight injustice, and discrimination, but as for hating those who are guilty of these things, remember the philosophy of the Jews whose plight has been similar to your own: "Vengeance is mine; I will repay, saith the Lord."

I am convinced that the liberal-minded and far-seeing among us will eventually realize that, as a people, we can be no happier or stronger than our most miserable and weakest group.

The doctrine of laissez faire in interracial relations has characterized national administrations since the reaction from reconstruction days. Under Franklin D. Roosevelt this attitude has changed. He has realized, as no other President since Lincoln seemed to realize, that the mere existence in the Federal

Constitution of the 13th, 14th and 15th amendments is no guarantee of their enforcement. Among his many humane and far-sighted acts has been that of a vigorous policy of justice toward Negroes. His administration of relief, in which Negroes have received the same consideration as whites, has given the members of the Negro race a standing which they have not enjoyed since they became citizens. Of course, the prejudices that have been fostered and built up for 60 years cannot be done away with over night, but the greatest advance since the Civil War toward assuring the Negro that degree of justice to which he is entitled and that equality of opportunity under the law which is implicit in his American citizenship, has been made since Franklin D. Roosevelt was sworn in as President on March 4, 1933.

There is appearing today among Negroes a newer, abler and more forthright leadership. It is a self-respecting leadership. They come not as suppliants or wards. It is gratifying to observe the approach of these leaders to the problems of the time and the sanity and justice of their demands for their race. It is perfectly proper that they should, as they do, regard themselves as citizens entitled to all the rights and privileges that go with that status. The record of Negroes throughout the history of America is one of which any group might well be proud. In every aspect of the Nation's life they have made significant contributions. And now, properly, the day has arrived when they are asking for a fulfillment to them of the promise of "Life, Liberty, and the Pursuit of Happiness."

Negroes are demanding that the ideals and principles upon which the Nation was founded shall be translated into action, and made to apply to themselves as well as to other citizens. They are not asking the Government to coddle them nor to direct their activities, but they do want the Government to assure them a fair chance and an equal opportunity in their desire to attain a fuller life.

Your Government at the present time is not insensitive to this plea, for it comports with its own conception of its responsibility. It is attempting to build a new social order and to set up higher ideals for all of its citizens. In helping the common man to achieve a life that is more worth while, this Administration is seeking the greatest good for the greatest number of the people.

Especially are citizens asking today that human life and personality be accorded the respect that is due them. This is especially in point at this time when intolerance is on the upgrade and mob violence appears to be on the increase. That "vile form of collective murder—lynch law— . . . has broken out in our midst again." No language is too forceful to characterize these blights on America's honor. No measures of the Government would be too strong that effectively would stamp out such un-American practices. The President of the United States has put the weight of his voice and the prestige of his high office against these evil manifestations. Many organizations and numerous law-abiding citizens everywhere have protested. Mass murders, mob rule, and terrorism are subversive of our most cherished ideals as embodied in the Declaration of Independence and the Constitution. The weak, the helpless, and the unprotected elements in our population have a right to expect protection from their Government. If for no other reason than that of self-preservation, it is imperative that the Nation become aroused to this insidious danger that threatens it.

In addition to the protection of their lives, liberty and property, citizens have a right to expect their Government to make it possible for them to improve their status along all lines—economic, political, and social. I am happy to tell you that the present Administration is conscious of its responsibility in this regard also. . . .

51 • W. E. B. DuBois: *Can Federal Action Change the South?*

W. E. Burghardt Du Bois (1868-1963) was the towering Negro intellectual figure of the first half of the twentieth century. At the start of the century, he clashed with Booker T. Washington over the latter's caution that the Negro should not demand full social and political equality. Du Bois helped found the National Association for the Advancement of Colored People in 1911, edited its magazine *Crisis* for many years, taught sociology at Atlanta University, and later came into collision with more conservative Negroes at the university and in the NAACP. His book *The Souls of Black Folk* (1903) is a passionate evocation of the feelings of a Negro in America. His *Black Reconstruction* (1935) written in the New Deal era, pioneered in the rewriting of the history of Reconstruction, stressing the contributions of Negroes in the Radical governments of the South. In the article below, Du Bois notes that after seven years of New Deal reform, the problem of poverty in the South remains. Yet he points to the possibility that the federal government might play a crucial role in building a new South.

. . . Years ago I was fairly well acquainted with the Southern States both city and country; and then after an absence of twenty-five years I returned to pick up the threads of my acquaintanceship. In the last four or five years I have lived in Atlanta and visited central and south Georgia. I have made two or three trips to Florida and Alabama; I have crossed the Mississippi, and visited Louisiana and eastern Texas. From

From W. E. B. Du Bois, "Federal Action Programs and Community Action in the South," *Social Forces*, XIX (March 1941), 375-380. Prepared for the Fifth Annual Meeting of the Southern Sociological Society, April 5, 1940. Reprinted with the permission of The University of North Carolina Press, publisher of *Social Forces*.

these casual glimpses I seem to have received some idea of current Southern thinking so far as the general mass of people are concerned.

Uppermost I think I perceive bewilderment and lack of logical coherence in the face of drastic change; and even of upheaval in certain basic ideas. These ideas stemmed from that powerful eighteenth century, when freedom became predominantly freedom for industrial enterprise and when political democracy was more and more refused practical operation in the realm of economic development. This situation has been stressed in England, France, and the northern United States, but perhaps it has not always been so clearly pointed out that the freedom which industrial enterprise had in industrialized States became in the Cotton Kingdom, freedom for agricultural enterprise, which left the plantation with its monarchial constitution, its aristocracy, clients and slaves largely outside the realm of government and reduced government to the narrowest functions. This was not so much a throw-back to seventeenth century paternalism as a new nineteenth century pattern. The dream of developing this new discreet economy into a ruling expanding imperialism was curbed by the Civil War, and followed by the extremest attempt at democracy ever made in modern times,—the ideal of a democracy which would include ex-slaves as well as freemen and which tried to extend the political power of that democracy over all manner of work and industry. This trial was not conscious nor wholehearted but its main movement would have denied the false divorce between democracy and work which the eighteenth century initiated. The double task failed, not because it was wrong nor impossible, but because in the setting in which it was tried the opposing patterns and forces were far too strong. Neither the South nor the whole of the North believed in allowing black folk to have voice in their own government; but it was more especially because the industrial North and the ruins of the planting South still wanted to keep political power separated from industry. This was finally accomplished by setting up in the South political institutions which deserve more thorough and critical study than they have received. First of all the real methods of government were elaborately concealed. Effective political rule was a matter of secret conference and manipulation, aided by secret police. It became not only difficult for the mass of people to know what government really was, but even the persons in power were not at all clear as to what was being done and how it was being accomplished. The only power that emerged concentrated and clear in its object was the organization of industry including agriculture, and the one widely believed political tenet was what we may call the mud-sill theory of society: namely, that it was to the advantage of the State and to all persons in the State to have at the bottom of society a mass of laborers with the lowest standards of living, the most curtailed wage and with periodic unemployment. Industry thrived on this dogma and industry ruled politics and the State. . . .

On this peculiar relation of politics and industry fell the depression. There came unemployment and relief; there came into sudden and direct contact with the citizen of the Southern community, the far-off and not too well-liked Federal Government. This Federal Government came not as a tax collector but as an alms giver. A new and direct connection between the Federal Government and the individual citizen arose such as the South had never experienced before; but much more than that, there came a direct connection between politics and industry, between government and work, between voting and wages, such as the South was born believing was absolutely impossible and fundamentally wrong.

This approach of the Federal Government to the citizen did not take place suddenly and did not begin with the depression. It began with a certain breakdown of efficiency in local government and a failure of our economic organization to supply resulting needs. Gradually this government had been approaching armed with reasonable bribes and inducements. The Federal Government said build good roads and we will help pay for them; protect forests against fires and we will furnish funds; we will contribute to public health especially that of mothers and children; and we will help in certain kinds of vocational education. Then came even more intimate and practical aid: subsidies to low-cost housing and social security for the old and the young, the blind and the cripple. There came the astonishing work of the PWA and WPA by which the Federal Government cooperated with localities to assist all sorts of public works and their local improvements. The political power of the Federal Government even encroached upon territory long sacred to private industry, insuring bank deposits, protecting mortgaged property and building cheap homes; and finally the actual furnishing of jobs and food. And it did this in the South at a time when the local government was powerless because of lack of funds and unwillingness to distribute jobs or furnish any kind of economic security.

Now the great influence and meaning of this coming of the Federal Government into the provincial South was the fact that here was a political agency attending to economic matters; attending to precisely those economic matters in which as the South had long believed politics had no place. Or if it did have a place it was by secret and unacknowledged methods. Cities and counties attended to their own roads through the agencies of profit-making contractors. Banks were run for the benefit of bankers and, if they could not pay their depositors, they calmly failed. Mortgages were private profit-making investments and homes were built chiefly to sell and not to use. But above all the matter of employment and unemployment was primarily the field and dominion of private industrial enterprise. For a government to furnish jobs simply because a man was out of work, or to give away food simply because a man was starving, was at best an exceptional and unorthodox method of enterprise. Above all private industry furnished jobs and, if jobs failed, private industry when ready would restore them. Capitalists gave work. They were to be commended for their generosity, while laborers out of a job were looked upon with suspicion as probably shiftless.

The laziness of the South, especially of the blacks and the poor whites, had become proverbial and a matter of widespread mirth. Always philosophers pointed out that in this happy land the farm was ready to give any person a living who was willing to dig for it. But here and now in the South this old conception was breaking down; the farmers were badly bankrupt and the tenants worse than bankrupt. Industry was slowing down and wage earners being laid off. However, in steps the Federal Government and no matter with what difficulty or with what waste, with what new interpretation of law and intricacy of administration, it accomplished things. It gave the South food and work and it gave it certain intangible ideals in architecture and industrial planning, in equality of burdens and treatment despite wealth.

Now it seems to me that the essential influence of all this on the South was to bring a question as to the relation of politics to industry; of voting and administration to what had been looked upon always as profit-making business. The Marxian dogma of the fundamental place of economics in the building of civilization was brought home suddenly and effectively to the ordinary and even unlettered Southern citizen: "that in every historical epoch the prevailing mode of economic production and exchange, and the social organization necessarily following from it, form the basis upon which is built up, and from which alone can be explained, the political and intellectual history of that epoch." If ever in modern time a region illustrated this dogma it is the South. Moreover, beyond this a new economic lesson is being subtly and widely instilled in the Southern consciousness. Business itself in the public mind is gradually beginning to disintegrate into schemes for making money and schemes for public usefulness. I am not sure just how far this distinction has gone but I have noticed with great interest WPA enterprises all over the South; beautiful buildings arising, parks being terraced, roads being ditched, schoolhouses being built; people working together not for the orthodox purpose of making something that can be sold for profit, but for the unorthodox and yet very logical purpose of doing something that needs to be done. There were often clear cases of malingering and of work, the necessity of which was not clear; and yet the basic division in man's thought between useful work and work which, in addition to its use or necessity, must return a profit is, it seems to me, growing clearer and clearer throughout the land.

I cannot prove how clear this new conception of the basic relations of political activity to economic well-being has become, how deeply it is sunk but certainly the political instrument known as the Federal Government has rescued the South from the depths of depression, and sooner or later there is bound to come the question: how can this political instrument which is the Federal Government be used more widely and efficiently for the well-being of the mass of people? The same thought has come in other parts of the country, but in no section does it meet with greater inherent difficulties of conception of action than in the South. If in local government, politics in the South has meant low taxes and friends in office, with now and then an anti-Negro excursion, in Federal Government it has shown itself through an organized rotten borough system which by widespread disfranchisement of blacks and whites, gives the Southern voter from five to ten times as much power as the Northern or Western voter. It happens that in this crisis the political power of the South is supporting the man and machines who have so drastically increased the field and function of government, and brought relief to the common man. But this is neither logical nor natural to the South. The natural place of the South, according to its post-Civil War training in politics, and its post-Reconstruction surrender to Northern capital, would be to oppose the increased functions of government and any intrusion of politics in industry.

Something of this reaction to be sure we see, but it is held back by this counter thought; by this deeper questioning: can political activity in the South guide the new relation of politics to industry and, if indeed it can, how shall it do it and toward what ideal? This brings increasing necessity in the South of facing new problems of democracy, of harking straight back to that attempt made in Reconstruction to include all human beings in the realm of democratic control. If this be not done then the South, still prisoned and controlled by old bars and patterns including not only the color line but the eighteenth century conception of freedom of industrial enterprise, becomes the pensioner of a Federal Government with all the difficulties of local administration in a region where local government is neither democratic nor efficient.

How far now between these two extremes can the South find resting place? There can be no doubt of the strong and persistent desire to preserve in the South the social mudsills represented by the poorest workers mostly black, but largely white. Any real democracy has got to share political power with these. The economic mudsill is kept in place by the industrial organization and, until the industrial pattern is changed, the political pattern cannot be free to establish democracy. It is in this way that Southern economic conditions make political freedom impossible. Is the South today ready for such economic revolution? Not yet.

As I look around to these areas with which I have become more or less familiar in the last five or six years, I see in Atlanta and Georgia the old idea of industrial exploitation dominant; the glee at seeing Northern industry pour into the South in search of cheap labor, of lack of governmental interference and machine politics, of the secret grafting type dominating government activities. This is still the pattern of Atlanta thought no matter what other thinking may be or must be seething below. In Houston, Texas, the old pattern goes on. The mass of farmers and farm tenants deserting the wide surrounding land pour into this fabulous city which is probably today the largest in the South. Deserted lands lie dead round about in wide areas but the city is wild with activity, the crowds push and seethe; there is commerce foreign and domestic; there is cotton; there is oil; there is food and profit-making is the great ideal; the machine is dominant and yet across the way in Louisiana there rises the statue of a man who with ruthless dishonesty gave Louisiana bridges instead of dividends.

At Tuskegee rises an institution, facing as it always faced, a paradox. It was placed there by Booker Washington, and his effigy on a United States stamp emphasizes the fact today that the Negro must become a prosperous and efficient farmer; but the Negro has not done this, and, with agriculture in the South, in the United States and in the world over in the plight which it is, he cannot do it. Only revolution in industry and politics such as will restore markets and prices to essential raw material and food can restore the farmer to civilization. So Tuskegee has waited and waits.

But in Florida perhaps comes the most disconcerting contrasts: rich and beautiful land bursting with fruit whose greatest object seems increasingly to be the pampering of the idle rich and pandering to their waste and gambling. Yet the mass of the people here are poor people struggling for a living and not sure whether that living is coming from digging in the soil or the tips of the rich.

Thus contradiction and enigma are before the South, under this increased and increasing function of government. There lingers undoubtedly the thought that the South will not be compelled to find a new way and new formulae that old conditions one of these days will be restored when the Federal Government will recede to its former distance and inactivity and where the employer will give jobs and give alms. But all this wishful thinking is in vain. Change has come and the South will be more and more compelled to put politics in industry, to reconstruct government so as to give and direct work, and to make that government democratic. I feel that the South is more or less consciously thinking of these things and groping toward solution; and that this thinking is not so much the work of its intellectual leaders, of its colleges and writers, as of the man to whom the Federal Government has given bread.

PART TEN

THE CONSTITUTION AND SOCIAL PROGRESS

52 • Felix Frankfurter: *Social Issues Before the Supreme Court*

Felix Frankfurter (1882-1965) came to the United States at an early age from Austria, graduated from Harvard Law School, and served from 1914 as a distinguished member of the Law School faculty until his appointment by FDR to the Supreme Court in 1939. An outspoken liberal, he wrote frequently on topics of public interest, and attracted nationwide attention as a defender of Sacco and Vanzetti, two Italian immigrants executed on charges of murder and armed robbery in Massachusetts in 1927. He had been a friend of Roosevelt for many years, and became an unofficial adviser to the President soon after the election. Frankfurter often sent bright young Harvard Law School graduates to Washington to work with the administration; through them and through his long correspondence with Roosevelt, he became one of the most influential of FDR's advisers.

The Supreme Court, in the early years of the twentieth century, and up through the 1920's, had proved a bulwark of conservatism, striking down one after another attempts by states to pass welfare legislation, whether laws to restrict child labor, or to set maximum hours, or minimum wages, or to regulate big business. In the article below, Frankfurter anticipates what would become, four years later, the philosophy of the Court itself.

In this the fourth winter of our discontent it is no longer temerarious or ignorant to believe that this depression has a significance very different from prior economic stresses in our national history. The more things change the more they remain the same is an epigram of comfortable cynicism. There are new periods in history, and we are in the midst of one of them. . . .

In our scheme of government, readjustment to great social changes means juristic readjustment. Our basic problems—whether of industry, agriculture, or finance—sooner or later appear in the guise of legal problems. Professor John R. Commons is therefore justified in characterizing the Supreme Court of the United States as the authoritative faculty of economics. The foundation for its economic encyclicals is the Constitution. Plainly, however, constitutional provisions are not economic dogmas and certainly not obsolete economic dogmas. A classic admonition of Mr. Justice Holmes cannot be recalled too often —"A constitution is not intended to embody a particular economic theory, whether of paternalism and the organic relation of the citizen to the State or of *laissez faire*. It is made for people of fundamentally differing views, and the accident of our finding certain opinions natural and familiar or novel and even shocking ought not to conclude our judgment upon the question whether statutes embodying them conflict with the Constitution of the United States."

By its very conception the Constitution has ample resources within itself to meet the changing needs of successive generations. For "it was made for an undefined and expanding future and for a people gathered and to be gathered from many nations and of many tongues." Through the generality of its language the Constitution provided for the future partly by not forecasting it. If the Court, aided by the bar, has access to the facts and heeds them, the Constitution is flexible enough to respond to the demands of modern society. . . .

Public law is thus a most potent instrument of public policy. The significant cases before the Supreme Court are not just controversies between two litigants. They involve large public issues, and the general outlook of the Justices gives direction to their judicial views. In law also, where one ends, depends much on one's starting point. . . .

The Justices of the Supreme Court are arbiters of social policy because their duties make them so. For the words of the Constitution which invoke the legal judgment are usually so unrestrained by their intrinsic meaning or by their history or by prior decisions that they leave the individual Justice free, if indeed they do not compel him, to gather meaning not from reading the Constitution but from reading life. Only an alert and self-critical awareness of the true nature of the judicial process in these public controversies will avert the translation of discredited assumption or unconscious bias into national policy.

In a period of rapid change like ours, the pace of social adjustments must be quickened. Poignant experience has made us realize the public implications of interests heretofore treated as private. Such interests must be stripped of many of their past immunities and subjected to appropriate responsibility. Courts will thus be called upon to make and to sustain extensive readjustments.

For example, the law must become more sophisticated in its conception of trustees' obligations. It must sharpen and extend the duties incident to the fiduciary relations of corporate directors and officers. The whole process of corporate salaries disproportionate to services rendered must be fearlessly faced, but especially the abuse of agreement for swollen contingent compensation. The Bethlehem Steel bonus system is a notorious example. Another instance, recently before the courts, merits recital. The directors of the American Tobacco Company in 1912 initiated a by-law authorizing six senior officers to divide among themselves ten per cent of any annual profits in excess of those earned by the Company in 1910. Since 1921, $10,000,000 has been thus distributed. In addition to his regular salary of $168,000 and "special cash credits" of $273,000, the President of the Company in 1930 received a bonus of $840,000. Even these rewards, apparently, did not provide sufficient incentive. The directors therefore adopted an Employee Stock Subscription Plan, which resulted in the sale to themselves, as officer-employees, of 32,000 shares of stock at $25 a share when the market price was $112. The millions which the President and Vice-President of the American Tobacco Company thus received appeared to a majority of the United States Circuit Court of Appeals, in New York, only reasonable compensation for making Lucky Strike the most popular cigarette in the world. That Court seemed impressed by the fact that both schemes were approved by the stockholders. To which Judge Thomas W. Swan, with real insight into the actualities of corporate management, suggested, in his dissent, that the shareholders when they adopted the by-law in 1912 could hardly have anticipated that they were conferring upon their President in 1930 a bonus five times his salary, or that through the Employee Stock Subscription Plan three-fifths of the stock would be allotted to directors by themselves. Equally unreal seems the Court's failure to explore whether the conventional assent by proxies really signifies considered approval. . . .

Mr. Justice Stone admirably expressed the far-reaching objections to the considerations of parochialism to which the Supreme Court, most surprisingly in the light of precedents, deferred in this case: "Extension of corporate activities, distribution of corporate personnel, stockholders and directors through many States, and the diffusion of corporate ownership, separated from corporate management, make the integrity of the conduct of large business corporations increasingly a matter of national rather than local concern, . . . to which the

Federal courts should be quick to respond, when their jurisdiction is rightly invoked."

The case furnishes an illuminating glimpse into the traditional operations of big business and its opportunities for socially indefensible profit to the insiders. The law cannot long continue to give such unbridled rein to the acquisitive motive. Our social health cannot afford it. . . .

Indeed, we must recognize the profound shift in the very purposes of taxation. Senator Root once reminded the American bar that "the vast increase of wealth resulting from the increased power of production is still in the first stages of the inevitable processes of distribution." Mr. Root was himself a member of an Administration which employed the taxing power as one of the instruments for such distribution. Theodore Roosevelt was the first President avowedly to use the taxing power as a direct agency of social policy. More and more, it is bound to serve as a powerful means for directing the modern flow of wealth to social uses. The historical ambitions of American democracy and fiscal necessities alike demand it. . . .

The Supreme Court is indispensable to the effective workings of our federal government. If it did not exist, we should have to create it. I know of no other peaceful method for making the adjustments necessary to a society like ours—for maintaining the equilibrium between state and federal power, for settling the eternal conflicts between liberty and authority—than through a court of great traditions free from the tensions and temptations of party strife, detached from the fleeting interests of the moment. But because, inextricably, the Supreme Court is also an organ of statesmanship and the most powerful organ, it must have a seasoned understanding of affairs, the imagination to see the organic relations of society, above all, the humility not to set up its own judgment against the conscientious efforts of those whose primary duty it is to govern. So wise and temperate a scholar as the late Ernst Freund expressed this judgment after a lifetime's study of our government: "It is unlikely that a legislature will otherwise than through inadvertence violate the most obvious and cardinal dictates of justice; gross miscarriages of justice are probably less frequent in legislation than they are in the judicial determination of controversies." And the Supreme Court itself has told us that "it must be remembered that legislatures are ultimate guardians of the liberties and welfare of the people in quite as great a degree as the courts."

Unfortunately, the Supreme Court forgets at times to remember its own wisdom. In view of the tasks in hand, the price of judicial obscurantism is too great. . . .

Finally, what of the Supreme Court's attitude towards the most inclusive of all our problems, namely, how to subdue our anarchic competitive economy to reason, how to correct the disharmonies between production and consumption? This issue was raised last spring in the now famous Oklahoma Ice case. On the basis of watchful scrutiny of the actual operation of the ice industry in Oklahoma, the legislature of that State, acting upon the recommendation of its Corporation Commission, availed itself of a well-tested instrument of public control—the device of a certificate of public convenience and necessity—to subject the ice business to a regulated instead of a wildcat economy. By this means, Oklahoma, within the limited area of the ice industry, endeavored to avoid excessive equipment and the demoralization of deflation and unemployment, and thereby promote stability. But the majority of the Court struck down this very modest essay in regulated economy. It denied Oklahoma's right to act upon its own experience, and, for a time at least, unbridled competition was given the sanction of the United States Constitution.

Against such an attitude, Mr. Justice Brandeis raised his magistral voice. It is not hazardous prophecy to believe that Mr. Justice Brandeis's opinion (concurred in by Mr. Justice Stone, Mr. Justice Cardozo taking no part in the decision) merely anticipates history, even the history of future opinions of the Court. The closing observations of this memorable dissent deserve quotation:

"To stay experimentation in things social and economic is a grave responsibility. Denial of the right to experiment may be fraught with serious consequences to the Nation. It is one of the happy incidents of the federal system that a single courageous State may, if its citizens choose, serve as a laboratory; and try novel social and economic experiments without risk to the rest of the country. This Court has the power to prevent an experiment. We may strike down the statute which embodies it on the ground that, in our opinion, the measure is arbitrary, capricious or unreasonable. We have power to do this, because the due process clause has been held by the Court applicable to matters of substantive law as well as to matters of procedure. But in the exercise of this high power, we must be ever on our guard, lest we erect our prejudices into legal principles. If we would guide by the light of reason, we must let our minds be bold."

The faith and enterprise which built this nation are unimpaired. Our intrinsic resources are greater than ever. We have also the unparalleled advantage of a fluid society. Under the guidance of a Supreme Court responsive to the potentialities of the Constitution to meet the needs of our society, it would now lie within our power to have an enduring diffusion of the goods of civilization to an extent never before attainable.

53 · Morris R. Cohen: *Fallacies About the Court*

In May 1935, in the *Schechter Case,* the Supreme Court delivered a great blow to the New Deal by declaring the National Recovery Act unconstitutional. The Act, the Court said, delegated to the

From Morris R. Cohen, "What to do with the Supreme Court?" *The Nation,* XCLI (July 10, 1935), 39-40. Reprinted with the permission of the publisher.

President too many powers that rightfully should be exercised by Congress. Furthermore, the NRA stretched the interstate commerce clause of the Constitution beyond its limits, the Court maintained, by using it as a justification for regulating all kinds of business establishments. The decision in the *Schechter Case* inaugurated a bitter battle, in Washington and throughout the country, on the role of the Supreme Court in the American scheme of government. Joining that battle was Morris Cohen (1880-1947), one of the most influential of twentieth-century American philosophers, who wrote many books and had a long teaching career at City College in New York. His argument below is a cogent exposition of what is sometimes called the "sociological interpretation" of constitutional law.

That the people of the United States favor the NRA was made obvious by the unprecedented Congressional majority accorded to the Administration in the election of 1934. What, then, prevents Congress from passing a bill enlarging the Supreme Court with ten additional judges who, on a rehearing, are sure to vote for the constitutionality of the original act?

There is a general impression that this would be dishonest. Why so? Because, according to the traditional assumption, judges have nothing to do with making the law, their decisions following with logical necessity from "the solemn will of the people expressed in the Constitution," and if the results are bad, we should go through the laborious ordeal of changing the Constitution rather than the composition of the court. This view has so often been repeated that it is generally accepted as axiomatic. Nevertheless, it rests on a number of rather obvious fallacies.

1. That the judges merely find the meaning of the Constitution and in no way make or mold it has long been characterized among scientific jurists as a childish fiction. No one can seriously maintain that all of our constitutional law as to what constitutes interstate commerce, the police power of the states,

or due process of law follows logically from the wording of the Constitution and has not been affected by the social, economic, and political opinions of different judges. The law took a different direction under Taney than under Marshall. Indeed, how could the people in 1789—or the small proportion of them who had the right to vote then—have foreseen all the modern inventions and made definite provisions for them? It is certainly not through anything written in the Constitution that the power to regulate interstate commerce includes the power to prohibit the sending of liquor into certain states but not the power to regulate insurance. A thousand similar distinctions may be mentioned which, whether justified or not by their practical consequences, are certainly judge-made and might have been different if other judges had ruled.

Specificaly the NRA is declared unconstitutional because it delegates legislative power to the President. But the fact is that all effective legislation for the future must inevitably delegate some subsidiary lawmaking to the executive authority. Justices Stone and Cardozo recognized this and claimed that in this case there was too much delegation. But the line between proper and improper delegation is not laid down in the Constitution itself. Where to draw it is a question of political wisdom. Why should the courts rather than Congress determine it? The usual answer is that the Constitution declares itself to be the supreme law of the land, and its interpretation must therefore be left to the courts. This, however, cannot be consistently maintained. The Constitution provides that every state shall be guaranteed a republican form of government. What does that mean? In the Oregon case, when the issue was raised as to whether the referendum was compatible with a republican form of government, the Supreme Court declared it a political question and *not* for the courts to decide. There are in fact many express provisions of the Constitution which the courts cannot or dare not enforce. Thus for more than ten years Congress refused to obey the Constitution and to apportion representation according to the latest census. Would our courts have dared to declare the acts of the counter-constitutional congresses between 1922 and 1932 unconstitutional? Certainly not, though if they did so, they would be on logically firmer ground than in deciding that Congress could not pass a minimum-wage law for the District of Columbia.

The truth, then, is that constitutional law is just what judges make it. A leading conservative newspaper put it aptly when it said that the United States Supreme Court is a continuous constitutional convention. This it is in fact. But we do not generally recognize it, else we should demand that the work of this constitutional convention be ratified by the people before it goes into effect, or at any rate that the delegates be more responsive to, and in closer touch with, popular needs.

2. We are frequently told that the Constitution represents the eternal principles of justice, or at least those principles of liberty and right which are characteristic of Anglo-Saxon civilization. The first of these claims is obviously question-begging; specific decisions which strike people as unjust can certainly not be defended that way. The second claim is even more readily disposed of by the fact that our English cousins have never given their courts power to set aside legislation on grounds of unconstitutionality.

3. Quite fallacious also is the rhetorical argument that without this power vested in the courts we should be at the mercy of legislative majorities. This argument ignores the historic fact that in few, if any, actual cases have the majority of our people felt themselves saved from Congressional oppression by judicial intervention. On the contrary, Congress being more responsive to popular demand, our people as a whole have felt more resentment at being at the mercy of small judicial majorities than at being at the mercy of very large legislative majorities. Besides, the mischief of Congressional wrongs can be readily remedied at the next election, while the mischief

of wrong judicial decisions in the name of the Constitution requires the laborious consent of two-thirds of each house of Congress and three-quarters of the state legislatures.

If we need watchers to protect us from bad legislation, why not watchers against bad judicial decisions? The fact is that the people of England, France, Switzerland, or the Scandinavian countries feel as free as we do, and their rights are as amply protected, without their courts having the power to set aside legislation as unconstitutional.

4. It is quite fallacious to argue that our system assures a maximum security of legal rights and thus encourages business enterprise. The actuality is rather the other way. In no other civilized country would people endure a legal system in which such a question as that of the legality of certain codes could remain undetermined for two years. In no other country also is there such a complete separation between power and responsibility as in ours, where those who have the final word on all questions of law are in no way answerable to the popular will or to any other earthly authority.

5. It is generally urged that the judicial veto over legislation has been in force since the case of Marbury vs. Madison in 1803 and it is too late to change it. This argument is historically untenable. What that famous case did decide was that the court would not issue a mandamus to compel a Democratic Secretary of State to deliver certain commissions to some Federalists, even though an act of Congress authorized it to do so. The actual decision was a quite satisfactory victory for the Democratic Administration and not something over which the country got excited. In his written opinion Marshall did, in the fashion of his day, indulge in speculations about constitutions written for all time and superior to acts of Congress; but most of it was mere dictum. It is obviously one thing for a court to refuse to follow a coordinate department of the government to constrain the Executive, and quite another to say to the peo-

ple at large that they are under no obligation to obey a general law enacted to Congress. Marshall argued that judges swear to obey the Constitution and must therefore live up to their oath. But Members of Congress and the Executive likewise swear to obey the Constitution and must therefore also follow what they regard as the meaning of the Constitution. From the chaos which would follow a consistent adherence to the theory of three independent departments of the government we have been saved by the process of practical accommodation and the extra-legal party system.

The first case in which the Supreme Court exercised the right to set aside a law of general importance was the Dred Scott case, and the decision and the dicta in that case were repealed by force of arms. It is only in recent times that declaring acts of Congress unconstitutional may be said to have become a practice.

6. The subordination of Congress to the courts has often been defended on the ground that under this system we have greatly prospered. This is a rather naive example of the fallacy of *post hoc ergo propter hoc*. Our prosperity, if it is a fact, may be due to our unrivaled natural resources, to the practical skill of our people, and the like. And it may well be argued that our present depression is in part due to such judicial vetoes as those of the Lochner case, the Adair case, the child-labor cases, the minimum-wage cases, and others, which by depressing the economic power of the laboring classes have depressed our home markets.

7. When we realize that the important questions which come before our highest court involve political, economic, and technical issues, then if we lay aside pious rhetoric we must admit that far from being the strongest, the judiciary is the weakest part of our governmental system—for it has the least opportunity of getting adequate information. No one who wants to inform himself thoroughly on any question will be satisfied to

do so on the basis of listening for a few hours to two lawyers who have submitted argumentative briefs.

8. Space does not permit discussion of the relation of our federal courts to state legislation. But if the virtue of a federal system be the opportunity for different experiments in different states, that virtue has been effectively minimized by the way in which the Supreme Court has turned the Fourteenth Amendment—intended by the people as a protection for the Negroes—into a prohibition of experiments in the field of social legislation.

54 · Franklin D. Roosevelt: *The Court Needs "New and Younger Blood"*

After its decision on the NRA, the Supreme Court dealt another blow to the New Deal legislative program in 1936, when it declared the Agricultural Adjustment Act unconstitutional, in *Butler* v. *U. S.* The Court argued that the AAA improperly used the taxing power for the regulation of agriculture. That same year, in *Carter* v. *Carter Coal Company*, it struck down the Guffey Coal Conservation Act, which sought to regulate prices and labor conditions in the coal industry. And in still another case it declared unconstitutional a New York State minimum-wage law. Roosevelt, fearful that even more New Deal laws would fall, decided upon a plan to change the nature of the Supreme Court. The Constitution gives Congress the power to fix the number of Supreme Court justices; in February 1937, FDR sent to Congress a proposal to add a new justice to the Supreme Court every time one of its members reached the age of seventy and did not retire. The following month, in one of those

From *The Public Papers and Addresses of Franklin D. Roosevelt*, VI, 122-133.

radio addresses that became memorable as "Fireside Chats," Roosevelt defended his plan before the nation.

. . . Tonight, sitting at my desk in the White House, I make my first radio report to the people in my second term of office.

I am reminded of that March, four years ago, when I made my first radio report to you. We were then in the midst of the great banking crisis. . . .

The American people have learned from the depression. For in the last three national elections an overwhelming majority of them voted a mandate that the Congress and the President begin the task of providing that protection—not after long years of debate, but now.

The Courts, however, have cast doubts on the ability of the elected Congress to protect us against catastrophe by meeting squarely our modern social and economic conditions.

We are at a crisis, a crisis in our ability to proceed with that protection. It is a quiet crisis. There are no lines of depositors outside closed banks. But to the far-sighted it is far-reaching in its possibilities of injury to America.

I want to talk with you very simply tonight about the need for present action in this crisis—the need to meet the unanswered challenge of one-third of a Nation ill-nourished, ill-clad, ill-housed.

Last Thursday I described the American form of Government as a three-horse team provided by the Constitution to the American people so that their field might be plowed. The three horses are, of course, the Congress, the Executive and the Courts. Two of the horses, the Congress and the Executive, are pulling in unison today; the third is not. Those who have intimated that the President of the United States is trying to drive that team, overlook the simple fact that the President, as Chief Executive, is himself one of the three horses.

It is the American people themselves who are in the driver's seat. It is the American people themselves who want the furrow plowed.

It is the American people themselves who expect the third horse to pull in unison with the other two. . . .

But since the rise of the modern movement for social and economic progress through legislation, the Court has more and more often and more and more boldly asserted a power to veto laws passed by the Congress and by State Legislatures in complete disregard of this original limitation, which I have just read.

In the last four years the sound rule of giving statutes the benefit of all reasonable doubt has been cast aside. The Court has been acting not as a judicial body, but as a policy-making body.

When the Congress has sought to stabilize national agriculture, to improve the conditions of labor, to safeguard business against unfair competition, to protect our national resources, and in many other ways to serve our clearly national needs, the majority of the Court has been assuming the power to pass on the wisdom of these Acts of Congress—and to approve or disapprove the public policy written into these laws.

That is not only my accusation. It is the accusation of most distinguished Justices of the present Supreme Court. I have not the time to quote to you all the language used by dissenting Justices in many of these cases. But in the case holding the Railroad Retirement Act unconstitutional, for instance, Chief Justice Hughes said in a dissenting opinion that the majority opinion was "a departure from sound principles," and placed "an unwarranted limitation upon the commerce clause." And three other Justices agreed with him.

In the case holding the Triple A unconstitutional, Justice Stone said of the majority opinion that it was a "tortured construction of the Constitution." And two other Justices agreed with him.

In the case holding the New York Minimum Wage Law unconstitutional, Justice Stone said that the majority were actually reading into the Constitution their own "personal economic predilections," and that if the legislative power is not left free to choose the methods of solving the problems of poverty, subsistence and health of large numbers in the community, then "government is to be rendered impotent." And two other Justices agreed with him.

In the face of these dissenting opinions, there is no basis for the claim made by some members of the Court that something in the Constitution has compelled them regretfully to thwart the will of the people.

In the face of such dissenting opinions, it is perfectly clear that, as Chief Justice Hughes has said: "We are under a Constitution but the Constitution is what the Judges say it is."

The Court, in addition to the proper use of its judicial functions, has improperly set itself up as a third House of the Congress—a super-legislature, as one of the Justices has called it—reading into the Constitution words and implications which are not there, and which were never intended to be there.

We have, therefore, reached the point as a Nation where we must take action to save the Constitution from the Court and the Court from itself. We must find a way to take an appeal from the Supreme Court to the Constitution itself. We want a Supreme Court which will do justice under the Constitution—not over it. In our Courts we want a government of laws and not of men. . . .

What is my proposal? It is simply this: Whenever a Judge or Justice of any Federal Court has reached the age of seventy and does not avail himself of the opportunity to retire on a pension, a new member shall be appointed by the President then in office, with the approval, as required by the Constitution, of the Senate of the United States.

That plan has two chief purposes. By bringing into the Judicial system a steady and continuing stream of new and younger blood, I hope, first, to make the administration of all Federal justice, from the bottom to the top, speedier and, therefore, less costly; secondly, to bring to the decision of social and economic problems younger men who have had personal experience and contact with modern facts and circumstances under which average men have to live and work. This plan will save our national Constitution from hardening of the judicial arteries.

The number of Judges to be appointed would depend wholly on the decision of present Judges now over seventy, or those who would subsequently reach the age of seventy.

If, for instance, any one of the six Justices of the Supreme Court now over the age of seventy should retire as provided under the plan, no additional place would be created. Consequently, although there never can be more than fifteen, there may be only fourteen, or thirteen, or twelve. And there may be only nine.

There is nothing novel or radical about this idea. It seeks to maintain the Federal bench in full vigor. It has been discussed and approved by many persons of high authority ever since a similar proposal passed the House of Representatives in 1869. . . .

Those opposing this plan have sought to arouse prejudice and fear by crying that I am seeking to "pack" the Supreme Court and that a baneful precedent will be established.

What do they mean by the words "packing the Supreme Court"?

Let me answer this question with a bluntness that will end all honest misunderstanding of my purposes.

If by that phrase "packing the Court" it is charged that I wish to place on the bench spineless puppets who would disregard the law and would decide specific cases as I wish them to be decided, I make this answer—that no President fit for his office would appoint, and no Senate of honorable men fit for their office would confirm, that kind of appointee to the Supreme Court.

But if by that phrase the charge is made that I would appoint and the Senate would confirm Justices worthy to sit beside present members of the Court who understand modern conditions—that I will appoint Justices who will not undertake to override the judgment of the Congress on legislative policy—that I will appoint Justices who will act as Justices and not as legislators—if the appointment of such Justices can be called "packing the Court," then I say that I, and with me the vast majority of the American people, favor doing just that thing—now. . . .

If such a law as I propose is regarded as establishing a new precedent—is it not a most desirable precedent?

Like all lawyers, like all Americans, I regret the necessity of this controversy. But the welfare of the United States, and indeed of the Constitution itself, is what we all must think about first. Our difficulty with the Court today rises not from the Court as an institution but from human beings within it. But we cannot yield our constitutional destiny to the personal judgment of a few men who, being fearful of the future, would deny us the necessary means of dealing with the present.

This plan of mine is no attack on the Court; it seeks to restore the Court to its rightful and historic place in our system of Constitutional Government and to have it resume its high task of building anew on the Constitution "a system of living law." The Court itself can best undo what the Court has done. . . .

55 • The Supreme Court Retreats: *Minimum-Wage Laws are Constitutional*

FDR's proposal to add to the number of Supreme Court Justices turned out to be one of the worst mistakes of his political career.

West Coast Hotel Co. v. *Parrish,* 300 U.S. 379 (1937).

Most Americans, even when they objected to the Court's decisions, considered it a foundation of democratic government, and many liberals as well as conservatives wanted to keep it structurally intact. But while the "court-packing plan" was encountering difficulty, a remarkable change was taking place in the Supreme Court. Associate Justice Owen Roberts and Chief Justice Charles Evans Hughes began to join the court liberals in a number of decisions that favored the New Deal philosophy of economic reform. The turning point, in March 1937, was a decision holding constitutional a Washington minimum-wage law. This was a dramatic reversal of the *Adkins* case (1923), which held that such laws violated the Fourteenth Amendment's "due process" clause. That decision appears below, as does Justice Sutherland's minority view, which in retrospect seems the last stand of conservatism on the Court. After this, the Supreme Court became a New Deal Court: some of the older justices retired or died, Roosevelt began to appoint new members to the bench, and a succession of decisions found constitutional the Wagner Act, the Social Security Act, and the Wage-Hour Act.

. . . More than twenty-five years ago we set forth the applicable principle in these words, after referring to the cases where the liberty guaranteed by the Fourteenth Amendment had been broadly described:

"But it was recognized in the cases cited, as in many others, that freedom of contract is a qualified and not an absolute right. There is no absolute freedom to do as one wills or to contract as one chooses. The guaranty of liberty does not withdraw from legislative supervision that wide department of activity which consists of the making of contracts, or deny to government the power to provide restrictive safeguards. Liberty implies the absence of arbitrary restraint, not immunity from reasonable regulations and prohibitions imposed in the interests of the community."

This power under the Constitution to restrict freedom of

contract has had many illustrations. That it may be exercised in the public interest with respect to contracts between employer and employee is undeniable. . . . In dealing with the relation of employer and employed, the legislature has necessarily a wide field of discretion in order that there may be suitable protection of health and safety, and that peace and good order may be promoted through regulations designed to insure wholesome conditions of work and freedom from oppression.

The point that has been strongly stressed that adult employees should be deemed competent to make their own contracts was decisively met nearly forty years ago, where we pointed out the inequality in the footing of the parties. We said:

"The legislature has also recognized the fact, which the experience of legislators in many States has corroborated, that the proprietors of these establishments and their operatives do not stand upon an equality, and that their interests are, to a certain extent, conflicting. The former naturally desire to obtain as much labor as possible from their employees, while the latter are often induced by the fear of discharge to conform to regulations which their judgment, fairly exercised, would pronounce to be detrimental to their health or strength. In other words, the proprietors lay down the rules and the laborers are practically constrained to obey them. In such cases self-interest is often an unsafe guide, and the legislature may properly interpose its authority."

And we added that the fact "that both parties are of full age and competent to contract does not necessarily deprive the State of the power to interfere where the parties do not stand upon an equality, or where the public health demands that one party to the contract shall be protected against himself." "The State still retains an interest in his welfare, however reckless he may be. The whole is no greater than the sum of all the parts, and when the individual health, safety and welfare are sacrificed or neglected, the State must suffer." . . .

We think that the views thus expressed are sound and that

the decision in the *Adkins* case was a departure from the true application of the principles governing the regulation by the State of the relation of employer and employed. . . .

With full recognition of the earnestness and vigor which characterize the prevailing opinion in the *Adkins* case, we find it impossible to reconcile that ruling with these well-considered declarations. What can be closer to the public interest than the health of women and their protection from unscrupulous and overreaching employers? And if the protection of women is a legitimate end of the exercise of state power, how can it be said that the requirement of the payment of a minimum wage fairly fixed in order to meet the very necessities of existence is not an admissible means to that end? The legislature of the State was clearly entitled to consider the situation of women in employment, the fact that they are in the class receiving the least pay, that their bargaining power is relatively weak, and that they are the ready victims of those who would take advantage of their necessitous circumstances. The legislature was entitled to adopt measures to reduce the evils of the "sweating system," the exploiting of workers at wages so low as to be insufficient to meet the bare cost of living, thus making their very helplessness the occasion of a most injurious competition. The legislature had the right to consider that its minimum wage requirements would be an important aid in carrying out its policy of protection. The adoption of similar requirements by many States evidences a deepseated conviction both as to the presence of the evil and as to the means adapted to check it. Legislative response to that conviction cannot be regarded as arbitrary or capricious, and that is all we have to decide. Even if the wisdom of the policy be regarded as debatable and its effects uncertain, still the legislature is entitled to its judgment.

There is an additional and compelling consideration which recent economic experience has brought into a strong light. The exploitation of a class of workers who are in an unequal position with respect to bargaining power and are thus relatively defenceless against the denial of a living wage is not only detrimental to their health and well being but casts a direct burden for their support upon the community. What these workers lose in wages the taxpayers are called upon to pay. The bare cost of living must be met. We may take judicial notice of the unparalleled demands for relief which arose during the recent period of depression and still continue to an alarming extent despite the degree of economic recovery which has been achieved. It is unnecessary to cite official statistics to establish what is of common knowledge through the length and breadth of the land. While in the instant case no factual brief has been presented, there is no reason to doubt that the State of Washington has encountered the same social problem that is present elsewhere. The community is not bound to provide what is in effect a subsidy for unconscionable employers. The community may direct its law-making power to correct the abuse which springs from their selfish disregard of the public interest. . . .

Our conclusion is that the the case of *Adkins* v. *Children's Hospital, supra,* should be, and it is, overruled. The judgment of the Supreme Court of the State of Washington is

Affirmed.

Mr. Justice Sutherland, dissenting:

Mr. Justice Van Devanter, Mr. Justice McReynolds, Mr. Justice Butler and I think the judgment of the court below should be reversed. . . .

The judicial function is that of interpretation; it does not include the power of amendment under the guise of interpretation. To miss the point of difference between the two is to miss all that the phrase "supreme law of the land" stands for and to convert what was intended as inescapable and enduring mandates into mere moral reflections.

If the Constitution, intelligently and reasonably construed in the light of these principles, stands in the way of desirable legislation, the blame must rest upon that instrument, and not upon the court for enforcing it according to its terms. The remedy in that situation—and the only true remedy—is to amend the Constitution. Judge Cooley, in the first volume of his Constitutional Limitations (8th ed.), p. 124, very clearly pointed out that much of the benefit expected from written constitutions would be lost if their provisions were to be bent to circumstances or modified by public opinion. He pointed out that the common law, unlike a constitution, was subject to modification by public sentiment and action which the courts might recognize; but that "a court or legislature which should allow a change in public sentiment to influence it in giving to a written constitution a construction not warranted by the intention of its founders, would be justly chargeable with reckless disregard of official oath and public duty; and if its course could become a precedent, these instruments would be of little avail. . . . What a court is to do, therefore, is *to declare the law as written,* leaving it to the people themselves to make such changes as new circumstances may require. The meaning of the constitution is fixed when it is adopted, and it is not different at any subsequent time when a court has occasion to pass upon it."

The *Adkins* case dealt with an act of Congress which had passed the scrutiny both of the legislative and executive branches of the government. We recognized that thereby these departments had affirmed the validity of the statute, and properly declared that their determination must be given great weight, but we then concluded, after thorough consideration, that their view could not be sustained. . . .

In support of minimum-wage legislation it has been urged, on the one hand, that great benefits will result in favor of underpaid labor, and, on the other hand, that the danger of such legislation is that the minimum will tend to become the maximum and thus bring down the earnings of the more efficient toward the level of the less-efficient employees. But with these speculations we have nothing to do. We are concerned only with the question of constitutionality.

That the clause of the Fourteenth Amendment which forbids

a state to deprive any person of life, liberty or property without due process of law includes freedom of contract is so well settled as to be no longer open to question. Nor reasonably can it be disputed that contracts of employment of labor are included in the rule. *Adair* v. *United States,* 208 U. S. 161, 174-175; *Coppage* v. *Kansas,* 236 U. S. 1, 10, 14. In the first of these cases, Mr. Justice Harlan, speaking for the court, said, "The right of a person to sell his labor upon such terms as he deems proper is, in its essence, the same as the right of the purchaser of labor to prescribe the conditions upon which he will accept such labor from the person offering to sell. . . . In all such particulars the employer and employé have equality of right, and any legislation that disturbs that equality is an arbitrary interference with the liberty of contract which no government can legally justify in a free land."

In the *Adkins* case we referred to this language, and said that while there was no such thing as absolute freedom of contract, but that it was subject to a great variety of restraints, nevertheless, freedom of contract was the general rule and restraint the exception; and that the power to abridge that freedom could only be justified by the existence of exceptional circumstances. This statement of the rule has been many times affirmed; and we do not understand that it is questioned by the present decision. . . .

We then pointed out that minimum-wage legislation such as that here involved does not deal with any business charged with a public interest, or with public work, or with a temporary emergency, or with the character, methods or periods of wage payments, or with hours of labor, or with the protection of persons under legal disability, or with the prevention of fraud. It is, simply and exclusively, a law fixing wages for adult women who are legally as capable of contracting for themselves as men, and cannot be sustained unless upon principles apart from those involved in cases already decided by the court. . . .

PART ELEVEN

CRITIQUES AND PERSPECTIVES

56 • Frances Perkins: *FDR Was "A Little Left of Center"*

Few people were in a better position to comment on Franklin D. Roosevelt's "ideology" than Frances Perkins. When he was governor of New York, she had worked with him on factory and labor laws, her specialty. And when he became President, he named her Secretary of Labor, the first woman ever appointed to a cabinet position. (See Document 41.) Aside from her long friendship with Roosevelt, Frances Perkins was sufficiently sympathetic with his approach to social problems to attempt to describe the special quality of his liberal conservatism, as she does in this selection from her reminiscences.

I knew Roosevelt long enough and under enough circumstances to be quite sure that he was no political or economic radical. I take it that the essence of economic radicalism is to believe that the best system is the one in which private ownership of the means of production is abolished in favor of public ownership. But Roosevelt took the status quo in our economic

From Frances Perkins, *The Roosevelt I Knew* (New York: The Viking Press, 1946), pp. 328-333.

system as much for granted as his family. They were part of his life, and so was our system; he was content with it. He felt that it ought to be humane, fair, and honest, and that adjustments ought to be made so that the people would not suffer from poverty and neglect, and so that all would share.

He thought business could be a fine art and could be conducted on moral principles. He thought the test ought to be whether or not business is conducted partly for the welfare of the community. He could not accept the idea that the sole purpose of business was to make more and more money. He thought business should make and distribute goods with enough profit to give the owners a comfortable living and enable them to save something to invest in other productive enterprises. Yes, he felt that stockholders had a place and right and that a business ought to be conducted so that they would earn modest interest, while the workers got good wages and the community profited by low prices and steady work.

But he couldn't see why a man making enough money should want to go on scheming and plotting, sacrificing and living under nervous tension, just to make more money. That, of course, made him unable to sympathize with the ambitions and drive of much of the American business fraternity. But he liked and got along well with those businessmen who shared, as many did, the point of view that business is conducted partly for the welfare of the country as well as to make money. They liked and trusted him and understood his objectives. Gerard Swope of the General Electric Company, Thomas J. Watson of the International Business Machines Company, Ernest Draper of the Hills Brothers Company, Donald and Hugh Comer, southern textile manufacturers, who had a humane if not a trade union conception of the rights of their workers and of the employers' duty in relation to them, were all comprehensible to the President. He liked Walter Chrysler, although I am not sure that Chrysler fully embraced the idea that enough is enough, particularly if his rivals were making more. But he did have some of the attitude that there was nothing remarkable in itself about making money.

It is true that Roosevelt never met a payroll, and many businessmen took it into their heads that he could not possibly comprehend business unless he had had that experience. This, of course, is part of the limitation of the business fraternity itself.

Roosevelt was entirely willing to try experiments. He had no theoretical or ideological objections to public ownership when that was necessary, but it was his belief that it would greatly complicate the administrative system if we had too much. He recognized, however, that certain enterprises could best be carried on under public control. He recognized that we probably would never have enough cheap electric power to supply the needs of the people if the Government did not undertake vast programs in the Tennessee and Missouri valleys, and he believed that plenty of power at low rates was necessary for the development of a high standard of living and for business progress. Just as the need for production in wartime is so great that the government must take a hand in it, so he was able to accept the idea that in peacetime too the Government must sometimes carry on enterprises because of the enormous amount of capital expenditure required or the preponderance of the experimental element. He was willing to concede that there were some fields in which such Government participation might be required permanently. But he always resisted the frequent suggestion of the Government's taking over railroads, mines, etc., on the ground that it was unnecessary and would be a clumsy way to get the service needed.

A superficial young reporter once said to Roosevelt in my presence, "Mr. President, are you a Communist?"

"No."

"Are you a capitalist?"

"No."

"Are you a Socialist?"

"No," he said, with a look of surprise as if he were wondering what he was being cross examined about.

The young man said, "Well, what is your philosophy then?"

"Philosophy?" asked the President, puzzled. "Philosophy? I am a Christian and a Democrat—that's all."

Those two words expressed, I think, just about what he was. They expressed the extent of his political and economic radicalism. He was willing to do experimentally whatever was necessary to promote the Golden Rule and other ideals he considered to be Christian, and whatever could be done under the Constitution of the United States and under the principles which have guided the Democratic party.

The young reporter, or his editor, did not think the answer had any news value, and nothing was printed about it. I suppose if the President had answered that he thought there was something remarkable in Communism or capitalism, it would have been a headline story.

I am certain that he had no dream of great changes in the economic or political patterns of our life. I never heard him express any preference for any form of government other than the representative republic and state-federal system which have become the pattern of political organization in the United States under the Constitution. At the beginning of his administration, and also, I think, at the end, he would have said that the states and their administrative systems should be strengthened and maintained. Nevertheless, federal legislation and administration must occur in some fields. If there could be greater co-operation among the states, that would be fine. But they should permit federal intervention on behalf of certain things that could not be done by them alone.

He believed in leadership from the office of the President, a leadership based upon the immense sources of information and analysis which the Executive Department had and which were available to the President. He fully recognized, however, the importance of Congress and the desirability of maintaining the strength of our congressional system. For that reason he wished at times that the people of the country would be more careful about whom they sent to Congress, to be sure that the congressman elected would not only represent his constituents but take part, intelligently and constructively, in making laws for all the people.

When he came to Washington, he had no idea whatever of reforming, changing, or modifying the Supreme Court. He believed strongly that Congress and its law-making powers should be seriously regarded by the Court, and that all the courts ought to exercise extreme care not to interfere with the development of law and procedures as times changed. As witness his casual reference that EPIC, even if it won in California, would "make no difference in Dutchess County, New York"—or other states or counties. He believed that Congress, suitably advised by its own legal committees, should be permitted to decide what was best for the country, and that the will of the people as expressed by an act of Congress should not be frustrated by overmeticulous decisions on abstract constitutional lines.

Roosevelt was not very familiar with economic theory. He thought of wealth in terms of the basic wealth in agriculture, transportation, and services which were the familiar pattern of his youth. He recognized or took for granted the changes that had come about in our economy in his own lifetime: the shift in emphasis from agriculture to industry and distribution, the importance of the financial elements. Honorable methods in all business matters seemed to him imperative and to be insisted upon, by changes in the law if necessary. And under "honorable" he instinctively included wages and working conditions of the best, together with friendly, fair industrial relations. But, he had, I am sure, no thought or desire to impose any overall economic or political change on the United States. Some of the high-strung people who advised him from time to time did, I think, have ideas of this sort, but he always laughed them off and used their brillant analyses for some project that would do some immediate good to people in distress.

It was his way to be concerned about the concrete situations.

One recalls his ideas for salvaging and preserving the fertility of the soil where this was needed, his plans to develop and preserve the forests for their value not only as timber but as aids to the soil and the water supply. He had ideas for developing water power all over the country by great dams and irrigation systems and for distributing electric power and light to remote areas at low prices. He had plans for a transcontinental through highway with a network of feeders to serve farmers and city folks. He had plans for a chain of small hospitals all over the country with medical service available as the people needed them.

The objective of all these plans was to make human life on this planet in this generation more decent. "Decent" was the word he often used to express what he meant by a proper, adequate, and intelligent way of living.

If the application of these and similar ideas constitute revolution, then the phrase "Roosevelt revolution," used half in jest, may be correct. If such it was, it was a social revolution—a revolution in living—not an economic or a political revolution.

Radicals were always getting angry at Roosevelt for not being interested in overall economic and political changes. For him, the economic and political measures were not the end but the means. He was not even a vigorous anti-monopolist. Big enterprises, if morally and socially responsible, seemed entirely all right. Efficiency interested him only as it produced more comforts for more people and a better standard of living. Bigness did not frighten him as it did many people. He would insist on moral and social responsibility for all the institutions of human life; for the school, for the family, for business and industry, for labor, for professional services, for money management, for government—yes, even for the Church. He would insist in his way of thinking that all of these institutions should accept and practice a moral responsibility for making the life of the individuals who make up the life of the common people "more decent," and in the common people he included the rich and the poor alike. I remember that he wanted to find a way for well-to-do boys, as well as relief boys, to go to CCC camps (to get the advantages of the training and democratic living).

What he cared about was improvement in people's lives. If economic changes were necessary, he would make them, but only to do a specific task. When he said of himself that he was "a little to the left of center" he described accurately his thinking and feeling in political and economic matters.

57 • Benjamin Stolberg and Warren Jay Vinton: *The New Deal "Moves in Every Direction at Once"*

One of the liveliest and most acute critiques of the New Deal program was contained in a pamphlet of 1935 written by Benjamin Stolberg (1891-1951), long active in radical causes and in the labor movement, and Warren Jay Vinton (1889-   ), who was in the field of public housing. The selection below compresses much of the complaint leveled against Roosevelt by radicals who felt the administration was indecisive because of its failure to break with the traditional economic system.

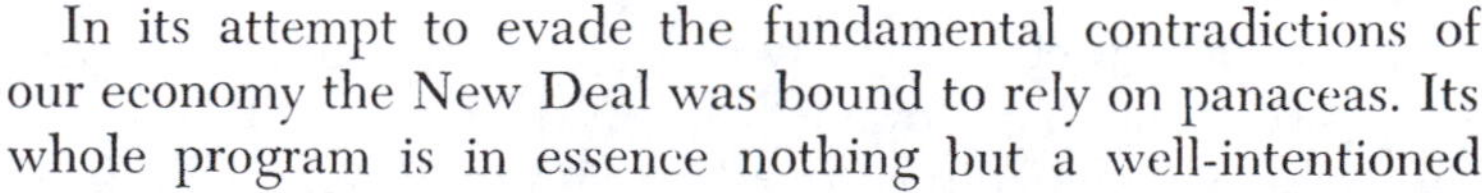

In its attempt to evade the fundamental contradictions of our economy the New Deal was bound to rely on panaceas. Its whole program is in essence nothing but a well-intentioned synthesis of errors. What it accomplishes in one direction it

From *The Economic Consequences of the New Deal*, copyright, 1935, by Benjamin Stolberg and Warren Jay Vinton; renewed, 1963, by Mary Fox Herling and Warren Jay Vinton. Reprinted by permission of Harcourt, Brace & World, Inc.

undoes in another. It is like the Russian peasant who cut some cloth from the front of his pants to patch the hole in the seat; and then cut from the leg of his pants to patch the front. After repeating this operation a dozen times he wound up, very much like the New Deal, with his pants all in patches and the migratory hole still there. (Of course the Moujik finally got himself a new pair of pants, but that is another story.)

The strangest of all the New Deal illusions is its dream of making Big Ownership accept an economy of abundance. But, unfortunately for this Utopian vision, capitalism is an economy of measured scarcity. Business is successful to the extent to which it gauges correctly that optimum point of profit at which a maximum price coincides with a maximum demand. And the more nearly it succeeds in curtailing production at that point, the better business it is. The vital concern of Big Industry is to prevent an abundance of goods from flooding the market.

In boom times production is tempted into abundance and scarcity gets out of hand. Capitalist recovery from the ensuing depression lies in the reorganization of scarcity. During the New Era Big Industry blundered into a disastrous abundance. And its potential productivity is now so great that it cannot get out of the depression under its own power. It needed the aid of government to reestablish scarcity and to enforce recovery; and that is exactly what the National Recovery Administration is all about. The codes, avowedly written for the "regulation of competition," are obviously an apparatus for industrial scarcity-mongering.

In order to protect Big Ownership in its scarcity program, the New Deal had to integrate agriculture into the same program. For agriculture during the World War had so increased its production that the collapse of its price structure became a permanent threat to manufacturing prices. And the organization of agricultural scarcity is exactly what the Agricultural Adjustment Administration is all about.

The inner drive of labor, however, is always for greater

abundance, for more goods for less money, for shops running at full speed. And so, to integrate labor into this program of anti-social scarcity, the New Deal has been forced, for all its liberal pretensions, to liquidate every expression of labor unrest. And that is exactly why the President insists on a truce between capital and labor, which it is the function of the National Labor Relations Board to achieve.

In short, the first and foremost of the New Deal panaceas, the N.R.A. and the A.A.A., have only served to render more explicit, through an enormous administrative apparatus, what has always been implicit in the nature of Big Ownership. Under capitalism scarcity is the life of trade. . . .

The World War was the greatest Public Works project in all history. And when it was over the profits which American Big Ownership had made out of this magnificent project were in part represented by $25,000,000,000 in government bonds which it held as a first lien against the American people. But what most pleased Big Ownership about this war-time project was that the Public Works created by it were immediately shot to hell in defence of its "freedom," and not left over to get funny and compete permanently with private property. The war correlated the destruction of Public Works with their construction.

But a peace-time Public Works project during a capitalist depression is a horse of a very different color. For one thing, such an unreasonably honest administrator as Mr. Ickes sees to it that profits are kept within bounds. Such honesty really amounts to a sabotage of our accustomed modes of doing business. But be that as it may, the real objection on the part of Big Ownership to a peace-time Public Works program—other than the kind which the G.O.P. used to call by the less elegant appellation of the Pork Barrel—is that it must build for permanent use and not for immediate destruction. Such Public Works would become a competitive threat to capital investments.

But the New Deal, with characteristic optimism, slurred over this contradiction in formulating its policy of Public Works. It thought of Public Works primarily as a stimulant to recovery, as a mere "priming of the pump." Naïvely it believed that if it only spent enough, heavy industry would start up again, consumers industries would follow, and business revival would gradually spread. It was Mr. John Maynard Keynes, the well-known English economist, who sold the President this bright idea. He estimated that $300,000,000 a month would turn the trick. But neither he nor anybody else can show just how this will in any way cure our fundamental malady, the maldistribution of wealth and income.

The moment the New Deal started looking for places to spend money it ran headlong into trouble. For one thing, the field traditionally reserved for government investment—post-offices, bridges, harbors, rivers, roads—had been pretty well exploited by that Great Engineer, Mr. Hoover, in his efforts toward recovery. Nor could the New Deal embark on a program of government-owned means of production, for this field is, of course, the jealously protected preserve of Private Initiative on which no government may poach. Nor could it persuade Big Ownership to borrow from it for expansion, because Big Ownership had already built far more plant and equipment than is workable under our system.

The one great and obvious field in which America has lagged in its physical equipment is housing. The masses of our people need decent, modern, and commodious shelter. And our potential productivity is more than enough to give it to them. During the depression we have wasted through enforced idleness $287,000,000,000 of possible production, far more than enough not only to clean out our slums but to house the American people in the luxury to which their natural resources entitle them. Capitalism has failed to meet this need. It fails to give its workers enough income to pay rent on the present price of modern housing. Nor can it get the cost of modern housing down to present wage levels, for to do so would mean writing down land values, reducing the price of building materials, and giving building labor such steady work that it would be justified in agreeing to a reduction in hourly wage scales.

The New Deal, for all its anxiety to put money into building and construction, has not dared to face these fundamental economic facts. Instead, the New Deal is exerting itself to sustain land values; through the N.R.A. it has been party to a 23 per cent increase in the price of building materials; and, lacking a long-range and extended housing program, it cannot very well ask building labor to reduce its high hourly wage in exchange for a steady annual income. Nor has the New Deal challenged the rate of return on funds invested in housing. It is charging municipalities 4 per cent on the few housing loans it has made, though it has available $1,200,000,000 of workers' money in its postal savings bank at a cost to itself of only 2 per cent.

The upshot of all the excitement about rehousing the American people has been that the Public Works Administration, out of its $3,700,000,000, has allotted only $146,000,000 for low cost housing. And of this sum only a few millions have actually been spent in eighteen months. . . .

There is no doubt that the T.V.A. means well. Whether it does well is up to the New Deal. If the New Deal steels itself to press for "national planning" in the Tennessee Valley, instead of being content to use the T.V.A. merely as a "yardstick" to measure the just price of a kilowatt hour of electricity, then it can boast that it has offered some challenge to Big Ownership.

We shall see what we shall see. But one thing is certain. The very existence of the T.V.A. is an invaluable lesson to the American people in the possibilities of social control. . . .

The economic consequences of the New Deal have been exactly what might have been foreseen by a competent Brain Trust. Capitalist recovery, on the classic lines of laissez-faire, has not only been impeded but arrested. And its only economic alternative, social planning on socialist lines, has been sedulously avoided.

The New Deal is trying to right the unbalance of our economic life by strengthening all its contradictions. For Big Ownership it tries to safeguard profits and to keep intact the instruments of its financial domination. For the middle classes it tries to safeguard their small investments, which only serves to reintrench Big Ownership. For labor it tries to raise wages, increase employment, and assure some minimum of economic safety, while at the same time it opposes labor's real interests through its scarcity program. In trying to move in every direction at once the New Deal betrays the fact that it has no policy.

And it has no policy because as a liberal democracy it must ignore the overwhelming fact of our epoch, the irreconcilable conflict between capital and labor. The result is that we are today neither an economy of balanced scarcity, nor an economy of progressive abundance, nor in transit from one to the other. We are today in an economy of stalemate.

During the last year of Mr. Hoover's régime this country was in a state of complete economic disintegration. There was no confidence, there was no hope. Our business structure was collapsing all about us. Finally the banks closed.

When Mr. Roosevelt took office confidence surged back. During its first few months the New Deal staged an inflationary boom. As soon as the bankers returned from their Holiday, Mr. Woodin, then Secretary of the Treasury, sold the public on the idea that the very same credit structure which had collapsed two weeks before had miraculously become sound again. The Administration announced that prices were going to rise, and invited the public to buy while the buying was good. We went off the gold standard, the dollar went down, prices went up, and the public started to buy. Retailers replenished their stocks. Manufacturers laid in raw materials and began to produce in a hurry before the Blue Eagle could "crack down" on them.

As a result the index of business activity was pumped up in

four months from 58 in March, 1933, to 89 in July. There it was punctured abruptly and business activity fell off as rapidly as it had risen. By November it was down to 68. During the first five months of 1934 there was a slow improvement, but by June the increased margins of profits and higher prices of the N.R.A., applied to our anemic purchasing power, began to show their inevitable effects. Business fell off again, and by October, 1934, it was back to 70.

Of course business conditions are somewhat better than they were in the moribund year of 1932. But since June, 1933, there has been no forward progress. Indeed, there has been regression. In October, 1934, which is the last month for which we have available figures, business activity was 2.6 per cent less than a twelvemonth before. Industrial production had declined 6.4 per cent. The steel, lumber, automobile, and textile industries were all less active. Freight car loadings, a sound index of distribution, were 6.1 per cent less. Building construction, measured by value of contracts awarded, was 6.7 per cent lower, despite the heroic efforts of Mr. Ickes to stimulate public works.

When production dropped labor's position naturally worsened. During the same period—from October, 1933, to October, 1934—unemployment increased by 5.4 per cent, while the real weekly wages of industrial workers who still had jobs decreased 2.0 per cent. The number of those on relief increased 33 per cent and the cost of relief almost doubled.

Yet Big Business, with the aid of the N.R.A., has been extracting greatly enlarged profits from our stricken society. Our great industrial corporations increased their profits during the first nine months of 1934 by 76 per cent as against the same period in 1933. According to the *New York Times*, "the chemical companies reported a 45 per cent increase; the mines and metals group, 360 per cent; office equipment, 157 per cent; and tobacco, 166 per cent." And dividends rose 17 per cent in the twelve months ending October, 1934.

When profits rise while wages lag it means but one thing. It means that behind the vivid confusion of the New Deal, the redistribution of the national income is stealthily and fatally progressing *upwards,* and that the power of Big Ownership is steadily enlarging. And unless the government succeeds in reversing this disastrous process, Big Ownership is bound to intensify the crisis in the long run.

There is nothing the New Deal has so far done that could not have been done better by an earthquake. A first-rate earthquake, from coast to coast, could have reestablished scarcity much more effectively, and put all the survivors to work for the greater glory of Big Business—with far more speed and far less noise than the New Deal.

58 • Floyd B. Olson: *A New Party to Challenge Capitalism*

The upsurge of radical thinking in the depression brought into political office in various parts of the country men bold enough to speak of the need for a new economic system. One of these was the Governor of Minnesota, Floyd B. Olson (1891-1936), who felt that Roosevelt and the Democratic Party were not doing enough to solve the basic problems of American life. In this article, he presents his case for a new political party.

A great deal of printers' ink has been spilled to tell the world that a third party movement is impossible of success in America—is something foreign to our soil. It is certain that much of

From Floyd B. Olson, "My Political Creed," *Common Sense,* IV (April 1935), 6-7.

this is sheer propaganda designed to discourage formation of a political party which will be representative of the aspirations of the masses.

If it were true that there is some characteristic inherent in American life which must defeat a liberal and radical political expression in the form of a political party, the outlook for fundamental economic changes would be well-nigh hopeless. It is virtually certain that neither the Democratic nor Republican parties will ever become the vehicle for bringing about such changes.

But the premise is fallacious. Although the American people in the past were never ready to support a genuinely radical movement, a history of American politics reveals that new and successful political parties came into existence when there was a real and legitimate challenge to the existing order, and one which found no expression through, or champion in, any of the then existing parties.

The needs of the agrarians more than one hundred years ago gave birth to what is now called the Democratic party. To the Tories of that day, Jefferson symbolized the radical and destructionist. When he was elected president, the Tories hurriedly made John Marshall chief justice so that he might control interpretation of the Constitution. Through his interpretations Marshall virtually wrote a new constitution. He held that the Supreme Court had the power to declare unconstitutional any act passed by Congress. It is historically known that the delegates to the Constitutional Convention purposely left that question to the wisdom of future generations for determination; diaries kept by delegates disclose that this question threatened to split the convention.

It is doubtful whether either Jefferson or Jackson would recognize their political step-children of today, who may be found in the leadership of the Democratic Party.

The crisis of the Civil War, together with the rise of the industrialists, gave birth to the Republican Party. This has been the dominant political party in America, and although it has lapsed at times into periods of progressive—or rather semi-progressive—tendencies, it has been, is, and will remain the champion of the capitalistic system and financial plutocracy.

The political challenge to the basic claims and principles of capitalism, as we generally use the term, is not only certain to come, but in a measure already has arrived. The Farmer-Labor Party of Minnesota talks about the cooperative commonwealth. There might be some accusation that the term is vague and nebulous, but it is nevertheless an attack on the fundamental concepts of the present system. For a number of years—in fact quite a few years—an extremely liberal movement has been developing in Wisconsin, Nebraska, and other Middle Western states, which paraded under the Republican banner but never really belonged in that company. The Wisconsin movement already has divorced itself from the Republican party, which it should have done from its inception. EPIC in California put on the cloak of the Democratic party, but it did not fit. In fact the "respectable" leaders of the party sought to tear off the cloak. Mr. Huey Long's "Share the Wealth Society," rightly meets objection from the scientific, economic mind, but it derives its strength from the challenge to the present order which is in the air.

Not only is there a serious challenge to the capitalistic order today but that challenge is taking on a very definite form. The present depression brought to light and to public attention vital defects in the economic system which had been known to the student of economics for quite some time. The principal defect is its faulty and inequitable distribution of wealth. It did not require much deep thinking for the average person to deduct that there is something drastically wrong when people are starving in the midst of plenty.

It was only a few years ago, comparatively, that criticism attacking the fundamentals of our social and economic order was confined almost exclusively to so-called "soapbox" orators and "parlor reds" and "pinks." Professors of economics in our universities talked glibly about the law of supply and demand and told their students that all economic forces are determined by that law. Today these same professors are telling their classes that while we have perfected and brought to a high point of efficiency our system of wealth production, we have not kept pace in perfecting the machinery of wealth-distribution.

University professors are thus treading on what had been holy ground, because *when one questions our system of wealth distribution the line of thought must inevitably lead to conviction of the necessity of production for use as against production for private profit.*

The young people of today, particularly the college students, are open and almost violent in their criticism. Open forum discussions on economics and social problems are more popular on the university campuses than ever before and the influence of the liberal student is becoming felt. The American student is beginning to take the leadership in the fight against the inequities of the present order, whereas in the past he was not even a follower. Recently a "youth congress" was held in St. Paul of sufficient importance for the local newspapers to devote columns in reporting it seriously, despite the fact that the atmosphere was decidedly radical. This fact is indicative of the vitality in the new challenge to capitalism.

But it is not only in college class rooms that we encounter discussions of that nature. We hear it at every kind of gathering, social and otherwise. People who formerly would regard such discussions as sacrilege, when accused of reactionary tendencies, apologetically say: "My mind is open. I know some changes may be necessary."

No matter what inherent injustices a system possesses, it will remain in power as long as the great majority of people feel a sense of economic security under it. Agitators shouting from improvised platforms on every corner of the land cannot do much to weaken it. But when the majority of the people begin losing that sense of economic security, the system is doomed—its days are numbered. Recurrent depressions, economic inequalities, poverty, unemployment, hunger, all so needless in the presence of our actual and potential wealth, are causing men to lose faith in the infallibility of the capitalistic system.

There have been financial depressions before but never one exactly like this—never one for which the defenders of the system could find so little justification. The old shibboleths no longer have their catch and power. Rotary clubs and Lions clubs are at a loss to create "pep." It is hard to find something to cheer for. The average person laughs when the business man talks of restoration of confidence. Industrial leaders no longer speak of prosperity just around the corner; an audience would howl a speaker down if he made such a reference.

The capitalistic system always had its toll of human wreckage, but its propagandists succeeded pretty well in putting over the idea that those who fell by the wayside, fell because of their own shortcomings and not because of the shortcomings of the system . . . "they were too lazy to work" . . . "tramps" . . . "anti-social creatures." The philosophy preached was that the world owes nobody a living, but that everybody who really wanted to find work in the capitalistic world could find it. Criticism was ascribed to "green-eyed" envy of those who were rewarded because of their industry and ability. That rot can no longer be preached!—not when millions of able-bodied men and women are clamoring for work to do.

If the depression did one thing it brought home to the people the knowledge that private industry in itself has not the stuff to keep our people unemployed, give security of employment, and make a contented nation. This thought in itself is destructive of the very basis of the capitalist theory, which is that the material needs and comforts of the nation can be provided through a system of wealth production motivated by private profit. The alternative to such a system is one in which wealth production is motivated by social needs. This can only be brought about when government actually takes over the important industries of the country. *A third party must arise and preach the gospel of government and collective ownership of the means of production and distribution.*

Here we have the vital economic issue, which will have to be fought on the political field.

The platform of a third party must be based upon this vital economic issue. It must demand the taking of any and all steps necessary to guarantee human liberties and a decent standard of living. It must have an American concept based upon the rights of the people to "life, liberty and the pursuit of happiness." It must educate people to the realization that government is but an instrument for the attainment of these "inalienable rights." Many now know that American capitalism cannot be reformed so as to give happiness to the masses. Many more can be convinced that government can be used for the attainment of a common happiness.

The Communist Party, bogged down with Marxian dogma, and clumsy Stalinite strategy, offers no hope as a political instrument for changing our prevailing system. It is all or nothing with the Communists. Otherwise stated—it is Communism or Fascism. Those who profess to see another course are denounced as enemies of the masses and champions of capitalism. And the throwing of a brick through a window during a Communist demonstration is hailed as the beginning of the "Revolution." . . .

And what of the Democratic Party? Despite a program which curtails production in order to produce profits—in the face of a great need for increased production—Mr. Roosevelt is undoubtedly sincere in his endeavor to attain a "fuller life" for the masses. Evidences that the Tories will no longer follow him are apparent. When Mr. [James] Farley has dispensed the last of his patronage, these evidences will increase. Mr. Roosevelt, if he desires to move to the "left," may find it necessary to join a new party in the same spirit as might have moved him to run as an independent in 1932, had he not been nominated by the Democratic convention.

And what of the differences between left-wingers? They may be adjusted if left-wingers cease being pure individualists and become collective-minded. The aggravation of the economic crisis and the rise of Fascism will demand it, and, in all probability, bring it about.

If the "pursuit of happiness" is to be a moving human emotion and not an empty phrase, many liberals and radicals must be brought together under a single political banner.

59. • Norman Thomas: *Socialism, Not Roosevelt's Pale Pink Pills*

Norman Thomas (1884-   ), a graduate of Princeton, and then a Presbyterian minister in New York, became a pacifist and Socialist during World War I. After the death of Eugene Debs in 1924, he became the foremost figure in the Socialist Party in the United States. He ran for mayor of New York City twice, for governor of New York State twice, and for President six times. By 1936, liberals and Socialists were especially attracted to the policies of the New Deal, for the previous year had seen a definite turn of the Roosevelt administration toward the laboring part of the population, with the Wagner Labor Relations Act, and the Social Security Act. Norman Thomas, campaigning for president again in 1936, gave his reasons for not supporting FDR, in a speech delivered at the Manhattan Opera House.

From Norman Thomas, "Shall Labor Support Roosevelt?" (New York: Socialist Party, 1936).

What is our Socialist attitude to Labor's Non-Partisan League for Roosevelt (whose chairman is Major George L. Berry, president of the Printing Pressmen) and to its New York state expression, the recently organized American Labor Party? . . .

There is, or there was, a Negro farmer near Earle, Arkansas, named Frank Weems. He was a local strike leader for the Southern Tenant Farmers' Union in the struggle to get for field workers more than 75 cents a day. He led a peaceful demonstration and meeting. A planters' mob broke it up and beat Weems until he fell dead or unconscious to the ground. Then they took him away. His friends have not seen him since that day. When Rev. Claude Williams and Willie Sue Blagden went to arrange for the funeral they were whipped by some of Major Berry's Democratic comrades. The Democratic sheriff of the county, the Democratic governor, the Democratic Senator Robinson—Roosevelt's friend and Senate floor leader—all delegates to the Democratic Convention at Philadelphia, denied that Weems was dead and said that he would be produced. That was almost three months ago. They have not produced Weems. Will the Berry committee stop cheering the "great humanitarian" long enough to ask: "Where is Frank Weems?"

For Weems, like John Brown, has become a symbol; a symbol of the struggle of the most exploited of all workers, the plantation serfs, black and white, to be free. Robinson is the symbol and representative of the system which keeps them in serfdom, deprived of an effective ballot, subject to peonage, exploitation, organized theft, terrorism, murder. President Roosevelt knows this. But in Little Rock, Arkansas, he eulogized Robinson, and his secretary refused an appointment to a union committee when the presidential party was in the state.

In general, whatever may have been the President's original good intentions, his administration has widened the gap between planters and share-croppers and worsened the latter's plight. It has kept some of its promises to them of help. Roosevelt has pale pink pills to cure the hurt of the workers in Pennsylvania and New York but none in Arkansas. You worry to keep Robinson & Co. on his side.

Nor is Arkansas unique. Consider the decline in civil liberty under Roosevelt—the epidemic of loyalty oaths, the ride of the vigilantes in California, military law in Indiana: flogging and murder in Florida. "Not his fault," you may say? Well, maybe. But what has he done against it? When did he as President of his country and leader of his party speak out? Did he ever put an anti-lynching bill on his *must* list? Did he protest when Democratic governors in 1934 made a new record in the use of military force against the textile strikers? Would he see me when I tried to tell him the story of North Carolina during the textile strike? The answer is *No.*

But he is the great humanitarian whom Socialists and radical workers must support or be dubbed the allies of fascism! While American labor shuts its eyes to the record which I have listed, American labor will never be free.

Or turn to the subject of war and peace. On peace depend our lives and all our hopes. But who has been President while America has expanded her military and naval expenditures until, despite our favorable position, they are the highest in the world? Who was President while naval maneuvres were held nearer the coast of Japan than the United States for the first time in history! Who had enormous power yet did not use it to take the profit out of war and preparation for war; to proclaim a policy of genuine neutrality, or to declare what America is defending—her shores, her trade, or that vague thing, "her honor?" Whose ambassadors have steadily backed the forces of reaction in Cuba against the workers? Who has not even answered my appeal to keep American exports away from ports where they aid the fascist rebels who endanger the peace of the world? Franklin Delano Roosevelt, exponent of "democracy against fascism!"

But anyway, the non-partisan committee may say, he has helped most of the workers, including the unemployed, and he has made it easier to organize them. Yes, as compared with Hoover, yet how little has been done.

Help for the unemployed? More than ten million still in the sorrowful ranks of men, workless and unwanted. Not the 3½ million Roosevelt promised to put to work at relief jobs, but some 2 million. And those at wages as low as $19 a month in certain regions. Relief shot through with politics. An insecurity, not a security, law which puts the burden of unemployment insurance on the workers as consumers and gives the bosses a premium on increasing technological unemployment. No program of new housing to aid employment and end slums, not even a presidential *must* behind the inadequate Wagner bill.

Prosperity for the workers? Listen to Col. Leonard Ayres' estimate: Business recovery 12% below normal; employment 25% and industrial payrolls 31% below normal. Or to this: Corporation profits this year 50 to 75% above 1935; production for the first quarter of the year only 15% above '35.

Aid in organizing bona fide unions? Some. But how much? Even while NRA was alive, surely you remember that the bosses not the workers got the best of it in the automobile, steel and rubber codes and settlements. The bosses dominated the code authorities. The Administration itself broke the Colt Arms strike at Hartford by insisting that, codes or no codes, strike or no strike, it must have its guns and by giving continually new orders for them to the bosses.

You say: "The President would have done better except for the Supreme Court." Maybe. But observe that he has not yet had the courage to outline a real program for dealing with the courts or the Constitution. Rumor persists that he may fill the first Supreme Court vacancy with Joe Robinson. Then God save the Republic! Major Berry can't!

"But anyway we have recovery." How much and for how long? Two such different authorities as John T. Flynn and

Roger Babson see fresh collapse in less than four years. "Recovery" has brought low wages, lagging employment, a staggering burden of debt to the bankers, which the producers must bear. To the consumers it has brought rising prices, sales taxes but no pure food and drug act.

This, my friends, is the record that Berry, Hillman and their publicity agents, and the communist candidate, with varying intensity applaud. Even they do not find in the Democratic Platform any reason to look for its marked change for the better. Roosevelt's next four years with a Democratic Congress will be less, not more radical—as Americans use the word—than his first term. But this is what they offer as your defense against fascism.

I do not write this record primarily as a personal indictment of the President. Why and how should he have done better if labor is so easily satisfied? Not the old deal, nor the new, but the capitalist game is at fault. This more than ever Socialists must insist.

Whatever the differences between Roosevelt and Landon they are not enough to prevent the drift to war and fascism. We lose precious months in fighting over the lesser of two evils. There was a difference between Wilson and Hughes in 1916. It did not keep us out of war. There was a difference between Hindenburg and Hitler in Germany. Labor's support of the former and labor's achievements of economic reforms, far more thoroughgoing than Major Berry of Tennessee and his comrades demand, did not save Germany from the Nazis. And yet they ask Socialists and other radicals to stultify themselves by supporting Roosevelt! Such support would be suicide to our Party and almost mortal injury to our cause.

Let the communists with their peculiar chameleon philosophy, organization and tactics play with this sort of thing. I do not think it will help them. It will not help the working class. We cannot and will not play with it. We will keep faith with the struggle of the working-class toward its destined end. . . .

Each day makes it clearer that Socialism is the world's one hope. There is no time to lose. The way to get Socialism is to proclaim the Socialist message, not to declare a moratorium on it during an election campaign when men and women are thinking on political issues. If we are silent now, or hide our real opinions, we shall lose and deserve to lose our own respect and the respect of others. If we shadow-box now, we shall never deserve to win. Everything that has made Socialists, every argument that now bids workers in farm, city, school, factory or profession to be Socialist, compels us to work this year for the Socialist Party and the straight Socialist ticket.

I want to go out, I know I shall go out in this all important campaign, with the knowledge that the Socialist Party and its friends in New York are fighting for Socialism as never before. That way, and that way only, lies not only our best service to a real farmer-labor party, but our eventual hope of victory over war and fascism and the triumph of the federated cooperative commonwealths of mankind. The Party of the Socialist prophets and heroes throughout the world, the Party in America of London and Berger, Hillquit and Debs, the Party of loyal Jimmy Higginses who have made it, that Party is on the march. Fall in line!

60 • John Maynard Keynes: *The Maintenance of Prosperity Is Extremely Difficult*

As FDR was struggling to get the nation out of the sudden recession of mid-1937, one of the world's most distinguished econ-

John Maynard Keynes to Franklin D. Roosevelt, February 1, 1938, ms., from the papers of Franklin D. Roosevelt, Franklin D. Roosevelt Library, Hyde Park, New York.

omists, John Maynard Keynes (1883-1946), offered advice. Although Roosevelt's spending and public-works policies had often been called "Keynesian," New Dealers had only brief and indirect contact with Keynes himself. In December 1933, Keynes had addressed an open letter to Roosevelt, making several suggestions in the way of "reasoned experiment within the framework of the existing social system." And the following year, Keynes had talked with FDR in the White House. Now, he attempted to prod the President gently in the direction of a larger spending program for public works, housing, and other useful ventures. Roosevelt's reply to Keynes was brief and evaded the issues the economist had posed. In a few months he resumed spending, but on nothing like the scale called for by Keynes, or by American economists like Alvin Hansen (See Document 28).

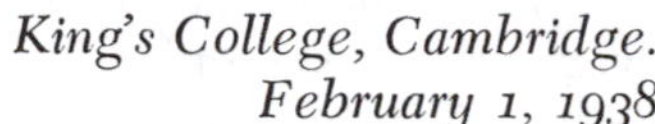

King's College, Cambridge.
February 1, 1938

DEAR MR. PRESIDENT,

You received me so kindly when I visited you some three years ago that I make bold to send you some bird's eye impressions which I have formed as to the business position in the United States. You will appreciate that I write from a distance, that I have not re-visited the United States since you saw me, and that I have access to few more sources of information than those publicly available. But sometimes in some respects there may be advantages in these limitations! At any rate, those things which I think I see, I see very clearly.

1. I should agree that the present recession is partly due to an "error of optimism" which led to an over-estimation of future demand, when orders were being placed in the first half of this year. If this were all, there would not be too much to worry about. It would only need time to effect a readjustment; —though, even so, the recovery would only be up to the point required to take care of the *revised* estimate of current demand,

which might fall appreciably short of the prosperity reached last spring.

2. But I am quite sure that this is not all. There is a much more troublesome underlying influence. The recovery was mainly due to the following factors:—

(i) The solution of the credit and insolvency problems, and the establishment of easy short-term money;

(ii) the creation of an adequate system of relief for the unemployed;

(iii) public works and other investments aided by Government funds or guarantees;

(iv) investment in the instrumental goods required to supply the increased demand for consumption goods;

(v) the momentum of the recovery thus initiated.

Now of these (i) was a prior condition of recovery, since it is no use creating a demand for credit, if there is no supply. But an increased supply will not by itself generate an adequate demand. The influence of (ii) evaporates as employment improves, so that there is a dead point beyond which this factor cannot carry the economic system. Recourse to (iii) has been greatly curtailed in the past year. (iv) and (v) are functions of the forward movement and cease—indeed (v) is reversed—as soon as the position fails to improve further. The benefit from the momentum of recovery as such is at the same time the most important and the most dangerous factor in the upward movement. It requires for its continuance, not merely the maintenance of recovery, but always *further* recovery. Thus it always flatters the early stages and steps from under just when support is most needed. It was largely, I think, a failure to allow for this which caused the "error of optimism" last year.

Unless, therefore, the above factors were supplemented by others in due course, the present slump could have been predicted with absolute certainty. It is true that the existing policies will prevent the slump from proceeding to such a disastrous degree as last time. But they will not by themselves—at any rate, not without a large scale recourse to (iii)—maintain prosperity at a reasonable level.

3. Now one had hoped that the needed supplementary factors would be organised in time. It was obvious what these were—namely increased investment in durable goods such as housing, public utilities and transport. One was optimistic about this because in the United States at the present time the opportunities, indeed the necessity, for such developments were unexampled. Can your Administration escape criticism for the failure of these factors to mature?

Take housing. When I was with you three and a half years ago the necessity for effective new measures was evident. I remember vividly my conversations with Riefler at that time. But what happened? Next to nothing. The handling of the housing problem has been really wicked. I hope that the new measures recently taken will be more successful. I have not the knowledge to say. But they will take time, and I would urge the great importance of expediting and yet further aiding them. Housing is by far the best aid to recovery because of the large and continuing scale of potential demand; because of the wide geographical distribution of this demand; and because the sources of its finance are largely independent of the Stock Exchanges. I should advise putting most of your eggs in this basket, *caring* about this more than about anything, and making absolutely sure that they are being hatched without delay. In this country we partly depended for many years on direct subsidies. There are few more proper objects for such than working class houses. If a direct subsidy is required to get a move on (we gave our subsidies *through* the local authorities), it should be given without delay or hesitation.

Next utilities. There seems to be a deadlock. Neither your policy nor anyone else's is able to take effect. I think that the litigation by the utilities is senseless and ill-advised. But a great deal of what is alleged against the wickedness of holding companies as such is surely wide of the mark. It does not draw the right line of division between what should be kept and what discarded. It arises too much out of what is dead and gone. The real criminals have cleared out long ago. I should doubt if the controls existing to-day are of much *personal* value to anyone. No-one has suggested a procedure by which the eggs can be unscrambled. Why not tackle the problem by insisting that the *voting power* should belong to the real owners of the equity, and leave the existing *organizations* undisturbed, so long as the voting power is so rearranged (e.g. by bringing in preferred stockholders) that it cannot be controlled by the holders of a minority of the equity?

Is it not for you to decide either to make real peace or to be much more drastic the other way? Personally I think there is a great deal to be said for the ownership of all the utilities by publicly owned boards. But if public opinion is not yet ripe for this, what is the object of chasing the utilities round the lot every other week? If I was in your place, I should buy out the utilities at fair prices in every district where the situation was ripe for doing so, and announce that the ultimate ideal was to make this policy nation-wide. But elsewhere I would make peace on liberal terms, guaranteeing fair earnings on new investments and a fair basis of valuation in the event of the public taking them over hereafter. The process of evolution will take at least a generation. Meanwhile a policy of *competing* plants with losses all round is a ramshackle notion.

Finally the railroads. The position there seems to be exactly what it was three or four years ago. They remain, as they were then, potential sources of substantial demand for new capital expenditure. Whether hereafter they are publicly owned or remain in private hands, it is a matter of national importance that they should be made solvent. Nationalise them if the time is ripe. If not, take pity on the overwhelming problems of the present managements. And here too let the dead bury their dead. (To an Englishman, you Americans, like the Irish, are so terribly historically minded!)

I am afraid I am going beyond my province. But the upshot is this. A convincing policy, whatever its details may be, for promoting large-scale investment under the above heads is an urgent necessity. These things take time. Far too much precious time has passed.

4. I must not encumber this letter with technical suggestions for reviving the capital market. This is important. But not so important as the revival of sources of demand. If demand and confidence re-appear, the problems of the capital market will not seem so difficult as they do to-day. Moreover it is a highly technical problem.

5. Business men have a different set of delusions from politicians; and need, therefore, different handling. They are, however, much milder than politicians, at the same time allured and terrified by the glare of publicity, easily persuaded to be 'patriots', perplexed, bemused, indeed terrified, yet only too anxious to take a cheerful view, vain perhaps but very unsure of themselves, pathetically responsive to a kind word. You could do anything you liked with them, if you would treat them (even the big ones), not as wolves and tigers, but as domestic animals by nature, even though they have been badly brought up and not trained as you would wish. It is a mistake to think that they are more *immoral* than politicians. If you work them into the surly, obstinate, terrified mood, of which domestic animals, wrongly handled, are so capable, the nation's burdens will not get carried to market; and in the end public opinion will veer their way. Perhaps you will rejoin that I have got quite a wrong idea of what all the back-chat amounts to. Nevertheless I record accurately how it strikes observers here.

5. Forgive the candour of those remarks. They come from an enthusiastic well-wisher of you and your policies. I accept the view that durable investment must come increasingly under state direction. I sympathise with Mr. Wallace's agricultural policies. I believe that the S.E.C. is doing splendid work. I regard the growth of collective bargaining as essential. I approve minimum wage and hours regulation. I was altogether on

your side the other day, when you deprecated a policy of general wage reductions as useless in present circumstances. But I am terrified lest progressive causes in all the democratic countries should suffer injury, because you have taken too lightly the risk to their prestige which would result from a failure measured in terms of immediate prosperity. There *need* be no failure. But the maintenance of prosperity in the modern world is extremely *difficult;* and it is so easy to lose precious time.

I am

Mr. President

Yours with great respect and faithfulness,

J. M. KEYNES

61 · John Dewey: *The Old Problems are Unsolved*

By 1939, Europe was on the verge of war; FDR was thinking more and more about foreign affairs; and the New Deal was reaching the end of its long list of economic reforms. Much had been accomplished; but those critics who had seen in the economic crisis an opportunity for a thoroughgoing reconstitution of the social order kept reiterating their creed. One of these was the philosopher John Dewey who, in this essay of 1939, pointed to what remained to be done.

. . . Events after the war in this country seemed to give the lie to the hopes then entertained. "Return to Normalcy" was not only the slogan but the practice—"normalcy" meaning the old

From John Dewey, "The Economic Basis of the New Society," in *Intelligence in the Modern World* (New York: Random House, Inc., 1939), pp. 416-433. Reprinted with the permission of Joseph Ratner.

social-economic regime. Attempts at radical social change were defeated in Europe in every country save Russia. Italy and Germany moved into Fascist dictatorships and other European and South American countries in that direction. Social reorganization did take place but in a direction opposite to that of the hopes entertained by liberals and radicals in the earlier period. Nevertheless, the forecast of "serious internal disorder and unrest" has been fulfilled.

After the world depression of 1929, the earlier idea of reconstruction revived, not under that name but, in this country, under the slogan of the New Deal. It has become increasingly evident that the conditions which caused the World War remain in full force, intensified indeed by the growth of exacerbated Nationalism—which is the direction in which "internal social reorganization" has in fact mainly moved. Failure of the world communities to "meet and forestall" needed change with "sympathy and intelligence" has left us with the old problems unsolved and new ones added. . . .

How much progress has been made in the intervening years? How does the situation now stand? We have a recognition which did not exist before of social responsibility for the care of the unemployed whose resources are exhausted in consequence of unemployment. But at best, the method we employ is palliative: it comes after the event. The positive problem of instituting a social-economic order in which all those capable of productive work will do the work for which they are fitted remains practically untouched. As a result, the conduct of relief and charitable care is almost never at what was termed "at the best." The personal deterioration that results from enforced idleness is a coercion which excludes the idle from the factors that contribute most effectively to decent self-respect and to personal development. While the mass of unemployed have met the situation with patience and even dignity, there can be no question that the corroding influence of living without work, upon the charity of others, private and public, is operating. In the long run, it would be difficult to find anything more destructive of the best elements of human nature than a continued prospect of living, at least of subsisting, in more or less parasitical dependence upon charity, even if it is public.

In saying these things, I am expressing no sympathy for those who complain about the growing amount of money spent upon taking care of those thrown out of productive work and the consequent increase in taxation. Much less am I expressing sympathy with the reckless charges brought against the unemployed of loving idleness and wishing to live at the expense of society. Such complaints and charges are the product of refusal to look at the causes which produce the situation and of desire to find an alibi for their refusal to do anything to remove the causes—causes which are inherent in the existing social-economic regime. The problem of establishing social conditions which will make it possible for all who are capable to do socially productive work is not an easy one. I am not engaging in criticism because it has not been solved. I am pointing out that the problem is not even being thought much about, not to speak of being systematically faced. The reason for the great refusal is clear. To face it would involve the problem of remaking a profit system into a system conducted not just, as is sometimes said, in the interest of consumption, important as that is, but also in the interest of positive and enduring opportunity for productive and creative activity and all that signifies for the development of the potentialities of human nature.

What gain has been made in the matter of establishing conditions that give the mass of workers not only what is called "security" but also constructive interest in the work they do? What gain has been made in giving individuals, the great mass of individuals, an opportunity to find themselves and then to educate themselves for what they can best do in work which is socially useful and such as to give free play in development of themselves? The managers of industries here and there have learned that it pays to have conditions such that those who are employed know enough about what they are doing so as to take an interest in it. Educators here and there are awake to the need of discovering vocational and occupational abilities and to the need of readjusting the school system to build upon what is discovered. But the basic trouble is not the scantiness of efforts in these directions, serious as is their paucity. It is again that the whole existing industrial system tends to nullify in large measure the effects of these efforts even when they are made. The problem of the adjustment of individual capacities and their development to actual occupations is not a one-sided or unilateral one. It is bilateral and reciprocal. It is a matter of the state of existing occupations, of the whole set-up of productive work, of the structure of the industrial system. Even if there were a much more widespread and searching concern with the capacities of individuals and much more preparation of them along the lines of their inherent fitness and needs than now exists, what assurance is there in the existing system that there will be opportunity to use their gifts and the education they have obtained? As far as the mass is concerned, we are now putting the social cart before the social horse.

If we take the question of production, what do we find? I pass by the basic fact that real production is completed only through distribution and consumption, so that mere improvement in the mechanical means of mass production may, and does, intensify the problem instead of solving it. I pass it over here because recurring crises and depressions, with the paradox of want amid plenty, has forced the fact upon the attention of every thoughtful person. The outcome is sufficient proof that the problem of production cannot be solved in isolation from distribution and consumption. I want here to call attention rather to the fact that the present method of dealing with the problem is *restriction* of productive capacity. For scarcity of materials and surplus of those who want to work is the ideal situation for profit on the part of those situated to take advantage of it. *Restriction of production* at the very time when *expansion* of production is most needed has long been the rule of *industrialists*. Now the Government is adopting the same policy for agriculturalists. Those who practice restriction of production in their own businesses cry out loudly when the Government, following their example, intervenes to kill pigs, plow under cotton, and reduce the crop of cereals, and does it, moreover, when there is the most urgent need for food. Here again, as in the case of public relief, critics prefer to complain about symptoms rather than to face the cause: The inherent exigencies of the existing social-economic system. Anyone can wax eloquent about the high social function of those who farm, mine and quarry, providing the raw materials not only of food, clothing and shelter but also of all later forms of production of both capital and consumer goods. Anyone can wax pathetic over the plight of agriculture. But under present conditions, the former course is to put the burden of carrying society upon the class now least competent to bear it, and the latter course is to engage in idle sentiment.

The ultimate problem of production is the production of human beings. To this end, the production of goods is intermediate and auxiliary. It is by this standard that the present system stands condemned. "Security" is a means, and although an indispensable social means, it is not the end. Machinery and technological improvement are means, but again are not the end. Discovery of individual needs and capacities is a means to the end, but only a means. The means have to be implemented by a social-economic system that establishes and uses the means for the production of free human beings associating with one another on terms of equality. Then and then only will these means be an integral part of the end, not frustrated and self-defeating, bringing new evils and generating new problems.

The problem today remains one of using available intelligence, of employing the immense resources science has put at our disposal: a pooled and coördinated social intelligence, not the mere scattered individualized intelligences of persons here and there, however high their I.Q.'s may be. Mere individual intellectual capacities are as ineffective as are mere personal good intentions. The existence of social objective intelligence brings us back to the point where we started. Social control effected through organized application of social intelligence is the sole form of social control that can and will get rid of existing evils without landing us finally in some form of coercive control from above and outside.

A great tragedy of the present situation may turn out to be that those most conscious of present evils and of the need of thorough-going change in the social-economic system will trust to some short-cut way out, like the method of civil war and violence. Instead of relying upon the constant application of all socially available resources of knowledge and continuous inquiry they may rely upon the frozen intelligence of some past thinker, sect and party cult: frozen because arrested into a dogma.

That "intelligence," when frozen in dogmatic social philosophies, themselves the fruit of arrested philosophies of history, generates a vicious circle of blind oscillation is tragically exemplified in the present state of the world. What *claims* to be social planning is now found in Communist and Fascist countries. The *social* consequence is complete suppression of freedom of inquiry, communication and voluntary association, by means of a combination of personal violence, culminating in extirpation, and systematic partisan propaganda. The results are such that in the minds of many persons the very idea of social planning and of violation of the integrity of the individual are becoming intimately bound together. But an immense difference divides the *planned* society from a *continuously planning* society. The former requires fixed blueprints imposed from above and therefore involving reliance upon physical and psychological force to secure conformity to them. The latter means the release of intelligence through the widest form of coöperative give-and-take. The attempt to *plan* social organization and association without the freest possible play of intelligence contradicts the very idea in *social* plann*ing*. For the latter is an operative method of activity, not a predetermined set of final "truths."

When social "planning" is predicated on a set of "*final*" truths, the social end is fixed once for all, and the "end" is then used to justify whatever means are deemed necessary to attain it. "Planning" then takes place only with respect to means of the latter sort, not with respect to ends, so that planning with respect to even means is constrained and coercive. The social result is that the means used have quite other consequences than the end originally set up in idea and afterwards progressively reduced to mere words. As the events of the past twenty years have shown, the seizure of political power by force signifies the continued maintenance of power by force with its continued suppression of the most precious freedoms of the individual spirit. Maintenance of power in order to use force becomes the actual end. Means used determine the end actually reached. The end justifies the means only when the means used are such as actually bring about the desired and desirable end.

Only when reflection upon means and choice of ends are free can there be actual social planning. Every arrest of intelligence (and every form of social dogma is an arrest) obstructs and finally suppresses free consideration and choice of means. The method of social intelligence is primarily concerned with free determination of means to be employed. Until that method of social action is adopted we shall remain in a period of drift and unrest whose final outcome is likely to be force and counterforce, with temporary victory to the side possessed of the most machine guns.

62 • The New Republic: *"Extraordinary Accomplishments" and "Failure in the Central Problem"*

In May 1940, as Roosevelt's second term was coming to a close, the liberal magazine *The New Republic* printed a long summary and evaluation of the record of the Roosevelt administration from 1936 to 1940. The closing passages of that evaluation are reprinted below.

One need only recall what conditions were in 1932 to realize the amazing change in our national thinking that has taken place in eight years. While there is still complaint about paternalism and centralized government (from the Republicans who were the great exponents of these ideas, applied under special circumstances, for the first seventy-five years of their party's life) it is obvious that even the critics are only half-hearted in what they say.

As a nation we have agreed, once and forever, that the individual must not bear the sole responsibility for his failure to cope with economic problems of unemployment or old age which are, quite obviously, beyond his powers, and that society as a whole must take over a substantial part of the burden.

We have at last learned that laissez-faire has been dead for years, that the unguided lust of the business man for profit does not infallibly produce Utopia.

And finally, we have reaffirmed in these past eight years an early American doctrine that had been all but forgotten in preceding decades: that the country exists for the welfare and happiness of all its inhabitants; and that when this condition is

From "New Deal in Review 1936-1940," supplement to *The New Republic,* CII (May 20, 1940), 707-708. Reprinted by permission of *The New Republic.*

not met, reformation is in order no matter how drastic it may be or how much it may be disliked by existing privileged minorities.

The New Deal, even in its second term, has clearly done far more for the general welfare of the country and its citizens than any administration in the previous history of the nation. Its relief for underprivileged producers in city and country, though inadequate to the need, has been indispensable. Without this relief an appalling amount of misery would have resulted, and a dangerous political upheaval might have occurred. Since the expenditure of money for relief—even the insufficient amounts recently appropriated—has been the principal target of the administration's conservative enemies, this accomplishment alone would be sufficient reason for support of the New Deal. The assertion of the reactionaries that if the federal budget were balanced by cutting expenses, business would revive sharply enough to absorb the unemployed and make relief expenditures unnecessary, is incapable of proof and seems highly improbable.

In addition, the New Deal in this second period has accomplished much of permanent benefit to the nation. Perhaps its most important achievement was the National Labor Relations Act, the result of which was to inhibit employers' opposition to union organization and true collective bargaining, so that trade-union membership was more than doubled. This was not a mere act of justice; it was the laying of a solid foundation for our society in the future. Without a strong, alert and independent labor movement a modern industrial nation is in constant danger from the enemies of political and social democracy. Second only to the strengthening of unions is the establishment of minimum labor standards. The fury with which reactionaries have attacked these two labor measures is an index of their importance.

Other permanent improvements are the impetus given to conservation of soil and forests, the manysided TVA, a great road-building program, flood control, a good beginning at slum clearance and adequate housing for those not provided for by private construction, great hydro-electric projects, extension of electricity at reasonable rates through the Rural Electrification Administration, and the inauguration of insurance against unemployment and the other forms of social security.

The government as an instrument of democratic action in the future has also been strengthened and renovated. This is not merely a matter of the addition of many new agencies, but of the more efficient organization of the whole executive department—including a planning board under the President which so far has been relatively unimportant but is capable of future development. The Courts, too, have been revivified, partly by legislation, but principally by excellent new appointments, so that we now have a Supreme Court which is abreast of the times.

It is improbable that these more permanent changes will be or even can be destroyed by any new administration.

All these extraordinary accomplishments must be remembered when we speak of the points at which the New Deal has been disappointing in its second phase. The most important of these is of course its failure to discover or apply a genuine remedy for the stagnation of our economy, and for unemployment. These years have seen no return to the conditions of 1932 or 1933, to be sure, but on the other hand no great or permanent improvement in national income, production or employment above the level already achieved in 1936. Nor have they seen the adoption of any important new means of bringing about such improvement. The President has apparently been hoping continually that business and investment would gain momentum of their own accord, while business spokesmen have been blaming what they called the hostile attitude of the New Deal for a lack of confidence which they charged with responsibility for retarding advance. It is doubtful, however, whether they are right about this, in the view of economists who have studied the problem intensively.

On two occasions during the past few years the President has heeded business advice, at least in part, by trying to cut recovery expenditures in the hope that a permanent improvement in business was in prospect—once in 1937 and again in 1939. On both occasions a sharp slump followed. The upswing which was occurring when the cuts were made turned out to have been due to an accumulation of inventories by business, which overshot the demand from consumers, and reaction under such circumstances was inevitable.

The reason for the failure of our economy to come back to really prosperous levels is not known with certainty, but there is no such mystery about it as many believe. Economists of varying schools have pointed out several causes, each of which undoubtedly plays a part. The question concerns how large a part each plays, but we do not need to wait for the answer to that question in order to devise and apply remedial action.

One assigned reason is the failure of construction fully to revive. Closely associated with this is the high price of steel, other capital goods, and high building costs themselves. Such progress as has been made is largely due to government efforts to reduce the price of and access to capital for home-owners through the FHA, and the valuable but insufficient work of the USHA in organizing and financing large low-cost housing projects. The anti-trust prosecutions of the Department of Justice may help in the future.

Another assigned reason is high prices of industrial products in general. Too few privately controlled industries follow the policy of low prices leading to enlarged sales. Anti-trust action may remedy this in the relatively few cases in which illegal monopoly exists, but that is hardly enough.

The third important reason is the lack of old or rapidly expanding new industries in which capital investment may take place. The government might remedy this situation by a drastic railroad-reorganization program, or by a carefully planned scheme of large-scale public investment. It has not moved in either direction.

The President's failure to make more progress in tackling the central problem of our economy is probably due mainly to two things—the strengthening of conservative opposition, especially since the 1938 election, and concentration on the European situation. The country is weaker, whether for war or for peace, because of this slackening of pace in the New Deal. If our foreign policy can avoid involvement in the war, we shall be fortunate. But in any case we should not rely on war, whether we are in it or not, to do for us the domestic job that remains. If the New Deal is to deserve our support in the future, it must not rest on what it has already done, great as that is, but tell us how it is going to finish the task.

INDEX